Photoshop® Elements 13

All-in-One

FOR

DUMMIES®

A Wiley Brand

by Barbara Obermeier
and Ted Padova

FOR
DUMMIES®
A Wiley Brand

Photoshop® Elements 13 All-in-One For Dummies®

Published by: **John Wiley & Sons, Inc.,** 111 River Street, Hoboken, NJ 07030-5774, www.wiley.com

Copyright © 2015 by John Wiley & Sons, Inc., Hoboken, New Jersey

Published simultaneously in Canada

For general information on our other products and services, please contact our Customer Care Department within the U.S. at 877-762-2974, outside the U.S. at 317-572-3993, or fax 317-572-4002. For technical support, please visit www.wiley.com/techsupport.

Wiley publishes in a variety of print and electronic formats and by print-on-demand. Some material included with standard print versions of this book may not be included in e-books or in print-on-demand. If this book refers to media such as a CD or DVD that is not included in the version you purchased, you may download this material at http://booksupport.wiley.com. For more information about Wiley products, visit www.wiley.com.

Library of Congress Control Number: 2014944992

ISBN 978-1-118-99860-1 (pbk); ISBN 978-1-118-99859-5 (ebk); ISBN 978-1-118-99861-8 (ebk)

Manufactured in the United States of America

10 9 8 7 6 5 4 3 2 1

Contents at a Glance

Table of Contents

Introduction

*W*e live in a photo world. And Photoshop Elements has become a tool for both professional and amateur photographers who want to edit, improve, manage, manipulate, and organize photos and other media. Considering the power and impressive features of the program, Elements remains one of the best values for your money among computer software applications.

This book is an effort to provide as much of a comprehensive view of a wildly feature-rich program as we can. Additionally, this book is written for a cross-platform audience. If you're a Macintosh user, you'll find all you need to work in Elements 13, including support for placing photos on maps and more consistency with Windows features.

Elements is overflowing with features, and we try to offer you as much as possible within a limited amount of space. We begged for more pages, but alas, our publisher wants to get this book in your hands in full color and with an attractive price tag. Therefore, even though we may skip over a few little things, all you need to know about using Photoshop Elements for designing images for print, sharing, the web, versatile packaging, emailing, and more is covered in the pages ahead.

Because Photoshop Elements has something for just about everyone, we know that our audience is large and also that not everyone will use every tool, command, or method we describe. We offer many cross-references throughout to help you jump around. You can go to just about any chapter and start reading. If a concept needs more explanation, we point you in the right direction for getting some background.

Conventions Used in This Book

Throughout this book, especially in step lists, we point you to menus for keyboard commands. For accessing a menu command, you may see something like this:

Choose File⇨Get Photos⇨From Files and Folders.

You click the File menu to open its drop-down menu, click the menu command labeled Get Photos, and then choose the command From Files and Folders from the submenu that appears. It's that simple.

We also refer to *context menus,* which open where your cursor is positioned and show you a menu of options related to whatever you're doing at the time. These menus look like the ones you select from the top of the Elements workspace. To open a context menu, just right-click the mouse, or Control-click on a Mac if you don't have a two-button mouse.

When we mention that keys need to be pressed on your keyboard, the text looks like this:

Press Alt+Shift+Ctrl+S (Option+Shift+⌘+S on the Mac).

In this case, you hold down the Alt key on Windows/the Option key on the Mac, then the Shift key, then the Control key on Windows/the ⌘ key on the Mac, and then press the S key. Then, release all the keys at the same time.

Icons Used in This Book

In the margins throughout this book, you see icons indicating that something is important.

This icon informs you that this item is a new feature in Photoshop Elements 13.

Pay particular attention when you see the Warning icon. This icon indicates possible side-effects or damage to your image that you might encounter when performing certain operations in Elements.

This icon is a heads-up for something you may want to commit to memory. Usually, it tells you about a shortcut for a repetitive task, where remembering a procedure can save you time.

A Tip tells you about an alternative method for a procedure, giving you a shortcut, a workaround, or some other type of helpful information.

Elements is a computer program, after all. No matter how hard we try to simplify our explanation of features, we can't entirely avoid some technical information. If a topic is a little on the technical side, we use this icon to alert you that we're moving into a complex subject. You won't see many of these icons in the book because we try our best to give you the details in nontechnical terms.

Beyond the Book

We have online content that you can enjoy in conjunction with this book:

- ✔ **Cheat sheet:** The cheat sheet for this book includes a detailed look at the Elements photo editing workspace, Tools panel shortcuts, tricks for selecting objects, and more. You can find it at www.dummies.com/ cheatsheet/photoshopelementsaio.

- ✔ **Online articles:** We couldn't fit everything we wanted into this book, so you can find additional content at www.dummies.com/extras/ photoshopelementsaio. A few of the topics covered are organizing and importing photos, dynamically updating saved searches, finding and loading actions, and adjusting brightness/contrast with the Smart Brush tool. But there's much more than these few topics. Be sure to check these out.

Where to Go from Here

If you're totally new to Photoshop Elements, Book I helps orient you to the different workspaces (one for organizing and another for editing) and tools within those workspaces. After you have a feel for navigating among the different workspaces in Elements, feel free to jump around based on your interests and pay special attention to the cross-referenced chapters, in case you get stuck on a concept.

We hope you have much success and enjoyment in using Adobe Photoshop Elements 13, and it's our sincere wish that the pages ahead provide you with an informative and helpful guide to the program.

Book I
Getting Started with Elements

Contents at a Glance

Chapter 1: Examining the Elements Environment

In This Chapter

- ✔ **Working with the Organizer**
- ✔ **Setting up your workspaces**
- ✔ **Moving through the Menu bar and context menus**
- ✔ **Picking settings in the Options panel**
- ✔ **Playing around with panels and bins**
- ✔ **Shortening your steps with shortcuts**
- ✔ **Getting a helping hand**

*P*hotoshop Elements 13 continues to evolve with new tools and features. Both Windows and Macintosh users also have continued support for the Organizer and its file management, creation, and file-sharing opportunities.

In this release, there is greater consistency between Macintosh and Windows version. For example, the Slide Show creation that was previously limited to Windows users is now available on the Mac. Photo Mail, which was also a Windows-only feature, has been eliminated from the Share panel, making the Create and Share panels identical on both operating systems.

This chapter starts with some essential tasks to make your photo management and editing experiences an easy process. This chapter's content may not be the most fun part of this book, but it's a critical first step for anyone new to Elements. Stay with us while we break down all the areas in the Photoshop Elements workspace, where you can turn that photo of Aunt Gina into something that Whistler's mom would envy.

Launching Elements

After running the installer from the Photoshop Elements DVD-ROM or down-loading the program from the Adobe Store (or Apple App Store for Mac users), double-click the program icon to launch Elements. When the program launches, you see the Adobe Photoshop Elements Welcome screen, as shown in Figure 1-1.

Figure 1-1: The Photoshop Elements Welcome screen for Windows.

On the Welcome screen, you find two buttons for opening the Organizer and the Photo Editor. Click one of these buttons, and you open the respective Elements application:

- **Organizer:** Click the Organizer button, and Elements opens the Organizer, the window where you take care of a plethora of file-management and organization tasks. Among your other options, you can choose to load pictures in the Organizer window so that they're ready to use for all your projects. The Organizer is available to Macintosh users in Photoshop Elements 9 and above as well as to Windows users.

- **Photo Editor:** Click the Photo Editor button to open the Photoshop Elements Photo Editor, where you perform all the editing for your photos.

- **Settings:** Click Settings (the sprocket icon) to open the Adobe Photoshop Elements 13 preferences for the startup window. Here, you can choose to show the window on startup, open only the Organizer, or open only the Photo Editor. By default, the Welcome screen is set to always open when Elements is launched.

✔ **Close:** Click the X on the Welcome screen to close it. Closing the Welcome screen has no effect on the Editors or the Organizer. If either or all are open, they remain open when you close the Welcome screen.

First glance at eLive

Whether you launch the Organizer or Photo Editor for the first time, you may see the eLive tab selected by default. The next time you launch Elements, the last tab you selected from your last session opens the respective tab.

eLive is a new feature in Elements that offers you help, tutorial assistance, and information related to updates. When you first begin to explore Elements, take a look at the various options you have for learning more about the program.

eLive has three separate categories and a View All category (called Everything) where all options are shown in the eLive window. You select a category by opening the drop-down menu from the left side of the window. Here you find:

✔ **Learn:** Click this item to learn various techniques in editing photos.

✔ **Inspire:** Click this item to view some inspirational creations.

✔ **News:** Click this tab to view updated Elements news items such as updates and announcements.

The "Live" reference in the name of the eLive tab is because the tab shows updated information as Adobe posts it. The interface is web based, and new updates to the individual items occur routinely. Be sure to explore eLive to keep updated with new ideas and announcements.

Getting familiar with your hardware

Wait! Stop! Hold on! Before you launch Elements, be advised that there are certain minimum hardware requirements necessary to run the programs. The minimum requirements recommended by Adobe include the following:

✓ **Common requirements for all systems:** 1GB of RAM (2GB for HD video functions), 4GB of available hard-disk space (additional space is needed for installation), DVD drive (optional for installing from a DVD drive), and an Internet connection for product activation.

✓ **Windows requirements:** Microsoft Windows XP with Service Pack 3, Windows Vista with Service Pack 2, Windows 7, or Windows 8. Note that Windows XP offers only limited functionality for Camera Raw files. See Book III, Chapter 4, for an introduction to Camera Raw.

You also need the following on a Windows computer: 1.6 GHz or faster processor (including single core support), color monitor with 16-bit color video card, 1024 x 768 monitor resolution, and Microsoft DirectX 9 compatible display driver.

New in Elements 13 is support for 64-bit Windows operating systems. You can use eaither 32-bit or 64-bit computers.

✓ **Macintosh requirements:** 64-bit Multi-core Intel processor, Mac OS X v10.7, 1024 x 768 display resolution, QuickTime 7 software required for multimedia features.

Note that the preceding specifications are what Adobe recommends for problem-free operation. You may be able to run Elements with older operating systems and less hardware power, but Adobe does not recommend it.

Every time you launch Photoshop Elements, the Welcome screen is the first item you see on your monitor, unless you change the default to Organizer or Photo Editor. From the Welcome screen, you choose the kind of tasks you want to accomplish in a session. If you want to change from one window to another, for example, or change from the Organizer to the Photo Editor, you can easily navigate workspaces after you open one editing environment, as we explain in the section "Navigating the Different Modes," later in this chapter.

The window you see in Figure 1-1, along with any of the help information displayed there, may be slightly different from what you see on your monitor when you launch Elements. The Welcome screen displays dynamic content, and Adobe changes the content routinely.

Opening the Organizer

The Organizer is one of several workspaces available to you with Photoshop Elements. Unless you have an immediate task at hand for editing a photo in the Photo Editor workspace, the Organizer is often going to be your first workspace to visit. In the Organizer, you can manage photos and navigate to every other editing workspace that Elements provides you.

The Organizer is almost identical on both Windows and Macintosh computers. Many screenshots showing the Organizer in this book equally apply to both Windows and Macintosh users.

To open the Organizer, click the Organize button on the Welcome screen. When you install Elements and first open the Organizer, you see an empty screen, as shown in Figure 1-2.

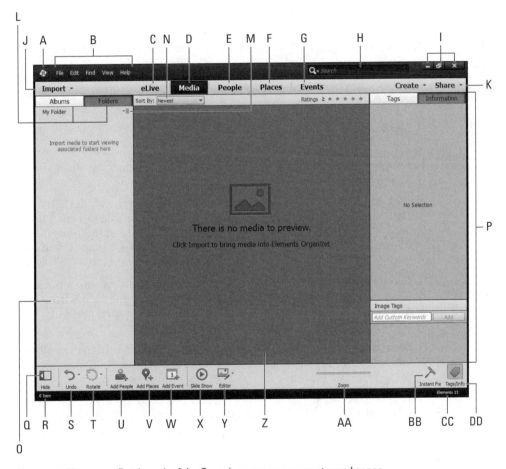

Figure 1-2: Upon your first launch of the Organizer, you see an empty workspace.

You can add photos to the Organizer window by using a variety of options that we cover in Book II, Chapter 1. For now, we focus on looking at the Organizer tools and understanding how they work. Some of the more important tools in the Organizer include

A. Elements Organizer button: On a Windows machine, clicking this button opens a menu where you can choose to close, minimize, and maximize the Organizer workspace. The icon represents the Organizer. In other workspaces, such as the Photo Editor, clicking the icon returns you to the Organizer window. On the Mac, no such icon exists.

B. Menu bar: The menus contain all the commands you use in the Organizer workspace. On the Macintosh, the menu bar is positioned above the Organizer workspace and a menu item titled Elements Organizer appears in the menu bar. Throughout this book, we talk about using menu commands.

C. eLive. In Elements 13, you find five tabs at the top of the Organizer window above the Media Browser (see Y). The first tab, called eLive, is a new addition to Elements 13. When you click this tab you find a number of help articles, tutorials, and examples to assist you in learning more about Elements.

D. Media: When you click Media, thumbnail images of your media appear in the Media Browser.

E. People: Click this tab, and all images with people tags are shown in the Media Browser.

F. Places: Click the Places tab, and you see images in the Media Browser that have been tagged as locations. When you click this tab and click the Tags/Info button (item GG), the Map button appears at the bottom of the Panel Bin (item S). Click the Map button, and a Google map is displayed in the Panel Bin.

G. Events: The fifth tab above the Media Browser is the Events tab. Click this tab, and all images tagged as events appear in the Media Browser. You additionally see a calendar in the Panel Bin for sorting events according to dates.

H. Search: Type text in the text box to search for photos in the Organizer window. After typing text in the text box, click the magnifying glass icon to perform the search.

I. Features buttons: The three buttons represented by tiny icons include, from left to right, (H) Minimize, (I) Restore, and (J) Close (on the top right in Windows and on the top left on a Mac where they are Close, Minimize, and Zoom, from left to right). These buttons work the same as they do in almost all Windows or Mac applications.

J. Import panel: The Import panel displays Albums and Folders (item L). In Figure 1-2, media has not yet been imported into the Organizer. Therefore, no folders appear in the Import panel.

K. Create/Share buttons: Click a button to open a drop-down menu for the respective panel in the Panel Bin (item S). The panels include

- *Create:* Click the Create tab to make creations you can print or share online.

- *Share:* Options in this panel provide you with many different opportunities to share photos and creations.

L. Albums/Folders tabs: Notice two different tabs appearing in the Import panel. To view Albums, click the Albums tab. To view imported photos, click the Folders tab. You can add new albums by clicking the + (plus) icon (appearing when the Albums tab is selected and choosing New Album from the drop-down menu).

M. Tree/List Views: When you have folders added to the Folders tab, you can view the folders as a hierarchical *Tree* or as an alphabetical *List.* Choose from the menu that opens when you click the icon.

N. Sort By: A drop-down menu permits you to choose how images are sorted in the Media Browser: Newest files first, Oldest files first, or by Import batch.

O. My Folders: As you add media, the media are added as folders. You can create folders on a hard drive and add a folder name and the media contained within the folder.

P. Panel Bin: The default Panel Bin displays keyword tags, information, and image tags. Additional panels are opened in the Panel Bin by clicking the Create and Share button at the top of the panel and by clicking icons appearing at the bottom of the panel.

In Elements 13, another sort option was added to this menu. You find Name as a choice that permits you to sort files according to filename.

Q. Hide Panel: Click this button, and the Import panel disappears, providing you more space in the Media Browser to look for photos. When hidden, the button changes to Show Panel. Click the Show Panel button, and the Import panel reappears.

R. *N* **Item:** The number of items in the catalog appears as a readout here. In Figure 1-2, no media is loaded in the Organizer, hence the readout is 0 Item.

S. Undo/Redo: You use these tools to undo and redo edits.

T. Rotate: Click the Rotate tool to display the Clockwise and Counterclockwise tools. Select a photo in the Media Browser and click one of the tools, and you can rotate the image. When you rotate an image, you don't need to save anything. The Organizer remembers rotated images, and they continue to appear as you perform a rotation in all subsequent Organizer sessions.

U. Add People: Select one or more photos and click this button to tag photos for people recognition.

V. Add Places: Select one or more photos and click this button to display a map where you can tag photos with geospatial locations.

W. Add Event: Click this button, and the Add Event panel opens in the Panel Bin. The Add Event panel permits you to add new event tags to photos with dates and descriptions.

X. Slide Show: Click this button and a Full Screen view window opens, where you can view all files in the Media Browser as a slide show.

Y. Editor: Click the button, and the Elements Photo Editor opens. If you have photos selected in the Media Browser, the photos open in the Photo Editor. Click the down arrow adjacent to the icon, and a menu provides choices for editing with an External Editor, Edit with Photoshop (if installed), edit with the Elements Photo Editor, and Edit with Premiere Elements (if installed). If you choose External Editor and you haven't identified an editor in the Editing preferences, Elements opens the Preferences dialog box, where you identify the external editor you want to use.

Z. Media Browser: The main window in the Organizer is called the Media Browser. Here is where you find thumbnail images of photos added to your catalog and thumbnail icons representing PDF files, music files, and video files.

Commit the term *Media Browser* to memory. This area is where thumbnail images are shown in the Organizer, and we make reference to the Media Browser throughout this book.

AA. Adjust Size of Thumbnail: Move the slider to change the size of thumbnail images appearing in the Media Browser. (See item CC for more on the Media Browser.)

BB. Instant Fix: Click this button, and the Quick editing tools open in the Panel Bin. You can make many adjustments to your photos without leaving the Organizer.

CC. Catalog Name: The name of the open catalog appears here. Click the text, and you open the Catalog Manager. A catalog contains thumbnail images of all the photos you add from your hard drive or media disk.

DD. Tags/Info: Click this button, and the default panels display keyword tags, information, and image keywords.

For maximum viewing of photos in the Media Browser, click the Hide Panel button and the Keyword/Info button. Both panels collapse from view, and the Media Browser occupies the entire Organizer window horizontally.

Adding Images to the Organizer

To manage photos and apply edits, you need to load some photos into the default catalog that appears (empty, obviously) when you first launch Elements.

If you used earlier versions of Elements, the Organizer prompts you to convert an earlier catalog to the new version when you first launch the program. If you want to convert an earlier catalog, follow the onscreen directions, and your photos are loaded in the Media Browser.

To add photos to the default catalog, do the following:

1. **Copy some photos to your hard drive.**

   On the Macintosh, you're prompted immediately when you launch the Organizer the first time to add photos from your iPhoto library. If you have photos stored in iPhoto, click the Import button to add photos to a new catalog.

   Make a new folder on your hard drive and name it My Photos or another descriptive name and copy photos to the new folder.

2. **Launch Elements.**

   Double-click the program icon or use the Start menu to open Elements. On the Mac, click the icon on the Dock or in Launchpad.

3. **Click the Organizer button on the Welcome screen.**

4. **Choose File⇨Get Photos and Videos⇨From Files and Folders.**

   The Get Photos and Videos from Files and Folders dialog box opens, as shown in Figure 1-3.

Navigate to the drive and folder that holds your photos.

Select photos to import.

Figure 1-3: You select photos to import in a catalog from the Get Photos and Videos from Files and Folders dialog box.

You can also import photos using the Import drop-down menu in the upper-left corner of the Organizer. Open the menu and choose From Files and Folders.

5. **Navigate your hard drive to locate the folder where you copied your photos and then select the photos to import.**

   If you want to import all photos from a given folder, press Ctrl+A (⌘+A on the Mac). If you want to select individual photos, click a photo and press the Ctrl (⌘) key while clicking additional photos.

6. **Click the Get Media button to import the photos into your catalog.**

   You have other options available in the Get Photos and Videos from Files and Folders dialog box. Select the Get Photos from Subfolders check box if you have subfolders containing images. Click the Get Media button and leave all other items at their defaults.

   An alert dialog box opens, informing you that you need to click the All Media button if you want to see all the photos in your catalog. This button appears at the top of the Organizer window, as shown in Figure 1-4.

Figure 1-4: Click the All Media button above the image thumbnails to show all the photos in your catalog.

7. **Click OK in the alert dialog box.**

8. **View the photos in the Organizer.**

   As shown in Figure 1-5, photos appear in the Organizer window. In this view, we hid the Import panel and the Panel Bin to provide maximum viewing area in the Media Browser.

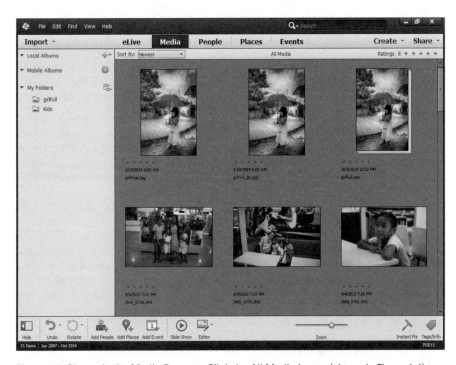

Figure 1-5: Photos in the Media Browser. Click the All Media button (shown in Figure 1-4) to view all photos in your catalog.

Each time you add new photos to the Organizer, only the new photos are shown in the Media Browser. To see all the photos in your catalog, click the All Media button.

A number of file-management options are available in the Organizer for sorting images, tagging files with keywords, and creating albums of photos. We cover all you can do with file management in Book II, Chapters 2 and 3.

Navigating the Different Modes

Elements provides you with three editing modes. If you're in the Organizer, you access the different editing modes in the Photo Editor. Click the Photo Editor button at the bottom of the Organizer window or click Photo Editor on the Welcome screen when you launch Elements from your desktop. The editing modes are as follows:

- **Expert:** In Expert mode, you have access to all tools and commands, which provide you with limitless opportunities for editing your pictures.

- **Quick:** Use this mode when you need to polish an image in terms of brightness, contrast, or color adjustment or other, similar editing tasks. You can perform quick edits in the Photo Editor or within the Organizer by clicking the Instant Fix tool.

- **Guided:** This marvelous tool gives you step-by-step instructions to — produce an editing result, such as removing a color cast or perfecting a portrait image. Three new Guided photo edits have been added in Elements 13 — Black and White, B&W Selection, and B&W Color Pop.

After you have files loaded in the Organizer, you can easily open an image in an editing mode.

You can move around in the Photo Editor to explore panels and different modes. When you change from Expert mode to another mode or explore options in the Panel Bin, you lose the Tools panel on the far left of the Photo Editor screen. When you want to regain access to the Tools panel, click Expert at the top of the Photo Editor window.

Visiting Expert editing mode

Don't let the term *Expert* dissuade you from exploring options in this mode. It's not really a mode used only by experts. Rather, the Expert moniker simply distinguishes it from the other modes, because the Expert mode is where you apply limitless edits to your photos.

Assuming that you want to edit a picture, follow these steps to launch the Photo Editor workspace from the Organizer:

1. **Click an image thumbnail in the Organizer.**

   Following this step presumes that you've added photos to the Organizer, as we describe in the section "Adding Images to the Organizer," earlier in this chapter.

2. **Click Editor at the bottom of the Organizer window.**

After you select the mode, the selected image appears in the Photo Editor's Expert mode workspace, as shown in Figure 1-6. Notice the tabs at the top of the window for changing the modes.

3. **To return to the Organizer, click the Organizer button at the bottom of the Editor window, as shown in Figure 1-6.**

These tabs indicate your current mode and enable you to switch modes.

Figure 1-6: To return to the Organizer from the Photo Editor workspace, click the Organizer button.

When you open a file from the Organizer or change to another workspace while the Organizer is open, you have two workspaces open in Elements. The second workspace (such as the Photo Editor) opens while the Organizer remains open. When you toggle between modes, both modes remain open until you exit one mode or the other.

Visiting Quick editing mode

If you've worked in earlier versions of Elements, you may expect the Organizer to provide a direct link to each editing mode in the Photo Editor: Expert (formerly Full Photo Edit mode), Quick (formerly Quick Fix), and Guided.

In Elements 13, you have just *one* place to switch to from the Organizer — the Photo Editor. You get to the Photo Editor by clicking the Editor button at the bottom of the Organizer window. In the Photo Editor, Elements shows you the last mode you chose (Expert, Quick, or Guided). To switch to a different editing mode, click the tab at the top of the window. So, for Quick editing mode, you click the Quick tab.

If you're in the Organizer, you don't have to switch to the Photo Editor to make quick fixes to your images. Click Instant Fix at the bottom of the Panel Bin, and Photo Fix Options are displayed for making quick edits while you remain in the Organizer.

If you arrive at the Photo Editor via the Welcome screen, you see the same tabs for each mode at the top of the Photo Editor. To enter Quick mode, click the Quick tab and Quick mode appears, as shown in Figure 1-7.

Notice in Figure 1-7 that you find the Move tool in the Tools panel. Earlier versions of Elements didn't have the Move tool in this mode. Now in Elements 13, the Move tool has been added to the Tools panel.

Figure 1-7: While Elements is in the Photo Editor, you can easily open Quick mode by clicking Quick at the top of the Photo Editor window.

Quick switching between interfaces

Your operating system has a built-in Application Switcher. In Windows, press the Alt key and then the Tab key. Keep the Alt key depressed, release the Tab key, and click the application you want to use. On the Macintosh, press the ⌘ key and then the Tab key. Keep the ⌘ key depressed, release the Tab key, and click the application you want to use. You can also use the left and right arrows to move between applications in the Application Switcher. The following figure shows the Application Switcher in Windows (left) and on the Macintosh (right).

When you're using the Organizer and want to quickly open the Photo Editor or you're using the Photo Editor and want to switch to the Organizer, use the Application Switcher. If you need to open the Desktop view, use the Application Switcher to quickly change to the Desktop view. All the applications remain open, and you can toggle back and forth between programs.

Getting help with Guided mode

Although the Guided panel isn't entirely a separate mode, it changes the appearance of the Panel Bin to offer you help with many editing tasks. In the Photo Editor, click Guided at the top of the Photo window. The Guided panel opens in the Panel Bin.

If you've worked with earlier versions of Elements, you'll notice immediately that the default appearance of the Guided panel has changed. Adobe made things much more organized by adding categories in the Guided panel. As you can see in Figure 1-8, there are four categories: Touchups, Photo Effects, Camera Effects, and Photo Play. Click one of the four category names and the panel expands, showing you the options available for that category. In Figure 1-8, we expanded Photo Play, and the various options are shown in the panel.

Figure 1-8: Click a category in the Guided panel, and options for the given category are shown.

You have a number of choices for editing tasks. In our example, we chose a very simple edit process to straighten a photo, as shown in Figure 1-9.

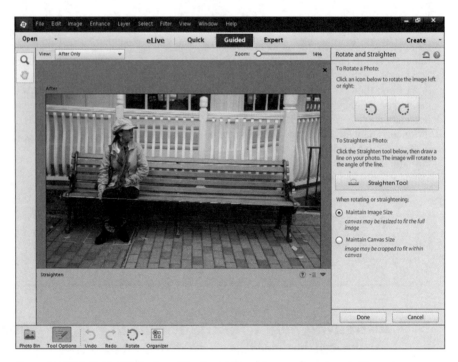

Figure 1-9: Click Guided at the top of the Panel Bin and expand a category. Then choose a Guided edit task in the Panel Bin.

One common item that appears with many different editing tasks is a mini-toolbar. Whenever you see a toolbar, remember to click the check mark to accept your edits. Or, if needed, click the icon with a circle and diagonal line to dismiss the edits and return to the image's previous state.

In Photoshop Elements 13, three new Guided editing tasks have been added to the Photo Effects category:

- **Black and White** provides step-by-step instructions for converting color photos to black and white.

- **Selective Black and White** walks you through steps to convert selective areas in a photo to black and white.

- **B&W Color Pop Guided Edit** (see Figure 1-10) enables you to convert a photo to black and white while retaining a color you can choose from options in the Guided panel.

Figure 1-10: The new B&W Color Pop effect.

Click other items in the Guided panel and find helpful steps to guide you through a number of common image-editing tasks.

Moving through the Menu Bar

As with most programs on your computer, Elements offers you a number of drop-down menus with many different commands that invoke actions. Don't bother to memorize all the menu commands. Instead, try to develop an understanding of the types of actions included in a given menu. A general understanding of the menus helps you find commands much faster.

Take a look at the menus in the Organizer. Among the Organizer menus, you find

✔ **File:** On the File menu, as you might expect, you find commands to open and browse files on your hard drive. You also find a number of options for saving files, such as writing images to CD-ROMs and DVDs (Windows). Commands for managing catalogs, moving files, and printing images are also located in this menu.

- ✔ **Edit:** Many commands you're familiar with — copy, undo, delete, and so on — are located on the Edit menu. In the Organizer, you also find many options for sorting files and options for managing color. In addition, you find a number of quick-access commands for editing photos similar to options you find in Quick mode.

- ✔ **Find:** The Find menu is all about finding images on your computer. You have many choices for searching photos based on a wide range of criteria.

- ✔ **View:** The View menu handles commands related to viewing images in the Organizer window. You can choose the types of media to display in the Organizer, show and hide files, and show and hide certain data associated with files such as the filenames. Choices you make in this menu relate to the display of images in the Organizer's Media Browser.

- ✔ **Help:** As you might expect, the Help menu contains menu commands that provide help when working in Elements. Certain Help commands open your default web browser and open Help web pages on the Adobe website.

Keep in mind that the Organizer is distinct from the editing modes. The commands you find in the editing modes are, for the most part, quite different from the menu items found in the Organizer. The Photo Editor contains the following menus:

- ✔ **File:** You find file-opening and -saving options as well as printing commands on the File menu. The File menu also contains some options for combining images and batch-processing files.

- ✔ **Edit:** The Edit menu offers a number of editing tasks, such as copying and pasting, merging copies, pasting into selections, setting up files, and using patterns and brushes. You also find color-management options that are identical to the commands on the Organizer Edit menu.

- ✔ **Image:** The Image menu contains commands used for changing images, such as cropping and resizing photos, changing color modes, converting color profiles, and transforming images or selections. Notice that you find no image corrections for brightness and color adjustments. These commands are on the Enhance menu.

- ✔ **Enhance:** The Enhance menu is all about working with images in terms of color and brightness corrections and altering their visual appearance.

- ✔ **Layer:** The Layer menu lets you work with layers and gives you access to the many tasks you can do with layers.

✔ **Select:** You use the Select menu to create, modify, and use selections. One of the most frequent phases of an edit is creating a selection, and the Select menu provides a number of commands and tools to help you perfect your selection of image content.

✔ **Filter:** For artistic edits, take a look at the Filter menu and explore the many filter effects you can add to your pictures. You don't need to be a Photoshop Elements expert. The program makes it easy for you by keeping all filters in one place so that with a click of the mouse button, you can create some dazzling effects.

✔ **View:** Viewing options in the Photo Editor relate to zooming in and out of photos, showing rulers and guides, and creating new windows.

✔ **Window:** The Window menu displays a list of panels that can be opened and closed. You also find a list of all open files, to a maximum number of windows you determine in the Elements preferences.

✔ **Help:** The Help menu connects you to an online Help document describing most of what you can do in Elements, tutorials, a Photoshop Elements forum, program updates, and the Inspiration Browser that's a Flash-based tutorial guide offering tips and techniques.

Using Context Menus

Context menus are found in just about every Adobe program. One of the helpful things about context menus is that if you want to perform an action using a menu command or tool, chances are good that you may find just what you're looking for on a context menu.

You open a context menu by right-clicking the mouse button (Windows or Mac) or Control-clicking (Mac). Depending on the tool you're using and the mode you're working in, the menu commands change.

If you're a Mac user with a two-button mouse, you can right-click to open a context menu. And, if you're a Mac user employing a trackpad, you can click with two fingers to open a context menu.

In Figure 1-11, we opened an image in the Photo Editor and created a selection. If you right-click the mouse button, the context menu changes to reflect edits you can make relative to a selection.

When you change tools and editing modes, the context menu choices change to reflect what you can do with the selected tool and in your current editing mode.

Figure 1-11: We created a selection in the Photo Editor mode and opened a context menu.

Selecting Settings in the Options Panel

A number of tools and options exist in several places in each mode. One area you frequently visit when you edit pictures is the Options panel. The Tool Options panel provides several choices for every tool you select in the Photo Editor. In Figure 1-12, we opened the Photo Editor and clicked the Straighten tool. The Tool Options panel changes to reflect the choices you have when working with this tool.

As you click different tools in the Tools panel, the Tool Options panel changes to offer the choices for working with the selected tool.

In photography, straightening is often needed when you can clearly see the horizon line. Double-check your photos to be certain they're straight before you post them online or print your pictures.

If you used Photoshop Elements prior to version 11, pay particular attention to the Tool Options panel at the bottom of the Photo Editor window. Earlier versions of Elements had pop-out toolbars in the Tools panel where you could select different tools from a tool group. In Elements 11 through 13, the Tools panel does not have any pop-out toolbars. You make all tool choices

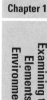

first in the Tools panel and can then choose related tools from the tool group in the Tools Options panel. Notice that in Figure 1-12, the Magnetic Lasso and Polygon Lasso tools appear adjacent and below the Lasso tool in the Tool Options panel.

Figure 1-12: Click the Straighten tool, and the Tool Options panel changes to display settings options you can use with the Straighten tool.

Playing with Panels

The Panel Bin contains many choices for editing files, assembling projects, and working with different tools. Each workspace and mode you visit (Organizer or Photo Editor and Expert, Quick, or Guided mode) support panels and a variety of options from panel menus and tools. In the Photo Editor, you see the Effects panel open in the Panel Bin with the Filters tab in view, as shown in Figure 1-13.

At the top of the Panel Bin are tabs in the Effects panel. Clicking a tab (Filters, Styles, or Effects) changes the tools and options you see. Notice that you also have drop-down menus on some tabs. In Figure 1-13, the Artistic menu is shown. Also, an Options drop-down menu is available: To open it, click the series of horizontal lines and a tiny down-pointing arrow shown in the upper-right of Figure 1-13. When you see this icon on any panel, click to open the menu, where you find menu commands for choosing additional options.

Getting choosy in the Favorites panel

You use the Favorites panel to add your favorite settings in the Photo Editor, such as the filters you like to apply to images. By default, you don't see the Favorites panel open. Open the panel by clicking the Favorites icon at the bottom of the Panel Bin.

Elements provides you with a number of Favorites contained in the panel, as shown in Figure 1-14. To add one of the graphic items to an image in the image window, double-click the favorite item in the panel. You can also open the Options menu and choose Apply.

Exploring other panels

The icons at the bottom of the Panel Bin open different panels. By default, the Layers panel is in view; when you're editing an image, you typically use this panel more often than the other panels.

On the far-right bottom of the Panel Bin, you see the More icon. Click this item, and a pop-up menu appears, as shown in Figure 1-15. From the menu options, you can choose additional panels to open in the Panel Bin.

At the bottom of the pop-up menu you find Custom Workspace. In Elements 11, some panels were docked in the Panel Bin and could not be removed. Other panels appeared as floating panels but could not be docked in the Panel Bin. In Elements 12 and 13, you can select Custom Workspace and dock/undock all panels as you like to create your own custom workspace.

When you open a panel by clicking one of the icons below the Panel Bin, such as Layers, Effects, Graphics, and Favorites, the panels are fixed in a docked position in the Panel Bin unless you choose Custom Workspace. If Custom Workspace is selected, you can drag panels out of the Panel Bin.

Figure 1-13: The Effects panel open in the Panel Bin.

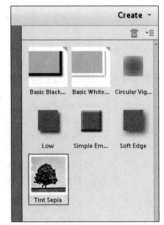

Figure 1-14: The Favorites panel, opened in the Panel Bin.

All the panels you open from the Others pop-up menu are not docked by default: They open as a *floating window* — meaning that they open in a window that you can move around the Photo Editor workspace. Notice, in Figure 1-16, the Actions panel opens as a floating window. Once again, if you choose Custom Workspace, you can dock the floating panels in the Panel Bin.

| Actions |
| Adjustments |
| Color Swatches |
| Histogram |
| History |
| Info |
| Navigator |
| Custom Workspace |

Figure 1-15: Click the Other icon to open a pop-up menu where you can select other panels.

In Figure 1-16, you see Actions at the top of the panel that appears like a tab. When you open additional panels, the newly opened panels open in the same space and appear as tabs, as shown in Figure 1-17. In essence, additional panels dock to the open floating window. If you want panels in separate windows, you can drag them out and away from the original floating window, thereby producing multiple floating windows.

In Figure 1-17, the panels in the lower-left corner where you see History, Histogram, and Color Swatches are docked together in a single panel. You can tear away any one of the panels, or you can dock any one of the floating windows to any other panel. You do this simply by clicking and dragging the panel tabs.

Figure 1-16: The Actions panel opens as a floating window.

Panels grouped into tabs

Click and drag to see a panel in a separate window.

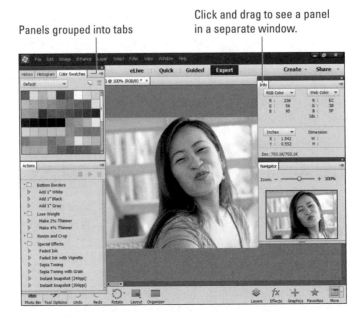

Figure 1-17: Several panels open from the Others pop-up menu and appear as tabs in a single floating panel.

On the Others pop-up menu, you find the following panels:

✔ **Actions:** In earlier versions of Elements, you found Actions nested in the Guided panel. Actions have graduated and now appear within their own panel.

Actions are like macros where you can automate different sequences. In Elements, you still can't record a series of steps and produce your own custom action, but you do have many choices for preset actions that Adobe provides you. You can also add actions from recorded action sets that are produced in Adobe Photoshop. We cover more on actions in Book I, Chapter 2.

✔ **Adjustments:** From the drop-down menu on the top-right corner of the panel you can choose to apply a variety of Adjustment Layers for brightness and color adjustments.

✔ **Color Swatches:** The Color Swatches panel displays a color set from which you can choose colors to apply to images and artwork. We talk about using the Color Swatches in Book V.

✔ **Histogram:** The Histogram panel shows a histogram of the brightness values in an image open in the image window. For more on understanding histograms, see Book VIII.

✔ **History:** The History panel shows a historical view of your edits beginning from the last edit made and backward. You can return to an edit in the History panel by clicking the item you want to return to in the panel list of edits.

✔ **Info:** The Info panel displays information related to mouse cursor position in the image window and assesses color values beneath the cursor. You can also choose to view different color models. We cover more about the Info panel in Chapter 3 of this minibook.

✔ **Navigator:** The Navigator provides you with a method for viewing a photo in the image window in zoomed views. It's like zooming on steroids. We talk more about the Navigator in Chapter 3 of this minibook.

Each panel you open in Expert mode in the Photo Editor has associated Options menus. Click the icon in the upper-right corner to look over your options when working in any one of the panels.

Using the Photo Bin

You might have several images you want to edit in Elements. You might have some image data you want to copy from one image and paste into another image, or maybe you want to enhance a series of images so that the brightness and color appear consistent in several images taken in the same lighting conditions.

The photos are added to the Organizer, and you can easily see their thumbnail images in the Media Browser. But you don't want to continue returning to the Organizer to open one image or another in an editing mode.

Fortunately, thumbnails for all your open images appear in the Photo Bin, as shown in Figure 1-18. To see the thumbnails, click the Photo Bin button at the bottom your editing workspace.

Additionally, notice the top of the image window. All open files appear nested in the image window as tabs with the filename displayed for each open image. You can close an image by clicking the X to the right of the filename.

You can change the behavior of windows in the preferences. Options exist for making the panels default as floating windows or tabbed in the Panel Bin. See Chapter 4 of this minibook for more on setting preferences.

A tab for each open file

Open images appear in the Photo Bin

Figure 1-18: Several images opened in the Photo Editor appear in the Photo Bin.

You can easily access the images shown in the Photo Bin by clicking the respective filenames above the image window. You can also open several files in the Photo Editor and create a project from the files, such as a calendar or photo book. What you see in the Photo Bin are the files that are open in the Photo Editor in Expert mode.

In Figure 1-18, we opened six images, and they all appear in the Photo Bin when we hide the Panel Bin. (Click Layers, and the panel disappears.) If we want to work on the images and do something like move image data between the photos, we need to organize the photos in the image window a little differently. To work between photos, we need to view each photo in its own separate window.

We can easily undock the photos and have them appear in separate windows by choosing options on the Layout menu. Click Layout at the bottom of the Photo Editor workspace and choose an option to view photos differently in the image window. In our example, we chose All Grid, as shown in Figure 1-19. The photos then are displayed individually in separate windows.

Figure 1-19: Choose an option in the Layout pop-up menu to change the display in the image window.

Getting Productive with Shortcuts

Every Adobe program supports keyboard shortcuts, and Elements makes use of many different keystroke actions that open menus and select various tools. As a matter of fact, the keystroke commands available to you are so numerous that you would spend considerable time committing them all to memory.

Fortunately, Elements provides you with many hints as you organize and work on your photos. You find hints for using keyboard shortcuts in the following places:

✔ **Menus:** When you open a menu and skim the commands, you find that many commands list a keyboard shortcut, as shown in Figure 1-20.

Look at Figure 1-20. If you want to use Auto Smart Tone (the first menu item), press Alt+Ctrl+T (⌘+Option+T on the Mac) to invoke the menu command. Using the

Enhance	Layer	Select	Filter	View	Window
Auto Smart Tone...					Alt+Ctrl+T
Auto Smart Fix...					Alt+Ctrl+M
Auto Levels					Shift+Ctrl+L
Auto Contrast					Alt+Shift+Ctrl+L
Auto Color Correction					Shift+Ctrl+B
Auto Sharpen					
Auto Red Eye Fix					Ctrl+R
Adjust Smart Fix...					Shift+Ctrl+M
Adjust Lighting					▶
Adjust Color					▶
Convert to Black and White...					Alt+Ctrl+B
Unsharp Mask...					
Adjust Sharpness...					
Photomerge®...					▶

Figure 1-20: The items to the right of the menu commands display keyboard shortcuts.

keyboard shortcut results in exactly the same action as selecting the menu command. The Auto Smart Tone feature is a marvelous tool that helps you adjust tonality in a photo. Move the target (circle) around the photo to change the tones in different regions, as shown in Figure 1-21.

Figure 1-21: Move the circle around the photo to change tonality.

✔ **Tools:** When you move the cursor over a tool in the Tools panel, a pop-up tooltip opens, as shown in Figure 1-22. To the right of the tool name, you see a character within parentheses. Typing the character on your keyboard accesses the tool. For example, in the figure, you see the Horizontal Type tool below the selection arrow. The character in the tooltip is *T.* If you press T on your keyboard, the Horizontal Type tool is selected. You select each tool by typing individual characters on the keyboard. To scroll through tools in a given group, press the Shift key and press the respective key. For example, to scroll through the Type tools, press T to access the Horizontal Type tool and press Shift+T to scroll through the different Type tools. Note that whether you need to use the Shift key is determined in the General preferences.

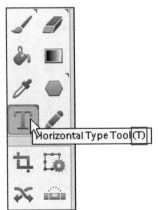

Figure 1-22: A tooltip displays the keyboard shortcut for the tool.

The best way to figure out keyboard shortcuts is to observe the menus and tools when you perform edits. For edits you use frequently, try to commit their keyboard shortcuts to memory. As you figure out more shortcuts, you'll find that working in Elements goes much faster.

Finding Help When You Need It

We hope this book provides you with helpful information on using all the features you have available when working in Photoshop Elements. However, you don't have to page through the book for every edit you make.

For speedy access to readily available Help information or when you want to expand your knowledge of commands, tools, and procedures, you have several sources of Help information.

Using the Help menu

Open the Help menu, and you find a menu command to access the Photoshop Elements Help guide. The web-based Help guide is hosted on the Adobe website. You need an Internet connection to access the file.

After choosing Help⇨Photoshop Elements Help or pressing the F1 key (Windows) or Help key or ⌘+? (Mac), you can search for keywords. Press the Enter key after typing the words you want to search for, and the panel that Elements opens on the left lists areas where you can find answers. Double-click an item, and the right pane provides you with Help information.

Reading PDFs from the Installer DVD-ROM

On the Installer DVD-ROM, you find several PDF documents. You need to have Adobe Reader installed on your computer to see these files on Windows. On the Mac you can see the PDF files in the Mac OS Preview application. The Installer disc contains the Adobe Reader installer. Double-click the installer to install Adobe Reader. Then take some time to browse the contents of the DVD-ROM for PDF documents.

If you have an earlier version of Adobe Reader on a Windows computer and you want to install a newer version from the Elements DVD-ROM, you must first uninstall the earlier version of Adobe Reader before installing a newer version.

Reading tooltips

We cover tooltips earlier in this chapter in the section "Getting Productive with Shortcuts." As you place the cursor over tools and in panels, you can observe the tooltips. They contain helpful information concerning the types of edits you want to perform or notifications of actions that take place when you click an object or a command.

Checking dialog boxes

When you open many different dialog boxes, you find some text adjacent to a light bulb icon, beginning with Learn More About and followed by blue text, as shown in Figure 1-23. Click the blue text, and the Adobe website opens to web pages where Help information is available.

Every time you see a light bulb icon appearing in a dialog box, you're one click away from Help information.

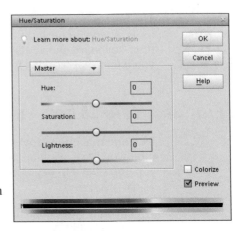

Figure 1-23: You can find links to Help information in dialog boxes.

Chapter 2: Getting to Know the Tools

In This Chapter

✓ **Looking at the Tools panel**

✓ **Understanding the tool groups**

✓ **Automating your image edits**

Y ou edit photos by using menu commands and tools. Elements knows that, so it provides you with a toolshed chock-full of tools to perform all sorts of editing tasks. These tasks include selecting image content areas, refining and sharpening photos, drawing and painting, adding text, and more.

In addition to using tools for manually changing the characteristics of a photo, you can use a number of different tools to magically automate tasks. In this chapter, you take a look at the Tools panel and all the tools at your disposal for modifying photos in many ways.

Examining the Tools Panel

The Tools panel opens by default when you enter Expert mode in the Editor. As you may recall from Chapter 1 of this minibook, you can open the Editor directly from the Welcome screen by clicking the Photo Editor button or by clicking Editor in the Organizer.

The tools you see in Figure 2-1 are listed by name and their keyboard shortcuts. If you press the key adjacent to a tool name shown in Figure 2-1, you select its respective tool. (See Chapter 1 in this minibook for more on keyboard shortcuts.)

The tools in the Tools panel include the ones in the following list, from top to bottom (sort of). To get you into the habit of using keyboard shortcuts, we list the shortcut associated with each tool and describe what you can do with each one.

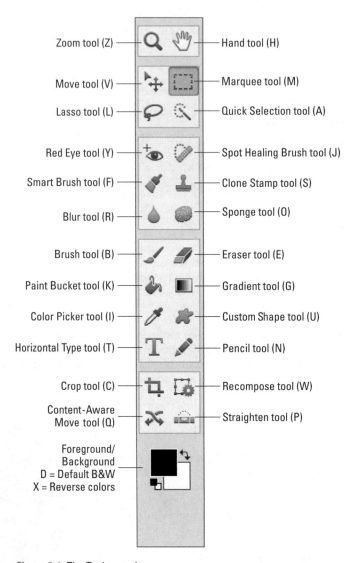

Figure 2-1: The Tools panel.

Z Zoom: Click with this tool to zoom in on an image. Press the Alt (Option on the Mac) key when the tool is selected and click to zoom out.

H Hand: Move an image around the image window. If you zoom in on a photo and see scroll bars on the right and left sides of the image window, you can drag the image around the window to display hidden areas.

V Move: Move either content within a selection, a layer, or an entire image.

M Marquee: One of many tools you can use to select part of an image.

L Lasso: Select part of an image in a free-form manner.

A Quick Selection: Similar to the Magic Wand tool, lets you click and drag to select part of an image.

Y Red Eye: Remove red-eye from photos.

J Spot Healing Brush: Repair images by removing dust and scratches.

F Smart Brush: Brighten or add contrast to areas you specify by "brushing over" the image.

S Clone Stamp: Clone an image area.

R Blur: Soften edges, particularly when you paste new image content into a photo and want to blur the edges of the pasted data slightly.

O Sponge: Add or remove color saturation on a photo.

B Brush: Paint over a photo using a number of brush tips.

E Eraser: Erase part of an image.

K Paint Bucket: Fill an area with a foreground color.

G Gradient: Create gradients.

I Color Picker: Sample color in an image. Click anywhere in a photo, and the foreground color swatch changes to the sample taken with the Color Picker tool. Press the Alt (Option) key and click the Color Picker tool to sample color for the background color.

If you're using other marking tools, such as Brush, Pencil, Blur, and so on, pressing Alt (Option) temporarily switches to the Color Picker tool. Release the Alt/Option key and you return to the last selected tool.

U Custom Shape: Create a vector shape on a new layer. This is one of many Shape tools you can choose in the Tool Options panel.

T Horizontal Type: Add text to a photo.

N Pencil: Draw free-form as if you're using a pencil.

C Crop: Crop images.

W Recompose: Recompose an image by making selections and resizing selected areas of an image.

Q Content-Aware Move Tool: Select an area in a photo and move the selection away. Elements automatically fills the empty space with content so the photo appears with a background similar to the surrounding area.

P Straighten: Straighten images — particularly useful for scanned images.

X Switch Foreground and Background Colors: Toggle between the foreground and background colors.

D Default Foreground and Background Colors: Return the foreground color to default black and the background color to default white.

Many tools in the Tools panel have companion tools that form a group. For example, the Lasso tool is contained among a group with the Magnetic Lasso and Polygon Lasso tools. Prior to Elements 11, tools within common groups appeared in pop-out toolbars. You accessed the toolbar by pressing the mouse button down on a tool that displayed a tiny arrow below and to the right of the tool.

Photoshop Elements 11 through 13 have eliminated the pop-out toolbars in the Tools panel. All tools within tool groups are now accessed in the Tool Options panel. (For more information on the Tool Options panel, see Chapter 1 in this minibook.)

Elements supports touch-screen capability on both Windows and Mac platforms. If you have a touch-screen monitor, or an iPad with a VNC (Virtual Network Computing) application, you can browse images in the Organizer by simply flicking with your fingers. What's even cooler is that you can retouch and enhance images by using all the tools in the Tools panel with your fingers. Mouse? We don't need no stinkin' mouse!

After you know the keyboard shortcuts for accessing tools, you can select tools within common tool groups by pressing the keystroke to access a tool plus the Shift key. For example, if you press L, you access the Lasso tool. When you press Shift+L, you access the Magnetic Lasso tool. Press Shift+L again, and you access the Polygon Lasso tool. You can also bypass adding the Shift key in the General preferences. If you disable Use Shift Key for Tool Switch, you can change tools simply by pressing the key for the respective character.

You can think of the tools in the Tools panel as part of individual categories. Knowing a little about the categories can help you decide where to look first when you want to make edits to a photo. The rest of this chapter discusses each tool in its category.

Using Selection Tools

You use *selection tools* to create selections of pixels in a photo. Unlike the objects you find in programs such as Microsoft PowerPoint, graphics you import in Microsoft Word, or artwork you create in illustration programs such as Adobe Illustrator or CorelDraw, photos are composed of tiny pixels. In other programs where objects are available, you can just click the mouse button with the cursor placed on an object to select it. In Photoshop Elements, you surround pixels with a selection tool to select part of a photo.

Clicking an object is easy, but selecting pixels requires some careful steps. You must also use the best tool to make a given selection. You can easily run into problems when little contrast and slight color difference exist between the areas you want to select and the areas you want to remain unselected in a photo.

You can also use certain keyboard modifiers to manage selections when using a selection tool. Such modifiers include

- **Shift key:** If you select a geometric selection tool and then press the Shift key while dragging the mouse, shapes are constrained to a square or circle. Also, if you make a selection on a photo and then press the Shift key and drag a new selection, you get to add that selection to the one you've already made. If you've made a selection on a photo and don't use the Shift key when you create a new selection, the first area you chose becomes deselected by default.

- **Alt (Option on the Mac) key:** When you press the Alt (Option) key and drag a geometric selection tool, you draw the selection from the center outward. If you already have a selection and then press the Alt (Option) key and drag through the first selection, you remove that segment from the current selection.

- **Shift+Alt (Shift+Option on the Mac):** If you already have a selection drawn, pressing the Shift key and the Alt (Option) key while dragging through that selection creates a new selection at the intersection with the original selection.

- **Spacebar:** If you press the spacebar while drawing a selection, you can move a selection to another area in a photo without changing the size of the selection.

- **Tool Options panel:** Don't forget the Tool Options panel below the Media Browser. When you click a selection tool, you find additional choices available by clicking one of the choices in the Tool Options panel. Choose from Creating a New Selection, Add to a Selection, Subtract from a Selection, or Intersect with a Selection.

The following sections introduce you to the tools, and you find out details about how to create selections with them in Book IV.

Geometric selection tools

The geometric selection tools include the Rectangular Marquee tool and the Elliptical Marquee tool. By default, the Rectangular Marquee tool appears "on top" in the Tools panel, whereas the Elliptical Marquee tool is hidden from view. So how do you find the hidden tool? Easy — look down at the Tool Options panel. In the Tool Options panel, you see all tools within the selected tool's group as well as attribute choices for setting options for the tools, as shown in Figure 2-2.

All tools in the tool
group appear here.

Click to dismiss the Tool Options panel.

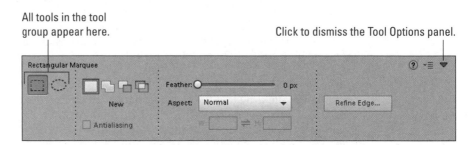

Figure 2-2: When you click the Rectangle Marquee tool, the Elliptical Marquee tool appears beside the Rectangle Marquee tool in the Tool Options panel.

Using geometric selection tools is straightforward. Click either the Rectangular Marquee tool or the Elliptical Marquee tool and drag on a photo to create a rectangle or ellipse.

The Tool Options panel occupies the same space as the Photo Bin (see Chapter 1 in this minibook for more on the Photo Bin). If you want to return to the Photo Bin after selecting a tool, click Photo Bin at the bottom of the Editor window. If you want to dismiss the Tool Options panel (and the Photo Bin), click the down-pointing arrow in the upper right (shown in Figure 2-2).

Lasso tools

Whereas the geometric selection tools restrict you to creating rectangles and elliptical shapes, the Lasso tools are used to create irregular selections — similar to freehand drawing with a pencil. The following three types of Lasso tools are shown in the Tool Options panel in Figure 2-3:

- **Lasso:** Click this tool and draw on a photo in a free-form fashion to select pixels around irregular shapes.

- **Magnetic Lasso:** With this tool, you can click and drag around a shape, and Elements magically hugs the shape as you draw. If you have a fore-ground figure that you want to isolate from the background, you can drag this tool around the shape. Elements automatically refines the selection to grab the shape you're selecting.

✔ **Polygonal Lasso:** This tool behaves like a Polygon tool that requires you to click and release the mouse button and then move the cursor to click in another area on the photo. As you continue clicking, the selection shape takes the form of a polygon.

In Figure 2-3, the Magnetic Lasso tool is selected in the Tool Options panel, and the tool name appears above the tool. As you select a tool, the tool name appears similarly in the Tool Options panel.

Magic Wand tool

The Magic Wand tool is truly magical. This tool performs a few different actions. For example, when you click the tool in an area of a blue sky, the area you click is sampled for the selected pixel value. Immediately following the mouse click, Elements travels outward in a contiguous area (if the check box in the Tool Options is selected) to find pixels of similar value and includes them in the selection. If Contiguous area is not checked in Tool Options, Elements looks through the entire image to find a similar color value as the one you click.

Figure 2-3: Click the Lasso tool in the Tools panel and observe the companion tools in the Tool Options panel.

To determine the amount of variance of the pixel values picked up by the Magic Wand tool, tweak the Tolerance value in the Tool Options panel, as shown in Figure 2-4. You can change (by moving the slider or typing in the text box) the value so that the Magic Wand tool selects a wider range of pixels (a higher number) or narrower range of pixels (a lower value).

Figure 2-4: You can change the Tolerance value to select a wider or narrower range of pixels.

By default, the Tolerance value is set to 32, which means that the pixel you click produces a selection of 16 pixel values lower than the sample and 16 pixel values higher than the sample.

After you create a selection with the Magic Wand tool and you want to add another selection to the first selection, press the Shift key and click the Magic Wand tool in another area on the photo. If you grab too many pixels, you can press the Alt (Option) key and click the area you don't want to be selected. If you need to refine the selection, you can adjust the Tolerance value in the Tool Options panel before clicking the mouse button each time you add to or subtract from a selection.

Suppose that you make a selection with the Magic Wand tool and the selection appears with tiny gaps (unselected areas). You can quickly grab those tiny areas that were not selected by using a menu command. Choose Select⇨ Modify⇨Expand and type a small number in the Expand Selection dialog box (1 or 2 pixels). The selection expands. Now return to the Select menu and choose Modify⇨Contract. Type the same value in the dialog box (1 or 2 pixels) to contract the selection.

Quick Selection tool

The Quick Selection tool is similar to the Magic Wand tool. Click the tool in an area of a photo, and three check boxes in the Tool Options panel permit you to start a new selection, add to the current selection, or subtract from the current selection.

If the Quick Selection tool isn't visible in the Tools panel, click the Selection Brush or the Magic Wand tool and click the Quick Selection tool in the Tool Options panel (refer to Figure 2-4).

In Figure 2-5, we used the Quick Selection tool and clicked a few times in the sky area of the photo to create the selection.

After you have a selection — regardless of the tool you used to create the selection — other edits you perform in Elements apply to only the active selection. If no selection appears on your photo, edits are made to the entire layer.

Using Figure 2-6 as an example, we wanted to add a little more character to the sky. We first set the foreground color to a light blue, and then applied the Filter⇨Render⇨Clouds filter to artificially create a better sky. (For more information on using filters, see Book VII, Chapter 1.)

Selection Brush tool

Use the Selection Brush tool like a brush to change shapes and diameters and paint over an area in an image. The result is a selection. To find out more about the Selection Brush tool, see Book IV, Chapter 1.

Figure 2-5: Click the Quick Selection tool in a few areas with similar pixel values to create a selection.

Figure 2-6: After you create a selection, you can apply edits to just the selected area.

Using Drawing and Painting Tools

Drawing and painting tools provide you with a huge number of options for adding illustrations, paintings, and effects and modifying brightness and contrast in photos. Don't think of these tools strictly as tools you use to draw and paint. You can also use them for color correction, contrast adjustments, and other kinds of brightness enhancements. Check out the introduction to the tools here and flip to Book V to find steps to guide you through the process of using them.

Brush tools

Several types of Brush tools are tucked away in the Tool Options panel. To view all tools, click the Brush tool and look down to the Tool Options panel to see the additional Brush tools, shown in Figure 2-7.

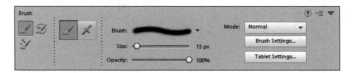

Figure 2-7: The Brush tools.

The tools that are available in the Tool Options panel are

- **Brush:** The Brush tool supports a number of different brush tips that you can choose from the Tool Options panel. You use the Brush tool as you would use a brush to apply paint to a canvas. You can paint within type selections, add color to selected areas, paint in selection channels, and more. For more information on selections, see Book IV, Chapter 1. For more on type selections, see Book V, Chapter 3. For more on selection channels and selection masks, see Book VI, Chapter 4.

- **Impressionist Brush:** This tool is designed to paint over a photo to make it look like a masterpiece by Renoir or Matisse. You can set various options that change the brush stroke style. Styles are chosen from a drop-down list in the Tool Options panel.

- **Color Replacement:** As its name suggests, you use this tool to paint over areas where you want to replace color.

- **Tablet support:** To the right of the three Brush tools, you see two more tools. These tools are only active when you use a tablet and stylus. The tools offer Brush mode (left) or Airbrush mode (right).

Smart Brush tools

The Smart Brush tools, shown in Figure 2-8, are located in the Tool Options panel. As you can see in Figure 2-8, the tools support options that you can select in a pop-up menu.

Using the Smart Brush and Detail Smart Brush tools is impressive and requires more than a brief explanation here. For a detailed view of using the brushes, see Book VIII, Chapter 2.

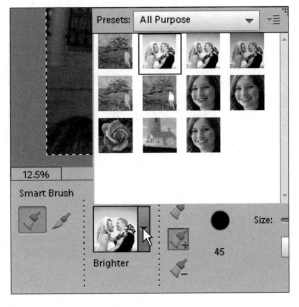

Figure 2-8: The Smart Brush tools.

Eraser tools

Three Eraser tools appear in the Tool Options panel, as shown in Figure 2-9:

- **Eraser:** The Eraser tool paints a color on a photo if you're erasing on the Background layer. The current background color is used when you paint with this tool on the Background layer. If your photo appears on a layer, the Eraser tool behaves like a normal eraser, removing pixels as you drag across a photo.

- **Background Eraser:** When you open a photo in the Editor, the photo appears on a background. Certain objects and types are added in layers that appear above the background. Two things happen when you make your first edit with this tool: The background is converted to a layer, and as you drag the cursor, the image data is removed from the layer.

Figure 2-9: The Eraser tools.

- **Magic Eraser:** The Magic Eraser tool sort of combines the Quick Selection tool and the Eraser tool. When you click and draw on a background, the area where you click is selected just as with the Quick Selection tool. Also, the background is converted to a layer, and the selected area is removed from the photo.

For details about working with each eraser, flip to Book VI, Chapter 4.

Paint Bucket tool

The Paint Bucket tool performs two separate actions when you click the tool in a photo. First it creates a selection similar to the one you create with the Magic Wand tool. After the selection is created, the foreground color fills the selected area. See Book V, Chapter 2, for more about the Paint Bucket tool.

Gradient tool

You can use the Gradient tool to create a gradient on a layer or within a selected area. You have a number of choices for gradient colors from the Tool Options panel, or you can add custom colors to create the gradient effect. Book V, Chapter 2, explains how to create and customize gradients.

Using Tools for Cloning and Healing

The cloning and healing tools are used for effects and when you need to clean up images. *Cloning* involves duplicating an image area to construct image content that wasn't in the original photo, whereas *healing* means (in an Elements context) removing dust, scratches, and imperfections in photos. Book VIII, Chapter 1, explains how to use these tools to fix problems in your images.

Cloning tools

Cloning tools are designed to duplicate image areas. You can use them for artistic effects and for reconstructing, repairing, and enhancing photos. The two tools are

- **Clone Stamp:** You use this tool by first sampling an area on a photo you want to clone. To sample, you place the cursor over the area to clone, press the Alt (Option) key, and then click the mouse button. You then move the cursor to an area where the clone image will appear and start painting with the cursor.

- **Pattern Stamp:** Use the Pattern Stamp tool to apply a pattern you select from a list of available patterns from the Tool Options panel. Select a pattern and paint with the cursor to apply the pattern to an area on a photo.

Healing brushes

Healing brushes are designed for photo-repair tasks, such as removing dust and scratches. The two Healing Brush tools are

- **Spot Healing Brush:** The Spot Healing Brush tool automatically samples neighboring pixels to correct image imperfections in one step. Unlike when you use the Healing Brush tool, you don't need to sample an area and then apply the brush strokes.

- **Healing Brush:** You use the Healing Brush tool by first pressing the Alt (Option) key and sampling an area you want to use as a source for the repair. Then move the cursor to a scratch or another imperfection and paint over the area.

Content-Aware Move tool

The Content-Aware Move tool gives you yet another way to fix photo imperfections. Suppose that you have a nice photo, but a trash can or some other object appears in the foreground. The Content-Aware Move tool enables you to easily move the object out of the way. You simply draw a selection around the object you want to move and then drag the selection away, as shown in Figure 2-10.

Before   After

Figure 2-10: The Content-Aware Move tool helps you move distracting foreground objects out of the way.

Creating Text with Typographical Tools

Elements offers you several tools for adding type to a photo. The tools, shown in Figure 2-11 reading from left to right and top to bottom, are

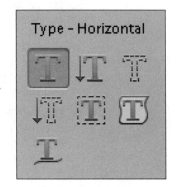

Figure 2-11: The Type tools.

- **Horizontal Type:** Click the cursor and type text horizontally. You can choose from various type attributes in the Tool Options panel.

- **Vertical Type:** Use this tool to add type vertically on a photo.

- **Horizontal Type Mask:** The Type Mask tools create selection outlines of the characters you type. As the tool name indicates, the text created with this tool is oriented horizontally.

- **Vertical Type Mask:** Use this tool to create a selection mask vertically.

- **Text on Selection:** Click this tool and make a selection. After completing the selection, you add text to the selection path.

- **Text on Shape:** Click this tool, and you can draw a shape (like a box). Move the cursor over the shape while the tool is still selected and add type to the shape. For example, add type around the sides of a box.

- **Text on Custom Path:** Click this tool, and you draw a line free-form — it's much like using a Pencil tool, but the cursor appearance is like a Pen tool. After drawing a line, click the cursor on the line to add text along the path.

Discover the tips and tricks of typography and see how to more precisely use the Elements 13 Type tools in Book V, Chapter 3.

Using Focus and Toning Tools

Use focus and toning tools to edit image brightness, contrast, and color. Several tools for making these adjustments are contained within the Tools panel. Book VIII, Chapter 1 explains how you use these tools to create your desired results.

Red Eye Removal tool

In Elements 13, two tools appear in the Tools Panel:

- **Red Eye Removal tool:** This tool is used to scrub over red-eye that frequently appears when taking pictures indoors with a flash.

✔ **Pet Red Eye tool:** This tool is new to Elements 13. We've had a red-eye correction tool available for people, but Adobe forgot about our pets that show up with green eyes when we're shooting with flash. This tool helps you correct red-eye (or green-eye) problems with your pets.

Toning tools

Toning tools are used to refine edges on pasted content of photos by softening edges, sharpening areas of a photo, and blending areas that might have been cloned or pasted into photos. The tools, as shown in Figure 2-12, are

✔ **Blur:** Scrub over an area to blur the pixels.

✔ **Sharpen:** Scrub over an area to sharpen it.

✔ **Smudge:** Scrub over an area to blend pixels.

Figure 2-12: The Toning tools.

Focus tools

You use *focus* tools for making edits similar to those traditionally used in photo darkrooms. The tools, shown in Figure 2-13, are

✔ **Sponge:** Use this tool on an area that you want to either saturate with more color or reduce saturation. The choices for saturation and desaturation are found in the Tool Options panel.

✔ **Dodge:** The process of dodging in a traditional darkroom holds back light during a print exposure resulting in a lighter image. Use this tool to scrub over areas in a photo that you want to lighten.

✔ **Burn:** Burning has the opposite effect as dodging. Use this tool to darken image areas.

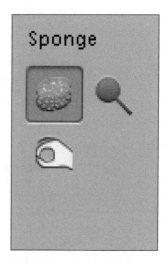

Figure 2-13: The Focus tools.

Creating Shapes

Use shapes to add artistic elements to photos or to mask out areas in a photo. We explain using shapes in layers and masks in Book VI. Find out your options in the following sections.

Cookie Cutter tool

When you click and drag the Cookie Cutter tool on a photo, the entire area outside the shape is eliminated from the layer. You can see some of the shapes available in Figure 2-14. Book VI, Chapter 4 cuts to the chase with steps for using this tool.

Shape tools

Shape tools, as shown in Figure 2-15, add different shape objects to your images.

This list describes what you can do with the Shape tools:

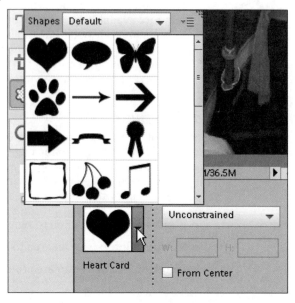

Figure 2-14: To change the Cookie Cutter shape, open the pop-up menu and click a different shape.

- ✔ **Rectangle:** Draw a rectangle.
- ✔ **Rounded Rectangle:** Draw rectangles with rounded corners.
- ✔ **Ellipse:** Draw elliptical shapes.
- ✔ **Polygon:** Draw polygonal shapes.
- ✔ **Line:** Draw lines.
- ✔ **Custom Shape:** Draw custom shapes from a choice of shapes identical to those available for the Cookie Cutter tool. Again, you make shape choices from a drop-down list in the Tool Options panel.

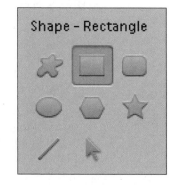

Figure 2-15: The Shape tools.

- ✔ **Shape Selection:** After a shape has been drawn, it appears as an object on a photo. Move it by clicking and dragging with this tool.

Viewing, Navigating, and Sampling Tools

Some of the tools in Elements are useful for zooming in and out of photos, moving photos around the image window, and sampling color.

Book I
Chapter 2

Getting to Know the
Tools

Color Picker tool

The Color Picker tool samples color and places the sample color in the Foreground color swatch. If you press the Alt (Option) key and click the Color Picker tool, the sampled color is placed in the Background color swatch.

Hand tool

Use the Hand tool to move a photo around the image window.

Zoom tool

Click the Zoom tool to zoom in on a photo. Press the Alt (Option) key to zoom out.

You find the same magnifying glass icon for the Zoom tool appearing in different dialog boxes. Whenever you see this tool icon, realize that in order to zoom out, you always need to press the Alt (Option) key and then click the photo.

When using any of the painting tools, pressing Alt (Option) shows you the Eyedropper tool. You can click to sample color; release the Alt (Option) key to return to the selected painting tool.

Other Editing Tools

Some miscellaneous tools are contained in the Tools panel to perform additional edits.

Move tool

Click and drag with the Move tool to move the selection (and all pixels contained within the selection) on the canvas. This tool is particularly helpful when moving layer content if you're creating layered files. If you press the Alt key (Option on the Mac) when you drag, you duplicate the content.

Crop tool

Use the Crop tool, shown in Figure 2-16, for cropping images.

The Crop tool has changed in Elements 13. No longer do you have options for Rule of Thirds and Golden Ratio. In Elements 13, you have

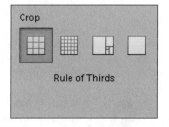

Figure 2-16: The Crop tool.

crop suggestions (as shown in Figure 2-17). Move the mouse cursor over the thumbnails to see the different suggestions Elements offers you for cropping a photo. To find out more about using the new features for the Crop tool and understanding the grid choices, see Book III, Chapter 1.

Figure 2-17: The Crop tool now offers you suggestions for cropping your photos.

Recompose tool

The Recompose tool was nested with the Crop tool in Elements 10. In Elements 11 and later, the Recompose tool occupies its own position in the Tools panel. This tool is marvelous when you have large gaps between subjects and want to narrow the gaps to bring people closer together in a group shot. For more information on using the Recompose tool, see Book IV, Chapter 1.

Straighten tool

Use the Straighten tool to straighten crooked images. This tool is especially useful for slightly tilted images. We used the Straighten tool in Chapter 1 of this minibook in Guided mode. Refer to Chapter 1 to see how the Straighten tool helps you straighten images.

In earlier versions of Elements, the Straighten tool left some gaps after straightening a photo. In Elements 13, you find a Content-Aware Fill applied to the Straighten tool, and the results are much improved.

Discovering the Automation Tools

Elements offers you some one-click steps to improve your images. Although these automated tasks aren't *tools* per se, we list them here as tools to simplify the message. In reality, you use menu commands to automate certain refinements for your photos. More authentic automation is available using the Actions panel.

Using one-click auto adjustments

To observe the automation tools available to you, click the Enhance menu and look over the first set of commands, as shown in Figure 2-18. If a menu command name begins with *Auto,* the command has something to do with an automated function.

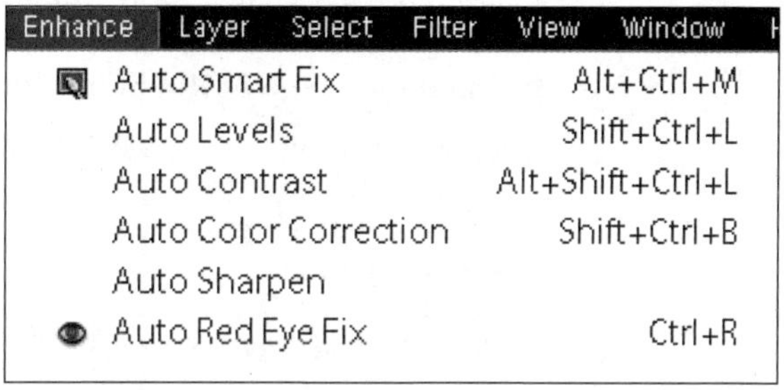

Figure 2-18: Some automated tasks in Elements are listed as menu commands in the Enhance menu.

The automated features you find in the Enhance menu are

- ✓ **Auto Smart Fix:** Use Auto Smart Fix to add more contrast, adjust brightness, and improve color by using only one menu choice.

- ✓ **Auto Levels:** The Levels adjustment is used to adjust image brightness. Elements takes a guess at the proper brightness level and automatically boosts the white and black points in your photos to render a pure white and rich black.

- ✓ **Auto Contrast:** Use this command when contrast is flat and without any snap.

- ✓ **Auto Color Correction:** Auto Color Correction improves color in images by removing color casts.

- ✓ **Auto Sharpen:** Use the Auto Sharpen command to sharpen dull images.

- ✓ **Auto Red Eye Fix:** You use this tool to remove red-eye in photos. If you have a group shot taken with a flash, you can use this command to remove red-eye from all subjects.

In previous versions of Elements, the auto-correction tools offered you corrections without regard to your personal preferences. For example, some people may like to see photos with a bit more contrast while others may want a little less contrast. In Elements 12 and 13, you find an implementation of Auto Correction with Learning. In essence, Elements learns some tweaks that you make to adjustments and applies the same tweaks to all subsequent images you correct. It's like an artificial intelligence application for your personal use with the auto-correction tools.

Running actions

An action is an automated set of sequences. You find several of these available in the Actions panel. To access actions, click More in the Editor at the bottom of the Panel Bin. From the pop-up menu, choose Actions. To perform an action on an image, do the following:

1. **Open an image in the Editor and open the Actions panel.**

2. **Look over the actions appearing in the panel. If you see one you like, skip to Step 4. If you don't find the action you want, open the Options menu and choose Load Actions, as shown in Figure 2-19.**

   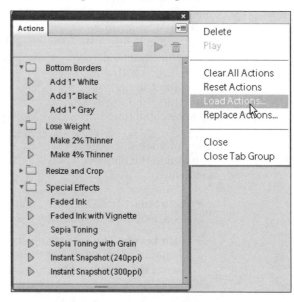

   After clicking Load Actions, the Load dialog box opens. Elements takes you to the Actions depository automatically. You don't have to search your hard drive for the Actions files.

   Figure 2-19: Open the Options menu and click Load Actions.

3. **In the Load dialog box shown in Figure 2-20, select the action set you want and click Load.**

   In our example, we chose the Image Effects actions.

4. **Run the action.**

   In our example, we want to use a simple action to create a sepia toning on an image. Click the action you want to use and click the Play Selection (right-pointing arrow), as shown in Figure 2-21. The action runs and produces the effect in a single step.

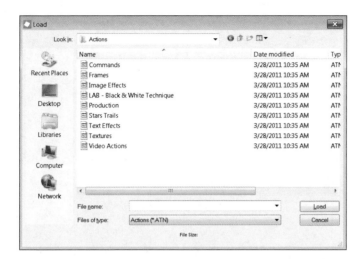

Figure 2-20: Select the action set you want to use and click Load.

Figure 2-21: Click the Play Selection button to run the action.

Many predefined actions are available in Elements. Have some fun and poke around, experimenting with the effects that the actions produce.

If you want a custom action that's not available in Elements, you can create actions (or have them created for you) in Adobe Photoshop. You can also find actions available for download from the Internet. Elements will run most of the actions you create in Photoshop or download from sites offering free or for-purchase action sets.

Chapter 3: Viewing and Navigating Images

In This Chapter

- ✓ Examining the Image window
- ✓ Changing zoom views
- ✓ Navigating images
- ✓ Seeing grids and guides
- ✓ Getting information from the Info panel
- ✓ Working with the Graphics panel

*O*ne of the most important aspects of working with images in an editor is navigation — knowing how to move around the image (as well as between images) and how to use tools and menu commands to help.

Many tools in Elements enable you to zoom in and out of images, acquire information about your photos, and examine them in detail. In this chapter, we talk about these tools and clue you in on the best methods to use for viewing files in an editor.

When you open the Photo Editor, you arrive at the last mode you viewed. You find four different modes — eLive, Quick, Guided, and Expert. Throughout this chapter, when we refer to the Photo Editor, we assume that you enter the Expert mode. After you select Expert in the Photo Editor, all future editing sessions open in the Expert mode.

Looking at the Image Window

The first thing you need to know about examining an image is how to open it in the Image window. The Image window in the Photo Editor is where your photos open, ready for editing. To open an image in the Photo Editor, you have a few options available to you.

Like almost all programs, Elements supports choosing File⊅Open. When you use that menu command, a dialog box opens, enabling you to navigate your hard drive and select a photo. Click the Open button, and the photo opens in the Image window.

Another method for opening photos is to use the Organizer, where you select one or more photos you want to edit. Because we cover the essential steps for using the Organizer in Book II, Chapter 2, we take a look here at opening a file from the Organizer in the Photo Editor:

1. **Open the Organizer.**

   You can launch Photoshop Elements and click the Organizer button on the Welcome screen to open the Organizer window; or, if you're in an edit mode now, click the Organizer button at the bottom of the Photo Editor window.

2. **Click a photo thumbnail in the Organizer window.**

   Following this step presumes that you have photos in the default catalog, as we explain in Chapter 1 of this minibook and elaborate more in Book II, Chapter 2.

3. **Click Editor at the bottom of the Organizer window or press Ctrl+I/⌘+I.**

   The photo opens in the Image window docked to the Elements workspace. By default, and unless you made any changes to the Photo Editor Preferences, the photo appears as a tab in the Photo Editor.

   If you want the photos to appear as floating windows as shown in In Figure 3-1, you need to make an adjustment in General Preferences. Open General Preferences by pressing CTRL/⌘+K. Check Allow Floating Documents In Expert Mode in the General Preferences and click OK. To undock a photo from the tabbed group, click the tab at the top of the image window and drag away from the top.

Figure 3-1 highlights several important items when you view photos in the Image window:

- The **filename** appears in the upper-left corner of the photo (above the center on the Mac). Double-check the name to be certain that the photo you want to edit is the correct image.

- **Scroll bars** become active when you zoom in on an image. You can click the scroll arrows, move the scroll bar, or grab the Hand tool in the Tools panel and then drag within the window to move the image.

- The **Magnification box** shows you at a glance how much you've zoomed in or out. Click in the box and you can type a zoom level.

- The **Information box** shows you the readout for a particular tidbit of information. You can choose which information you want to see in this area by choosing an option from the pop-up menu.

Filename   Close Button

Magnification Box

Information Box   Scroll Bars

Figure 3-1: The Image window.

When you're working on an image in Elements, you should know its physical image size, image resolution, and color mode. (We explain these terms in more detail in Book III, Chapters 1 and 2.) Regardless of which menu option you choose from the Information box, you can get a quick glimpse of these essential statistics by clicking the Information box, which displays a pop-up menu like the one shown in Figure 3-2.

> Width: 2211 pixels (30.708 inches)
> Height: 1504 pixels (20.889 inches)
> Channels: 3 (RGB Color, 8bpc)
> Resolution: 72 pixels/inch

Figure 3-2: Click the readout in the Information box to see important information about your file.

✔ The **Size box** enables you to resize the window. Move the cursor to the box, and a diagonal line with two opposing arrows appears. When the cursor changes, drag in or out to size the window smaller or larger, respectively.

You can also resize the window by dragging any other corner in or out.

- You can click the **Close button** that appears as an X in Windows (upper-right corner as shown in Figure 3-1) or like a red button (upper-left corner on the Mac) to close the active Image window and keep Elements open. Alternatively, you can press Ctrl+W (⌘+W on the Mac) or choose File⇨Close to close the active window.

When you're familiar with the overall Image window, we want to introduce you to the Information box's other drop-down menu, in which you choose the type of information you want to view in the Information box. Click the right-pointing arrow (not the information in the box itself) to open the menu, as shown in Figure 3-3.

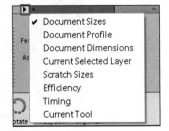

Figure 3-3: From the drop-down menu in the Information box, you select commands that provide information about your file.

Here's the lowdown on the options you find on the drop-down menu:

- **Document Sizes:** Shows you the saved file size.

- **Document Profile:** Shows you the color profile used with the file.

- **Document Dimensions:** Shows you the physical size in the default unit of measure, such as inches.

- **Current Selected Layer:** This item was added in Elements 12. When you click Current Selected Layer, the layer name appears adjacent to the right-pointing arrow that opens the pop-up menu.

- **Scratch Sizes:** Displays the amount of memory on your hard drive that's consumed by all documents open in Elements. The *scratch space* is the extension of RAM created by a space on your hard drive. For example, *20M/200M* indicates that the open documents consume 20 megabytes (M) and that a total of 200 megabytes is available for Elements to edit your images. When you add more content to a file, such as new layers, the first number grows while the second number remains static.

- **Efficiency:** Indicates how many operations are being performed in RAM as opposed to using your scratch disk. When the number is 100 percent, you're working in RAM. When the number drops below 100 percent, you're using the scratch disk.

Continually working below 100 percent is a good indication that you need to buy more RAM to increase efficiency.

- **Timing:** Indicates the time it took to complete the last operation.

- **Current Tool:** Shows the name of the tool selected from the Tools panel.

Don't worry about trying to understand all these terms. The important thing to know is that you can visit the drop-down menu to change the items at will during your editing sessions.

The Image window is just one small part of the user interface in Elements. To get the full picture, imagine that when a photo opens in the Photo Editor, you see the Image window contained within the workspace as a whole, where you have access to tools, panels, and menus to choose from a variety of editing options.

If you select multiple files in the Organizer and click the Editor button, all photos open in the Image window. Clicking the filename in the Image window brings forward a photo so that you can edit it. Likewise, double-click a thumbnail in the Photo Bin, and the photo moves forward and appears in the Image window. In the workspace interface, you see an arrangement similar to the one in Figure 3-4 when a photo is opened in the Image window and several other open photos appear in the Photo Bin. In Figure 3-4, the Panel Bin is visible. (If the Photo Bin is hidden, choose Window⮕Panel Bin or click the Layers icon at the bottom of the Photo Bin.)

Book I
Chapter 3

Viewing and
Navigating Images

Image window   Recycle Bin

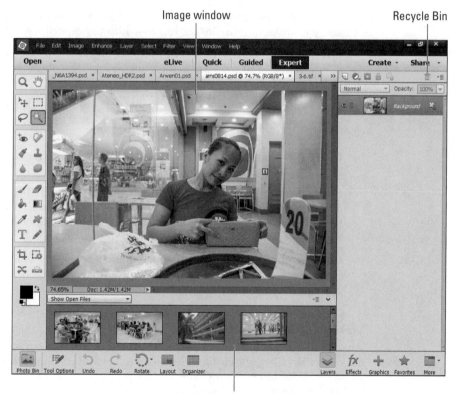

Open files in Photo Bin

Figure 3-4: One photo in the Image window with several open photos in the Photo Bin.

Zooming In and Out of Image Windows

Precision goes a long way toward making good edits on photos. When you're working carefully on image detail, zoom in on any part of a picture where you want to (carefully) apply some fine-tuning. Nothing looks worse than photos with obvious edits that were clumsily made.

Zooming with keyboard shortcuts

For some quick zooms in and out of photos, you can use keyboard shortcuts. Here are a few to keep in mind when you need to quickly change the zoom level:

- **Ctrl++ (⌘++ on the Mac):** Press the Ctrl (⌘) key and the plus (+) key, and you zoom in on a photo. Keep pressing the same keys to continue zooming in. By default, when you press these keys, the photo and the Image window zoom together.

- **Ctrl+– (⌘+– on the Mac):** Press the Ctrl (⌘) key and the minus (–) key, and you zoom out. Again, the Image window zooms along with the photo.

- **Ctrl+Alt++ (⌘+Option++ on the Mac):** Press both the Ctrl (⌘) and Alt (Option) keys and then press the plus (+) key. The photo zooms in, but the Image window stays fixed at one size.

- **Ctrl+Alt+– (⌘+Option+– on the Mac):** Press both the Ctrl (⌘) and Alt (Option) keys and then press the minus (–) key. The photo zooms out, but the Image window stays fixed at one size.

- **Ctrl+0 (⌘+0 on the Mac):** Press the Ctrl (⌘) key and then 0 (the zero key), and the photo zooms to fit the Image window.

- **Ctrl+spacebar (⌘+spacebar on the Mac):** This combination temporarily activates the Zoom In tool. For this shortcut to work on a Mac, you need to change the System Preferences and reallocate the Spotlight shortcut to another key combination.

- **Ctrl+Alt+spacebar (⌘+Option+spacebar on the Mac):** This combination temporarily activates the Zoom Out tool. You also need to reallocate the Spotlight shortcut on the Mac.

Using the Zoom tool

You can use the Zoom tool to zoom in and out of the Image window. You first click to select the Zoom tool in the Tools panel and then click the photo to zoom in. (To zoom out, press the Alt [Option] key when clicking the Zoom tool on the photo.)

While working on an image using another tool from the Tools panel, you can temporarily access the Zoom tool without clicking it in the Tools panel. Press Ctrl+spacebar (⌘+spacebar on the Mac), and the cursor changes to the Zoom In tool. To zoom out, press Ctrl+Alt+spacebar (⌘+Option+spacebar on the

Mac). When you release the keys on the keyboard, you return to the tool last selected in the Tools panel.

When you select the Zoom tool in the Tools panel, the Options panel shows your choices for zooming, as shown in Figure 3-5.

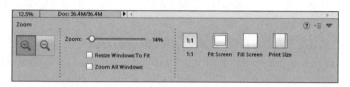

Figure 3-5: Click the Zoom tool, and the Options panel displays more options for zooming.

The tools available in the Zoom tool Options panel are

- ✔ **+/–:** The plus and minus icons are for zooming in and out of a photo in the Image window. Click one of the icons to zoom in or out.

- ✔ **Slider and Percent readout:** You can change the number in the text box to zoom to a percentage size. Drag the slider left/right to zoom out/in, respectively.

- ✔ **Resize Windows to Fit:** When you select the check box, the zoom resizes the window to the size of the image or the maximum size of the window.

- ✔ **Zoom All Windows:** If you have multiple photos open in the Image window, all photos are zoomed together when you zoom views.

- ✔ **Actual Pixels:** The ratio is reported in this text box. When the photo is shown at 100 percent size, the ratio reads *1:1.* The ratio changes as you change zoom views.

- ✔ **Fit Screen:** Zooms the current window to the screen size.

- ✔ **Fill Screen:** Click this button to zoom the image to the largest size that fits within the workspace.

- ✔ **Print Size:** Although the term suggests something relative to printing, clicking this icon just zooms the photo to 100%.

Moving with the Hand tool

When you zoom in to a size larger than the Image window can accommodate, scroll bars appear on the bottom and right sides of the photo. You can click and drag scroll bars to see more of the image area, or you can use the Hand tool to drag the image around the Image window.

While working with other tools from the Tools panel, you can temporarily access the Hand tool by pressing the spacebar. Press the spacebar and drag the image; then release the spacebar to return to the last tool selected in the Tools panel.

If you're typing text on an image, you can't use the spacebar to temporarily access the Hand tool. To move the Image window when you're typing text, click the Hand tool in the Tools panel and move the photo. Click the Type tool in the Tools panel, click in the text block you started, and continue typing.

Cruising with the Navigator panel

The Navigator panel is a handy tool to keep open when you need to zoom in and out of a photo while editing images. It allows you to zoom on a particular part of a photo while viewing a thumbnail preview of the entire image in the Navigator. You can do all your zooming in this panel — and you can keep it open during your editing session!

To open the Navigator panel, choose Window➪Navigator. The panel opens in a floating window, as shown in Figure 3-6.

Figure 3-6: The Navigator panel.

At the upper right adjacent to the slider, a readout displays the current zoom percentage. You can move the slider left to zoom out of a photo and right to zoom in on a photo. In the center of the panel, you see a view displaying the entire image and a red rectangle displaying the area corresponding to the zoom view in the Image window.

The rectangle in the center of the panel can be moved around the Navigator panel just as you use the Hand tool to move around an image. The lower-right corner is dragged out or in to size the panel larger or smaller, respectively.

You can quickly resize the zoom area in the Navigator panel by pressing the Ctrl key (⌘ on the Mac) and drawing a rectangle around the area you want to zoom.

Aligning Image Elements with Grids and Guides

Grids and guides are helpful when you're adding text to photos, working with layers, or working with selections. You can align content to guidelines for precise alignment. In addition, you can display rulers along the left and top sides of a photo.

To view the grid and guidelines, choose View⇨Grid. A nonprinting grid appears in your photo, like the one shown in Figure 3-7. To display rulers, choose View⇨Rulers.

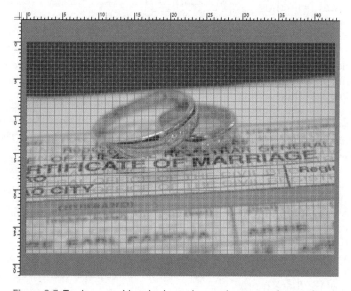

Figure 3-7: To show a grid and rulers, choose the appropriate options from the View menu.

To snap layers and objects to the grid and guides, choose View⇨Snap To. From the submenu, you can choose Guides and Grid. When the objects in your image are dragged, selected, or moved, they snap to the items you've selected on the Snap To submenu.

Using the Info Panel

The Info panel provides some feedback related to the cursor position and color information as you move the cursor around a photo. In addition, you can quickly examine the file size and other document information in the panel.

To open the Info panel, choose Window⇨Info. By default the panel is docked with the other More panels. You can make it a floating panel by dragging the Info tab away from the docked position, as shown in Figure 3-8.

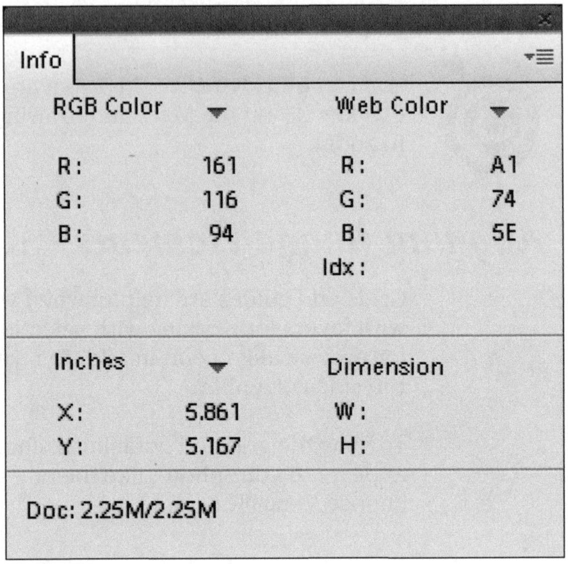

Figure 3-8: The Info panel.

Click the icon in the upper-right corner of the panel to open the Options menu, shown in Figure 3-9. Choose Panel Options from the menu, and the Info Panel Options dialog box opens. Here, you can choose what kind of information appears in the panel, such as providing information on color readouts and status information. Play around with the Info palette to see the kind of feedback it provides you.

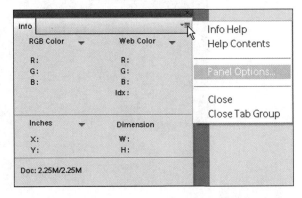

Figure 3-9: Click the down-pointing arrow to open the Info Panel Options dialog box.

Book II
Organizer Fundamentals

For more details and projects about Photoshop Elements, visit www.dummies.com/
extras/photoshopelementsaio.

Contents at a Glance

Chapter 1: Gathering Your Image Files

In This Chapter

✔ **Organizing your hard drive**

✔ **Acquiring photos from cameras, phones, scanners, and more**

✔ **Importing photos into the Organizer**

✔ **Backing up your photos and edits**

After you install Photoshop Elements, the first thing you want to do is open some photos. It stands to reason that, before you can jump into all the editing opportunities you have with the program, you need to have the image files ready to use, whether those photos are digital camera photos still on a memory card or files copied to your computer. You may also have a photo print you want to scan or photos you took on your cellphone.

Regardless of where you have photos stored, you want to get them into Elements and start working on them. In this chapter, we talk about getting your files onto your computer and imported into the Organizer. After you have your files loaded in the Organizer, you have a number of options for viewing, searching, and organizing photos in the Organizer, which we discuss in Chapters 2 and 3 of this minibook. (If you want to bypass the robust image-tagging and organization features that the Organizer offers and jump right into editing in the Photo Editor, skip to Book III.) You also find out about your options for backing up your images after you have them on your hard drive.

Organizing Image Files on Your Hard Drive

Although the Photoshop Elements Organizer is a marvelous tool for managing photos, you'll still get the best results from Elements if you first have a system for storing photos on your hard drive.

We recommend creating folders in a hierarchical order with folder names that represent logical divisions for where and when photos were taken. It's your call for how you want to develop the hierarchy. You might want to create separate folders for each year and inside those folders divide the images into other folders for people, family, business, events, occasions, and so on. How you organize the images is a personal choice. Just be certain that you keep the organization consistent and logical for your personal needs.

Dedicating a drive to just photos

If your photography is important to you and you have substantial numbers of images stored on a hard drive, you may want to look at acquiring a dedicated hard drive just for your photos. With prices dropping on large drives of ½ to 2 terabytes, you can pick up an additional drive and attach the drive to your computer. Use the drive for storing your photos only and keep all other data away from the drive.

Photoshop Elements offers you some backup options to store images *in the cloud* (a remote server accessible via the Internet) on Adobe Revel. But the free service is limited to 50 image uploads a month. These days, you can shoot 2GB of photos in a single photo shoot. All the free services you find aren't going to provide you with enough storage space if you're a serious photographer.

For backup purposes, it might be best to purchase a second drive for your photos. A 500GB to 1TB drive will serve you well for media storage and backup.

See the section "Protecting Your Assets," later in this chapter, for more details about backing up.

Viewing your hard drive's folder structure in the Organizer

When you get into the Organizer, you can use the marvelous viewing option for finding photos on a hard drive. As a matter of fact, your folder organization on your hard drive has become the default view in Elements 13. You see an Import panel and a list of folders where your photos are stored, as shown in Figure 1-1.

For a more traditional Explorer/Finder type appearance, you can change the view by clicking the folder tree icon in the Import panel (the icon is indicated by a red box in Figure 1-1). The view changes to a hierarchical view, as shown in Figure 1-2. To return to the original folder view, click the folder tree icon again. (It moves to the upper-right corner in the Import panel when the Explorer/Finder-style view is displayed.)

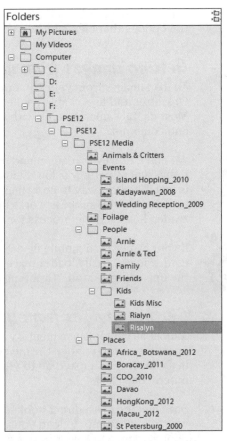

Figure 1-1: The Folder view in the Organizer.

Figure 1-2: The Hierarchical Folder view in the Organizer.

Don't worry now about how to use the Folder views and how to navigate folders. We cover all that and more in Chapter 2 of this minibook. For now, think about how you want your folders on your hard drive to be organized and create a structure that you can understand so that you can easily copy photos to the newly created folders.

Transferring Images to Your Computer

In the early days of Adobe Photoshop, circa early '90s and later when Photoshop Elements arrived, most photos were acquired from scanned prints, from scanned slides, from some point-and-shoot cameras, and occasionally from images stored on CDs. These days, you can add volumes of photos, not only from scanned images and CD/DVDs but also from digital cameras, cellphones, and tablets. The following sections walk you through the options that Elements and your computer make available to you.

Getting images from your camera

To load images from your camera in the Organizer window, you open the Organizer and use a cable connected to your camera and your computer. Most digital cameras come with USB cables that can connect to both camera and computer.

We don't, however, recommend uploading photos directly from your camera. If the camera battery is low, Elements stops the upload when the connection is lost. The best way to copy files to your computer is via a card reader. We explain how this process works in the next section. (If you don't have a reader, however, the process for a camera or reader is basically the same.)

If your camera is a mobile device instead of a digital camera with a memory card, you can easily load those images into the Elements Organizer, too. See the upcoming section, "Grabbing photos from mobile devices" for details.

Getting images from your card reader

Almost all cameras use memory cards to store photos. After shooting some photos, you can remove the memory card itself from the camera and place it in a card reader hooked up to your computer or in a direct slot on your computer if one exists.

Both methods — a direct hookup or a connection to a card reader — afford you an opportunity to load your photos into the Elements Organizer. To add photos to the Organizer from a card reader, do the following:

1. **Hook up a card reader via a cable; alternatively, if you have a built-in reader on your computer, you can insert the memory card into the slot for the built-in reader.**

   Use the cable supported by your card reader. When you connect your camera or card reader, the AutoPlay Wizard opens on a Windows PC or iPhoto opens on a Mac.

2. **Cancel the AutoPlay Wizard (Windows). If iPhoto or Image Capture opens on the Mac, close the application.**

   Click Cancel in the wizard or choose iPhoto⇨Quit to proceed.

   For Mac users, you can set Preferences in iPhoto to prevent iPhoto from being launched when you connect a camera or card reader. Open iPhoto and choose iPhoto⇨Preferences. On the General tab, select No Application from the Connecting Camera Opens pop-up menu. Click the Advanced tab and deselect the Importing Item: Copy Items to iPhoto Library check box.

3. **Open the Organizer.**

   Launch Photoshop Elements and click the Organizer button on the Welcome screen.

4. **In the Organizer, choose File⇨Get Photos and Video⇨From Camera or Card Reader or press Ctrl+G (⌘+G on the Mac).**

   The Elements Organizer – Photo Downloader Wizard appears. At the top of the wizard, you find a drop-down list that displays your hard drive and a source, such as a camera or card reader attached to your computer.

5. **In Windows, select a media source from the Get Photos from drop-down list, as shown in Figure 1-3. On the Mac, choose a source drive from the Devices list in the sidebar.**

Book II
Chapter 1

6. **Click the Browse button in the Location area and locate a folder where you want to copy your photos.**

   If you followed our advice and created folders on a hard drive as we explained in the section "Organizing Image Files on Your Hard Drive," earlier in this chapter, locate the folder where you want to copy the files. If you need a new folder, you can make a new folder in the Browse dialog box.

   After you choose a camera or card reader, the Downloader appears with the Get Media button active.

7. **Click the Get Media button and leave the other settings at their defaults.**

8. **Wait for the Downloader to complete downloading all images before continuing.**

   A progress bar displays the download progress. If you have many photos on your memory card, it may take a little time to complete the download. Be patient and wait for the download to finish.

   A dialog box opens when the download is complete. The download doesn't copy images to the Organizer.

9. **To import the copied images into the Organizer, click OK.**

10. **View the results.**

    After the photos have been imported in the Organizer, you see thumbnail images for all the photos acquired from the memory card.

After the photos are added to the Organizer, you can edit the images in the Editor's Expert or Quick mode. Book III helps you with opening images in the Editor.

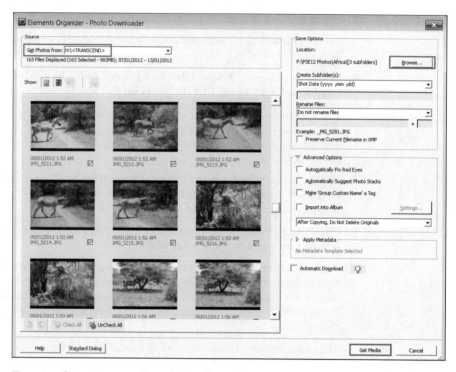

Figure 1-3: Choose a source from the Get Photos from drop-down list.

Each time you import photos in the Organizer, only the last import is visible as thumbnails. If you have other photos you previously imported and you want to see both the new import and the other files in the Organizer, click the Show All button at the top of the window.

Grabbing photos from mobile devices

If you're among the increasing numbers of people pulling a cellphone from your pocket to capture a moment or taking pictures with a tablet, this section is for you. Cellphones and tablets offer various options for transferring media from the handheld device to your computer. You typically have the following options:

- **USB:** Devices that support USB connections enable you to connect a cable through a USB port to your phone and your computer. With some devices, the computer sees the phone as an external media source, so you can drag photos from the device to a folder on your computer. In the Organizer, choose File➪Get Photos and Videos➪From Files and Folders. Or you can choose File➪Get Photos and Videos➪From Camera or Card Reader to load the files in an Organizer catalog from a folder on your hard drive or directly from the media storage source. See the preceding section for details about using these Organizer commands.

✓ **Bluetooth:** Many handheld devices support Bluetooth, a type of wireless connection. A Bluetooth support application makes a device discoverable, enabling you to copy photos from your device to a folder on your computer. Both Windows and the Macintosh operating systems support Bluetooth natively.

✓ **Email:** Although not a connection, emailing photos is available on many devices and used often for sharing photos. Simply email the photo to yourself from your device. Then log in to your email program on your computer and download the image attachment. You can then subsequently add the image to the Organizer.

The iPhone, iPad, and many Android devices use both USB connections and Bluetooth. In Figure 1-4, we hooked up a Samsung Galaxy Tab. After we mounted the device, we opened the Elements Organizer and chose File⇨Get Photos and Videos⇨From Camera or Card Reader. The Photo Downloader recognizes both the internal memory and the memory card. On the iPhone and iPad, you have only a single storage device: the internal memory card.

On the Macintosh, you can use the Apple iPhoto software to download photos and videos from the iPhone or iPad.

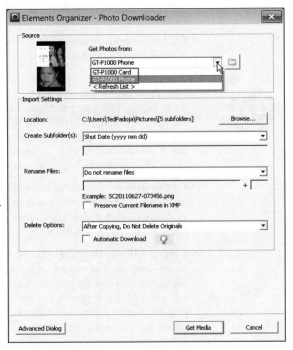

Figure 1-4: The Photo Downloader when your device is attached to your computer.

Scanning images

Scanners connect through the same ports as cameras and card readers. Most of today's scanners use either USB or FireWire. Almost all low-end scanners sold now are USB devices.

Even the lowest-end scanners provide 16-bit scans that help you get a little more data in the shadows and highlights. Like a digital camera, a scanner's price is normally in proportion to its quality.

Preparing before you scan

Just as you'd clean a lens on a digital camera and set various menu selections before clicking the shutter button, you should prepare a few things ahead of time before scanning:

- **Connect the scanner properly.** Make sure that you have all connections made to your computer according to the user manual that came with your scanner. If you just purchased a scanner, check for any lock bolts or tape and remove them according to the instructions.

- **Clean the scanner platen.** Use a lint-free cloth and some glass cleaner (applied to the cloth) to remove all dust and particles on the glass. The more dust particles you remove, the easier it is to edit your image in Elements.

- **Clean the source material.** Be certain that the print or film you want to scan is free of dust and spots.

If you have old negatives that are dirty or that have water spots or debris that you can't remove with a cloth and film cleaner, soak the film in *photo flo* (a liquid you can purchase at a photo retailer). Be certain that your hands are clean and then run the filmstrip between two fingers to remove the excess liquid. Turn on your shower full force with hot water only and hang film nearby to dry it. Remove the film when it's dry, and you should see a surprisingly clean filmstrip compared to your soiled original.

- **Get to know your scanner software.** When you scan in Elements, the software supplied with your scanner takes charge, and you use the options in this software before the image scan finally drops into an Elements image window.

- **Prepare the artwork.** If you plan on scanning pages in a book or pamphlet, remove the pages or try to make photocopies so that the piece you scan lies flat on the scanner platen. Make sure that you observe copyright laws if you're scanning printed works. For faxes and photocopies, try to improve originals by recopying them on a photocopier by using darker settings.

- **Find the scanner's sweet spot.** Every scanner has an area where you can acquire the best scans. This area is often called the *sweet spot.* To find the scanner's sweet spot, scan a blank piece of paper. The sweet spot is the brightest area on the resultant scan. Other areas should be darker. The sweet spot is most often in the upper-left quadrant, the lower-right quadrant, or the middle of the page. Note the area and place your source material within this area when scanning pictures.

Understanding image requirements

All scanning software provides you with options for determining resolution and color mode before you start a new scan. You should decide what output you intend to use and scan originals at target resolutions designed to accommodate a given output. Here are some examples:

✓ **Scan the artwork or photo at the size and resolution for the final output.**
Scan at 72 ppi for web use and 150 ppi to 300 ppi for print or archiving.
(See Book III, Chapter 2, for information about resizing images.)

✓ **Size images with the scanner software.** If you have a 4-x-6 photo that
needs to be output for prepress and commercial printing at 8 x 12 inches,
scan the photo at 4 x 6 inches at 600 ppi (enough to size to 200 percent
for a 300-dpi [dots per inch] image).

✓ **Scan properly for line art.** *Line art* is 1-bit black and white only —
something like a black-and-white illustration. When you print line art on
laser printers or prepare files for commercial printing, the line-art resolution should match the device resolution. For example, printing to a
600-dpi laser printer requires 600 ppi for a 1-bit line-art image. When
you're printing to an image setter at a print shop, or if it's going directly
to plate or press, the resolution should be 1200 dpi.

✓ **Scan grayscale images in color.** In some cases, it doesn't matter, but
with some images and scanners, you can get better results by scanning
in RGB (red, green, blue) color and converting to grayscale in Elements
by using the Hue/Saturation dialog box or the Convert to Black and
White dialog box, as we explain in Book III, Chapter 3.

✓ **Scan in high bit depths.** If your scanner is capable of scanning in 16
or 32 bits, by all means, scan at the higher bit depths to capture the
most data. See Book III, Chapter 2, for more information about working
with higher-bit images.

**Book II
Chapter 1**

**Gathering Your
Image Files**

Using scanner plug-ins (Windows only)

Generally, when you install your scanner software, a stand-alone application
and a plug-in are installed to control the scanning process. *Plug-ins* are
designed to work inside other software programs, such as Photoshop
Elements. When you're using the plug-in, you can stay right in Elements to
do all your scanning. Here's how it works:

1. **After installing a new scanner and the accompanying software, launch
   Elements and then open the Organizer by clicking the Organize button
   on the Welcome screen.**

   Macintosh users need to use a TWAIN plug-in. By default the plug-in is
   not available in Elements. In your Mac's Application folder, open the
   Adobe Photoshop Elements 13 and then open the Support Files folder.
   Copy the Import Modules folder and paste it into the Plug-ins folder.
   Relaunch the Photo Editor and you find your scanner accessible in the
   File⇨Import submenu.

2. **From the Organizer, open the Preferences dialog box by pressing Ctrl+K.**

3. **Click Scanner in the left column and adjust the Scanner preferences.**

When the Preferences dialog box sees your scanner, you know that the connection is properly set up and you're ready to scan. Assuming that all your connections are properly set up, here's how to complete your scan:

1. **To open the scanner software from within Elements, choose File⇨Get Photos and Videos⇨From Scanner.**

   You must be in the Organizer window to access this menu command.

   Elements may churn a bit, but eventually your scanner software appears atop the Organizer window, as shown in Figure 1-5. The window is the scanner software provided by your scanner manufacturer. (Your window looks different from the one in Figure 1-5 unless you use the same scanner we use.) Regardless of which software you use, you should have similar options for creating a preview; selecting resolution, color mode, and image size; scaling; and other options.

2. **Adjust the options according to your output requirements and the recommendations made by your scanner manufacturer.**

   If you have an option to Preview the scan, click Preview to be sure the image is cropped correctly.

3. **When everything is ready to go, click the Scan button.**

   The final image drops into an Elements image window.

Figure 1-5: When you scan from within Elements, your scanner software loads on top of the Elements workspace.

Searching for files

The last option you have on the Get Photos and Videos submenu in the Organizer is the By Searching item. Choose File➪Get Photos and Videos➪By Searching and a search dialog box opens. You can choose to search the media sources available from the Look In drop-down menu.

Searching is limited to searching for photos. You don't have options for searching for filenames or camera data. Most often, this option is the one you'll typically use less than the other submenu choices.

If you're a Macintosh user, save your scans and then acquire the scans either via iPhoto or choose File➪Get Photos and Videos➪From Files and Folders.

Scanning many photos at a time

If you have several photos to scan, you can lay them out on the scanner platen and perform a single scan to acquire all images in one pass. Arrange the photos to scan on the glass and set up all the options in the scanner window for your intended output. When you scan multiple images, they form a single scan, as you can see in Figure 1-6.

After you scan multiple images, Elements makes it easy for you to separate each image into its own image window, where you can save the images as separate files. Choose Image➪Divide Scanned Photos to

Figure 1-6: You can scan multiple images with one pass.

make Elements magically open each image in a separate window, as shown in Figure 1-7, while the original scan remains intact. See Book III for details about saving images after they're divided.

Adding images from any media via your file system

Your computer's file system (for the purposes outlined in this section) is the Windows Explorer or Mac Finder view, where you can make folders and copy files to folders. To get images from your storage media onto your computer using your file system, you can copy files to folders from a card reader,

CD/DVD, or some other device mounted on your computer and view the photos in the file system. Here are the steps to do so:

1. **Make sure that the media is connected to your computer or loaded into your CD/DVD drive.**

2. **Cancel out of any autoplay wizards and go to Windows Explorer or the Finder.**

3. **Open the source media and drag files to target folders on your hard drive.**

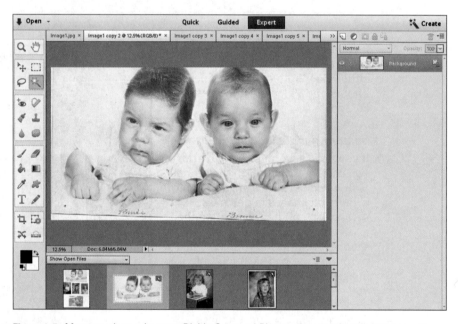

Figure 1-7: After you choose Image⇨Divide Scanned Photos, the scan is split into separate image windows.

If you shoot an event such as a birthday party and you additionally shoot some nature photos, you may want the photos to be organized in separate folders. Organizing photos into separate folders may be easier using the file system. (See the section "Organizing Image Files on Your Hard Drive," earlier in this chapter, for details.)

Importing Files from Your Hard Drive into the Organizer

After your image files are on your computer's hard drive, you want to work with them in Elements. If you want to use the viewing, searching, and organizing capabilities of the Organizer, your first step is loading files copied to your hard drive into the Organizer. In the following sections, you find out how to choose certain files you want to import or how to set up a special folder called a Watch Folder that helps you import images into the Organizer automatically.

Importing photos manually

When you want to choose specific files or a folder to import, follow these steps:

1. **Organize your image files into folders and subfolders on your hard drive.**

   See the "Organizing Image Files on Your Hard Drive" section, earlier in this chapter.

2. **Choose File⇨Get Photos and Videos⇨From Files and Folders.**

   The Get Photos and Videos from Files and Folders dialog box opens, as shown in Figure 1-8.

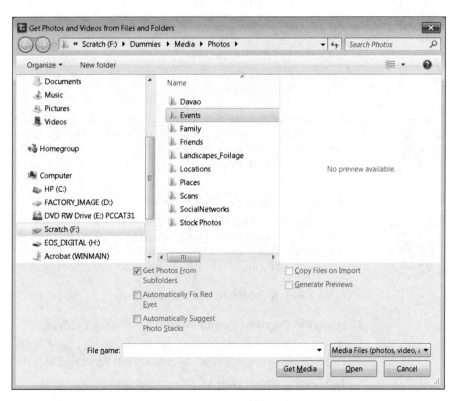

Figure 1-8: The Get Photos and Videos from Files and Folders dialog box.

3. **Select images to import.**

To import a folder full of images, select that folder to import all the images within it. If you nest folders, you can get files from a parent folder and all subfolders when you select the parent folder.

However, you only import one folder in the same level of your folder hierarchy at a time. So, if you want to import multiple folders at the same level, you have to repeat the steps here to import each folder's images into the Organizer.

If you want to import all photos within a given folder but not any sub-folders, click any file in the list and then press Ctrl+A (⌘+A on a Mac) to select all.

Alternatively, you can click and Ctrl-click (⌘-click) to select files individually in a noncontiguous order or click and Shift-click to select photos in a contiguous order.

4. **Specify your Fix Red Eyes and Photo Stacks options.**

We recommend leaving the other options, such as fixing red-eye and suggesting photo stacks, at the defaults where the check boxes are deselected. You have much better editing options in Elements, so don't use the automated features in the Get Photos and Videos from Files and Folders dialog box.

5. **Click the Get Media button.**

Wait for Elements to complete the import process. Your photos appear in a new Organizer window.

When you import photos, only those photos you imported are shown as thumbnails in the Organizer. To see all photos you imported from previous sessions as well as the new import, click the Show All button at the top of the Media Browser window.

Setting Up Watch Folders

One easy way to get files into the Organizer window is to use Watch Folders. *Watch Folders* are folders that you can identify on your computer. Each time new photos are added to the Watch Folders, Elements prompts you to confirm adding the files from the folders to your Organizer Catalog.

To set up a Watch Folder, follow these steps:

1. **Open the Organizer and choose File⇨Watch Folders.**

The Watch Folders dialog box opens, as shown in Figure 1-9. By default, your Pictures folder on your hard drive is already identified as a Watch Folder.

2. **To identify a new Watch Folder, click the Add button.**

3. **In the Browse for Folder dialog box that opens, locate a folder or make a new folder for adding photos. Click OK when you're done.**

   Each time you copy photos to any location shown in the Watch Folders dialog box, Elements sees the photos and either asks you whether you want to import them into your catalog or automatically adds the files to a catalog.

4. **Choose whether to be notified when Elements detects new files or to import new files automatically.**

   In the Watch Folders dialog

Figure 1-9: Choose File⇨Watch Folders in the Organizer to open the Watch Folders dialog box.

box, you find radio button choices for either notifying you when new files are found in a Watch Folder or for Elements to automatically import photos each time that new files are added to a Watch Folder. We recommend selecting the Notify Me radio button so that you're always aware of when new files are added to your catalog.

5. **Click OK to create your new Watch Folder.**

The next time you copy photos to the watched folder and launch the Organizer, a dialog box opens, prompting you to confirm adding photos (assuming that you chose Notify Me in the Watch Folders dialog box). Follow these steps to decide whether you want to import the newly detected photos:

1. **Click Yes in the dialog box shown in Figure 1-10.**

   The Add New Files from Watch Folder dialog box opens, where you find thumbnail previews for the new files found in a Watch Folder. By default, all the check boxes are selected, as shown in Figure 1-11.

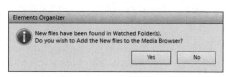

Figure 1-10: Click Yes to import new files in your catalog from files added to a Watch Folder.

2. **Deselect any photos you don't want to add.**

3. **Click OK, and the files are added to your catalog.**

Book II
Chapter 1

Gathering Your
Image Files

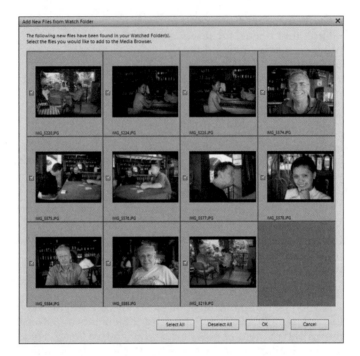

Figure 1-11: Deselect any photos you don't want to add to the Organizer and click OK.

When you add photos in the Organizer, only those photos you added appear in the Media Browser area of the Organizer. To see all photos, be sure to click the Show All button above the Media Browser.

Protecting Your Assets

At this point in your digital life, you probably have more data stored on computers from photo and other media files than any other document types. Other media, such as text documents, layouts, and spreadsheets, can often be easily reproduced. However, photos, once lost, are gone forever. That's why backing up your photos is important. If you take a lot of time to create and edit images and photos, you don't want to lose that work either.

We can save you aggravation right now before you spend any more time editing your photos in Elements. The following sections introduce you to a couple of backup options. You might choose one or more than one. We authors are so paranoid when we're writing a book that we back up our chapters on multiple drives, CDs, and DVDs when we finish them. The standard rule is that if you spend sufficient time working on a project and it gets to the point at which redoing your work would be a major aggravation, it's time to back up your files.

Backing up your catalog

When organizing your files, you want to back up the catalog file in case your catalog becomes corrupted. (You have a default catalog for all your images unless you create separate catalogs, as we explain in Chapter 2 of this minibook.)

Here's how you can use Elements to create a backup of your data:

Book II
Chapter 1

1. **In Windows, choose File⇨Backup Catalog to CD/DVD or Hard Drive to open the Backup Catalog to CD/DVD or Hard Drive Wizard (Windows) or Assistant (Mac). On the Macintosh, choose File⇨Backup to Hard Drive.**

   This wizard has three panes (Window) or two panes (Mac) that Elements walks you through; it's a pretty painless way to back up your files.

2. **Choose a backup option.**

   The first pane in the Burn/Backup Wizard offers two options:

   • *Full Backup:* Select this radio button to perform your first backup or when you're writing files to a new media source.

   • *Incremental Backup:* Use this option if you've already performed at least one backup and you want to update the backed-up files.

3. **Click Next and select a target location for your backed-up files.**

   Active drives, including CD/DVD drives attached to your computer (Windows), appear in the Select Destination Drive list, as shown in Figure 1-12. Select a drive, and Elements automatically assesses the write speed and identifies a previous backup file if one was created. The wizard also displays the total size of the files you've chosen to copy. This information is helpful so that you know whether you need more than one CD or DVD to complete the backup.

4. **If you intend to copy files to your hard drive or to another hard drive attached to your computer, click the Browse button and identify the path.**

   If you use a media source, such as a CD or DVD, Elements prompts you to insert a disc and readies the media for writing.

5. **Click Done, and the backup commences.**

   Be certain to not interrupt the backup. It might take some time, so just let Elements work away until you're notified that the backup is complete.

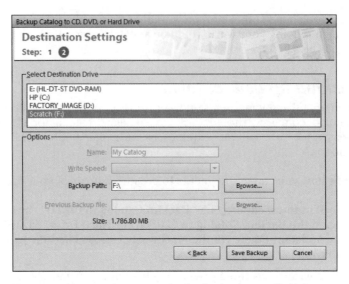

Figure 1-12: You can choose your destination backup media in the wizard.

Backing up photos and files (Windows)

With files stored all over your hard drive, manually copying files to a second hard drive, CD-ROM, or DVD would take quite a bit of time. Fortunately, Elements makes finding files to back up a breeze.

Choose File➪Make a CD/DVD and then, in the dialog box that opens, click Yes to confirm the action. The Make a CD/DVD dialog box opens. Select a hard drive or a CD/DVD drive, type a name for the backup folder, and click OK. Elements goes about copying all files shown in the Organizer window to your backup source.

Chapter 2: Viewing, Searching, and Sorting Images

In This Chapter

✔ **Working with catalogs**

✔ **Locating and viewing images**

✔ **Searching image metadata, content, and more**

✔ **Hiding and stacking files**

*W*hen you add files to the Organizer, you have many options for viewing, searching, and sorting your images. As your photo collection grows over time, these tools can help you sift through your images to find ones that meet specific criteria, whether they are images associated with a certain location or images of a friend or family member through the years.

This chapter covers the many types of viewing and searching options you have when working in the Organizer. In Chapter 3 of this minibook, you find out how to add tags, create albums, and use other organization tools that often work hand in hand with the viewing and searching features we explain in this chapter.

Cataloging Files

When you add files in the Organizer, they're contained within a catalog. You can have a single catalog showing thumbnail images of your media or several catalogs that contain media organized according to the events, time frames, or other organizational criteria you want. If multiple users are working on the same computer, you can create separate catalogs for each user.

Photograph courtesy of Don Mason

In the following sections, you find out about the benefits of organizing images in separate catalogs and see how to create a new catalog, import an old catalog, and move from one catalog to another after setting up catalogs the way you want them.

Creating a new catalog

If you have lots of pictures — perhaps numbering in the hundreds or even thousands — you can still add each and every one of these photos to a single catalog. However, doing so slows the performance in the Organizer and makes searching for photos a bit more difficult. A better option for dealing with large numbers of photos is to create separate catalogs.

You might have a number of photos that were taken at some event or special occasion and want to create a separate, new catalog to manage just those files. Here's how you go about creating a new catalog:

1. **In the Organizer, choose File⇨Manage Catalogs.**

   The Catalog Manager opens, as shown in Figure 2-1.

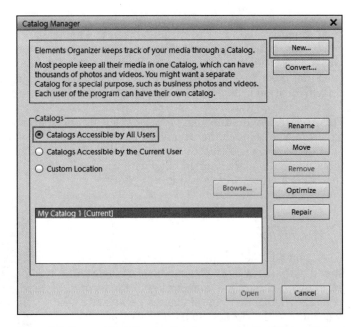

Figure 2-1: Choose File⇨Manage Catalogs to open the Catalog Manager.

2. **In the Catalogs section of the Catalog Manager, choose an accessibility level (Windows).**

   By default, your catalog is accessible to all users. If you have several logons for different users, all users can access the catalog.

On the Macintosh, the catalog is always accessible to the current user. If multiple users access the same computer, the catalog files created by other users cannot be viewed by the current user. For multiple user access, you can use the default OSX Public folder, shared folders, or use an external hard drive for storing photos.

If you want to make the catalog accessible only to you and not to others logging on to your computer, select the Catalogs Accessible by the Current User radio button.

3. **Choose a location.**

   If you don't choose one of the first two radio buttons and you want to save the catalog to the folder of your choice, select the Custom Location radio button and click the Browse button to select a folder on your hard drive in which you want to store the catalog.

4. **Click the New button in the upper-right corner of the Catalog Manager.**

   The Enter a Name for the New Catalog dialog box opens, as shown in Figure 2-2.

5. **Type a name for your new catalog.**

   If you want to import free music files for later use when creating slide shows, select the Import Free Music into This Catalog check box.

> Enter a name for the new catalog   ✕
>
> | Vacations |
>
> ☑ Import free music into this catalog
>
>   OK   Cancel

Figure 2-2: Type a name for the new catalog and click OK.

6. **Click OK.**

   You return to the Catalog Manager, and the new catalog is listed below your default catalog.

7. **Click OK in the Catalog Manager.**

   The new catalog opens in the Organizer with an empty screen. From here, you can add photos by importing images, using any of the methods described in Chapter 1 of this minibook.

One Elements limitation is that it has no option for moving images between catalogs.

If you decide that you want to move images from one catalog to another, you can import the images into the desired catalog and then delete those images from the old catalog. Or, if you like, the same images can appear in more than one catalog.

You can create multiple catalogs by following the same steps. To change a catalog, choose File➪Manage Catalogs. In the Catalog Manager, click a catalog name and click Open. The newly selected catalog is now the default and is available in all Elements sessions until you change the catalog again.

You can include the same photo in different catalogs.

Importing legacy catalogs

If you've used a previous version of Elements, you may want to convert an older catalog created in an earlier version of Elements to one that Elements 13 can recognize. Note that Elements prompts you to convert a legacy catalog when you first attempt to open it in Elements 13.

To convert a legacy catalog, follow these steps:

1. **Open the Catalog Manager by choosing File➪Manage Catalogs.**

2. **Click the catalog you want to convert and then click the Convert button in the Catalog Manager to open the Convert Catalog dialog box.**

3. **Select the Show Previously Converted Catalogs check box.**

   The list expands to display older catalogs, as shown in Figure 2-3.

   Additionally, you can click the Find More Catalogs button and locate catalogs that are saved to your hard drive.

4. **Click the Done button.**

   The catalogs are converted and displayed in the Catalog Manager.

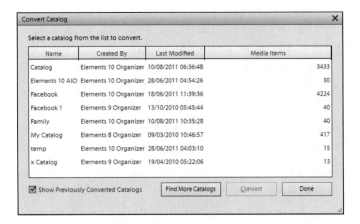

Figure 2-3: Select the Show Previously Converted Catalogs check box to expand the list.

Switching catalogs

As you create new catalogs, you switch back and forth between catalogs to view photos in the Organizer. If you make a catalog active, of course, you see only the photos you've previously added to that particular catalog.

To switch catalogs, follow these steps:

1. **Choose File⇨Manage Catalogs to open the Catalog Manager.**

2. **From the list of catalogs that appears, select the catalog that you want to open, as shown in Figure 2-4.**

3. **Click the Open button.**

    The photos added to the catalog appear in the Organizer, and you're ready to edit those pictures.

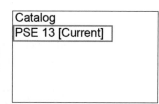

Book II
Chapter 2

Viewing, Searching, and Sorting Images

Figure 2-4: Click the catalog that you want to open.

Viewing Images in the Organizer

After you add images to a catalog, the default Organizer view — the view you're most likely to use in all your Elements work sessions — looks a lot like a light table (those tables with lights under the tabletop that enable you to easily view sheets full of negatives).

The Organizer window shows you all the files that have been added to a particular catalog. You can change the types of views you see in the Organizer to facilitate finding photos and managing them. In addition to the default view, here are a few of the other view options:

- ✔ Double-click a photo in the Organizer, and you see the image fill an Organizer window.

- ✔ Use the View menu to limit the images shown based on media type, date, and more.

- ✔ Examine your pictures one by one in a slide show.

- ✔ Compare images side by side.

If you're looking for one or more images to edit, you can select the desired images and then select an editor to use — whether from the Edit menu or from a context menu opened on a selected image. Or, instead of opening a menu, simply click the Editor button at the bottom of the Organizer window to switch to the Photo Editor.

In the sections that follow, you find just what you need to know about your viewing options in the Organizer.

Understanding the Media Browser

The central area in the Organizer where you see image previews of your photos is called the Media Browser. The Media Browser displays thumbnail images of photos and also displays icons for other file types, such as PDFs, videos, and audio files.

When you import photos in the Organizer, the Organizer doesn't create a copy of your image elsewhere on your hard drive or external drive. Instead, the Organizer keeps track of the locations of your files on your hard drive and creates links to the images. Therefore, the catalog doesn't get overburdened with the total file size for each image.

If you move a photo (or rename a photo or folder) to another folder on your hard drive, the link to the file is broken. When you click a thumbnail in the Media Browser where a photo has been moved to another location, Elements opens a dialog box and begins searching for the file. In the dialog box, you can click the Browse button and manually locate the file to reestablish the link.

When you import new media into the active catalog, only the media you last imported is shown in the Media Browser. To see all the media in your catalog (media that was previously imported as well as a new import), click the All Media button at the top of the

Figure 2-5: Click the All Media button to show all the media in the open catalog.

Media Browser, as shown in Figure 2-5.

Using Thumbnail view

When you open the Organizer, the default view is a Thumbnail display. Your photos, videos, projects, audio files, and so on are shown as mini-images or icons in the Media Browser that you can adjust to different sizes.

Below the Media Browser, you find a zoom slider. Move the slider left and right to size the thumbnail images.

Press Ctrl++ (Control plus the + key — Windows) or ⌘++ (Command plus the + key — Macintosh) to zoom in on the image thumbnails. To zoom out, press Ctrl+- (Control plus the – [minus] Key — Windows) or ⌘+- (Command plus the – [minus] key — Macintosh).

If you double-click a photo, the image thumbnail zooms into view as a single photo in the Media Browser. To return to a view where you see smaller thumbnails, click the icon to the left of the slider.

Using sort commands

One quick way to sort images in the Organizer is to use the menu on the Shortcuts bar in the Organizer window for date sorting. The following four options are available to you, as shown in Figure 2-6:

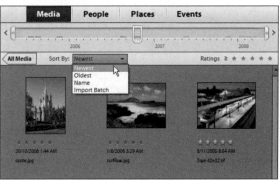

Figure 2-6: You can sort files quickly by Date (Newest First) order, Date (Oldest First) order, Name, or Import Batch.

✔ **Newest:** Select this option to view images according to the date you took the photos, beginning with the most recent date.

✔ **Oldest:** This option displays photos in chronological order, starting with the oldest file.

✔ **Name:** When you choose Name, files are sorted according to filenames.

✔ **Import Batch:** Import Batch organizes photos according to the date you import files. All files imported together are nested in groups according to the import.

Changing view options on the View menu

The View menu enables you to change views and sort images according to different preset views:

✔ **Media types:** The Media Browser displays thumbnail previews and icons for Photos, Videos, Audio files, Projects, and PDF documents. Choose View↪Media Types and select the types you want to display in the Media Browser or deselect to hide a media type. If you want only photos shown in the Media Browser, deselect each of the other media types on the Media Types submenu.

✔ **Hidden files:** Some files, such as different versions of the same document, may be hidden from view. Choose View⇨Hidden Files, and you can make choices for hiding files, showing all files, or showing only the hidden files. See the section "Hiding Files That Get in the Way," later in this chapter, for more about hidden files.

✔ **Sort by:** When you choose View⇨Sort By, you have the same options that are available on the Sort By menu that appears at the top of the Media Browser. The preceding section explains each of the sorting options.

✔ **Details:** You may want to keep the Details display as a default. Details displays star ratings if you rate files from 1 to 5 stars (Chapter 3 of this minibook explains how), and the dates the photos were taken. You can also include Filenames from the filename option in the View menu. In Figure 2-7, you can see some files with the Details and star ratings. Notice that adding Details takes up a bit more vertical space. However, the trade-off is slight when you review large catalogs and want to locate files by ratings, creation dates, or filenames.

Figure 2-7: Displaying Details helps you locate files by ratings, creation dates, and filenames.

✔ **Timeline view:** Choose View⇨Timeline, and a horizontal timeline appears above the Media Browser with a slider. (You can also see this view by pressing Ctrl+L or, on the Mac, ⌘+L.) Click All Media in the catalog; you can adjust the slider to narrow the thumbnail views to specific date periods; see Figure 2-8.

Be careful: The date is taken from the camera metadata. If a date isn't available from the camera data, the date is taken from the file's creation date and thus isn't likely to be the date you shot the photo.

✓ **Gridlines:** In Figure 2-8, you see lines dividing the thumbnail images into rectangles. When viewing Details, also shown in Figure 2-8, the Gridline view makes it easy to understand what detail belongs to a given thumbnail.

Figure 2-8: Move the slider on the Timeline to view photos within date ranges.

✓ **Expanding and collapsing stacks:** You can stack photos like a deck of cards, with only the top image appearing in the Media Browser. You can select two or more photos and stack them by choosing Edit➪Stack➪ Stacked Selected Photos. You can also have Elements automatically stack photos when importing media into the Organizer. See the section "Stacking 'em up," later in this chapter.

The View➪Expand All Stacks command expands stacks so that all photos within stacks are shown. Choosing View➪Collapse All Stacks returns the stacks to a collapsed view.

Viewing photos as a slide show and in Full Screen view

Are you ready for some exciting viewing in Photoshop Elements? To take an alternative view of your Organizer files, you can see your pictures in a self-running slide show (in Full Screen view), complete with transition effects and background music. Full Screen view takes you to a Slide Show view.

Elements 13 introduces a new short version of the Slide Show feature to enable you to quickly display your photos on your monitor. This view is the Slide Show view. For more options including transitions, playing music and a number of other features, you use the Full Screen view.

Viewing files in Slide Show mode can be helpful for quickly previewing the files you want to edit for all kinds of output, as well as for previewing photos that you might use for an exported slide show, which we explain in Book IX.

Creating a slide show and outputting it to a movie file is now supported on both the Macintosh and Windows.

Taking a quick view of the Full Screen view

To set up your slide show and/or enter Full Screen view, follow these steps:

1. **Open the Organizer and then select the images that you want to see in a slide show.**

   If no images are selected when you enter Full Screen view, all photos in the Media Browser are shown in Full Screen view.

2. **Choose View⇨Full Screen View.**

   Alternatively, press the F11 key (⌘+F11 on the Mac).

   After choosing the menu command, you jump right into the Full Screen view with some panels and tools displayed, as shown in Figure 2-9.

   Note that this view is accomplished only if you choose Full Screen view or use the modifier key. If you click the Slide Show button at the bottom of the Organizer window you get a completely different result.

4. **View the slides.**

   The slide show swipes photos at an interval you can specify in the Settings. By default, the photos change every 4 seconds. You can watch the slide show, or you can click the arrow keys at the bottom of the screen to move forward and back through the slides.

   You can also scroll through slides by pressing the left- and right-arrow keys on your keyboard.

5. **Exit the Full Screen view and press the Esc key on your keyboard to return to the Organizer window.**

Figure 2-9: Elements takes you right to Full Screen view after you click the Slideshow button or press the F11 key (⌘+F11 on the Mac).

You can also open Full Screen view by choosing View⇨Full Screen or pressing the F11 key (⌘+F11 on the Mac). Opening the Full Screen view is the same as clicking the Slideshow button in the Organizer. Laptop owners may need to use the Function key with the keystrokes to open Full Screen view.

Working with the Edit and Organize tools

Full Screen and Slideshow views provide you with several editing tools. When you open selected photos from the Organizer in Full Screen or Slideshow view, you find two panels on the left side of the screen:

- ✒ **The Edit panel** provides Edit tools for editing photos, such as sharpening images and removing red-eye.

- ✒ **The Organize panel** permits you to add keyword tags for easily organizing photos. (See Chapter 5 for more on adding keyword tags to photos.)

To open the Edit panel, click the vertical tab on the left side of the Full Screen view or click the Fix button on the Slideshow toolbar. The Edit panel opens, as shown in Figure 2-10.

As you move the mouse cursor over the tools, tooltips display the tool name. You can easily locate tools in the Edit panel and make image adjustments without leaving the Full Screen/ Slide Show view.

Elements provides you with many different editing options using the Quick Edit tools, and we cover each of the tools later in Book VIII, Chapter 1.

Working with the Organize tools

The other panel on the left side of the Full Screen/Slide Show window is the Organize panel. Click Organize on the left side of the window to open the panel or click the Organize button on the Slide Show toolbar.

Figure 2-10: The Edit panel offers tools for you to make image adjustments without leaving Full Screen view.

As you can see in Figure 2-11, this panel offers you choices for adding images to existing albums from the current images in the Full Screen/Slide Show view, and you can tag photos with keyword tags. For more information on creating albums and creating keyword tags, see Chapter 3 of this minibook.

Using the Slide Show toolbar

The toolbar shown in Figure 2-9 offers the following options for slide viewing (from left to right):

- ✔ **Previous Media:** Click the left arrow to open the previous photo or other media.

- ✔ **Play/Pause:** Click to play or pause a slide show.

- ✔ **Next Media:** Click the right arrow to advance to the next photo or other media.

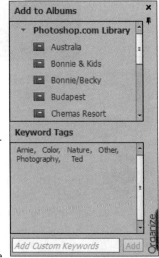

Figure 2-11: The Organize panel enables you to create albums and keyword tags.

- ✔ **Theme:** This item was named Transitions in earlier versions of Elements. Click the Theme tool, and the Select Transition dialog box opens, as shown in Figure 2-12. When you enter Full Screen view, this tool is selected. Four different transition effects are displayed in the dialog box. You can preview a transition effect by placing the cursor over one of the images. When you find an effect you like, click the image and click OK to change the transition.

✔ **Film Strip:** Click this tool to show or hide the filmstrip that appears at the bottom of the Full Screen window.

✔ **View:** The View tool displays a pop-up menu when you click the tool. From the pop-up menu, you have two choices: View media side by side horizontally or vertically. Choosing either option splits the screen where two media items are shown.

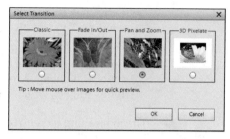

Figure 2-12: If you click the Theme tool, the Select Transition dialog box opens.

When one of these options is chosen, you can return to the default for a view of a single item onscreen by selecting the single monitor icon.

✔ **Sync Panning and Zooming:** This tool is only active when you view media side by side vertically or horizontally. Click the tool, and both media items sync when panning and zooming.

✔ **Settings:** Click to open the Full Screen View Options dialog box. (See Figure 2-13.) In this figure, you can choose a music file to play background music while viewing a slide show, set the page durations, and display items such as captions.

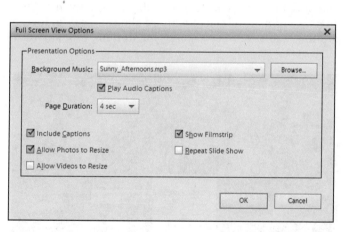

Figure 2-13: Click Settings and the Full Screen View Options dialog box opens.

✔ **Fix:** Click this tool to open the Edit panel.

✔ **Organize:** Click this tool to open the Organize panel.

✔ **Info:** Click this tool to open the Properties panel. This panel contains the same information and editing options as the Information panel discussed in Chapter 3 of this minibook.

✔ **Exit:** Click this tool to exit Full Screen view and return to the Organizer window. You can also press Esc to exit Full Screen view.

✔ **Show All Controls (right arrow):** Click the tiny left-pointing arrow on the right side of the toolbar, and the toolbar expands to reveal additional tools and changes to a left-pointing arrow to collapse the panel and hides the Fix, Organize, and Info tools.

The main thing to keep in mind is that the Full Screen view is a temporary viewing option you have in Elements. It's not permanent. You use the view for a quick display method on your computer when you want to show off some photos to family and friends. You have more permanent options for saving files as slide shows that they can share with other users, as we explain in Book IX.

Exploring more options in context menus

When you are in Full Screen view, you lose the top-level menus. If you're wondering how you can add the slide images to an album or create a slide show as a movie file (Windows only), you need a menu command. Because the menus are hidden, you must open a context menu in the Full Screen view.

In a context menu, you find options not available in the panels or the slide-show tools. Figure 2-14 shows a context menu opened in Full Screen view. You have menu commands for adding images to an existing album, removing an image from an album, creating a slide show (Windows only), marking for printing, and several commands for working with keyword tags.

Figure 2-14: Open a context menu when in Full Screen view to access menu commands.

When in doubt, always look for commands and features by opening a context menu.

Viewing photos in Slide Show view

When you select photos in the Organizer and click the Slide Show button at the bottom of the Organizer window, you find a very different experience than when viewing photos in Full Screen View.

The new Slide Show view is intended for a quick and easy viewing of your selected photos with a fixed transition and options for exporting the slide show to a movie file.

Select photos in the Organizer and click the Slide Show button and you open the photos in a Slide Show view, as shown in Figure 2-15.

Figure 2-15: The default Slide Show view.

Notice the options in the toolbar are fewer than the options you have in the Full Screen view toolbar (refer to Figure 2-14). If you click the Edit button, you're taken to the Slideshow Builder window (shown in Figure 2-16). Here you can add or delete photos from your slide show.

You can open the Export menu from either the first Slide Show screen or when in the Slideshow Builder. There are two options available for exporting: You can Export to a Local Disk and choose from one of three video export options, or you can choose to export a movie file direct to your Facebook account. We cover the video export options and uploading to Facebook thoroughly in Book IX, Chapter 3.

Figure 2-16: The Slideshow Builder enables you to add and delete photos from your slide show.

Searching for Images in the Organizer

The Organizer's Find menu is devoted entirely to searching for photos. From the Find menu, you can locate photos in albums and catalogs or based on a variety of search criteria. In addition, you have a Search text box at the top of the Organizer window.

To use the Organizer's search features, you need to have photos loaded in the Organizer. The following sections introduce the available search options and explain how each one works.

Typing search terms in the Search box

At the top of the Organizer window, you find Search with a text box. Type text in the box to search a given name or search criteria. Type any information in the text box related to filenames, captions, notes, and metadata.

Search is powerful and supports Boolean expressions (AND, OR, NOT). You can, for example type **Jack AND Jill** to find only files that match both words (not just one or the other). Or you can type **Jack OR Jill AND Harry** to narrow the search to files that contain either the word *Jack* or *Jill* but all of which match the word *Harry.* Or if you needed a photo of Jack and Jill together, but without Harry, the Boolean search **Jack AND Jill NOT Harry** would help you narrow your options.

After typing the search criteria, press Enter/Return to perform a text search, or you can choose from menu items to open other search items. Those items, shown in the drop-down menu in Figure 2-15, are explained later in this section.

Searching metadata

Metadata includes not only the information about your images that's supplied by digital cameras but also the custom data you can add to a file. Examples of *Metadata* includes such data as your camera name, the camera settings you used to take a picture, copyright information, and much more.

Searching metadata is easy. Just choose Find⇨By Details (Metadata) in the Organizer. The Find by Details (Metadata) dialog box opens. The first two columns in the dialog box offer a number of different choices for search criteria and for options based on the criteria. In the third column, you type search criteria into a text box to specify exactly what you want to search for. You can click the plus button to add new lines to your search criteria, as shown in Figure 2-17, which shows four lines of search criteria. Clicking the minus button deletes a line.

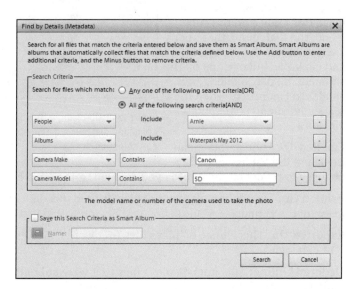

Figure 2-17: Choose Find⇨By Details (Metadata) in the Organizer to open the dialog box in which you specify metadata.

Searching by media type

You have the same choices here as you do when viewing media. Choose Find⇨By Media Type. From the submenu, choose Photos, Video, Audio, Projects, PDF, and/or Items with Audio Captions.

Searching by history

Elements keeps track of what you do with your photos, such as printing from within Elements, sharing photos, and performing various other tasks. If you want to base a search for files based on the file history, choose Find⇨By History, as shown in Figure 2-18. After you choose an option from the By History submenu, you see files that meet your criteria arranged by date and displayed in the Media Browser.

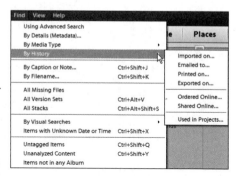

Figure 2-18: Choose Find⇨By History to search files based on their history.

Your options on the By History submenu include

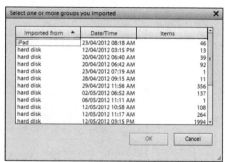

Figure 2-19: Choosing a By History submenu command displays a dialog box where you can select an item.

- ✔ **Imported On:** If you choose this option, you can select a date when files were imported into the current catalog. When you make this choice on the submenu, the dialog box that opens lets you select the import date and click OK. (All options on the submenu display a dialog box similar to Figure 2-19 when the respective menu command is chosen.)

- ✔ **Emailed To:** Choose this menu item, and the list in Figure 2-19 changes to reflect all the photos you emailed from within Elements.

- ✔ **Printed On:** This option displays all files printed in a date order for the print date and time.

- ✔ **Exported On:** This choice displays files that were exported from the current catalog.

- ✔ **Ordered Online:** This item displays files that were submitted to an online service.

- ✔ **Shared Online:** This choice displays files that were shared online.

- ✔ **Used in Projects:** This option displays files that were used in projects.

For details about importing photos, check out Chapter 1 of this minibook. If you need more info about emailing, printing, online sharing, or creating projects from within Elements, flip to Book IX.

Searching captions and notes

When captions or notes are added to files, you can search for the caption name, contents of a note, or both. Before you can search for captions and notes, though, you have to add them to your images similarly to the note we added in Figure 2-20.

Book II
Chapter 2

Viewing, Searching, and Sorting Images

Figure 2-20: The Information panel.

Adding captions and notes

Text captions and notes are easy to create. Although you can select a thumbnail image in the Organizer window and choose Edit⇨Add Caption, a better way is to use the Information panel. Just follow these steps:

1. **To open the Information panel, select a thumbnail image in the Organizer and click the Information panel in the Panel Bin.**

2. **Type a caption by adding text to the Caption text box.**

3. **Type text in the Notes area on the panel to add a note.**

    That's all there is to it, as shown in Figure 2-20. You can also record audio notes about an image.

> To record audio, click Audio in the Information panel, and a dialog box opens where you can click a button to make your recording.

Searching the captions and notes content

After you create captions and notes, you can search for the words contained in the descriptions.

To search for caption names and notes in your open catalog, follow these steps:

1. **Open the Organizer.**

   You should have images in a catalog and have files identified with captions and notes.

2. **Choose Find⇨By Caption or Note.**

   The Find by Caption or Note dialog box opens, as shown in Figure 2-21.

   Options in the dialog box are as follows:

   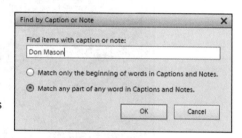

   Figure 2-21: Choose Find⇨By Caption or Note to open the dialog box in which search criteria for captions and notes are specified.

   • *Find Items with Caption or Note:* In the text box, type the words you want to locate.

   • *Match Only the Beginning of Words in Captions and Notes:* Select this radio button if you know that your caption or note begins with words that you type into the text box.

   • *Match Any Part of Any Word in Captions and Notes:* Select this radio button if you're not sure whether the text typed in the box is used at the beginning of a caption or note, or whether it's contained in the caption's name or the note's text.

3. **Click OK.**

   Your results appear in the Organizer window.

Searching by filename

Choose Find⇨By Filename, and a dialog box opens. Type the name of the file you want to find and click OK.

Searching missing files, version sets, and stacks

If you have files that appear in the Media Browser but Elements cannot find the file, you may want to search your hard drive to locate the files. Choose Find⇨All Missing Files, and a dialog box opens. Elements automatically searches locations on your hard drive to locate the missing files.

Remember that the Media Browser contains references to only the original files; so if you move photos to different locations on your hard drive, Elements loses the links to the photos.

You can create stacks and version sets where photos are grouped together, as we explain at the end of this chapter. Choose Find➪Stacks or choose Find➪Version Sets, and Elements displays only stacks or version sets in the Media Browser.

Searching by visual similarities

Elements enables you to search photos for visual similarities. You may have group shots, architecture, animal life, and so on and want to search for photos where objects in the photos are visually similar. To search for photos with visual similarities, choose Find➪By Visual Searches. From the submenu, you can choose Visually Similar Photos and Videos, Objects Appearing in Photos, and Duplicate Photos.

The features for finding people are integrated with Elements' tagging features and discussed in the sections about tagging in Chapter 3 of this minibook.

Searching visually similar photos

You may have a number of similar or near-duplicate photos. You may want to locate similar or near-duplicate images and delete some of them from your catalog.

Searching for visually similar images is a two-step process:

1. **Choose Find➪By Visual Searches➪Visually Similar Photos and Videos.**

   To help narrow your search, move the slider for Color/Shape back and forth. The results are immediately displayed in the Media Browser.

2. **Return to the Find➪By Visual Searches menu and choose Duplicate Photos.**

   Photos that are visually similar appear in horizontal rows.

In Figure 2-22, you can see one of the rows as it appeared after we performed a search. Notice the Stack button on the right side of the second figure in the second row. Click Stack, and the photos are stacked. If you want to delete photos, click a photo and click the Remove from Catalog button at the bottom of the window.

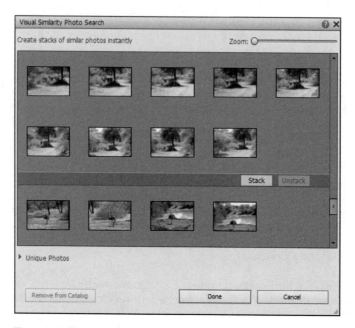

Figure 2-22: Here, we did a search for similar photos and then searched for duplicate photos.

Searching objects

You may have objects in photos, such as buildings, automobiles, trees, groups of people, and so on that you want to stack or delete. To search for objects, follow these steps:

1. **Choose Find⇨By Visual Searches⇨Visually Similar Photos and Videos.**

2. **Search again and choose Objects Appearing in Photos from the By Visual Searches submenu.**

    A rectangle appears on a selected photo that contains the object you want to search. You can move the rectangle and resize it.

3. **When you've identified the object, click Search Object, as shown in Figure 2-23.**

Searching for miscellaneous items

Other search items you have on the Find menu include Items with Unknown Dates, Untagged Items, Unanalyzed Content, and Items Not in Any Albums. These items are self-explanatory and make more sense when you run the Elements Auto Analyzer and work with Albums (see the section "Working with Albums" in Chapter 3 of this minibook).

Hiding Files That Get in the Way

Elements offers a few ways to hide files so that you can keep your images organized and easy to find.

With a simple menu command, you can mark selected files in the Organizer as *hidden*. You might have several files of the same subject and want to keep only one file visible in the Organizer window. However, you may not want to delete the other photos. You can hide files in the Organizer window — and show the hidden files later by using menu commands.

Figure 2-23: Mark the object you want to search and click Search Object.

Book II
Chapter 2

Viewing, Searching, and Sorting Images

Select files that you want to hide, and from either the Edit menu or a context menu, choose Visibility⇨Mark as Hidden. To see the files you marked as hidden, return to the same Visibility menu and choose Show Hidden. When you remove the check mark for Show Hidden, you hide the files. To toggle easily between showing and hiding files marked for hiding, choose View⇨Hidden Files. Selecting this menu command toggles between showing and hiding the files you marked for hiding.

The following sections explain how to hide files using stacks.

Stacking 'em up

Think of *stacks* as a stack of cards that are face up. You see only the front card, and all the other cards are hidden behind that card. Stacks work the same way. You hide one or more images behind a foreground image. At any time, you can sort the images or display all images in the stack in the Organizer window.

To create a stack, follow these steps:

1. **In the Organizer, select several photos.**

   You can select any number of photos. However, you can't stack audio or movie files.

2. **Choose Edit⇨ Stack⇨Stack Selected Photos.**

   Elements stacks your photos. The first image you select remains in view in the Organizer window. In the upper-right area, an icon that looks like a stack of cards appears on the image thumbnail when you've stacked some

Closed Stack

Open Stack

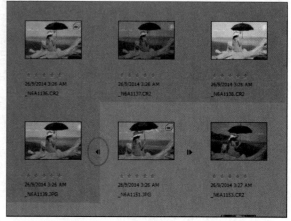

Figure 2-24: Viewing a stack in the Organizer.

images, as shown in Figure 2-24. When you click the photo to open the stack in the Organizer, you find the same icon in the upper-right corner shown at the bottom of Figure 2-24. You also see a right-pointing arrow to the right of the image thumbnail for a collapsed stack and left-pointing arrow to the right of the last photo in an expanded stack. To see all images in the stack, click the right-pointing arrow. To collapse the stack, click the left-pointing arrow that appears when a stack is expanded.

Chapter 3: Organizing Images with Tags, Albums, and More

In This Chapter

↙ **Tagging images with keywords**

↙ **Putting photos on a map**

↙ **Rating images with stars**

↙ **Organizing images into albums**

*W*hen you have a catalog with many photos, you'll want to organize the photos so that you can easily locate the pictures you want to share or use when making creations. Fortunately, Photoshop Elements offers a number of tools to help you organize and find images you want to use in editing sessions.

In this chapter, we extend our discussion from Chapter 2 of this minibook, where you find out how the view, search, and sort tools tell the Media Browser to display only files that meet certain criteria. These tools help you narrow down images so that you can easily apply tags, rate images with stars, and create albums, which are the tasks you find out how to do in this chapter.

As a bonus, after you develop a system for tagging your photos or rating them with stars, the viewing and searching features become even more robust. For example, after you add the tags and star ratings, you can then search for images based on a tag or rating. Or, if you want to collect several images with various tags, star ratings, or metadata for an image-editing project, you can use the view and search features to track down the images you want and then organize those images into an album so that they're all a click away as you work on your project.

Introducing Tags and the Tags Panel

In the Organizer window, the Tags panel helps you sort and organize your pictures. In the lower-right corner of the Organizer, the Tags/Info button toggles display of the panel so that it's hidden or visible. With the panel visible, simply click the Tags tab at the top to see the whole panel of tags and tools for working with them.

You use the Tags panel to identify individual images by using a limitless number of options for categorizing your pictures. In this panel, you can find Keywords tags, People tags, Places tags, and Events tags that help you neatly organize files. To create keyword tags, all the tools you need are right in the Tags panel. To tag people, places, or events, you can click the corresponding tab at the top of the screen to see additional tools that help you find and tag images based on the respective categories.

In Elements 12, Adobe has made the category divisions much easier for you by adding People, Places, and Events tags right under Keywords tags in the Tags panel.

Before you start adding different types of tags, here are a couple of basics you need to know before you get started:

✔ **You can create unique tags of each type.** Each of the four tag types shown in Figure 3-1 contains its own drop-down menu where new tags can be created. For example, when you open the People Tags drop-down menu, you find New Person as the first menu item. You use this command to add a new People tag. In the Places Tags area, you find Add a New Place. Choose this item to add a new Places tag. In the Events Tags portion, you find Add an Event. Use this item to add a new Events tag.

✔ **The hierarchy for each tag type has categories and subcategories.** When you add new tags, a category tag is at the top of the tag hierarchy. Below a category or subcategory, you can add additional subcategories. For example, you may want to create a Holiday category Keywords tag, and below it, you may want to add several different holidays, such as Valentine's Day, Groundhog Day, Independence Day, and so on. You might add people in the People Tags area and have subcategories for each person.

Tags are saved automatically with the catalog you work with. By default, Elements creates a catalog and automatically saves your work to it. If you happen to create another catalog, as we explain in Chapter 2 of this mini-book, your tags disappear. Be aware of which catalog is open when you create tags so you can return to them.

You can manage tags by using menu commands from the New drop-down menu and other commands from a contextual menu that you open by right-clicking a tag in the Tags panel.

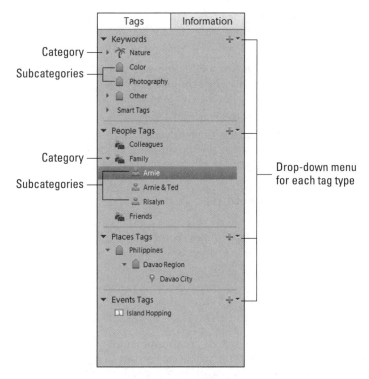

Figure 3-1: The four main tag categories.

On the New drop-down menu for Keyword tags, you can access the following commands:

- ✔ **New Keyword Tag:** Create a new keyword tag. The upcoming section "Creating a custom keyword tag," walks you through the process step by step.

- ✔ **New Sub-Category:** A *subcategory* is like a nested bookmark. Create a subcategory by selecting New Sub-Category from the New menu; a dialog box opens, prompting you to type a name for the new subcategory. As an example of how you would use keyword tags and subcategories, you might have a keyword tag category named Uncle Joe's Wedding. Then, you might create subcategories for Bride Dressing Room, Ceremony, Family Photos, Reception, and so on.

- ✔ **New Category:** Choose New Category to open a dialog box that prompts you to type a name for the new category. By default, you can find predefined category names for People, Places, Events, and Other. If you want to add your own custom categories, use this menu command.

- ✔ **Edit:** Click Edit, and the Edit Keyword Tag dialog box opens, where you can customize how your tag looks. See the section "Adding icons to keyword tags," later in this chapter, for details.

✔ **Import Keyword Tags from File:** If you export a keyword tag, the file is written as XML (eXtensible Markup Language). When you choose From File, you can import an XML version of a keyword tags file.

✔ **Save Keyword Tags to a File:** You can save keyword tags to a file that you can retrieve with the From File command. This option is handy when you open a different catalog file and want to import the same collection of names created in one catalog file to another catalog file.

✔ **Collapse All Keyword Tags:** Keyword tags appear like bookmark lists that you can collapse and expand. An expanded list shows you all the subcategory keyword tags. Choose Collapse All Keyword Tags to collapse the list.

✔ **Expand All Keyword Tags:** This command expands a collapsed list.

✔ **Show Large Icon:** Select this item on the menu and the icons appear larger. While in a larger view, you can see the icons associated with tags. If Show Large Icon is deselected, you won't see the icons you add with the Edit Icon dialog box.

Organizing Groups of Images with Keyword Tags

Elements provides you with a great opportunity for organizing files, in the form of keyword tags. After you acquire your images in the Organizer, you can sort them and add keyword tags according to the dates you took the pictures, the subject matter, or some other categorical arrangement.

Elements offers you a selection of keyword tags that you can use to tag your photos, and we refer to these tags as the *default tags*. We refer to *custom keyword tags* as those tags you create in the Tags panel. When you create a new tag, you end up with a custom tag that you can modify in regard to the appearance. With the default tags that Elements provides, you can make some changes to the tag appearances but in limited ways. For example, you have some preset icon images that Elements provides you, and you can choose one of the preset images for the icon appearance. However, you can't add a custom image for the tag icon.

In the following sections, you walk through the process of creating and customizing keyword tags in the Tag panel and tagging your photos.

Creating a custom keyword tag

To create a new keyword tag, follow these steps:

1. **Open the Organizer window by clicking the Organizer button in an editing mode or by clicking the Organizer button on the Welcome screen.**

At this point, we assume that you have images imported into the Organizer. If you don't have photos in a catalog, refer to Book I, Chapter 1, to see how to add images.

2. **If the Tags panel isn't already displayed, click the Tags/Info button in the lower right to display the panels and select Tags at the top of the panel bin.**

3. **To create a new keyword tag, click the plus (+) icon in the Tags panel to open a drop-down menu and then choose New Keyword Tag.**

   Alternatively, you can press Ctrl+N (⌘+N on the Mac) to create a new keyword tag.

   The Create Keyword Tag dialog box opens, as shown in Figure 3-2.

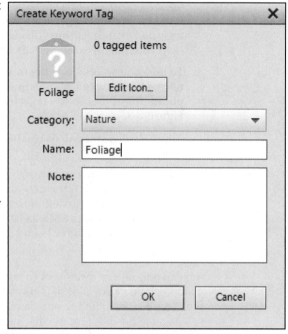

Figure 3-2: The Create Keyword Tag dialog box.

Book II
Chapter 3

Organizing Images with Tags, Albums, and More

4. **Click the Category drop-down menu and choose one of the preset categories listed on the menu.**

   See the section "Building your own categories and subcategories," later in this chapter, for instructions on customizing these categories.

5. **Type a name for the tag in the Name text box and add a note to describe the keyword tag.**

   You might use the subject matter or other descriptive information for the note.

6. **Click OK in the Create Keyword Tag dialog box.**

   You return to the Organizer window.

Tagging photos

After you create the tag you need, you're ready to apply that tag to your photos. Here's how it works:

1. **In the Organizer window, select the photos to which you want to add keyword tags.**

   Click a photo and Shift-click another photo to select photos in a group. Click a photo and Ctrl-click (⌘-click on the Mac) different photos scattered around the Organizer window to select nonsequential photos. The view and search features discussed in Chapter 2 of this minibook can help you narrow your choices based on specific criteria.

2. **To add a new keyword tag to a photo (or selection of photos), click one of the selected photos in the Organizer window and drag the photo thumbnail to the tag's icon in the Tags panel, as shown in Figure 3-3.**

   Alternatively, you can drag a tag to the selected photos.

   When you release the mouse button, the photos are added to the new keyword tag. The check box to the left of the tag name is used to display in the Media Browser only those photos that have been tagged with the respective tag name.

Figure 3-3: The Tags panel after adding some keyword tags.

You can add one or more tags to any photo. For example, if you take a lot of family photos, you might have a tag called Group Family Photos as well as a tag for different events, such as Reunion and Christmas. You'd likely have at least a handful of photos that you could tag with both the Group Family Photos tag and the Reunion tag for group photos taken at a family reunion.

Adding icons to keyword tags

In Figure 3-2, the Create Keyword Tag dialog box appears empty without an icon. If you want to add an image to the tag icon, you can handle it in a few ways. Perhaps the most reliable is to edit the icon by following these steps:

1. **In the Tags panel, open a context menu by right-clicking (Option-clicking on a Mac) a tag and then choose Edit.**

2. **When the Edit Keyword Tag dialog box opens, click Edit Icon.**

   The Edit Keyword Tag Icon dialog box opens. The dialog box displays the total number of images that are tagged with the current tag.

3. **Use the left and right arrows on either side of the Find button to scroll through all the images and choose one for an icon, as shown in Figure 3-4.**

4. **(Optional) Crop the image by moving handles on the rectangle displayed in the Edit Keyword Tag Icon dialog box.**

   Rest assured that this cropping just determines what part of your image will appear as the keyword icon. You don't actually crop your image in this step.

5. **Click OK when you finish editing the icon.**

   The icon is displayed in the Tags panel.

Modifying the default keyword tags

You can also modify the names for the default tags, and you can add some custom subcategories. To edit a default category tag, open a context menu and choose Edit in one of the predefined categories. The Edit Category dialog box opens, as shown in Figure 3-5.

Notice the Choose Color button in Figure 3-5. Click this button, and you can change the color of the tag icon. Also notice in Figure 3-5 that a row of icon images appears for choosing a category icon. Move the scroll bar horizontally and click the icon you want to use for the preset category. You're limited to the images that Elements provides for displaying icons on the predefined categories.

Book II
Chapter 3

Organizing Images with Tags, Albums, and More

Figure 3-4: The Edit Keyword Tag Icon dialog box enables you to add or change a tag icon.

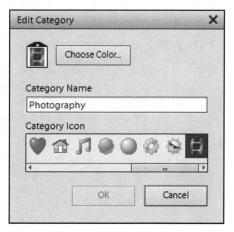

Figure 3-5: The Edit Category dialog box enables you to make some changes to the tag icon.

Building your own categories and subcategories

In the earlier section "Introducing Tags and the Tags Panel," you find out about the context menu that you can open for each tag type, as well as the way that tags have a hierarchy of categories and subcategories.

To create a category and/or subcategory, follow these steps:

1. **From the Keyword Tags drop-down menu in the Tags panel, choose New Category.**

   The Create Category dialog box appears.

2. **Provide a name and choose a color and icon for the appearance.**

3. **After creating a new category, choose New Sub-Category from the Keyword Tags drop-down menu.**

   The Create Sub-Category dialog box appears.

4. **Provide a Sub-Category name and click OK.**

5. **Repeat Steps 1 through 4 until you create all the subcategories you want.**

A Category tag you create using the context menu is limited to the same conditions you have with the default category tags. You can't use custom icons, and you're restricted to using the icons provided by Elements (refer to Figure 3-5). All the Sub-Category icons are predefined for you, as you can see in Figure 3-1, where three subcategories appear in the People Tags panel.

Finding and Tagging People in Photos

Elements provides a great, although not perfect, solution for identifying and labeling people. As people are identified, keyword tags are automatically added to the Tags panel. After you tag people, you can easily click the People tab at the top of the Organizer window and locate all the people you've tagged.

Before you start using Elements' facial recognition features, you'll find it helpful to understand Elements' strengths and weaknesses in determining whether a photo contains a person:

- Photos that show a person's whole face from the front are generally recognized by Elements as a photo with a person.

- Elements has more difficulty recognizing profile shots, people's faces at angles, and people wearing hats. Elements may also not detect a person in photos where harsh contrast appears along faces, such as partial shadow and partial bright sunlight.

With this in mind, you can't rely solely on Elements to identify people in photos. You have to fine-tune the automated features by hand. Here's the basic process for using Elements' automated facial recognition tool along with its manual people-tagging tool to make sure that the important people in your photos are all tagged:

1. **Tag on import.**

   Elements recognizes some photos when you import them into the Organizer, but the process isn't foolproof. Elements may not recognize that some photos containing people may need people tags. You can choose to supply names for people when the photos are imported or dismiss tagging people and handle the tagging later.

2. **Add people.**

   You can add people to a batch after you import it. However, you must have some photos tagged with people names for Elements to offer you suggestions and automate the tagging process. If you start in a catalog that has no people tags, you need to first identify some people in some photos using the Mark Face feature. After that, when Elements analyzes photos, it makes recommendations for tags that belong to people in photos. The next section walks you through this process.

3. **Individually tag photos where Elements missed people.**

   You can open a photo in the Media Browser and supply tag information individually on photos with the Mark Face feature. The upcoming section "Marking faces" explains how this process works.

Adding people

A great way to start adding people tags is by using the Add People button on the toolbar at the bottom of the Organizer window. This tool uses facial recognition to find photos that contain the same person and then asks you to confirm whether its analysis is correct. Here's how it works:

1. **Select the folder that you want to search in the Import panel. Or you can search the entire catalog if no folder or batch is selected.**

2. **Click the Add People button.**

   If you've tagged people in your catalog, Elements looks for visual similarities and asks you to confirm adding tags to people it thinks are the same as other tags in your catalog.

3. **If the people shown in the window match the names on the tagged photo, click the Save button. If not, skip to Step 4.**

   In Figure 3-6, you see the photo on the left identified and all the other photos that Elements thinks are a match.

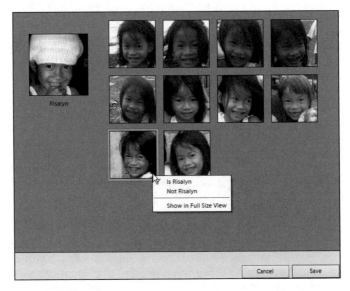

Figure 3-6: If all people are a match to the tagged photo, click Save.

4. **If some images aren't a match, click the photo, and a drop-down menu appears. Click Not (*Name*), as shown in Figure 3-6.**

   Elements may display several windows asking you to confirm matches. Click Save in each window, and eventually you may arrive at a window where Elements can't find any potential matches.

5. **If Elements detects a person but not a corresponding people tag, click the Who Is This? text and type names for each individual in the window, as you see in Figure 3-7.**

   Notice that when you click the text, Elements may offer suggestions below the text box for tags it thinks may belong to the photo. If one of the tags does belong to the photo, click the name below the text box. If no name appears that matches the photo, type the name of the person in the text box.

Marking faces

When Elements doesn't have a clue that a person appears in the photo, you have to go to its missing person's bureau and find someone. In Elements, that bureau is called the Mark Face button. For example, in Figure 3-8, Elements recognized the two figures on the left (Arnie and Irene). But Elements didn't recognize Malou on the right as a person.

Figure 3-7: Click the text and type a name to tag the photo.

Figure 3-8: Click the green check mark (Commit button) before closing
the window.

To use the Mark Face button, do the following:

1. **In the Organizer, locate a photo where a person isn't recognized.**

2. **Double-click the photo to open it in full view in the Media Browser.**

   You must double-click the photo in order for the Mark Face button to appear at the bottom of the Organizer.

3. **In the tools at the bottom of the Organizer window, click the Mark Face button.**

   A new rectangle appears in the photo.

4. **Move and size the rectangle around the face to position it.**

   When the cursor is placed inside the rectangle, you can click and drag the rectangle around the photo and to the person you want to tag. You resize the rectangle by dragging a corner of the rectangle in or out diagonally.

5. **Type the name of the person in the text box.**

6. **Click the Commit button (green check mark) to accept your edits.**

Mapping Photos with Place Tags

Photoshop Elements 11 reintroduced geospatial tagging in Elements with Google Maps and support for both Windows and Macintosh users. In addition, the Places view in the Organizer works in conjunction with maps. As a matter of fact, you won't see a Google map until you click the Places tab at the top of the Media Browser.

In Elements 13, tagging photos at map locations is easy as long as you know how it works, but quite frustrating if you don't know how the tools work.

GPS cameras and phones can tag photos with locations. Such photos appear on the map when you open the map associated with Places tags.

There are two ways to add Places tags to your photos:

- ✔ Select photos in the Media Browser. Next, open the Places panel and click the Plus icon to open the drop-down menu. Click the New Place button, and the Add New Place window opens where you can search the map to find the location for tagging the photos. Because you selected photos in the Media Browser, Elements assumes you want to add all the selected photos to the same place.

- ✔ Click the Add Places button at the bottom of the Organizer. You can do this by first selecting photos or not selecting any photos. In the Add Places window that opens after you click the Add Places button, a filmstrip appears at the top of the window. Click the photos you want to add to a common place.

To add geospatial tagging to photos you select in the Media Browser, do the following:

1. **Select photos in the Media Browser that you want to tag on a map location.**

2. **Open the Places panel and click the Plus icon to open the drop-down menu.**

   When you click the Add Places button, Elements opens the Add Places wizard, where you can search for a location and place photos on a map.

3. **Click Add New Place.**

   The Add New Place wizard opens.

4. **Search for the map location.**

   In the Add New Place wizard shown in Figure 3-9, type a location in the search text box and press the Return/Enter key.

5. **Click the green check mark (the Commit button) to tag the images to the map location as shown in Figure 3-9.**

Book II
Chapter 3

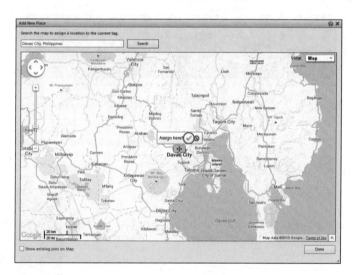

Figure 3-9: Click the green check mark to map the selected photos to the location.

6. **Click Done.**

7. **View the photos in the Media Browser.**

   Click the Places tab, and click a place listed in the panel (shown in Figure 3-10) to display photos tagged with a given place in the Media Browser.

If you first select photos in the Media Browser and click the Add Places button, the Add Places wizard opens with the selected photos appearing in a filmstrip as shown in Figure 3-11. You can choose which photos you want to add to a new place or a previously added place by dragging photos from the filmstrip to the map below the filmstrip.

Theoretically, if you haven't yet mapped any photos to a map location, you use the Places panel to add a new place. If later you want to add additional photos to the same place, select the photos in the Media Browser and click the Add Places button at the bottom of the Organizer window.

Figure 3-10: Click a place in the Places panel to see all the images tagged with that place.

Figure 3-11: The Add Places wizard with selected photos appearing as a filmstrip at the top of the wizard.

Tagging Events with the Events Tab

You may have occasions such as birthday parties, Christmas or other holiday celebrations, company picnics, and so on that you want to tag according to an event name.

When adding Events tags, you follow steps similar to when you add People and Places tags. Select photos in the Organizer, open the Events Tags panel, and click the Plus icon to open the drop-down menu. Click Add New Event in the menu, and the Events Tags panel appears as shown in Figure 3-12.

Figure 3-12: A new event added to the Events Tags panel.

Type a name for the event, and add the dates by either typing a date in the text box or clicking the calendar icon to open a calendar where you choose dates. Add a Description of the event and click Done.

Removing Tags

Invariably, you'll find yourself tagging a photo that doesn't belong to a tag group. For example, you may tag a person with the wrong name, add a photo to an event that doesn't belong in the group, or add Keywords tags to photos that shouldn't be tagged with a given tag name.

Photoshop Elements is not very intuitive when it comes to deleting tags from photos. You find no Delete Tag item in the drop-down menus in the different tags panels.

To remove a tag from a photo, you must follow some precise steps:

1. **In the Media Browser notice the tiny tag icon represented by a 1. Right-click the icon to open a context menu on the photo you want to untag.**

2. **Click Remove from *"tag name"* Event.**

    In our example, we click a photo not part of the bakery class event, as shown in Figure 3-13.

Book II
Chapter 3

Organizing Images
with Tags, Albums,
and More

Figure 3-13: Open a context menu in the Image Tags panel and choose Remove from *tag name.*

All the tags panels operate the same way when you want to remove tags. Display all photos having the same tag. Then, be certain to look at the Media Browser and remove the tags via a context menu.

Creating Smart Events

Elements can help you out in organizing photos by creating Smart Events for photos taken on the same date. Click the Events tab and you find a switch to turn on Smart Events, as shown in Figure 3-14.

Photos are automatically grouped together as individual Events according to the dates the photos were taken. Right-click a photo in the Events panel and you can supply a name. Subsequently the name is added as a new Event in the Events panel.

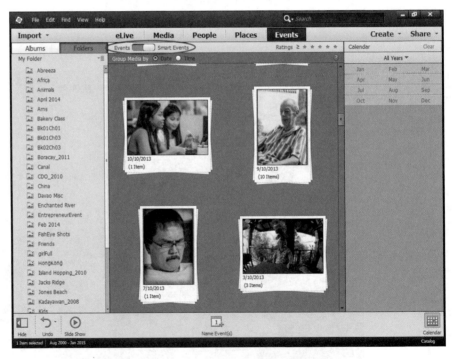

Figure 3-14: The Events tab contains a switch for turning on Smart Events.

Automating Tagging with Image Tags

The Image Tags feature at the bottom of the Tags panel puts the burden on Elements for sorting through photos and adding tags.

You use the Image Tags feature in conjunction with the Media Analyzer. By default, Media Analyzer is turned on. When you need to improve Elements' performance, turn the Media Analyzer off.

Using the Media Analyzer with a large catalog of files is especially burdensome to your system and can slow the performance of Elements. So unless you really need the Media Analyzer, you can keep it turned off in the Media Analysis Preferences.

In the Image Tags panel, Elements has predefined tags created for you, such as Two Faces, High Quality, Close Up, In Focus, and more. When you choose one of these tags from the pop-up menu that appears when you click in the Image Tags text box, Elements displays all the predefined tags; see Figure 3-15. When you run the Media Analyzer, these tag names are used to automatically tag photos. For example, the Media Analyzer searches through the photos for Two Faces, High Quality, and people names, and when Elements thinks a photo matches an item, it tags the photo automatically.

You can add more image tags by typing a new keyword in the Image Tags panel text box and then clicking the Add button.

The benefit of having image tags is that you can search any of the image tags in the Search item at the top of the Organizer window. When searching one of the criteria associated with Image Tags, Elements reports the number of found instances in the Search text box.

Figure 3-15: Click in the text box and a pop-up menu displays the predefined tags and additional tag names you add using the Tags panel.

Book II
Chapter 3

Organizing Images
with Tags, Albums,
and More

Rating Images with Stars

You can rate photos in the Organizer by tagging images with one to five stars. You might give exceptional photos a five-star rating and poor photos with lighting and focus problems one star. If you use stars to rate your photos, you can use the star rating as search criteria. Here's how star ratings work:

✔ **Giving a file a star rating:** Select a photo in the Media Browser and click Information in the Tags panel, shown in Figure 3-16. In the General pane, shown at the top of the panel, click a star. We clicked the fifth star, giving this file a five-star rating. (*Note:* You can remove a star rating by clicking the 1 star twice.)

✔ **Searching based on star ratings:** At the top of the Organizer window, you see Ratings followed by five stars. This item is used for searching images and not for rating them. After you rate files, you can search for all files with, for example, a three-star rating and above. Only those images rated with three, four, or five stars appear in the Media Browser. See Chapter 2 of this minibook for more details about searching in the Organizer.

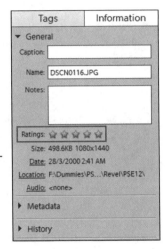

Figure 3-16: The Information panel.

Checking out image information

Image properties appear in the Information panel. Click Information in the Panel bin to open the panel.

The Information panel offers information about your files, including

✔ **Caption:** You type captions for photos in the text box.

✔ **Name:** The filename appears in a text box, and it is editable. You can change filenames by editing the text.

✔ **Notes:** If you want to add notes to images, you can type in the Notes text box.

✔ **Rating files:** You can assign ratings to files, as we describe in the nearby section "Rating Images with Stars."

✔ **Size:** The file size is reported in the panel.

✔ **Date:** The panel reports the date the picture was shot, a canvas was created, or a picture was scanned.

✔ **Location:** The panel displays the directory path for the file location on your hard drive.

✔ **Audio:** If the file contains a sound, the sound information is displayed.

✔ **Metadata:** Metadata, such as the camera data (camera model, f-stop, shutter speed, focal length of lens, and so on), are reported when you click the right arrow to open the Metadata pane.

✔ **History:** Open the History pane by clicking the right arrow, and you see the media's file history, such as date last modified, import date, import source, and the current location.

If you need to look up other data about your images, the Information panel is a great resource, as you can see in the other panes shown in Figure 3-15. See the nearby sidebar "Checking out image information" for details.

Working with Albums

Albums allow you to organize your photos in a way that's different from keyword tags or stars. Albums basically give you a special place to put photos you want to group together, no matter what the content or quality of the image is. You may want to organize an album for sharing photos with others on Adobe Revel, for creating a slide show, or just as a temporary holding spot.

The term *album* in Photoshop Elements nomenclature refers to a collection of images that aren't yet integrated into projects, such as photo books and photo collages. See Book IX for details about the projects you can create via the Create panel.

In the following sections, you find out a bit more about the benefits of albums and how to create and add photos to an album.

Exploring album benefits

Creating albums affords you many different exciting things that you can do with a collection of photos. Here are just a few ways that you might find albums helpful as you work in Elements:

- ✔ **Share your albums with friends and family.** Host albums online for others to view your photos, or write albums to CDs and DVDs (Windows) that you can view on your television set, on an Apple TV (Mountain Lion or greater Mac OS), or on another device for television viewing. In short, albums help you assemble a collection of photos that you can view on many devices and share with others. We explain much more about albums in Book IX, Chapter 1.

- ✔ **View albums as slide shows,** as we explain in Chapter 2 of this minibook.

- ✔ **Group a collection of images with different tags.**

- ✔ **Assemble a collection of photos to use in a project** and then later trash the album (without deleting the photos). Albums serve you well for quick assembly of different projects. After you add photos to an album, you don't need to be concerned with searching through a catalog when assembling a project.

What happened to Smart Albums?

In previous versions of Elements, we had a feature called Smart Albums, where Elements automatically added photos to your Smart Album as you imported them and tagged the photos with similar tags.

In Elements 13, you won't find Smart Albums. Adobe feels that when you create a search

and save your searches, the process is very similar to creating Smart Albums; therefore a bit of redundancy is removed from this version of Elements. Whether you agree or not, unfortunately you won't find Smart Albums in Elements 13.

Creating an album

To create an album, follow these steps:

1. **Sort photos in the Media Browser to find the photos you want to include in a new album.**

   In addition to tags and stars, discussed earlier in this chapter, Elements offers a variety of search and viewing options (discussed in Chapter 2 of this minibook) to help you track down specific photos in a large catalog.

2. **Click the plus (+) icon at the top of the left panel, as shown in Figure 3-17.**

Figure 3-17: Click the plus (+) icon to open the drop-down menu.

3. **From the drop-down menu, click New Album.**

   Notice in Figure 3-16 that you see the Albums menu on the left side of the Organizer window. When you create a new album, the remaining work you perform on an album — such as naming the album, categorizing the album, adding content to an album, and sharing an album — is all handled in the Panel Bin on the right side of the Organizer window.

The location of the menu is different than earlier versions of Elements, where the menu and the album options were all contained in the Panel Bin.

4. **Name the new album.**

   In the Panel Bin, you see the New Album panel. Type a name for the album in the Album Name text box and click OK, as shown in Figure 3-18.

5. **Drag photos from the Media Browser to the Content pane in the New Album panel, as shown in Figure 3-18.**

   Because we first started the steps to create an album with a star-rating sort, the only photos in the Media Browser are those files with a three or greater star rating. If you didn't sort files, you can do so now or simply pick and choose which photos to add to the new album from photos appearing in your catalog. If you want to include all photos in the Media Browser, press Ctrl+A/⌘+A to select all or choose Edit➪Select All. After the files are selected, drag them to the Content pane in the New Album panel (see Figure 3-18). If you don't have files sorted, click one or more photos and drag them to the Content pane. Repeat dragging photos until you have all photos you want to include in your new album.

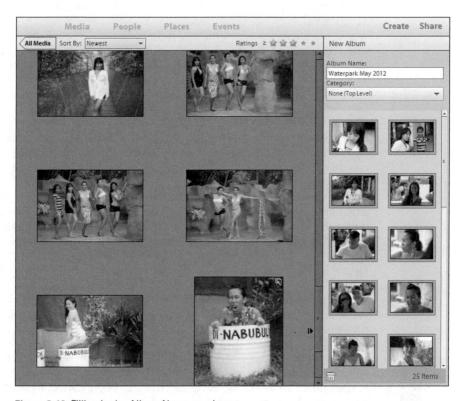

Figure 3-18: Filling in the Album Name text box.

6. **Click OK at the bottom of the panel.**

   After you create an album, you can add additional photos to the album by dragging photos to the album name in the Local Albums panel (the left side of the Organizer window).

   Your new album now appears listed in the Albums panel.

That's it! Your new album is created, and the photos you drag to the album are added to it. You can isolate all the photos within a given album by clicking the album name in the Albums panel.

Creating multiple albums uses only a fraction of the disk space that would be required if you wanted to duplicate photos for multiple purposes, such as printing, web hosting, sharing, and so on.

Using albums for temporary work

As you explore various features in Photoshop Elements, you may want to explore some of the creation and sharing items in the Create and Share panels. As you peruse the options, first create an album and add photos to it. Then proceed to explore the many features Elements offers you.

When you finish your exploration, right-click (or Ctrl-click on a Macintosh with a one-button mouse) to open a context menu and choose Delete *album name*. You can add an album for temporary work and then delete the album when you no longer need it.

Editing an album

After creating an album, you may want to change the album name, add more photos to an album, delete some photos from an album, change the album category, or do some other kind of edit.

Your first step in performing any kind of edit to an album is to look at the left side of the Organizer window. In the Import panel, you see a list of albums under the Albums category. To edit an album, open a context menu on an album name and click Edit. After clicking Edit, the album appears in the Panel Bin on the right side of the Organizer window, much like you see in Figure 3-18.

Other commands are available on the context menu you open from an album name in the Import panel. You can rename an album, delete an album, and add more media to your album.

If you want to use the context menu commands, you must close the New Album panel in the Panel Bin. While this panel is open, you can't open a context menu on an album name. Click either Done or Cancel to close the New Album panel in the Panel Bin.

Book III
Image Essentials

For more details and projects about Photoshop Elements, visit www.dummies.com/
extras/photoshopelementsaio.

Contents at a Glance

Chapter 1: Creating, Undoing, and Saving Images

In This Chapter

- Opening existing image files in the Editor
- Creating a new image from scratch
- Creating a new image from data copied to the Clipboard
- Unraveling errors with Elements' undo features
- Saving an image
- Closing an image versus quitting a workspace

To edit an image, your first step is to open an existing image or create a new one. It sounds simple, and it is. The same goes for saving images: Many times, you can just choose your favorite way of invoking the Save command that you find in almost any program. So why did we write a whole chapter about creating and saving images? Here are two reasons:

- First of all, Elements is packed with specialized tools. You'll find it helpful to know what commands and tools are at your disposal for opening, creating, and saving images. The primary focus of this chapter is introducing you to these commands and tools and explaining the basics of how they work.

- Secondly, you need to know when to pay attention to the options in the New and Save dialog boxes. When you create or save an image file, many of the options that you see exist for different outputs — namely, for prints or for displaying images online. As you walk through the basic steps for using the tools in this chapter, we point out when you need to understand an important image-editing concept (and where to find an explanation) so that your final image looks its best in your desired output.

View from the top

Resort and Restaurant

As you start learning how to create and edit your images — or even after you become pros like us — you're bound to make mistakes. As you begin your journey into image editing, this chapter bestows you with the magical gift of Undo. Elements' sophisticated Undo tools enable you to wipe away your errors in myriad ways. Whenever your image-editing experiments go awry, remember that you can undo. Then flip to this chapter for help.

Opening an Image in the Photo Editor

You may have a single photo that you want to edit without adding it to the Organizer. Perhaps you just want to apply some edits to an image you have on a media source or on your hard drive and then send it off via email or share the photo using one of several supported sharing services.

In this case, you can bypass the Organizer and start in the Photo Editor. To open an image in the Photo Editor, do the following:

1. **Launch Photoshop Elements.**

   If you open the Welcome screen, click the Photo Editor button to open the Photo Editor. If you're in the Organizer, click Editor at the bottom of the Organizer window.

2. **Choose File➪Open. Alternatively, you can click Open at the top of the Tools panel.**

3. **(Optional) If you want to search for photos saved within a given format, open the All Formats drop-down list (Format pop-up menu on the Mac) and choose the format for a file you want to open.**

   Selecting a format narrows the files displayed to only those files saved in the selected format. For example, if you have Camera Raw, JPEG, and TIFF images in a folder and you want to open only a JPEG file, you can select JPEG (*.JPG, *.JPEG, *.JPE) from the All Formats drop-down list (or JPEG from the Format pop-up menu [Mac]). Doing so displays only files saved in the format you choose.

   If you're not sure what format the file you want to open is, leave the default choice from the menu at All Formats.

   Macintosh users have an advantage here when searching for files. When you arrive at the Open dialog box (File➪Open or ⌘+O), you can use the Mac OS search feature, Spotlight, in the upper-right corner of the Open dialog box. Of course, if you haven't renamed your image from the default camera name (such as `img_3012.jpg`), you'll likely have a hard time remembering what filename to use in your search terms.

4. **From the list of photo files displayed, click the photo you want to open.**

5. **Click the Open button in the Open dialog box.**

   The file opens in the Photo Editor.

Using in Camera Raw

When you need to edit photos for brightness and color corrections, use the Camera Raw option. Camera Raw is a format supported by many higher-end digital cameras. However, you can open JPEG and TIFF files also in Camera Raw using this menu command. We cover all you want to know about Camera Raw, and why this would be an advantage when editing photos, in a web extra at www.dummies.com/extras/photoshopelementsaio.

Opening recently edited files

A quick way to open recently edited files is to choose File⇨Open Recently Edited File. The submenu lists these files. The number of files appearing in the submenu is determined in Preferences. You can also open recently edited photos from the Open drop-down menu.

If the file you want to open appears on the submenu, click the filename in the list, and the file opens in the Photo Editor.

The Recently Edited Files list also appears in the Organizer. If you want to open a recently edited image while in the Organizer workspace, choose File⇨Open Recently Edited File in Editor and select the file you want to open. The file opens in the Photo Editor.

**Book III
Chapter 1**

Creating, Undoing, and Saving Images

Opening an image within another image

In Elements, opening one image file inside another image is called *placing* an image file. You may have a piece of artwork you want to add to a photo. The artwork can be of any file type you find for the supported formats that you can open in Elements. Quite often, you may find a vector art drawing or a PDF file that contains the artwork you want to import into your current image file; however, you can use any of the supported formats for placing content on a photo.

For more information on placing PDF files, see our Web Extra on creating custom calendars at www.dummies.com/extras/photoshopelementsaio.

Before you place an image inside another image, you'll find it helpful to know whether you're working with vector versus raster art and how that impacts your ability to resize the placed image. Flip to Book III, Chapter 2, for an introduction to vector and raster images and image sizing.

Note that when you *place* an image, no matter what file format, it's inserted into your open file as a Smart Object. Smart Objects are essentially composed of two files, one inside the other, enabling the image's source data, whether pixel- or vector-based, to be embedded. Adobe uses the analogy of a new file, the *child,* which is embedded into the original file, the *parent.* What does this all mean to you? It means that you can repeatedly transform (size, skew, rotate) your image without losing any additional image quality because Elements uses your original source data to render the transformation and the Smart Object updates dynamically as you make edits. One caveat: With vector images, you can size up and down repeatedly and never worry about losing quality. With raster images, however, you can safely resize repeatedly, but you don't want to size larger than your original dimensions or else you risk resampling or degradation.

To place content in Elements, use the Place command as follows:

1. **Open an image file in the Photo Editor.**

   You must start with a file open in the Photo Editor to use the Place command.

2. **Choose File⇨Place.**

   The Place dialog box opens. This dialog box has the same options you find in the Open dialog box.

3. **Select a file to place.**

   Your file can be an image format, EPS, Adobe Illustrator (AI) or other type of vector format, PDF, or any other file type you see listed in the Files of Type drop-down list (Windows) or Format pop-up menu (Mac).

4. **Click Place.**

   When you place an image, you see handles around the image that can be used for sizing the image, as shown in Figure 1-1. Smart Objects always import into your file with an X over the image, which distinguishes them from regular images.

Figure 1-1: A placed vector art image.

5. **Size and position the image.**

   If you import a vector art image or PDF file containing vector art, you can drag the corner handles out to size up and/or rotate the image without losing image quality. Press the Shift key when sizing the image to constrain proportions and press the Enter (Return) key to accept your resizing edits. Click the image and move it to the desired position.

6. **Press Return and commit your layer.**

   The small black-and-white Smart Objects icon is in the lower-right corner of your layer thumbnail in the Layers panel.

Before you start creating new images from various sources and tools in Elements, we also suggest that you check out how layers work (see Book V) and see how the Photomerge tools help you combine images (see Book VIII, Chapter 3).

If you open a Camera Raw 16-bit image, you cannot place artwork on the photo. You must first convert the 16-bit image to an 8-bit image by choosing Image➪Mode➪8 Bits/Channel.

Creating a New Image

In Elements, you can create a new image from a totally blank canvas or from data you copied to the Clipboard. When you start with a fresh, new canvas, you can copy and paste content from other pictures, place objects, add shapes, and/or add text to create your own scene. To begin the process, you create a new image.

In either the Photo Editor or the Organizer, choose File➪New➪Blank File. Additionally you can open the Open drop-down menu in the Photo Editor and choose New Blank File. If you start in the Organizer, Elements switches workspaces from the Organizer to the Photo Editor, and the New dialog box opens, as shown in Figure 1-2.

The options you have here are covered thoroughly in Book III, Chapter 2. Look over that chapter for details on the options you have for creating new, blank files.

**Book III
Chapter 1**

Creating, Undoing, and Saving Images

New		
Name:	Untitled-2	OK
Preset:	Clipboard ▼	Cancel
Size:	None ▼	
Width:	1024	pixels ▼
Height:	768	pixels ▼
Resolution:	72	pixels/inch ▼
Color Mode:	RGB Color ▼	
Background Contents:	Transparent ▼	Image Size:
		2.25M

Figure 1-2: Choose File➪New➪Blank File to open the New dialog box from either the Organizer or the Photo Editor.

In Elements, you can also create a new image from data you copy to the Clipboard. If you copy data from somewhere else — such as text in Office applications or objects in Office applications, illustration programs, and other types of applications — Elements can convert the data on the Clipboard to a new image.

For example, you might want to copy a photo and save it as a new image when a family member posts a picture on Facebook or in another online album-sharing tool. You can create a new image from the photo you've copied and save it to your computer's hard drive.

Follow these steps to copy a photo from a web page, such as Facebook, and create a new file that you can add to your Organizer catalog:

1. **Log on to your Facebook, Flickr, Adobe Revel, or iCloud account, or another website where you can freely use an image.**

   Remember to observe copyright laws when copying online images. You should have permission to use the images you copy.

2. **Right-click a photo to open a context menu. (Ctrl-click on a Mac with a one-button mouse.)**

3. **Choose Copy (Internet Explorer) or Copy Image (in Firefox or Safari), as shown in Figure 1-3.**

Figure 1-3: Open a context menu to copy an image to the Clipboard.

4. **Open the Elements Organizer or the Photo Editor.**

   You can select the same menu command in either the Organizer or an editor mode.

5. **Choose File⇨New⇨Image from Clipboard.**

   The Clipboard contents appear in a new image window, as shown in Figure 1-4.

Figure 1-4: Clipboard contents appear in a new image window.

Using the steps outlined here, you can grab a bunch of images from a family member's online account without having to load images from a removable device or a media card.

Undoing in Elements

Back in 1984, Apple Computer brought windowing interfaces to the masses with the introduction of the Macintosh computer. Also tucked into that interface was the Undo command. Both innovations revolutionized the way people use personal computers. Together with the Cut, Copy, and Paste commands, these features became a standard in all programs that followed. Being able to undo your most recent edit in a program like Elements gives you the freedom to experiment, as well as the chance to correct mistakes immediately. Adobe broadened that initial Undo feature in Photoshop Elements so that you can retrace an entire series of editing steps with multiple undo actions, see a visual list of edits in the History panel, and work with different editing states.

In the following sections, you explore the many ways you can branch out, experiment a little, and retrace your editing steps (or overcome a series of editing mistakes) without having to save multiple versions of your photos.

Undoing what's done with the Undo command

As you might expect, the Undo command is found on the Edit menu. To undo an editing step, you simply choose Edit➪Undo or press Ctrl+Z or ⌘+Z. This simple command helps you correct a mistake or toss away an experimental edit that doesn't work for you.

When you open the Edit menu, you find the Undo command at the top of the menu. In addition, you find the name of the edit you last applied to the image. Figure 1-5 shows that we just applied a Brightness/Contrast adjustment. On the Edit menu, the menu command appears as Undo Brightness/Contrast.

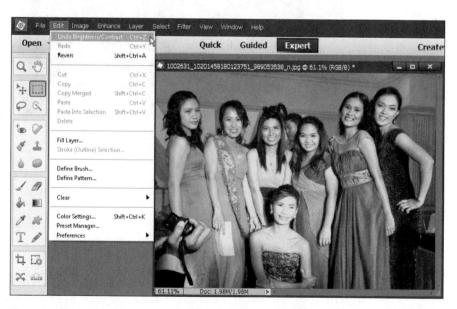

Figure 1-5: The Undo command appears listed on the Edit menu with the name of the last edit applied to the document.

You also have a command for Redo on the Edit menu. If you choose Undo from the Edit menu or press Ctrl+Z (⌘+Z) and then change your mind, you can always just redo that last undo: Choose Redo or press Ctrl+Y (⌘+Y), and the last undo returns to the state before you chose to undo the edit.

The number of redos you have is the same as the number of undos. By default, you can undo and thus redo up to 50 edits at a time.

Reverting to what's saved

At times, rather than undo a bunch of edits, you just want to toss all the edits away and return to the last saved version of your file. The Revert command on the Edit menu returns you to the last saved version of your photo.

If you make several edits and you like what you see, you can choose File↔Save or press Ctrl+S (⌘+S) to save your edits. If you then make several more edits and you don't like the results, choose Edit↔Revert to revert to the last save.

In many Adobe programs, you find a Revert command listed on the File menu. In Photoshop Elements, however, the Revert command is listed on the Edit menu. Keep this in mind when you perform edits in the Editor's Expert mode.

Working with the almighty History panel

Using menu commands and keyboard shortcuts enables you to travel back and forward in time to undo and redo edits using single menu choices or keyboard shortcuts for each undo/redo.

The History panel, on the other hand, gives you a capability that menu commands don't: You can target an undo (or redo) to go back (or forward) to a *specific* edit. For example, if you create a selection, apply an enhancement edit (such as changing image brightness), and then apply a filter, you can return to the selection with one mouse click. Instead of choosing Undo to undo the filter and Undo again to undo the image brightness, you simply click the selection edit in the History panel.

The following steps walk you through the process of undoing and redoing history states with the History panel:

1. **To open the History panel, choose Window↔History.**

   The History panel opens, as shown in Figure 1-6. As you make edits on an image, each edit is shown as a history state in the list in the panel.

2. **To return to an earlier edit in the History panel, find the history state you want to return to in the list and click it.**

   For example, say that you applied a number of edits for color and brightness adjustments. If you want to return to the state before the adjustments, click its corresponding history state in the History panel. In Figure 1-6, you might click on the Feather item to remove the Brightness/Contrast and Color Cast adjustments.

Figure 1-6: The History panel.

3. **If you decide that you went back too far in the list of history states, you can redo any grayed-out history states by clicking the most recent state you want to redo.**

   In our example, if we decide we want to redo the next two history states below the currently selected one, we'd simply click the third instance of the Clone Stamp in the list. That would restore the second and third use of the Clone Stamp in the list.

   As long as your history states remain in the list in the History panel, you can click backward or forward to undo and redo edits.

   You may need to manage the number of history states that appear in the History panel. By default, the panel provides 50 history states. When you come to the 51st edit, the first edit in the sequence is deleted from the panel, and you can't return to that state. As you make more new edits, you continually delete edits from the top of the panel. If you're making a lot of complicated edits to an image, you might be surprised by how quickly you use up all 50 states.

To manage the available history states in the History panel, you have the following options:

- **Increase the number of available history states.** To do so, open the Performance preferences and change the value in the History States text box.

  As you increase history states in the Performance preferences, the amount of memory required by Elements is increased. You may find the program getting sluggish if you significantly increase the number of history states.

✔ **Delete certain history states that you're certain you no longer need.**
You may have applied a series of edits to a document and then want to
return to an earlier history state. Suppose that you no longer need all
the history states made after the one to which you return. (This might
happen if you're experimenting with different edits and viewing the
results.) If you know that the history states following a particular state
are no longer needed, you can delete those history states from the list.

- *To delete the last history state in the History panel,* click the history
  state in the list and then right-click to open a context menu. From the
  menu choices, choose Delete. The selected history state is deleted
  from the list.

- *If you have a series of history states that you want to delete from the
  list,* click the first history state within a given list of edits to open a
  context menu. Then, when you choose Delete, you delete all the history states in the list that follow as well as the selected history state.

Keep in mind that *all* history states following a history state you target
for deletion are deleted when you open a context menu and choose
Delete.

If you want to delete a series of edits that are followed by edits you want
to retain, you have to delete the unwanted edits individually.

✔ **Clear the entire history.** If you don't need any of the history states in
the History panel, open a context menu and choose Clear History. The
list is cleared until you start editing your image again.

You also clear a file's history each time you save and close the image
file. If you apply a number of edits and just choose File⇨Save, the history states remain in the list of edits applied to the document before you
last saved it. Therefore you can undo edits after saving a file, as long as
the file remains open. However, if you close the file and reopen it, the
History panel is cleared.

Saving Files

In almost any program, the Save (or Save As) dialog box is a familiar place
where you make choices about the file to be saved. In Elements (as in most
other programs), choose Save when you want to save changes you've made
to the current image, overwriting the original. Choose Save As when you
want to save a copy of your image to edit and retain the original file.

To use the Save/Save As dialog box, follow these steps:

1. **Open an image and choose File⇨Save for files to be saved the first
   time or choose File⇨Save As for any file.**

   Either command opens a dialog box for you.

One exception: If you need to save a smaller version of a file for the web, you use a different dialog box than you do when you're saving files for other output. Choose File⇨Save for Web; the Save for Web dialog box opens. Flip to Book III, Chapter 3, for details about how to use the Save for Web dialog box.

2. **In the Filename (Windows) or Save As (Mac) box, type a name for your file in the text box if you haven't saved the file yet or would like to save it under a different name.**

This item is common to all Save dialog boxes.

3. **(Optional) From the Format drop-down list or pop-up menu, select a file format.**

If you do nothing to an image in terms of converting its color mode or changing bit depth (topics I explain in Book III, Chapters 3 and 5, respectively), you can save your edits to a file in the same format in which the file was opened.

However, in many circumstances, you open an image and prepare it for some form of output (web or print), which requires more thought about the kind of file format you use in saving the file.

For example, some format types require you to convert a color mode before you can use the format. Therefore a relationship exists between file formats and saving files. Additionally, bit depths in images also relate to the kinds of file formats you can use in saving files. Last but not least, not all file formats support all the Elements features. For example, if you add layers as you edit a file and want to preserve the layers for future editing, you need to save your file in a format that supports layers.

Before you go too far in Elements, we recommend familiarizing yourself with the file formats you use and the conversions you need to make to save in one format or another (as we explain in Book III, Chapter 3).

If you save in JPEG format, be aware that JPEG uses a *lossy* compression scheme, meaning that image data is tossed away with each save. Repeated saves from the same JPEG image degrade the image. After you open a JPEG file that was shot with your camera, save the file as PSD (Photoshop format). You can edit and save the file without losing data. When you need a final image in JPEG, use the Save As command and save in JPEG format. You can always return to the PSD file to edit more and then save again in JPEG format for output. To find out more about converting JPEG to other formats, see the section about exporting files in Book III, Chapter 3.

4. **(Optional) Set your options in the Save Options area.**

You see the following choices:

• **Include in the Organizer:** If you want the file added to the Organizer, select this check box.

- **Save in Version Set with Original:** You can edit images and save a version of your image, but only in the Photo Editor's Quick mode. When you save the file from Quick mode, this check box is active. Select the box, and a version of the original is saved and appears in the Organizer.

- **Color:** Select the check box for the ICC (International Color Consortium) Profile. Depending on which profile you use, the option appears for sRGB or Adobe RGB (1998). When the check box is selected, the profile is embedded in the image. Book IX, Chapter 2, explains how to use color profiles when you print.

- **Thumbnail (Windows):** If you save a file with a thumbnail, you can see a miniature representation of your image when viewing it in folders or on the desktop. If you select Ask When Saving in the Saving Files preferences, the check box can be selected or deselected. If you're choosing an option for Never Save or Always Save in the Preferences dialog box, this check box is selected or deselected for you and is grayed out. You need to return to the Preferences dialog box if you want to change the option.

- **Use Lower Case Extension (Windows):** File extensions give you a clue to which file format was used when a file was saved. Elements automatically adds the extension to the filename for you. Your choices are to use uppercase or lowercase letters for the extension name. Select the Use Lower Case Extension check box for lowercase or deselect the check box if you want to use uppercase characters in the filename. Lowercase extensions are preferable when you work with images that are hosted on websites.

5. **When you're done selecting your options, click Save.**

Closing and Quitting

You should understand a few important details when closing files and quitting Elements:

- When you're in the Photo Editor and have an image open in the Image window, you can close the image without quitting the Photo Editor workspace. Click the X button in the upper-right corner of the Image window or the red button in the upper-left corner (Mac), and the open file is closed. If the images appear as tabs in the Image Window, click the X to the right of the filename (Windows) or left of the filename (Mac).

- If you click the X (red button) in the upper-right corner of the Photo Editor workspace (Windows) or choose Photoshop Elements⇨Quit on the Mac, you quit the Photo Editor. Alternatively, you can press Alt+F4 (Windows) or Ctrl+Q (⌘+Q on a Mac).

**Book III
Chapter 1**

Creating, Undoing, and Saving Images

✔ If you happen to have the Organizer and the Photo Editor open and you quit one workspace, the other workspace remains open. For example, if the Organizer and the Photo Editor are both open when you quit the Organizer, the Photo Editor remains open and vice versa.

✔ If you make an edit on a photo in the Photo Editor and decide to quit the Photo Editor, Elements prompts you to save the file before quitting.

✔ If you have the Welcome screen open as well as the Organizer and the Photo Editor, quitting both the Organizer and the Photo Editor doesn't get you out of Elements. The Welcome screen remains open even though you've quit the workspaces.

✔ To completely shut down Elements, take a look at the status bar (Windows) or the Dock (Mac). If you see one workspace open, click the respective item in the status bar (or Dock) and then choose File⇨Quit, click the Close button (Windows), or press Ctrl+Q (⌘+Q on the Mac).

Chapter 2: Specifying Resolution and Changing Image Sizing

In This Chapter

✓ **Understanding image attributes**

✓ **Sizing images**

✓ **Scaling images**

✓ **Setting print and screen resolutions**

✓ **Altering the size of the canvas**

*W*hen you open a picture in Photoshop Elements, you're looking at a huge mass of pixels. These pixels are tiny, colored squares, and the number of pixels in a picture determines the picture's resolution. This relationship between pixels and resolution — important to understand in all your Elements work — relates to creating selections (as we explain in Book IV), printing files (Book IX, Chapter 2), and sharing files (Book IX, Chapter 3).

This chapter explains some essential points about resolution and image sizes and displaying images onscreen, especially in terms of the way these points affect how you end up modifying your images.

Examining Images Closely

Files you open in Elements are composed of thousands or even millions of tiny, square pixels. Each pixel has one, and only one, color value. The arrangement of the pixels of different shades and colors creates an illusion for your eyes when you're viewing an image onscreen. For example, you may have black and white pixels arranged in an order that creates the impression that you're looking at something gray — not at all those tiny black and white squares.

Just about everything you do in Elements has to do with changing pixels. You surround them with selection tools to select what appear to be objects in your image, you make pixels darker or lighter to change contrast and brightness, you change the shades and tints of pixels for color correction, and you perform a host of other possible editing tasks.

We have another term to throw at you when talking about pixels and Elements files: Your pictures are *raster images.* When you have pixels, you have raster data. If you open a file in Elements that isn't made of pixels, Elements can *rasterize* the data. In other words, Elements can convert other data to pixels if the document wasn't originally composed of pixels.

In addition to raster data, you can find vector data, which we talk more about in the section "Looking at raster versus vector images," later in this chapter.

To use most of the tools and commands in Elements, you must be working on a raster image file. If your data isn't rasterized, many tools and commands are unavailable.

Understanding resolution

The number of pixels per inch (ppi) in a file determines its image resolution. If you have 72 pixels across a 1-inch horizontal line, your image resolution is 72 ppi. If you have 300 pixels in 1 inch, your image resolution is 300 ppi.

For a simple understanding, you use 300 ppi photos for printing and 72 ppi images for screen views such as for web images and showing pictures on your monitor.

Image resolution is critical to properly outputting files when

- ✔ **You print images:** If the resolution is too low, the image prints poorly. If the image resolution is too high, you waste time and memory processing all the data that needs to be sent to your printer.

- ✔ **You show images onscreen:** Just as an image has an inherent resolution in its file, your computer monitor has an inherent — fixed — resolution at which it displays everything you see onscreen. Many computer monitors display images at 72 ppi (or 85 or 96 ppi) while newer computers such as the Apple's Retina displays show images with resolutions up to 227 ppi. With newer devices, such as cellphones and tablets, image resolution rises significantly. What's important to know is that you can always best display photos on your computer monitor at a 72-ppi image size in a 100-percent view. On cellphones and tablets, you need to look over the device specifications to see what the optimum resolution is for each device.

  As an example for viewing images on computer monitors, take a look at Figure 2-1: You see an image reduced to 50 percent and then at different zoom sizes. When the size changes, the resolution display on your monitor changes. When the size is 100 percent, you see the image in an optimum view. The 100-percent size represents the image displayed on your monitor at 72 ppi, regardless of the resolution of the file.

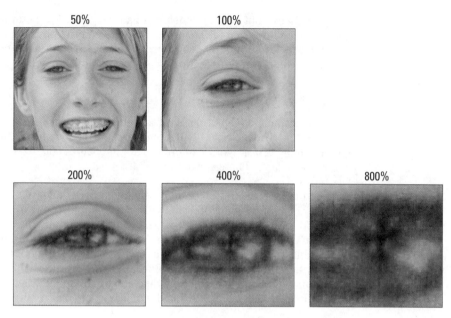

Figure 2-1: The same image, viewed at different zoom levels.

Book III
Chapter 2

Specifying
Resolution and
Changing Image
Sizing

This relationship between the image resolution and viewing the image at different zoom levels is tricky but vital. If, for example, you grab an image off the web and zoom in on it, you may see a view like the 800 percent view shown in Figure 2-1. If you acquire a digital camera image, you may need to zoom out to a 16-percent view to fit the entire image into the image window.

These displays vary so much because of image resolution. That image you grabbed off the web may be a 2-inch-square image at 72 ppi, and that digital camera image may be a 10-x-15-inch image at 240 ppi. You have to zoom in on the 240 ppi image if you want to fill the entire window with it — but when you zoom in, the resolution is lowered. The more you zoom in, the lower the resolution on your monitor.

When you zoom into or out of an image, you change the resolution as it appears on your monitor. *No resolution changes are made to the file.* The image resolution remains the same unless you use one of the Elements tools to reduce or increase image resolution.

Understanding image dimensions

Image dimensions involve the physical size of your file. If the size is 4 x 5 inches, for example, the file can be one of any number of resolution values. After the file is open in Elements, you can change the dimensions of an image, the resolution, or both.

When you change only the dimensions of an image (not the number of pixels it contains), an inverse relationship exists between the physical size of your image and the resolution: As image size increases, resolution decreases. Conversely, when you reduce the image size, you raise resolution.

Understanding camera megapixels

Digital-camera image resolution is measured in *megapixels* (millions of pixels) and is a factor in image size. If you have a 6-megapixel camera, the full-resolution images from your camera are about 3000 x 2000 pixels. The file size for a 6-megapixel image is about 5.7MB.

On the screen, the resolution of many digital camera images is 72 ppi (pixels per inch). Using the 6-megapixel image as an example, the resolution at 72 ppi produces an image that measures a little more than 41 x 27 inches. Regardless of whether your camera or cellphone takes pictures at 3, 5, or 8 megapixels or more, many images are captured at 72 ppi, but the dimensions vary according to the total number of pixels captured. With other cameras, you may find image resolutions like 230 ppi or some other variation. The higher resolutions typically produce images of smaller physical sizes.

Looking at raster versus vector images

Elements supports working with vector data in addition to raster data. Whereas raster data carries with it a fixed resolution, vector objects are not resolution-dependent. What does this mean, and more importantly, what advantages come from working with vector data?

A vector object might be a line of text or a shape that you add to a photo from an assortment of vector shapes. When you size vector text and shapes in Elements, the resizing has no effect on resolution. In other words, you can make a line of text or a shape as large as you want, and when the photo is printed, the text and shapes print clearly without distortion. Text and shapes remain resolution-independent until you flatten the layers. Then the shapes are converted to pixels and appear as raster images.

Vector images are created with mathematical algorithms instead of pixels, and thus are usually illustrations, line drawings, and basic shapes or letters. (You can't take or save a photo of your family as a vector image.)

Using the Image Size Command

When an image is too large, you need to reduce its resolution, physical size, or both. Or you may need a higher resolution to output an image at a larger size. This method of sizing — changing the size as well as the number of pixels — is called *resampling* an image.

You can reduce resolution by sampling fewer pixels (*downsampling*) or raise resolution by adding more pixels to the sample (*upsampling*).

Use caution when you resample images; when you resample, you're either tossing away pixels or manufacturing new pixels — and *neither activity particularly benefits image quality.* We discuss the sampling details in the section "Upsampling images," later in this chapter.

Downsampling images

You can change an image's size and resolution in a couple different ways. One method involves cropping images. You can use the Crop tool with or without resampling images. (For more information on using the Crop tool, see the section "Using the Crop tool," later in this chapter.) Another method involves the Image Size dialog box, which you use in many of your editing sessions in Elements.

When you use the Image Size dialog box to make an image smaller, you are *downsampling* the image. For example, you might downsample a high-resolution camera image from 14 inches wide and 240 ppi to 7 inches wide and 300 ppi before you send the image to a printing service. In Figure 2-2, you can see an image that was downsampled in Elements from more than 14 inches horizontal.

If you try to make an image larger, you are upsampling an image. Too much upsampling results in images of very poor quality, as shown in Figure 2-3.

Figure 2-2: Downsampling images usually produces satisfactory results.

Book III
Chapter 2

Specifying
Resolution and
Changing Image
Sizing

Follow these steps to downsample an image in Elements:

1. **Open a photo in the Photo Editor.**

   For these steps, you can use any photo you have handy.

2. **Choose Image➪Resize➪ Image Size.**

   Alternatively, you press Ctrl+Alt+I (⌘+Option+I on a Mac). The Image Size dialog box opens, as shown in Figure 2-4.

Figure 2-3: Upsampling images produces very poor results.

The Pixel Dimensions area in the Image Size dialog box shows the file size (such as 2MB [megabytes]). This number is the amount of space the image takes up on your hard drive. The width and height values are fixed unless you select the Resample Image check box at the bottom of the dialog box.

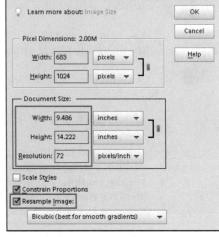

Figure 2-4: Choose Image⇨Resize⇨Image Size to open the Image Size dialog box.

3. **In the Document Size area, redefine the dimensions and resolution.**

   You have the following options:

   - *Width:* Type a value in the text box to resize the image's width; then, to implement the change, press Tab to move out of the field. From the drop-down list to the right of the text box, you can select a unit of measure: percent, inches, centimeters, millimeters, points, picas, or columns.

   - *Height:* The Height options are the same as the Width options, except there is no column setting. If you keep the sizing proportional — by selecting the Constrain Proportions check box — you typically edit either the Width or Height text box, but not both. When you alter either width or height, the resolution changes inversely.

   - *Resolution:* Edit the text box to change resolution and press the Tab key to change the value. When you edit resolution, the Width and Height values are changed inversely (if the Constrain Proportions check box is selected).

4. **If you're okay with resampling your image to get the desired size, select the Resample Image check box.**

   With this check box selected, you can change dimensions and pixels at the same time, which results in reducing or increasing the number of pixels. When the check box is deselected, the values for dimensions are linked. Changing one value automatically changes the other values.

   Before you resample your image, however, be sure to check out the following section.

5. **If you select the Resample Image check box, choose a resampling method as well as other resampling options.**

   In the drop-down menu, you find resampling-method choices. See Table 2-1 for details. The two check boxes above the Resample Image check box become active when you select the Resample Image check box. Here's what they do:

- *Scale Styles:* Elements has a Styles panel from which you can apply a variety of style effects to images. When you apply a style, such as a frame border, the border appears at a defined width. When you select the Scale Styles box and then resize the image, the Styles effect is also resized. Leaving the check box deselected keeps the style at the same size when the image is resized.

- *Constrain Proportions:* By default, this check box is selected; keep it that way unless you want to distort an image intentionally.

6. **When you're done selecting your options, click OK to resize your image.**

Table 2-1	Resampling Methods	
Method	*What It Does*	*Best Uses*
Nearest Neighbor	This method is the fastest, and the results produce a smaller file size.	This method is best used when you have large areas of the same color.
Bilinear	This method produces a medium-quality image.	You might use this option with grayscale images and line art.
Bicubic	This method is the default and provides a good-quality image.	Unless you find better results by using any of the other methods, leave the default at Bicubic.
Bicubic Smoother	This method improves on the Bicubic method, but you notice a little softening of the edges.	If sharpness isn't critical and you find that Bicubic isn't quite doing the job, try this method. This method tends to work best if you have to upsample an image.
Bicubic Sharper	This method produces good-quality images and sharpens the results.	Downsample high-resolution images that need to be output to screen resolutions and web pages.

**Book III
Chapter 2**

Specifying Resolution and Changing Image Sizing

Upsampling images

As a general rule, reducing resolution is okay, but increasing resolution isn't. If you need a higher-resolution image and you can go back to the original source (such as rescanning the image or reshooting a picture), try (if you can) to create a new file that has the resolution you want instead of resampling in Elements. Upsampling can severely degrade an image.

If you start with an image that was originally sampled for a web page and you want to print a large poster, you can forget about using Elements or any other image editor. Upsampling low-resolution images often turns them to mush, as shown in Figure 2-3.

You may wonder whether upsampling is useful for any purpose. In some cases, yes, you can upsample with satisfactory results. You can experience better results with higher resolutions of 300 ppi and more if the upsampling size isn't extraordinary. If all else fails, try applying a filter to a grainy, upsampled image to mask the problem. (Book VII, Chapter 1, has the details on filters.)

Some third-party tools do much better with upsampling images than the built-in sampling tools that Elements provides. For starters, take a look at OnOne Software's Perfect Resize 7.5 (formerly Genuine Fractals) at www. ononesoftware.com. When it's absolutely necessary to upsample images, you'll generally find favorable results using this product.

Using the Scale Command

When you open a photo in Elements, the photo rests on an underlying layer called the *canvas*. The canvas and the photo are at a 1:1 ratio. In essence, the canvas is the physical size of your image. You can keep the canvas size fixed while upsizing or downsizing the photo image. To do so requires using the Transformation tools.

Choose Image⇨Transform⇨Free Transform or press Ctrl+T (⌘+T on a Mac), and you see a number of handles on the sides of the transformation rectangle. To scale a photo up or down, grab one of the four corner handles by clicking one and holding down the mouse button; then you can move the handle in or out to size the image down or up, respectively.

If you open a context menu after you've selected Free Transform, you find several transformation commands, as shown in Figure 2-5. Choose the Scale command to size an image up or down. As you drag the corner handles, the scaling is made while constraining proportions.

The end result of scaling images is the same as using the Image Size dialog box to upsample and downsample images. As you scale an image up, the image loses resolution. As you scale an image down, it gains resolution. Therefore, when scaling images up, be certain that the image resolution is sufficient to support the new size.

In Figure 2-6, we scaled the image down by dragging a handle on the Transform rectangle and slightly rotated the image. The Transformation rectangle is shown before we commit the edit.

For more on transformations, see Book IV, Chapter 2.

Figure 2-5: Press Ctrl+T (⌘+T) and open a context menu to choose from different transformation commands.

Figure 2-6: The Transformation rectangle before committing the edit.

Book III
Chapter 2

Specifying
Resolution and
Changing Image
Sizing

Choosing a Resolution for Print or Screen

The importance of resolution in your Elements work is paramount when printing files. Good ol' 72-ppi images can be forgiving, and you can get many of your large files scrunched down to 72 ppi for websites and slide shows. Printing images is another matter. Among the many different printing output devices, resolution requirements vary.

For your own desktop printer, plan to print a variety of test images at different resolutions and on different papers. You can quickly determine the best file attributes by running tests. When you send files to service centers, ask the technicians what file attributes work best with their equipment.

For a starting point, look over the recommended resolutions for various output devices listed in Table 2-2.

Table 2-2	Resolutions and Printing	
Output Device	*Optimum Resolution*	*Acceptable Resolution*
Desktop color inkjet and laser printers	300 ppi	180 ppi
Large-format inkjet printers	150 ppi	120 ppi
Professional photo lab printers	300 ppi	200 ppi
Desktop laser printers (black-and-white)	170 ppi	100 ppi
Magazine quality — offset press	300 ppi	225 ppi
Screen images (web, slide shows, video)	72 ppi	72 ppi

For more information on printing photos, see Book IX, Chapter 2.

Changing the Canvas Size

When you scale images, you maintain the same canvas size. You might (for example) have a canvas size set up for printing a photo — say, 8 x 10 inches — and want to make an image a bit larger on the canvas. You might also add other images to create a photo collage and need to scale those added images up or down, again keeping the same canvas size.

For that matter, you might want to keep the image size the same but increase the canvas size to accommodate an area to include type, some content from the Content panel, or additional images.

You can also crop the canvas size with the Crop tool. The Crop tool is a more visual method for sizing the canvas.

Using the Canvas Size dialog box

To increase the canvas size, choose Image⇨Resize⇨Canvas Size. The Canvas Size dialog box opens, as shown in Figure 2-7. In this dialog box, you have several options to control, such as

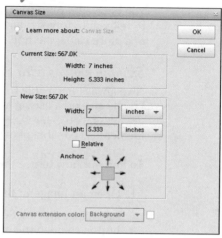

Figure 2-7: The Canvas Size dialog box.

- ✔ **Current Size:** The display for the Current Size shows you what your original canvas size is when you open the dialog box.

- ✔ **Width:** Type the new width in the text box.

- ✔ **Height:** Type the new height in the text box.

- ✔ **Relative:** By default, the new size is absolute. Select this check box if you want the new size to be relative to the dimensions.

- ✔ **Anchor:** By default, the canvas is increased from the center out. For example, if you have a 3-x-3-inch canvas area and you increase the size to 5 x 5 inches, 1 inch of canvas is added to all four sides of the photo. By clicking an arrow in the Anchor area, you can size the canvas relative to the photo from the upper-left corner, top, upper-right corner, left side, right side, lower-left corner, bottom, or lower-right corner.

- ✔ **Canvas Extension Color:** From the drop-down list, you can choose the current background, foreground, or some preset values for the color of the new canvas area. If you want a custom color, click the color swatch to the right of the drop-down list and make a new color selection from the pop-up color wheel.

In Figure 2-8, we added some canvas area to make the total size of the photo 8 x 10 inches. The new canvas color specified in the Tools panel is the same color as the background color.

Figure 2-8: A photo after a new canvas area was added from the center out.

Book III
Chapter 2

Specifying
Resolution and
Changing Image
Sizing

Using the Crop tool

You have a lot of toggles available in the Canvas Size dialog box. We're going to tell you to forget them all! It's old school, and you can now take advantage of a more visual method for sizing the canvas.

Sizing a canvas with the Crop tool

"I've always been able to trim a canvas with the Crop tool," you say, "But can I really size up a canvas with the Crop tool?" Yes, you can! In Photoshop Elements, you can resize the canvas with the Crop tool. The Crop tool in Elements is capable of expanding the canvas size as well as trimming it.

To find out how to use the Crop tool to size up a canvas, follow these steps:

1. **Open an image in the Photo Editor.**

   Any image will do. Select an image in the Organizer and click the Editor button to open the image in the Photo Editor.

2. **Select the Crop tool.**

   Press the C key to access the tool or click the tool in the Tools panel.

3. **Drag open a rectangle on the image and release the mouse button.**

   You can drag out a small rectangle or one to fill the entire size of the image. The size of the rectangle doesn't matter. Just be certain that you see a rectangle with eight handles (squares) along the dashed lines.

4. **Drag the rectangle handles out beyond the image size similar to what you see in Figure 2-9.**

5. **Press the Enter/Return key or click the green check mark to commit the new canvas size.**

   The canvas size is sized up to the rectangle boundaries.

What you see in Figure 2-9 is an overlay called the *Rule of Thirds,* where the grid appears with equal divisions in nine quadrants. Theoretically, the centermost rectangle is the area where a viewer of your photo makes eye contact; it should appear as the focal point for your photo.

You can also use numerical values as you do in the Canvas Size dialog box. Type values for the Width and Height fields and reshape the rectangle to include the area outside the image or crop the image down in size while retaining a fixed width and height.

Figure 2-9: Drag the crop rectangle outside the image area.

Book III
Chapter 2

Specifying
Resolution and
Changing Image
Sizing

Cropping a photo

In earlier versions of Elements, Adobe offered suggestions such as the Rule of Thirds and the Golden Ratio. These suggustrions appeared in the form of grids and overlays. In Elements 13, you find some more visual hints provided in the Tool Options panel when you select the Crop tool, as shown in Figure 2-10.

Move the mouse cursor over one of the suggestions and the result appears in the image menu. Click a suggestion and the crop is performed for the respective choice (after you click the Commit button or press Return/Enter).

Figure 2-10: Crop suggestions appear in the Tool Options panel when you select the Crop tool.

Chapter 3: Choosing Color Modes and File Formats

*W*hether you plan to use your images for print or screen (or both), you have to consider color mode and file format. The most common color mode for photos taken with a digital camera is RGB; you use it to prepare color files for printing on your desktop color printer or for sending to photo-service centers.

You can also use color modes other than RGB (red, green, blue) — bitmap or grayscale, for example. If you start with an RGB color image and want to convert to a different color mode, you have menu options for doing precisely that. Photoshop Elements uses an *algorithm* (a mathematical formula) to convert pixels from one mode to another. In some cases, the conversion that's made via a menu command produces good results; in other cases, you can use some different options for converting modes.

In this chapter, we introduce the modes that are available in Elements and explain how to convert from RGB to the mode of your choice: bitmap, grayscale, or indexed color.

File formats are also somewhat dependent on which color mode you choose for your files, so we tossed in a discussion about saving files in this chapter.

Selecting a Color Mode

When you open an image from a digital camera or scan an image, the image file contains a color mode. Typically, digital camera images are in RGB color mode. When you scan documents and photos on a scanner, you can choose from among line art (bitmap mode), grayscale, or RGB color.

Another mode you may have heard of is CMYK. Although CMYK mode isn't available in Photoshop Elements, you should be aware of it and its uses. CMYK, commonly referred to as *process color,* contains percentages of cyan, magenta, yellow, and black colors. This mode is used for commercial printing and also on many desktop printers. If you design a magazine cover in Elements and send the file to a print shop, the file is ultimately converted to CMYK. Also note that most desktop printers use different ink sets within the CMYK color space.

If you start in the Photo Editor and create a new blank document, you have a choice for defining the color mode of the new document. Choose File⇨New⇨Blank File, and the New dialog box opens, as shown in Figure 3-1. (Alternatively you can create a new blank file by clicking the Open drop-down menu at the upper left of the Photo Editor and choose New Blank File.) At the bottom of the dialog box, you make a choice for the color mode from the Color Mode drop-down list.

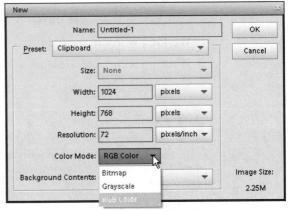

Figure 3-1: Define the color mode for a new blank document with the New dialog box.

When choosing a color mode, the options you have for importing images from digital camera shots, scanning images, and creating new documents are limited to the modes discussed thus far. To explore other modes or change a mode, you have to work with menu commands for converting color.

Converting Color Modes and Profiles

The most common scenario for photographers and users of Photoshop Elements is to start out with an RGB color image. This color mode is the center of your mode universe — and from here, you can convert from RGB to other color modes.

Converting to Bitmap mode

Bitmap mode is most commonly used in printing line art, such as black-and-white logos, illustrations, or black-and-white effects that you create from your RGB images. Also, you can scan your analog signature as a bitmap image and import it into other programs, such as Microsoft Office programs. If you're especially creative, you can combine bitmap images with RGB color to produce many interesting effects.

The Elements Bitmap mode isn't the same as the Windows BMP file format. In Elements, Bitmap mode is a color mode with only two color values — black and white. A Windows BMP file can be an image in RGB, Grayscale, or Bitmap color mode.

When you're working with color modes, keep in mind that when you combine images into single documents (as we explain throughout Book VI), you have to convert bitmap files to grayscale or color if you want to merge those images with an RGB image. If you convert to grayscale, Elements takes care of converting grayscale to RGB mode.

For an example of what happens when you combine grayscale and color images, look over Figure 3-2: The original RGB image was converted to a bitmap and then saved as a different file. The bitmap was converted to grayscale and dropped on top of the RGB image. Adjusting the opacity produced a grainy effect with desaturated color. (For more information on how to merge files, create layers, and blend the opacity of layers, see Book VI, Chapters 1 through 3.)

You can acquire Bitmap mode images directly in Elements when you scan images that are originally black and white — such as line art, logos, your signature, or a copy of a fax — in Bitmap mode. Additionally, you can convert your RGB color images to Bitmap mode.

Figure 3-2: Combining the same image from a bitmap file and an RGB file.

Converting RGB color to bitmap is a two-step process. You first convert to grayscale and then convert from grayscale to bitmap. If you use the Bitmap menu command while in RGB color, Elements prompts you to convert to grayscale first.

To convert RGB mode to Bitmap mode, do the following:

1. **Open an image that you want to convert to Bitmap mode in the Photo Editor, using either Expert or Quick mode.**

2. **Choose Image⊏>Mode⊏>Bitmap.**

   If you start in RGB mode, Elements prompts you to convert to Grayscale mode.

Book III
Chapter 3

Choosing Color
Modes and File
Formats

3. **Click OK.**

The Bitmap dialog box opens, providing options for selecting the output resolution and a conversion method.

4. **Select a resolution.**

By default, the Bitmap dialog box (see Figure 3-3) displays the current resolution. You can edit the text box and type a new resolution value or accept the default.

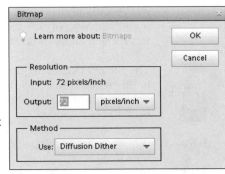

Figure 3-3: Type a resolution for your output; select a conversion method from the Use drop-down menu.

5. **Under the Method heading, select one of the following settings from the Use drop-down menu:**

- *50% Threshold:* This choice results in half the pixels turning white and the other half turning black. You see a piece of artwork that appears solid black and white.

- *Pattern Dither:* Dithering results in an illusion of gray pixels according to the placement of the blacks and whites. When using a pattern dither, the image is dithered according to a defined pattern.

- *Diffusion Dither:* This option results in the best view of a black-and-white photo where the dithering appears with grays as well as blacks and whites.

For more about dithering color, see the section "Converting to Indexed Color mode," later in this chapter. Look at Figure 3-4 to see a comparison of the different methods used in converting RGB images to bitmaps.

6. **Click OK to convert your image to Bitmap mode.**

Converting to Grayscale mode

Grayscale images have black and white pixels and any one of 256 levels of gray. By converting an RGB image to grayscale, you can make it look like a black-and-white photo.

We talk about 256 gray levels in many chapters in this book. An RGB color image is divided into three separate channels (one for red, one for green, and one for blue). Each of these channels contains 256 levels of grays. Adjusting the levels of grays affects the brightness and color in your images. (Look over Book VIII, Chapter 2 to understand more about the gray levels and adjusting them in Photoshop Elements.)

RGB Image

50% Threshold

Pattern Dither

Diffusion Dither

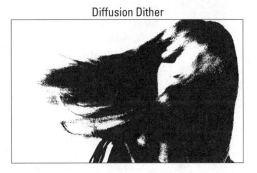

Figure 3-4: RGB image converted to bitmap by using 50% Threshold, Pattern Dither, and Diffusion Dither.

You can convert an image to grayscale in one of three ways, but we're here to tell you that one of these methods isn't as good as the others. In other words, avoid converting to grayscale by choosing Image⇨Mode⇨Grayscale. When Elements performs this conversion, it removes all the color from the pixels, so you lose some precious data during the conversion. You can't regain this color after conversion. If you use the Image⇨Mode⇨Grayscale command sequence to convert an image to grayscale and then save the file and delete the original from your hard drive or memory card, the color image is lost forever. You can save a secondary file, but this method is confusing and requires more space on your hard drive.

As an alternative to using the menu command for converting images to grayscale, follow these steps:

1. **Open an RGB image in Elements.**

2. **Duplicate a layer.**

    The default Project Bin contains the Layers panel. In this panel, you find a pop-up menu when you click the box in the upper-right corner. From the menu commands, choose Duplicate Layer. (For more information on working with layers, see Book VI, Chapter 1.) After duplicating the layer, you see a thumbnail of another layer in the Layers panel.

3. **Choose Enhance⇨Adjust Color⇨Adjust Hue/Saturation (alternatively, press Ctrl+U or ⌘+U on the Mac) to open the Hue/Saturation dialog box, shown in Figure 3-5.**

4. **Drag the Saturation slider to the far left to desaturate the image and click OK.**

   All color disappears, but the brightness values of all the pixels remain unaffected. (For more information on using the Hue/Saturation dialog box and the other Adjust Color commands, see Book VIII, Chapter 2.)

5. **Turn off the color layer by clicking the Eye icon.**

   In the Layers panel, you see two layers, as shown in Figure 3-6. You don't need to turn off the color layer to print the file in grayscale, but turning it off can help you remember which color layer you used the last time you printed or exported the file.

When you follow the preceding steps, your file will contain both RGB and grayscale versions of your image. If you want to print the color layer, you can turn off the grayscale layer. If you need to exchange files with graphic designers, you can send the layered file, and then the design professional can use both the color image and the grayscale image.

Another choice you have for converting color to black-and-white photos is to use the Convert to Black and White dialog box. Here's how it works:

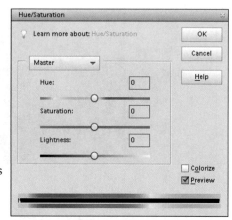

Figure 3-5: In the Hue/Saturation dialog box, move the Saturation slider to the far left to eliminate color.

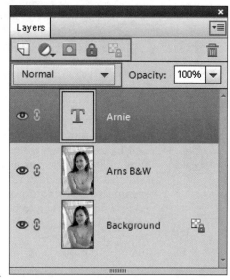

Figure 3-6: The Layers panel shows the grayscale and color layers. Click the Eye icon to turn layers on or off.

1. **Choose Enhance⇨Convert to Black and White in either Expert or Quick mode.**

   The Convert to Black and White dialog box appears, as shown in Figure 3-7. This dialog box contains many controls for adjusting brightness and contrast in images that you convert to grayscale.

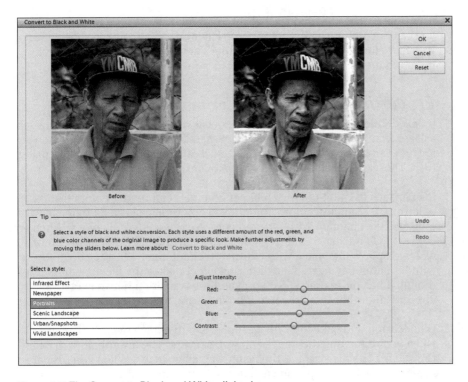

Figure 3-7: The Convert to Black and White dialog box.

2. **Select from preset options in the Select a Style list.**

3. **(Optional) To modify the settings that the preset applies, click and drag any of the Adjust Intensity sliders.**

   As you move the sliders in the Adjust Intensity area, you can see a dynamic preview displayed in the After thumbnail area.

4. **(Optional) If you want to keep your original RGB image in the same file as the grayscale version, duplicate the background by right-clicking a layer in the Layers panel and choosing Duplicate Layer from the context menu. Then click the background and choose Enhance⇨Convert to Black and White.**

   The conversion is applied only to the background, leaving the copied layer in the original color mode.

   Convert a photo by using the Convert to Black and White command, desaturate a photo by using the Hue/Saturation adjustment, or choose Enhance⇨Adjust Color⇨Remove Color. The photo appears as a black-and-white photo after using one of these techniques, but the color mode remains in RGB. From there you can tint a photo with a color Photo Filter or add a sepia-tone effect. See our Web Extra for more on creating sepia tones at www.dummies.com/extras/photoshopelementsaio.

Converting to Indexed Color mode

Indexed Color is a mode that you use occasionally with web graphics, such as saving in GIF format or PNG-8 (discussed later in this chapter). When saving indexed-color images, you can often create smaller file sizes than using RGB. These are ideal for using in website designs.

RGB images in 24-bit color (8 bits per channel) can render colors from a palette of 16.7 million colors. An indexed color image is an 8-bit image with only a single channel. With indexed color, you get only 256 colors. When you convert RGB images to indexed color, you can choose to *dither* the color, which displays the image with a dithered effect much like the effect you see with bitmapped images. This dithering effect makes the file appear as though it has more than 256 colors, and the transition between colors appears smoother than it would if no dithering were applied.

On occasion, indexed-color images have an advantage over RGB images when you're hosting the images on web servers: The fewer colors in a file, the smaller the file size and the faster the image loads. When you prepare images for web hosting, you can choose to use indexed color or RGB color. Whether you choose one over the other really depends on the quality of the image as it appears on your monitor. If you have some photos that you want to show on web pages, you should use RGB images and save them in a format appropriate for web hosting, as we explain in the section "Saving files for the web," later in this chapter.

If you have files composed of artwork, such as logos, illustrations, and drawings, you may find that the appearance of images using indexed colors is no different from the same images as RGB. If that's the case, you can keep the indexed-color image and use it for your web pages.

To convert RGB images to indexed color, choose Image➪Mode➪Indexed Color; the Indexed Color dialog box opens. Various options are available to you; fortunately, you can preview the results while you make choices. Get in and poke around. You can see the options applied in the image window.

Converting color profiles

Because we're talking about color conversions in this chapter, we also cover a little bit about color profiles (and converting color profiles) here. But for a more thorough discussion of color profiles, jump to Chapter 5 of this minibook.

Some image files contain embedded color profiles; an example is the one shown later in this chapter, in Figure 3-8, where the embedded profile is shown in the Save As dialog box.

Photoshop Elements can embed either one of two different color profiles in a photo: Adobe RGB and sRGB. The Adobe RGB profile uses a slightly larger color gamut (more available colors) than sRGB. Some printing devices work best when converting sRGB color to the printer's color. Other printers offer better support for Adobe RGB. (This is a nutshell view of color profiling for printing. For more detailed information, see Book IX, Chapter 2.)

If you want to print the file to a printer, you might want to convert the color profile. To do so, choose Image⇨Convert Color Profile and then make a choice from the submenu. Your options are

- ✔ **Remove Profile:** Choosing this option removes the color profile from the image.

- ✔ **Convert to sRGB Profile:** This choice applies the sRGB profile to the image.

- ✔ **Convert to Adobe RGB:** This option applies the Adobe RGB color profile to the image.

Choosing one of these options either removes a color profile or converts to the selected color profile. When you save your file, you have the option to embed the profile in the image.

Using the Proper File Format

As you edit your image files, be sure that you save frequently to update the work performed in your editing sessions. Continue saving as your work progresses to avoid data loss.

You can save Photoshop Elements files in a variety of formats. Some format types support only certain color modes, so you may need to convert a color mode before you can save in those formats. Put another way, a relationship exists between the color modes present in files and saving those files in formats that support those color modes. Additionally, an image's bit depth may also limit the kinds of file formats you can use when saving files. (See Chapter 4 in this minibook for more information about bit depth.)

Before you go too far in Elements, become familiar with file formats and the conversions necessary to save in one format or another. If you don't convert an image's modes or change its bit depth, you can save an edited file in the same format in which you opened it. Often, however, if you open an image and prepare it for some form of output, you have to give more thought to the kind of file format you should use when saving the file.

Book III
Chapter 3

Choosing Color
Modes and File
Formats

Using the Save/Save As dialog box

In almost any program, the Save (or Save As) dialog box is a familiar place where you make some choices about the file to be saved. With Save As, you can save a duplicate copy of your image or save a modified copy and retain the original file.

To use the Save (or Save As) dialog box, choose File⇨Save for files to be saved the first time, or choose File⇨Save As for any file, and a dialog box opens. In Figure 3-8, you can see the save options you have available in Windows (left) and on the Macintosh (right).

Windows   Macintosh

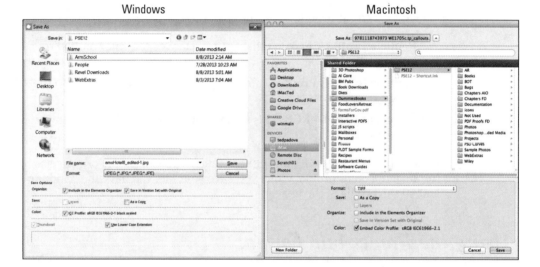

Figure 3-8: The Save As dialog box (Windows left, Mac right).

The standard navigational tools that you find in any Save dialog box appear in the Elements Save/Save As dialog box. Here are some standard options you find in the Elements Save/Save As dialog box:

- **File Name (Save As on the Mac):** This item is common to all Save dialog boxes. Type a name for your file in the text box.

- **Format:** From the drop-down menu, you select file formats. We explain the formats supported by Elements in the next section.

A few options make the Photoshop Elements Save/Save As dialog box different from other Save dialog boxes that you might be accustomed to using. The Save Options area in the Save As dialog box provides the following choices:

✓ **Include in the Elements Organizer:** If you want the file to be added to the Organizer, select this check box. (For more information about using the Organizer, see Book II, Chapter 1.)

✓ **Save in Version Set with Original:** You can edit images and save a version of your image, but only in Quick mode. When you save the file from Quick mode, this check box is active. Select the box to save a version of the original, which appears in the Organizer. The "Creating Versions" section, later in this chapter, introduces version sets.

✓ **Layers:** Select this check box if you have a file with layers and want to preserve the layers. This option is available only for PSD, TIFF, PDF, and PSE file formats.

✓ **As a Copy:** Select this check box to save a copy of the file without overwriting the original.

✓ **Color:** Select the check box for ICC (International Color Consortium) Profile. Depending on which profile you're using, the option appears for sRGB or Adobe RGB (1998). When the check box is selected, the profile is embedded in the image. (See the section "Converting Color Modes and Profiles," earlier in this chapter.)

✓ **Thumbnail (Windows):** If you save a file with a thumbnail, you can see a miniature representation of your image when viewing it in folders or on the desktop. If you select Ask When Saving in the Saving Files preferences, the check box can be enabled or disabled. If you select an option for Always Save or Never Save in the Preferences dialog box, this box is enabled or disabled (and grayed out). You have to return to the Preferences dialog box if you want to change the option.

✓ **Use Lower Case Extension (Windows):** File extensions give you a clue about the file format in which a file was saved. Elements automatically adds the extension to the filename for you. Your choices are to use uppercase or lowercase letters for the extension name. Select the check box for Use Lower Case Extension for lowercase; deselect the check box if you want to use uppercase characters in the filename. By default, you should always use lowercase extensions. Lowercase is required for some uses such as web-hosting images.

Understanding file formats

When you save files from Elements, you pick a file format in the Format drop-down menu found in both the Save and Save As dialog boxes.

When you choose from the different format options, keep the following information in mind:

✓ **File formats are especially important when you exchange files with other users.** Each format has a purpose, and other programs can accept or reject files depending on the format you choose.

✔ **Whether you can select one format or another for saving a file depends on the color mode and the bit depth, and whether layers are present.** If a format isn't present in the Format drop-down list when you attempt to save a file, return to one of the edit modes and perform an edit, such as changing a color mode or flattening layers, to save the file in your chosen format.

Figure 3-9 shows a number of different file formats you can use. However, in practicality, you're likely to use only a few on a routine basis. We talk about the most essential formats in this chapter. If you want to find out more about those formats we don't discuss here, consult the Elements Help files.

TIFF (*.TIF;*.TIFF)

| Photoshop (*.PSD;*.PDD) |
| BMP (*.BMP;*.RLE;*.DIB) |
| CompuServe GIF (*.GIF) |
| Photo Project Format (*.PSE) |
| JPEG (*.JPG;*.JPEG;*.JPE) |
| Photoshop PDF (*.PDF;*.PDP) |
| Pixar (*.PXR) |
| PNG (*.PNG) |
| TIFF (*.TIF;*.TIFF) |

Figure 3-9: Open the Format drop-down menu in either the Save or Save As dialog box to make the formats supported by Elements appear.

We could go into a lengthy explanation of each file format, but it's more important to know the format names and those that you're likely to use the most: JPEG and PNG are used for web graphics. PSD (native Photoshop document) and TIFF are used for editing and as final formats for higher-quality printing. PSE is a format used for Elements projects. Photoshop PDF is used for image files with vector graphics and text.

Saving files for the web

You save files for web hosting in a special dialog box — the Save for Web dialog box. It offers other options than the dialog boxes you use to save files for other output. You can use the Save for Web dialog box to optimize files, but before you open it — in fact, before you even save a file, set the physical size and resolution of the image. Choose Image⇨Resize⇨Image Size. In the dialog box that appears, you can adjust the dimensions and resolution. For web graphics, choose a resolution such as 72 ppi and downsample the image if necessary. (For more about downsampling, see Book III, Chapter 2.)

After your image is resized, choose File⇨Save for Web or press Ctrl+Alt+Shift+S (⌘+Option+Shift+S on the Mac) to open the Save for Web dialog box, as shown in Figure 3-10. As you can see, you have a lot of things to control in this dialog box. The settings are

A. Hand tool: When you are zoomed in on the Preview, use the Hand tool to move the image around the Preview area.

B. Zoom tool: Click the Zoom tool on one preview image to zoom in on both previews. Press the Alt (Option) key to zoom out.

C. Eyedropper tool: Sample a color in the image shown in the Preview area.

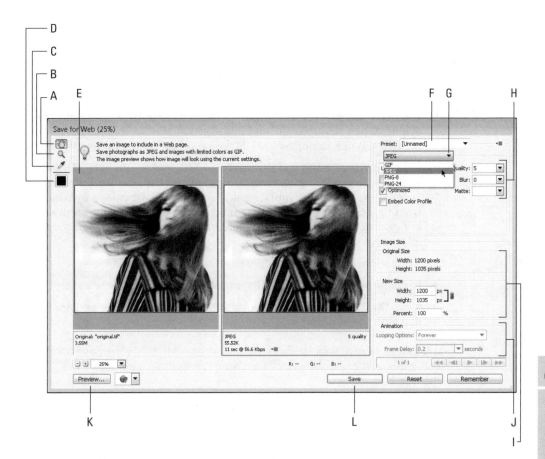

Figure 3-10: The Save for Web dialog box.

D. Eyedropper Color Picker color: This choice contains the current sampled color. Whatever color you sample can be used for the matte color, which is the transparent areas in your image, if any exist.

E. Previews: The first image displays the original image. The second preview displays a preview for how the file will look when saved. In Figure 3-10, JPEG is selected for the format option with a Quality of 5. The second preview displays the image with the JPEG settings. Notice that in the lower-left corner of the right-side preview area you see an estimate of how long the image will take to download with a certain modem speed. An image that can download in 11 seconds on a 56-Kbps modem, as shown in Figure 3-10, will download pretty quickly on most modern modems, which are usually high-speed broadband modems. You can use this area of the preview to make sure that you have the right balance between image quality and speedy downloads on the web.

F. Preset: A number of presets are available from the drop-down menu that will set up preconfigured settings for the options in this dialog box.

G. Image format: From the drop-down menu, choose a file format and adjust settings relative to the format. As you make choices, you can preview the results in the right-side preview area.

H. Quality settings: When saving your file as a JPEG, the Quality menu is visible. When saving in GIF and PNG-8, you have choices for the number of colors. When saving as PNG-24, you have an option for a matte color.

 I. Image attributes: You see the original width and height in the Original Size area. In the New Size area, you can adjust the size of your image by specifying a new width and height in pixels or a percentage by which you want to increase or decrease the image size relative to its current size. For example, entering 50 in the Percent box would size the image at 50 percent of its original size.

J. Animation: Settings here apply to animated GIF images.

K. Preview menu: This option displays the output preview.

L. Save: Click Save when you have all the adjustments made and are satisfied with the results.

This is a brief review of the options you have available in the Save for Web dialog box. For examples related to using the options, see Book IX, Chapter 3.

Creating Versions

Versions enable you to create and save several versions of an image in only one file. After you edit an image in the Photo Editor, saving the image with a *version set* permits you to save the original plus the edited version in the same file.

To create a version set, follow these steps:

1. **Open an original image file in the Photo Editor.**

2. **Edit the image to the point where you want to save a version.**

   You can choose from many different menu commands to edit the image. For example, change the color mode to Indexed Color by choosing Image⇨Mode⇨Indexed Color.

3. **Save a version by choosing File⇨Save As.**

4. **In the Save Options area of the Save As dialog box, select the Include in the Organizer and the Save in Version Set with Original check boxes.**

5. **Click Save.**

   The edit made in the Photo Editor is saved as another version in your version set.

After you create a version set, the Organizer offers menu commands that you can use to manage the version set. In the Organizer, choose Edit➪Version Set or open a context menu on a version set and then choose Version Set. The submenu, as shown in Figure 3-11, opens with the following options:

Figure 3-11: Opening a submenu for a version set.

- ✓ **Expand Items in Version Set:** Click a version set and choose this menu command to expand the items in the version set.

- ✓ **Collapse Items in Version Set:** When items are expanded, you can return them to a collapsed view by selecting this command.

- ✓ **Flatten Version Set:** Be careful here. If you choose this command, you lose all items in the version set except the top image.

- ✓ **Convert Version Set to Individual Items:** This command removes items from the version set and adds each version as a separate image to the Organizer window.

- ✓ **Revert to Original:** This command deletes the version set and returns you to the original, unedited version of the file.

- ✓ **Remove Item(s) from Version Set:** This option removes any selected item (or items) from a version set.

- ✓ **Set as Top Item:** When viewing an expanded version set, click one of the images and choose this item to move it to the top.

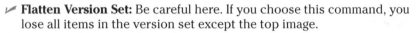

Batch-Processing Files

Elements provides you with some automated features for processing batches of photos. You can export multiple files from one format to another file format, and you can export files, changing file formats if you like. In addition, you have a limited number of other editing tasks you can automate.

The method you use and the features you want depend on whether you choose Export in the Organizer or Process Files in the Photo Editor. The following sections explain how each tool works.

**Book III
Chapter 3**

**Choosing Color
Modes and File
Formats**

Exporting files in the Organizer

You may need to export files from one format to another for a number of reasons. For example, when you open JPEG images and save back to a JPEG format, you're adding file compression to the saved images. JPEG is a *lossy* file format, which means that you lose image data when you save in this format. If you edit a JPEG image many times and save back to JPEG format each time, you continually lose more image data.

In some cases, you may want to convert multiple JPEG files to a file format that doesn't toss away data. You can use formats such as Photoshop PSD, PNG-24, or TIFF (without JPEG compression), and no data is thrown away when you save the file.

For a single instance when you want to convert a JPEG image to a PSD or TIFF image, you can open the file in Elements and choose File⇨Save As. From the Files of Type drop-down list (Windows) or Format pop-up menu (Mac), choose the desired format.

If you have multiple files and you want to convert the file type more efficiently, you can process a folder of files using a single command. To use a batch process to convert multiple files from one format to another (in Windows only), do the following:

1. **Open the Organizer.**

   You should have a collection of photos in the Organizer saved as JPEG or some other format that you want to convert to a newer format.

2. **Select files in the Organizer that you want to convert.**

   Click a file and press Shift and click the last file in a group, or you can click and press Ctrl and click all the photos you want to convert.

3. **Choose File⇨Export as New Files.**

   The Export New Files dialog box opens, as shown in Figure 3-12.

4. **Select a File Type option.**

   If you're converting JPEG files, you might want to choose PSD for the file format. The PSD format does not compress files. See the earlier section "Understanding file formats" for an explanation of each file type.

5. **Select a Size and Quality.**

   Select Original if you want to maintain the same image dimensions and resolution. If you want a different size for the saved images, make a choice from the Photo Size drop-down list.

6. **Click the Browse button in the Location area.**

   You can target a folder on your hard drive if you don't want to use the default folder shown in the Export New Files dialog box.

Figure 3-12: The Export New Files dialog box.

7. **Select an option under Filenames.**

   You can save the files to a new folder with the same names without over-writing the original files or save to the same folder adding a common base name. If you select the Common Base Name option, you can type a base name in the text box. Type something like Hawaii, for example, and the files are saved as `Hawaii001`, `Hawaii002`, and so on.

8. **Click the Add or Remove button to add more files or remove some from the list, respectively.**

   If you want to add more files, click the Add (+) icon.

   To remove a file, you can scroll the list of thumbnails, click the photo to remove from the group to be exported, and click the Remove (–) icon.

9. **Click the Export button.**

   Wait for the progress to complete before moving on.

   After the export progress finishes, the Exporting Files Complete dialog box opens.

10. **Click OK.**

    The file export task is completed.

Processing multiple files

The Export as New Files command in the Organizer provides a batch process for converting file formats with a rather limited set of options. In the Photo Editor, the Process Multiple Files command is more powerful than the Organizer's export tool and can make several enhancements to the new files saved. As shown in Figure 3-13, you have far more options available to you in the Process Multiple Files dialog box than you have in the Export New Files dialog box shown earlier in Figure 3-12.

To access the Process Multiple Files tool in the Photo Editor, choose File➪Process Multiple Files to open the dialog box shown in Figure 3-13.

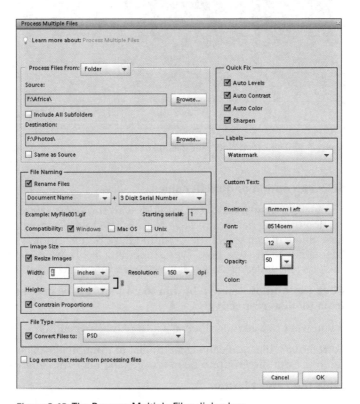

Figure 3-13: The Process Multiple Files dialog box.

In the left pane of the dialog box, you can make choices for file-naming conventions, locations for saved files, image size and resolution, and file formats. On the right, you see options for automating some basic edits to your images. Here's a brief introduction to each area of the dialog box:

✔ **Process Files From:** Use the options in this area to select the location of the images you want to process. You most likely want to corral all the images you want to process into a folder, select the location of the folder in the Source area, and select a different folder where Elements will save the processed files in the Destination area.

From the drop-down menu at the top, you can also choose to process files on import (from, say, a camera) or to process currently open files.

✔ **File Naming:** When you select the Rename Files check box, you can choose to rename the files using the current document name, numbers, dates, and letters. The example shown below the drop-down lists of options displays a preview of a filename that your selections will generate.

✔ **Image Size:** When you select the Resize Images check box, you can adjust the width, height, and resolution of a batch of images. Chapter 2 of this minibook explains how these options work.

✔ **File Type:** If you select the Convert Files To check box, the processing changes the file format of your images. The options here reflect all the options you see in the Save As dialog box. See the section "Understanding file formats," earlier in this chapter, for details about each format.

✔ **Quick Fix:** Here, you can select the check boxes for the image enhancements you want to make. For a complete description of these items, see Book VIII, Chapter 1.

✔ **Labels:** You can apply watermarks with custom text and choose the font attributes and placement for the text added to the new saved files. Leave the Custom Text box blank if you don't want to add text to your images. See Book V, Chapter 3 for details about adjusting the opacity of text.

After you click OK, your files are converted and saved to the target folder that you identified in the dialog box.

Chapter 4: Using and Managing Color

In This Chapter

✓ **Using foreground and background colors**

✓ **Selecting color from pickers, swatches, and images**

✓ **Working with Adobe Kuler**

✓ **Managing color**

✓ **Setting up the work environment**

✓ **Using color profiles**

*T*o produce great output, you have to understand color and how Elements treats color. If you want to carry around a laptop computer to show off your photos, you can basically adjust color for that particular computer. However, sharing photos with other users, printing your pictures, and hosting photos on websites require that you know something about the way color is displayed on other devices and in photo prints.

There's a lot to know about handling color, including setting up color workspaces, managing color, and working with color profiles. In this chapter, we talk about these issues and offer some key concepts for understanding and using color as it pertains to Photoshop Elements.

Dealing with Foreground and Background Colors

Foreground and background colors appear in the Tools panel as large color swatches. What you see in the two-color swatches represents the currently selected color for a foreground and the currently selected color for the background.

 By default, the foreground color is black, and the background color is white. You can change the foreground and background colors by making color selections from the Color Picker or the Swatches panel or by clicking the Color Picker tool and lifting a color from an image. (You find out how each method works in the next section.)

You can use colors that appear in the Foreground Color Swatch to fill type selections, shapes, and strokes, as well as when using tools to apply color. You can also use the current background color when using the Eraser tool to erase to the background color.

A couple of keyboard shortcuts are helpful when working with the foreground and background color swatches. You'll use the following keyboard shortcuts frequently, so you might as well commit them to memory:

✔ **D:** Press the D key to return to the default black for the foreground color and the default white for the background color.

✔ **X:** Press the X key, and the foreground and background colors are reversed. You might want to use this keyboard shortcut when painting black and white areas with one of the marking tools.

You can also click the two arrows adjacent to the upper right of the Foreground Color Swatch to reverse colors, or click the tiny icon adjacent to the lower right of the Foreground Color Swatch to return to default colors.

Defining Color

When you want to use a color for the foreground or background other than the default black and white colors, you make your color assignments using tools, panels, or dialog boxes.

All the colors available for a given color mode are accessible from the Swatches panel and the Photoshop Elements Color Picker. The range of colors shown in an image is also accessible through sampling color with the Color Picker tool.

Poking around the Color Picker

The Color Picker provides you with a color spectrum displaying all the colors available within a given color mode. If you're in RGB mode, you can choose from a color panel of more than 16.7 million colors. (See Chapter 3 of this minibook for an introduction to RGB mode.)

To open the Color Picker, click the Foreground Color Swatch in the Tools panel. The Color Picker pops up in a dialog box, as shown in Figure 4-1. The choices you have for selecting color and the options available to you in this dialog box are as follows:

A. Color panel: The large color swatch displays colors according to the position of the color spectrum slider.

B. New Color Choice: Clicking a color in the color panel selects a new color for the foreground color.

C. Warning: Not Web Safe Color: Not all colors display equally in both the Mac and Windows operating systems in 8-bit mode when you're viewing web pages. If a color is out of the Web Safe color palette, a cube icon appears.

The Web Safe palette was introduced more than 15 years ago to create a color palette that used common colors between com-

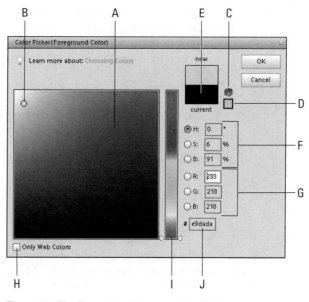

Figure 4-1: The Photoshop Elements Color Picker.

puter systems with 8-bit video cards. It's almost nonessential today because nearly all computer systems use 24-bit color. You can safely ignore this warning.

D. Select Closest Web Safe Color: Click this icon to select the closest Web Safe color value relative to the new color.

E. Current Foreground Color: When you open the Color Picker, the color that appears in the Foreground Color Swatch in the Tools panel is displayed here. The Current Foreground Color Swatch and the New Color Choice Swatch show you a *before/after* difference between the current color and any new color that you select in the color panel.

F. HSB values: This measure relates to Hue, Saturation, and Brightness. These values are the RGB equivalents for HSB.

G. RGB values: The numeric values for Red, Green, and Blue. As you choose other colors in the large color panel or by sliding the color spectrum slider, these values and the HSB values change to reflect the new color swatch at the top of the Color Picker.

H. Only Web Colors: Select this check box if you want to view only Web Safe colors.

I. Color Spectrum slider: Move the slider up or down to change the hue and display a new hue range in the large color panel.

J. Hexadecimal values: Colors are defined using specific hexadecimal values (or *hex* values for short). The hex value is displayed here for the new color. You may find hexadecimal numbers valuable when integrating

Elements photos and projects with programs such as Adobe Fireworks Adobe Dreamweaver and any application designed for web creations. These programs specify color in hex values, which are sometimes used to specify color in web page design.

To define a new foreground color, do the following:

1. **Click the Foreground Color Swatch in the Tools panel.**

   The Color Picker opens.

2. **Move the color spectrum slider to the hue range that you want to use for the new color.**

   For example, if you want to select a blue color, move the slider up to the range of blues.

3. **Click the cursor in the large color panel to select a color.**

   This sets saturation/lightness for a given hue. The new selected color appears as a rectangle in the New area above the current foreground color. (Refer to Figure 4-1.)

4. **Click OK.**

   The new foreground color selected in the Color Picker appears in the Foreground Color Swatch.

If you want to change the background color, click the Background Color Swatch in the Tools panel, and the same Color Picker opens. (Refer to Figure 4-1.) Any changes you make in the Color Picker are applied to the background color.

Grabbing color from the Color Swatches panel

Selecting color in the Color Picker is fine when you want to make a single color selection and use it once. However, if you want to create your own custom color panel and reuse colors, you want an easier method for choosing foreground and background colors — and a way to reuse the same colors easily.

The Color Swatches panel provides you with exactly what you need to create a personal color panel and easily access colors when painting on a canvas or filling selections in an image.

To open the Color Swatches panel, choose Window➪Color Swatches. The Color Swatches panel, shown in Figure 4-2, opens as a floating panel.

When you open the Color Swatches panel, you see a default panel of colors. Elements provides you with a number of different color panels that you can load into the Color Swatches panel. The choices also enable you to create your own custom color panel, as we describe later in the section "Creating a custom swatch set."

Using preset color panels

If you open the Default drop-down list in the Color Swatches panel, you find several preset color panels that you can load in the Color Swatches panel, as shown in Figure 4-3. Here's a quick introduction to each of your choices:

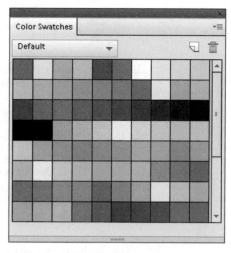

Figure 4-2: The Color Swatches panel.

✔ **Mac OS:** If you're using a Mac and looking at an image created on a Windows machine, choose this option to load a color panel that displays color accurately on the Mac. If you're using OS X Snow Leopard or higher, the colors are identical between platforms.

✔ **Photo Filter Colors:** This swatch set is a narrow range of colors consistent with those you apply using Photo Filters. (For a look at how Photo Filters are used, see Book VII, Chapter 1.)

✔ **Web Hues:** This swatch set displays hues that are Web Safe colors. Because most computers use 24-bit color, you needn't be concerned with Web Safe colors for web designs.

✔ **Web Safe Colors:** This set of swatches displays colors in a Web Safe panel. As with hues, you aren't likely to use Web Safe colors for any designs.

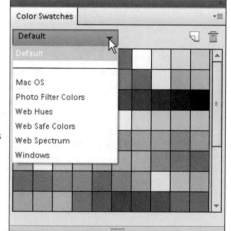

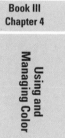

Figure 4-3: Preset choices in the Color Swatches panel.

✔ **Web Spectrum:** This swatch set displays the entire spectrum of Web Safe colors.

✔ **Windows:** This color set contains all the colors that display properly on a Windows machine.

Creating a custom swatch set

The Color Picker has all the colors you can use in a given color mode. You may want to add more colors to one of the color swatch sets when you select different colors in the Color Picker. You might also want to delete

Book III
Chapter 4

Using and
Managing Color

some colors from a swatch set, or you may want to save your new swatch set as a library that you can load in Elements so that you can use the new custom colors.

All this is possible in Elements, and here's how you go about creating your own custom panel of color swatches:

1. **Choose Window⇨Color Swatches to open the Color Swatches.**

2. **Delete colors from the Default panel.**

   Choose a color that you don't want to appear in your custom color panel. Press the Alt (Option) key, and the cursor changes to a Scissors icon. Click a color swatch with the Alt (Option) key depressed to delete the color. Continue deleting all the colors that you don't want in your custom color set.

3. **Select a new color to add to your custom color set and make that new color the foreground color.**

   Click the Foreground Color Swatch in the Tools panel. When the Color Picker opens, click a color that you want to add to your new set. Click OK, and the new color appears as the foreground color.

4. **Add the foreground color to the set.**

   Click the Panel menu icon in the Color Swatches panel to open a flyout menu. From the menu choices, choose New Swatch. The Color Swatch Name dialog box opens, as shown in Figure 4-4. The color is derived from the current foreground color to the left of the Name text box. Type a name for the color swatch and click OK. The new swatch is added to the Color Swatches panel.

   Figure 4-4: Type a name and click OK to add a color to your Color Swatches panel.

5. **Add additional colors.**

   Repeat Steps 3 and 4 to add new colors to the Swatches panel.

6. **Save the swatches.**

   Open the Panel menu and choose Save Swatches. A Save dialog box opens with the Color Swatches folder selected as the target folder. Be sure to not change the folder location. Type a name for your new swatches and click OK.

If you want to share color swatches with other Elements users or users of many Adobe programs such as Adobe InDesign, Illustrator, Photoshop, and Flash Pro, use the menu option Save Swatches for Exchange. For more on exchanging swatches, see the section "Using Adobe Kuler," later in this chapter.

You have saved a set of swatches without disturbing the original Default set. You can always return to the Default set by selecting Default. The original set remains intact.

Loading swatches

If you created a custom set of color swatches and then chose one of the presets from the Default drop-down list, the custom colors you created aren't visible in the Color Swatches panel. To see them there and use them, you have to load the swatches back into the Color Swatches panel.

To load swatches, open the Panel menu and choose Load Swatches. A Load dialog box appears with the target folder pointing to the Elements Color Swatches folder. Here you find all the custom color swatches you saved from the Color Swatches panel. Select a file in the Load dialog box and click Open. The custom color swatches set opens in the Color Swatches panel.

Replacing swatches

If you want to replace colors in an existing Color Swatches panel, you can do so by choosing Replace Swatches on the Panel menu. After the Load dialog box opens, select a file in the Custom Colors folder, and the colors in the file you selected replace the existing swatches.

Another item on the menu is Save Swatches for Exchange. If you want to exchange the palette with another user, choose this command. A Save dialog box opens that defaults to the Color Swatches folder location inside your Elements 13 folder. When you provide a name and click Save, the file is saved with an ASE extension. ASE is the Adobe Swatch Exchange format. You can save color swatches in this format, and you can load swatches saved in this format in a number of different Adobe applications, including Elements 12. If you send the ASE file to another Elements user, he or she can then load the palette into Elements by following the steps outlined in the section "Loading Adobe Kuler themes into Elements," later in this chapter.

Lifting and sampling color

If you have a photo that has colors you want to add to your Color Swatches, you can sample colors in an open image.

Click the Color Picker tool and click anywhere on a photo in the image window, and the Color Picker samples the color. We call this technique *lifting* color, although the color isn't removed from the photo. (It merely replaces the current foreground color.) If you want to replace the background color, press the Alt key (Option on the Mac) and click the Color Picker tool on a color you want to sample.

In the Options panel, you find a few settings for the Color Picker tool. Click the Color Picker tool in the Tools panel and click one of the three choices in the Options panel, as shown in Figure 4-5. The list items are

✔ **Point Sample:** This selection is the default. When you click the Color Picker tool to sample color, the pixel you click is the sampled color.

✔ **3 by 3 Average:** This menu choice averages 3 x 3 pixels, and the sampled color is the result of combining the color at the sample point with eight surrounding colors.

✔ **5 by 5 Average:** This menu choice averages 5 x 5 pixels, and the sampled color is the result of combining the color at the sample point with 24 surrounding colors.

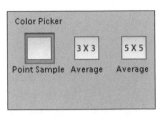

Figure 4-5: Click the Color Picker tool and click a choice in the Options panel.

You can sample colors in a photo and use the sampled colors to create a custom Color Swatch library.

Using Adobe Kuler

For people without skill in fine art, one of the difficult aspects of working with color is creating color palettes. What colors are complementary? What colors work well together? What color combinations are visually pleasing in designs?

Adobe Kuler (http://kuler.adobe.com) is a free community that can help you answer these questions. On the Kuler website, you can explore color themes that you might want to use in Elements projects and share color themes that you create with other users. In the following sections, you find out how to start using Adobe Kuler and explore the tools and sharing services it offers.

Getting started with Adobe Kuler

Before you log on to the Adobe Kuler website, you need to acquire an Adobe ID. You can visit the site without an Adobe ID, but to acquire themes that you can load in the Elements Photo Editor Color Swatches panel (which we describe earlier, in the section "Loading swatches"), you need to have an Adobe ID.

After you've acquired an Adobe ID, visit http://kuler.adobe.com. When the web page opens, provide your logon information (email address and password) and click Sign In. That's it. You're in and ready to acquire some color themes.

If you ever need help using Adobe Kuler, click the User Forums link at the bottom of any page to visit the Adobe Community page for Kuler. Here, the best place to find help with a topic is the Frequently Asked Questions section.

Exploring color themes

On the Kuler website, the color themes are the main attraction. To see themes that others have uploaded, click the Explore link, and you arrive at a screen like the one shown in Figure 4-6. You can limit the selection based on criteria such as the newest themes or the most used themes. Or use the search box to type a keyword that reflects the colors you want to explore, such as *skies, leaves, foliage, landscapes,* or *retro.*

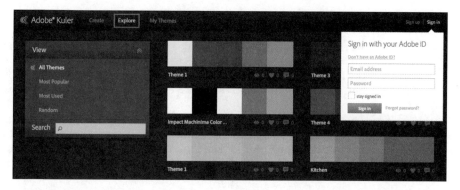

Figure 4-6: Log on to the Kuler website and click Explore, to see color themes that others have uploaded, which you can edit or download for your own use.

When you click a theme, you see options for editing the theme, copying the link, and downloading the color as a color swatch file that you can load in Photoshop Elements (refer to Figure 4-7).

Figure 4-7: When you click a color theme, you see more options that enable you to add as a favorite, edit the theme, copy the link or, download the swatch file.

When you hover over a theme or select it to see its details, Adobe Kuler offers you a few options:

✔ **Favorite:** Click the heart-shaped Favorite icon to save a theme to a list of your personal favorites so that you can find it again easily. To see your favorite themes, move to the MyThemes area and then click My Favorites.

✔ **Edit:** Click the Edit icon with three sliders and you're able to customize someone else's theme to your liking. For example, you can make one hue a little darker or lighter, or change some colors altogether. To do so, use the color slider under each color, or search for another starting swatch by moving the swatch's corresponding dial on the color wheel. When you're done editing the theme, you can save a copy of it to your My Themes area.

✔ **Copy Link:** Clicking this chain-link icon copies a link to the color theme to your computer's Clipboard. You can the paste the link wherever you like by pressing Ctrl+V or choosing the Paste command from a context menu.

✔ **Download:** When you move the cursor over a Theme and click the Download button, the file is downloaded to your computer. If you save that file to your hard drive, you can then use the file to upload the theme into Elements, as we explain in the section "Loading Adobe Kuler themes into Elements," later in this chapter.

Creating your own color theme in Kuler

You have two choices for creating a color swatch. You can move colors around the color wheel to select five different colors. The values are displayed below the five different swatches. When you have the colors selected, click the Save button and the new color set is saved to your personal Themes. See Figure 4-8.

The other choice you have is to upload a photo. When the photo is uploaded Kuler creates a sample of the colors. You can resample different areas of the photo using the Color Picker tool. When you have the colors you want, click the Save button and the swatch set is saved to your personal Themes.

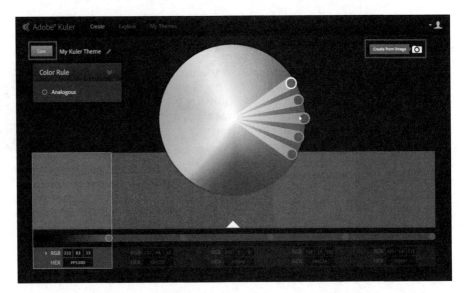

Figure 4-8: Click the Create button.

If you like creating color themes from photos and have an iPhone, check out the Adobe Kuler iPhone app. Just load a photo from your Camera Roll into the app. Kuler can then plot five points that create a theme from the colors in your photo. You can move the points around the photo and modify the color set from those colors you want to use. In the future, expect to see a similar feature available to everyone (not just iPhone users) on the Adobe Kuler website.

Getting themes from master artists

One truly great opportunity that's available with Search is exploring color combinations used by master artists. You might like wonderful earth tones used by Cézanne; bright colors used by Matisse; consistency across colors used by Da Vinci; or the colors used by Van Gogh, Picasso, Michelangelo, Rembrandt, Rivera, and more.

Just type the artist's name and press Enter/Return or click the search icon adjacent to the Search text box. The search results display color sets used in various paintings by the artist you entered as shown in Figure 4-9, where we searched for Van Gogh.

You can also search for colors contained in a variety of different themes such as skies, earth tones, landscapes, and so on.

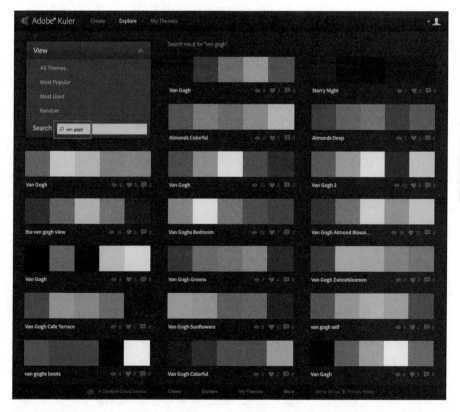

**Book III
Chapter 4**

**Using and
Managing Color**

Figure 4-9: Type search criteria in the Search text box and press Enter/Return to see the search results.

Loading Adobe Kuler themes into Elements

This section explains how to load a theme you've downloaded from Kuler into the Elements Color Swatches panel. (For an introduction to this panel, see the earlier section "Grabbing color from the Color Swatches panel.")

In Kuler, you can export any color theme you like as an ASE file by clicking the Download tool when your cursor hovers over a Theme. To then load the theme for use in Elements, follow these steps:

1. **Save the ASE file to the Elements Color Swatches folder on your hard drive.**

   You can save your color swatch anywhere on your hard drive, but if you want it to be available in the Color Swatches panel, save the file to the Color Swatches folder.

   In Windows, the directory path is `Program Files\Adobe\Photoshop Elements 12\Presets\Color Swatches`.

   On the Macintosh, the path is `Applications/Adobe Photoshop Elements 13/Settings/Presets/Color Swatches`.

2. **Load the color set by choosing Load Swatches from the Color Swatches panel menu in the Photo Editor.**

3. **When the Load dialog box opens, select Swatch Exchange (*ASE) from the Files of Type drop-down list (Windows) or Format pop-up menu (Macintosh).**

4. **Select the file or files you want to load in Elements.**

   If you want several color sets in a single color palette, download individual color sets from Kuler. Delete all colors in your Color Swatches panel and load each of your downloaded color sets. Save the final composite as a single color palette to the Color Swatches folder inside the Elements 13 folder.

Understanding Color Management Essentials

In Elements, the challenge with color isn't understanding color theory or definitions, but rather matching the RGB color you see on your computer monitor as closely as possible to your output. That output can be a printout from a color printer, a screen view on a web page, or an image in a photo-slide presentation.

We say match "as closely as possible" because you can't expect to achieve an exact match; you have far too many printer and monitor variables to deal with. However, if you properly manage color, you can get a very close match.

To match color in your monitor and your output, you must calibrate your monitor and then choose a color workspace profile. In the following sections, you can find all the details on how to do just that.

Discovering color channels

Your first level of color mastery in Photoshop is to understand what RGB is and how it comes about. *RGB* stands for *red, green,* and *blue.* These are the primary colors in the computer world. Forget about what you know about primary colors in an analog world; computers see primary colors as RGB.

RGB color is divided into *color channels.* Although you can't see the individual channels in Elements, you still need to get a handle on color channels. When you see a color *pixel* (a tiny, square dot), the color is represented as different levels of gray in each channel. (This may sound confusing at first, but stay with us for just a minute.) When you have a color channel, such as the red channel, and you let all light pass through the channel, you end up with a bright red. If you screen that light a little with a gray filter, you let less light pass through, thereby diluting the red color. That's how channels work — individually, they all use different levels of gray that permit up to 256 different levels of light to pass through them. When you change the intensity of light in the different channels, you ultimately change the color.

Each channel can have up to 256 levels of gray that mask out light. You can calculate the total number of possible colors that you can create in an RGB model by multiplying the values for each channel (256 × 256 × 256). The result is more than 16.7 million; that's the total number of colors a computer monitor can display in RGB color.

This is all well and good as far as theory goes, but what does that mean in practical terms? Actually, you see some of this information in tools and dialog boxes you work with in Elements. As an experiment, open a file in Elements and choose Enhance➪Adjust Lighting➪Levels (or press Ctrl+L/⌘+L); the Levels dialog box, shown in Figure 4-10, opens.

The Channel drop-down list shows you Red, Green, and Blue as individual channels, as well as a composite RGB selection. Furthermore, the Output Levels area shows you values ranging from 0 on the left to 255 on the right. Considering that 0 is a number, you have a total of 256 different levels of gray.

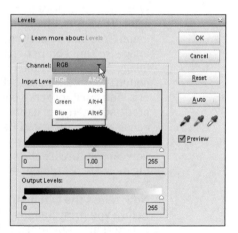

Figure 4-10: Choose Enhance➪Adjust Lighting➪Levels to open the Levels dialog box.

What's important is that you know that your work in color is related to RGB images that make up three different channels. Each channel can let 256 different levels of gray through — that is, hold back different amounts of light — to change brightness values and color.

Understanding bit depth

Another important item to understand about channels is *bit depth*. A *bit* holds one of two values; one value is for black, the other for white. When you have 256 levels of gray, you're working with an 8-bit-per-channel image — 8 bits with 2 possible values each is 2^8, or 256 possible levels of gray. Multiply 8 bits per channel times your 3 channels, and you get 24 bits, which is the common bit depth of images you print on your desktop printer.

Now take a look at the Image⇨Mode submenu. You should see a menu selection that says 8 Bits/Channel, as shown in Figure 4-11. When you open an image in Elements, if this menu command is grayed out, it means that you're working with a 24-bit image — an image of 8 bits per channel.

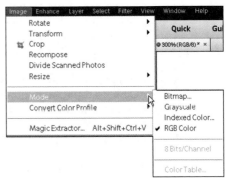

What does it mean when you can select the 8 Bits/Channel menu command? You can be certain that your image *isn't* an 8-bit-per-channel image. You may be able to select this command because some digital cameras and most low-end, consumer-

Figure 4-11: When you can choose 8 Bits/Channel, the image bit depth is higher than 8 bits per channel.

grade scanners can capture images at higher bit depths. Using a scanner, you can scan a photo at 16 bits per channel. When you do, you end up with many more levels of gray. When you take a picture with a quality digital camera, you can capture 32-bit-per-channel images, and you end up with a file containing more than 4 billion levels of gray. That's a lot!

Now, here's the catch: All files have to be reduced to 8 bits per channel before you print them — because that's all the information any printer uses. In addition, many tools, commands, and panel options work *only* with 8-bit-per-channel images. So, you ask, "What's the benefit of acquiring images at higher bit depths than I can print?"

If you attempt to adjust brightness, contrast, or other image enhancements in an 8-bit-per-channel image, you often destroy some data. You can cause some noticeable image degradation if you move adjustment sliders too far while working with 8-bit-per-channel images. When you edit your 16-bit and 32-bit images, you don't destroy data — you simply inform Elements *which* 256 levels of gray (of the total number available) you want to use. The result is an image with more continuous gray tones than you can achieve in 8-bit-per-channel images.

Calibrating your monitor

You need to calibrate your monitor to adjust the gamma and brightness; correct any color tints or colorcasts; and generally to display, as precisely as possible, accurate colors on your output. You have a few choices for which tool you can use to adjust monitor brightness, ranging from a low-cost hardware device that sells for less than $100 to expensive calibration equipment of $3,000 or more — or you can skip the hardware and use tools provided by Adobe, Windows, or your Mac.

Gamma is the brightness of midlevel tones in an image. In technical terms, it's a parameter that describes the shape of the transfer function for one or more stages in an imaging pipeline.

We skip the high-end costly devices and software utilities that don't do you any good and suggest that you make, at the very least, one valuable purchase for creating a monitor profile: a *hardware profiling system*. On the low end of the price scale, some affordable versions of this device go a long way toward helping you adjust your monitor brightness and color balance, including the following:

- **Datacolor Spyder4Express S4X100 Display Calibration Device by Datacolor:** For as low as $99, you can purchase an easy-to-use, three-step calibration device to balance the color on your monitor and adjust it for optimum brightness. This device is receiving five-star ratings at online resellers, including Amazon.com.

- **X-Rite CMUNSML ColorMunki Smile:** This device is an easy-to-use profiling tool that works with CRT displays, LCDs, and laptop computers. It sells for $99. You attach the unit via a USB port and click a few buttons in the software application accompanying the hardware. The profile you create is used automatically by your operating system when you start your computer. When the profile kicks in, your monitor is balanced with the settings that were determined when the device performed the calibration.

On LCD monitors, you adjust the hardware controls to bring your monitor into a match for overall brightness with your photo prints. Make sure that you run many test prints and match your prints against your monitor view to make the two as similar as possible.

You have a lot to focus on to calibrate monitors and get color right on your monitor and your output. (We talk more about color output in Book IX, Chapter 2.) For a good resource for color correction and printing using Photoshop Elements, we recommend that you look at *Color Management for Digital Photographers For Dummies,* by Ted Padova and Don Mason (published by Wiley).

Establishing your color settings

After you adjust your monitor color by using a hardware profiling system, your next step is to choose your color workspace. In Elements, you have a choice between one of two workspace colors: either sRGB or Adobe RGB (1998). You access your color workspace settings by choosing Edit⇨Color Settings. The Color Settings dialog box opens, as shown in Figure 4-12.

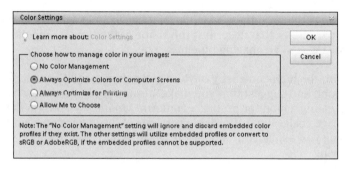

Figure 4-12: The Color Settings dialog box.

The options you have in the Color Settings dialog box are

- **No Color Management:** This choice turns off all color management. *Don't choose this option for any work you do in Elements.* You use No Color Management when you work with files that have color profiles embedded in the photos. Most likely you won't be using these types of photos. (For more about when you might use this option, see Book IX, Chapter 2.)

- **Always Optimize Colors for Computer Screens:** Selecting this radio button sets your workspace to sRGB. sRGB color is used quite often for viewing images on your monitor. But this workspace often results in the best choice for color printing, as well. Many color printers can output all the colors you can see in the sRGB workspace. In addition, many photo services, such as the Kodak EasyShare services (discussed in Book IX, Chapter 2), prefer this workspace setting.

✔ **Always Optimize for Printing:** Selecting this option sets your color workspace to Adobe RGB (1998). This workspace has more available colors than can be seen on your monitor. If you choose this workspace, you need to be certain that your printer is capable of using all the colors in this color space.

✔ **Allow Me to Choose:** When you select this option, Elements prompts you for a profile assignment when you open images that contain no profile. This setting is handy if you switch back and forth between screen and print images.

Understanding how profiles work

You probably created a monitor color profile when you calibrated your monitor. You probably also selected a color profile when you opened the Color Settings dialog box and selected your workspace color. When you start your computer, your monitor color profile kicks in and adjusts your overall monitor brightness and correction for any color casts. When you open a photo in Elements, color is automatically converted from your monitor color space to your workspace color.

At print time, you use another color profile to output your photos to your desktop color printer. Color is then converted from your workspace color to your printer's color space. In Book IX, Chapter 2, we show you how to use color profiles for printing. For now, just realize that the proper use of color profiles determines whether you can get good color output. From here, you can jump to Book IX, Chapter 2, and understand how the color profiles are used at print time.

**Book III
Chapter 4**

**Using and
Managing Color**

Book IV
Selections

For more details and projects about Photoshop Elements, visit www.dummies.com/
extras/photoshopelementsaio.

Contents at a Glance

Chapter 1: Making Selections

In This Chapter

- ✓ Creating selections with the Marquee tools
- ✓ Roping your selections with the Lasso tools
- ✓ Selecting pixels with the Magic Wand tool
- ✓ Choosing with the Selection Brush
- ✓ Using the Quick Selection tool to save time
- ✓ Cropping and transforming with the Recompose tool

Sometimes you get lucky, and what you capture in the camera's view-finder is exactly what you want to edit, print, or share online. But at other times, you may want to work with only a portion of that image. Maybe you just need to adjust the contrast in a certain area, or you want to combine part of one image with another. In these instances, you have to make a selection before you can go on to do the real editing work.

Being able to make accurate selections is a valuable skill. Fortunately, Elements offers an assortment of tools for making selections. In this chapter, we give you the foundation to use the basic selection tools. If, after you make a selection, you want to modify or transform that selection, check out the next chapter. Finally, masking is another way to make a selection. Be sure to look at Book VI, Chapter 4, for the lowdown on masking.

Defining Selections

Defining a selection means that you specify which part of the image you want to work with. Everything within a selection is considered *selected*. Everything outside the selection is *unselected*. Seems simple enough. It is, except that you can also have partially selected pixels, which allow for soft-edged, diffused selections. You can create *partially selected* pixels by feathering, masking, or anti-aliasing the selection. We cover feathering and anti-aliasing in this chapter. Masking is covered in Book VI, Chapter 4.

When you make a selection, a moving dotted outline known as a *selection border* (also called a *selection outline* or *selection marquee*) appears around the selected area. After you've made a selection, any adjustments or edits you apply affect only that portion. The unselected areas remain unchanged. You can also make a selection in one image and then copy and paste it into another image. If you can't squeeze in that trip to Europe this year, no worries: Select yourself from a family photo, choose Edit⇨Copy, open a stock photo of the Eiffel Tower, and then choose Edit⇨Paste. Nobody will know that you never made it to the City of Lights.

When making selections, be sure that you're working in the Photo Editor, in Expert mode, and not in Quick or Guided modes, or in the Organizer. For more on various modes in Elements, see Book I, Chapter 1.

Selecting a Rectangular or an Elliptical Area

The Marquee tools are the easiest selection tools to use. Basically, if you can use a mouse or a trackpad without much difficulty, you can become a marqueeing expert.

The Rectangular Marquee tool creates rectangular or square selections. Use this tool when you want to grab just a portion of an image and copy and paste it into a new, blank document or into another image. The Elliptical Marquee tool creates elliptical or circular selections. You can select clocks, doughnuts, inner tubes, and other round objects with this tool.

Follow these steps to make a selection with the Rectangular Marquee tool:

1. **Select either the Rectangular or Elliptical Marquee tool from the Tools panel.**

   The tool looks like a dotted square or oval. You can also use the keyboard shortcut — press the M key. If the tool isn't visible, press M again, or you can select either tool from the Tool Options.

2. **With the Rectangular Marquee tool, click and drag from one corner of the area that you want to select to the opposite corner. With the Elliptical Marquee tool, position the crosshair near the area you want to select, and then click and drag around the element.**

   While you drag, the selection border appears. The border follows the movement of your mouse cursor (a crosshair or plus sign icon).

3. **Release your mouse button.**

   You now have a selection, as shown in Figure 1-1.

© iStockphoto.com/gilaxia Image #20557146, © iStockphoto.com/Brosa Image #3771244

Figure 1-1: The Marquee tools select rectangular or circular portions of your image.

 If your selection isn't quite centered on the element, move the selection border by clicking and dragging inside the border with either the Rectangular or Elliptical Marquee tool. You can also move a selection with either tool *while* you're drawing by pressing the spacebar.

Fine-tuning squares and circles

If you want to create a perfect square or circle, hold down the Shift key after you begin dragging your mouse. When you have a selection, release the mouse button first and then release the Shift key.

You may find it easier to create an elliptical selection by dragging from the center outward. To do so, click and hold down the mouse button in the center of an element. Then press the Alt key (Option key on the Mac) and drag from the center outward. After you have your selection, release the mouse button first and then the key.

If you want to draw from the center outward and you want a perfect circle (or square), hold down the Shift key as well. When you have a selection, release your mouse button first and then press Shift+Alt (Shift+Option on the Mac).

 You can also achieve a perfect circle or square by specifying a 1:1 aspect ratio on the Tool Options.

Using the Marquee options

The Tool Options provide oodles of other options when you're making Marquee selections. Some of these options allow you to make precise selections by specifying exact measurements. Others enable you to make soft-edged, feathered selections.

You must select the options in the Tool Options, as shown in Figure 1-2, *before* you make your selection with the Marquee tools. The only exception is that you can feather a selection after you have created it. Note that to feather a selection, you must choose the menu command Select⇨Feather.

Figure 1-2: Specify Marquee settings in the Tool Options.

Here's the scoop on each Marquee option:

- **Feather:** *Feathering* softens, or feathers, the edges of a selection. The amount of softening depends on the value — the higher the value, the softer the edge, as shown in Figure 1-3. The radius measures how far in all directions the feather effect extends. You can use small amounts of feathering to create natural transitions between selected elements in a collage. Use larger amounts to create a special effect where one image gradually fades into another. If you just want a selected element to have a soft edge without the background, choose Select⇨Inverse and then delete the background.

  To feather while you're selecting, select the Feather option in the Tool Options before you use the Marquee tools. You can feather a selection after the fact by choosing Select⇨Feather.

- **Anti-aliasing:** Whereas feathering completely softens edges, anti-aliasing just slightly softens the edge of an elliptical or irregularly shaped selection so that extremely hard, jagged edges aren't quite so prominent, as shown in Figure 1-4. An anti-aliased edge is always only 1 pixel wide.

We recommend keeping the Anti-aliasing option selected, especially if you plan on creating a collage of images. Anti-aliasing helps create natural-looking transitions and blends between multiple selections. However, if you want a supercrisp edge, deselect this option.

Feather 6 pixels

Feather 30 pixels

© iStockphoto.com/OwenPrice Image #04795551

Figure 1-3: Feathering a selection softens the edges.

anti-aliased

not anti-aliased

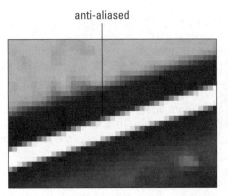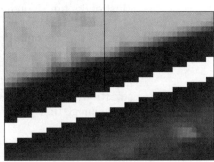

Figure 1-4: Anti-aliasing barely softens selection edges.

✔ **Aspect:** The Aspect drop-down menu contains three settings:

- *Normal:* This option enables you to freely drag a selection to any dimension.

- *Fixed Ratio:* This setting allows you to specify a fixed ratio of width to height in a selection. For example, if you enter 2 for width and 1 for height, the Marquee selection you create is *always* twice as wide as it is high, no matter what the size.

- *Fixed Size:* This setting lets you specify values for the width and height. It comes in handy when you need to make multiple selections that must be the same exact size, such as in a school yearbook. Note that the marquee is immediately drawn when you click your canvas. The click point is the upper-left corner of the marquee.

✔ **Width and Height:** When you select Fixed Ratio or Fixed Size from the drop-down menu, you also enter values in the Width and Height text boxes. To swap the Width and Height values, click the double-headed arrow button.

Even though the default unit of measurement in the Width and Height text boxes is pixels (px), you can enter any unit of measurement that Elements recognizes — pixels, inches (in), centimeters (cm), millimeters (mm), points (pt), picas (pica), or percent (%). Enter the value and then type the word or abbreviation of a unit of measurement.

The Refine Edge option is also available, but because you most likely won't need it for a selection made with the Marquee tools, we explain it in the next section on Lasso selections.

Free-Form Selecting with the Lasso Tools

Unfortunately, not much in life is perfectly rectangular or elliptical in shape. Most of the time, you have to deal with irregular shapes that have undulations of some kind or another. That's where the Lasso tools come in handy. This group of tools enables you to make any free-form selection your heart desires.

Elements offers three Lasso tools: Lasso, Polygonal Lasso, and Magnetic Lasso. Each Lasso tool has its own special purpose in the world of free-form selections, and they're simple to use. You just have to drag around the part of the image that you want to select. All that's required is a decaffeinated, steady hand.

The selection you make is only as good as your accuracy in tracing around an element. If you don't make an exact selection the first time around, don't worry. You can always go back and make corrections, as described in the next chapter.

The Lasso and Polygonal Lasso tools have three settings in the Tool Options — Feather, Anti-aliasing, and Refine Edge. The first two options work exactly as they do with the Marquee tools. To find out about Feather and Anti-aliasing, see the preceding section. The Refine Edge option does exactly that — cleans up the edges of your selection. You also find this command in the Tool Options for the Marquee, Magic Wand, and Quick Selection tools. Keep in mind that you can apply this option to any existing selection, no matter how you created the selection, by choosing Select➪Refine Edge.

Here's the scoop on the settings for the Refine Edge options:

✔ **View Mode:** Choose a mode from the drop-down menu to preview your selection. For example, Marching Ants shows the selection border.

Overlay lets you preview your selection with the edges hidden and a semi-opaque layer of color in your unselected area. On Black and On White show the selection against a black or white background. Hover your cursor over each mode to see a tooltip. Show Original shows the image without a selection preview. Show Radius displays the image with the selection border.

✓ **Smart Radius:** Select this option to have Elements automatically adjust the radius for hard and soft edges near your selection border. If your border is uniformly hard or soft, you may not want to select this option. This enables you to have more control over the radius setting.

✓ **Radius:** Specify the size of the selection border you will refine. Increase the radius to improve the edge of areas with soft transitions or a lot of detail. Move the slider while looking at your selection to find a good setting.

✓ **Smooth:** Reduces jaggedness along your selection edges.

✓ **Feather:** Moves the slider to create an increasingly softer, more blurred edge.

✓ **Contrast:** Removes artifacts while tightening soft edges by increasing the contrast. Try using the Smart Radius option first before playing with Contrast.

✓ **Shift Edge:** Decreases or increases your selected area. Slightly decreasing your selection border can help to *defringe* (eliminate undesirable background pixels) your selection edges.

✓ **Decontaminate Colors:** Replaces background fringe with the colors of your selected element. Note that because decontamination changes the colors of some of the pixels, you will have to output to, or create, another layer or document to preserve your current layer. To see the decontamination in action, choose Reveal Layer for your View mode.

✓ **Amount:** Changes the level of decontamination.

✓ **Output To:** Choose whether you want to output your refined, decontaminated selection to a selection on your current layer, layer mask, layer, layer with layer mask, new document, or new document with layer mask.

✓ **Refine Radius tool:** Brush around your border to adjust the area you are refining. To understand exactly what area is being included or excluded, change your View mode to Marching Ants. Use the right and left brackets to decrease and increase the brush size.

✓ **Erase Refinements tool:** If your refinements were not so refined after all, brush around the border to restore your original edge.

✓ **Zoom tool:** Enables you to zoom into your image to see the effects of your settings.

✓ **Hand tool:** Lets you pan around the document window to see the effects of your settings on various portions of your image.

**Book IV
Chapter 1**

Making Selections

Using the Lasso tool

Making a selection with the Lasso tool is basically like tracing an outline around an element on a sheet of paper.

To make a selection by using the Lasso tool, follow these steps:

1. **Select the Lasso tool from the Tools panel.**

   It's the tool that looks like a rope — hence the moniker *lasso.* You can also use the keyboard shortcut by pressing the L key. If the Lasso isn't visible, press L again to cycle through the various Lasso tools or grab your desired tool from the Tool Options.

2. **Position the cursor anywhere along the edge of the element you want to select.**

   The *hot spot* (the leading point) of the Lasso cursor is the end of the rope. If you need a little visual help, press the Caps Lock key, which switches your cursor to a crosshair.

   Zoom in on the image a bit if you need to better see its edges.

   In our example, we started at the bottom of the butterfly wing, as shown in Figure 1-5.

3. **Hold down the mouse button and trace around the element, trying to include only what you want to select.**

   While you trace, an outline forms that follows the movement of your mouse.

   Don't release the mouse button until you complete the selection by closing the loop and returning to your starting point. When you release the mouse button, Elements assumes that you're done and closes the selection from wherever you release the mouse button to your starting point.

4. **Continue tracing until you return to your starting point; release the mouse button.**

   Elements rewards you with a selection border that matches your Lasso path, as shown in Figure 1-6.

Selecting straight sides with the Polygonal Lasso tool

The Polygonal Lasso tool is at its best when selecting straight-sided subjects, such as city skylines, buildings, and stairways. Unlike the Lasso tool, the Polygonal Lasso tool has rubber band–like qualities, and instead of dragging, you click and release the mouse button at the vertices of the object you're selecting.

Lasso cursor

Selected area

© iStockphoto.com/TammyFullum Image #00354144

© iStockphoto.com/TammyFullum Image #00354144

Figure 1-5: The Lasso tool is for free-form selections.

Figure 1-6: After tracing around your object, release the mouse button to obtain a selection border.

Follow these steps to select with the Polygonal Lasso tool:

1. **Select the Polygonal Lasso tool in the Tools panel.**

   You can also use the keyboard shortcut by pressing the L key. If the Polygonal Lasso isn't visible, press L again to cycle through the Lasso tools or select the tool from the Tool Options. The Polygonal Lasso tool looks like the Lasso tool but has straight sides.

2. **Click and release at any point along the edge of the desired element.**

   We like starting at a corner.

3. **Move (don't drag) the mouse and click and release at the next corner of the element; continue clicking and releasing at the various corners of the object.**

   The line stretches out from each corner you click, like a rubber band.

4. **To close a selection, return to your starting point and click and release.**

When you place the cursor over the starting point, a small circle appears next to the cursor, indicating that you're at the right place for closing the selection. A selection marquee that matches your Polygonal Lasso path appears, as shown in Figure 1-7.

© iStockphoto.com/rustemgurler Image #019040480

Figure 1-7: Select straight-sided elements with the Polygonal Lasso tool.

Some objects have both curves and straight sides. No problem. Hold down the Alt key (Option key on the Mac) and then click and drag to select the curves. Your Polygonal Lasso tool temporarily transforms into the regular Lasso tool. Release the Alt (or Option) key to return to the Polygonal Lasso tool. This trick also works with the other Lasso tools.

Hugging edges with the Magnetic Lasso tool

The last Lasso tool is the Magnetic Lasso, which works by analyzing the colors of the pixels between the elements in the foreground and the elements in the background. Then it snaps to, or hugs, the edge between the elements, as though the edge had a magnetic pull.

Not always the easiest tool to manipulate, the Magnetic Lasso tool performs best when your image has a well-defined foreground object and good contrast between that object and the background — for example, a dark mountain range against a light sky or a black silhouette against a white wall.

The Magnetic Lasso tool has some unique settings, found in the Tool Options, which you can adjust to control the sensitivity of the tool and thus aid in your selection task.

We recommend starting out by experimenting with the Magnetic Lasso tool using its default settings. If the tool isn't cooperating, play with the options.

The Feather, Anti-aliasing, and Refine Edge options work as they do with the Marquee and Lasso tools. Here are the remaining options:

✔ **Width:** This option, measured in pixels from 1 to 256, determines how close to the edge you have to move the mouse before the Magnetic

Lasso tool snaps to that edge. Decrease the value if the object's edge has a lot of indentations and protrusions or if the image has low contrast. Increase the value if the image has high contrast or smooth edges.

✓ **Contrast:** Measured in percentages from 1 to 100, this option specifies the contrast required between the object and its background before the Magnetic Lasso tool snaps to the edge. If the image has good contrast between the foreground element and its background, use a high percentage.

✓ **Frequency:** This setting, measured in percentages from 0 to 100, specifies how many *fastening* points (points anchoring the selection line) to place on the selection line. The higher the value, the more fastening points used. If the element you want to select has a fairly smooth edge, keep the value low. If the edge is jagged or has a lot of detail, try a higher value to create a more accurate selection.

✓ **Tablet Pressure (Pen icon):** If you own a pressure-sensitive drawing tablet, select this option to make an increase in stylus pressure to cause the edge width to decrease.

Follow these steps to use the Magnetic Lasso tool:

1. **Select the Magnetic Lasso tool in the Tools panel.**

   You can also press the L key if the tool is visible. If it isn't, press L again to cycle through the Lasso tools. The tool looks like a straight-sided lasso with a magnet on it.

2. **Click and release on the edge of the element you want to select to place the first fastening point.**

   Start anywhere, but be sure to click the edge between the element you want and the background you don't want.

3. **Move your cursor around the object without clicking.**

   The Magnetic Lasso tool creates a selection line similar to the other lasso tools while placing fastening points that anchor the selection line (see Figure 1-8). Think of it as the way you might cordon off an area of your yard with ropes and stakes.

Fastening points

© iStockphoto.com/swilmor Image #03160253

Figure 1-8: The Magnetic Lasso tool snaps to the edge of your element.

Here are a couple tips to keep in mind when working with the Magnetic Lasso tool:

- *If the Magnetic Lasso tool starts veering off the edge of your object,* back up your mouse and click and release to force a fastening point farther down along the edge.

- *If the Magnetic Lasso tool adds a point where you don't want one,* simply press the Backspace (Delete on a Mac) key to delete it.

- *If the Magnetic Lasso is misbehaving,* you can temporarily switch to the other Lasso tools. To select the Lasso tool, press the Alt key (Option key on the Mac) and then press the mouse button and drag. To select the Polygonal Lasso tool, press the Alt (or Option) key and click; don't drag.

4. **Continue moving the mouse around the object and then return to your starting point; click and release the mouse button to close the selection.**

A small circle appears next to your cursor, indicating that you're at the correct place to close the selection. The selection border appears when the selection is closed.

Performing Wand Wizardry

The Magic Wand has been around since the early days of the digital-imaging era. You'd think with a name like Magic Wand, it'd grant your every selection wish with a mere click. Well, yes and no. The success of the Magic Wand depends on your particular image.

The Magic Wand is a no-brainer to operate: Click the element you want within your image, and the Magic Wand makes a selection. This selection is based on the color of the pixel (the *target* pixel) directly under the cursor when you click. If other pixels are similar in color to your target pixel, Elements includes them in the selection. What's sometimes hard to predict, however, is how to determine *how similar* the color has to be to get the Magic Wand tool to select it. That's where the Tolerance setting comes in. First, here's a little info on tolerance so that you can better wield the Wand.

Talking about tolerance

The Tolerance setting determines the range of color that the Magic Wand tool selects. The issue is that most images contain a few shades of a similar color. For example, consider an image of a field of grass. A few shades of green make up that field. Using the Magic Wand tool, if you click a darker shade of green, it selects all similar shades of green, but the lighter shades remain unselected, which is a sign that you need to increase the tolerance level to select all shades of the green grass. Tolerance is based on brightness levels that range from 0 to 255. That being said,

✔ Setting the tolerance to 0 selects only one color.

✔ Setting the tolerance to 255 selects all colors, or the entire image.

The default setting is 32, so whenever you click a pixel, Elements analyzes the value of that base color and then selects all pixels whose brightness levels are between 16 levels lighter and 16 levels darker.

What if an image contains a few shades of the same color? It's not a huge problem. You can try different Tolerance settings:

✔ **If you didn't quite pick up what you wanted in the first try,** as shown in Figure 1-9, try a higher Tolerance setting.

✔ **If your wand selects too much,** you can also lower your Tolerance setting, or you can make multiple clicks of the Magic Wand, with the Shift key pressed down, to pick up additional pixels that you want to include in the selection.

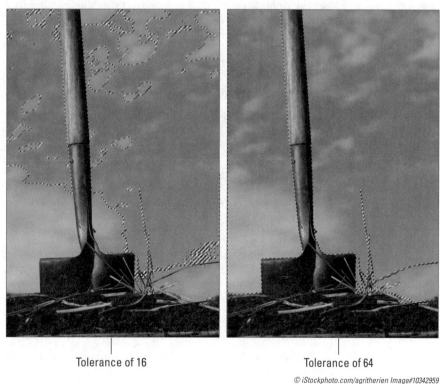

Tolerance of 16   Tolerance of 64

© iStockphoto.com/agritherien Image#10342959

Figure 1-9: Finding the right Tolerance setting is the key to selecting with the Magic Wand.

Book IV
Chapter 1

Making Selections

Selecting with the Magic Wand tool

The Magic Wand tool works best when you have high-contrast images or images with a limited number of colors. For example, the optimum image for the Wand is a solid-colored object on a white background. Skip the Wand if the image has a ton of colors and no real definitive contrast between your element and the background.

To make a selection with the Magic Wand tool, follow these steps:

1. **Select the Magic Wand tool in the Tools panel.**

   It looks like, well, a wand. You can also press the A key. If the Magic Wand isn't visible, press A again to cycle through the tools. Or simply choose the Magic Wand in the Tool Options.

2. **Click the portion of the image you want to select, using the default Tolerance setting of 32.**

   The pixel you click (the *target* pixel) determines the base color. Remember that the default value of 32 means that the Magic Wand tool selects all colors 16 levels lighter and 16 levels darker than the base color.

   If you selected everything you wanted the first time you used the Magic Wand tool, give yourself a pat on the back. If you didn't (which is probably the case), go to Step 3.

3. **Enter a new Tolerance setting in the Tool Options.**

   If the Magic Wand tool selected more than you wanted it to, lower the Tolerance setting. If it didn't select enough, raise the setting.

   Here are a few other options to specify:

   - *Sample All Layers:* If you have multiple layers and enable this option, the Magic Wand selects pixels from all visible layers. If it's deselected, the tool selects pixels from the active layer only. For more on layers, see Book VI.

   - *Contiguous:* When this option is selected, the Magic Wand tool selects *only* pixels that are adjacent to each other. When this option is deselected, the Magic Wand tool selects all pixels within the range of tolerance on the active layer (unless Sample All Layers is selected), regardless of whether they're adjacent to each other.

   - *Anti-aliasing:* This option subtly softens the edge of the selection. See the section "Using the Marquee options," earlier in this chapter, for details.

   - *Refine Edge:* This option enables you to clean up the selection edges. See the earlier section "Free-Form Selecting with the Lasso Tools" for details on this option.

4. **Click the portion of the image that you want to select.**

   Changing the tolerance level doesn't adjust the current selection, so you must start again by clicking your image. The Magic Wand tool then deselects the current selection and makes a new selection — based on the new Tolerance setting, as shown in Figure 1-10. If it still isn't right, you can adjust the Tolerance setting again. Unfortunately, it's all about trial and error.

Painting with the Selection Brush

© iStockphoto.com/clintscholz Image #2556066

Figure 1-10: Select a portion of your image with the Magic Wand tool.

If the action of painting on a canvas is more up your alley, try out the Selection Brush. Using two different modes, you can either paint over areas of an image that you want to select or paint over areas you don't want to select. The Selection Brush also lets you make a basic selection with another tool, such as the Lasso, and then fine-tune the selection by brushing additional pixels into or out of the selection.

Follow these steps to paint a selection with the Selection Brush:

1. **Select the Selection Brush from the Tools panel or simply press the A key.**

   If the Selection Brush isn't visible, press A again to cycle through the tools. Or simply choose the Selection Brush in the Tool Options. This tool works in either Expert or Quick mode.

2. **Specify your Selection Brush options in the Tool Options.**

   Here's the scoop on each option:

   - *Mode (note that this drop-down menu is not labeled as such):* Choose between Selection and Mask. Choose Selection if you want to paint over what you *want* to select. Choose Mask if you want to paint over what you *don't* want to select. If you choose Mask mode, you must choose some additional overlay options. An *overlay* is a layer of color (that shows onscreen only) that hovers over your image, indicating protected or unselected areas. You must also choose an overlay opacity between 1 and 100 percent. You can also choose to change the overlay color from the default red to another color. This option can be helpful if the image contains a lot of red.

   - *Brush Presets:* Choose a brush from the presets drop-down panel. To load additional brushes, click the down-pointing arrow to the left of

Default Brushes and choose the preset library of your choice. You can select the Load Brushes command from the panel menu.

- *Size:* Enter a brush size from 1 to 2500 pixels. You can also drag the slider.

- *Hardness:* Set the hardness of the brush tip, from 1 to 100 percent.

3. **If your mode is set to Selection, paint over the areas you want to select.**

You see a selection border. Each stroke adds to the selection. (You'll notice the Add to Selection button in the Tool Options is automatically selected.) If you inadvertently add something you don't want, simply press the Alt key (Option on the Mac) and paint over the undesired area. You can also click the Subtract from Selection button in the Tool Options. After you finish painting what you want, your selection is ready to go.

4. **If your mode is set to Mask, paint over the areas that you *don't* want to select.**

While you paint, you see the color of your overlay. Each stroke adds more to the overlay area, as shown in the left image in Figure 1-11. When working in Mask mode, you're essentially covering up, or *masking,* the areas you want to protect from manipulation. That manipulation can be selecting, adjusting color, or performing any other Elements command. Again, if you want to remove parts of the masked area, press the Alt key (Option on the Mac) and paint.

When you're done painting your mask, choose Selection from the Mode drop-down menu or simply choose another tool from the Tools panel to convert your mask into a selection border, as shown in the right image in Figure 1-11.

© iStockphoto.com/PKM1 Image #3217961

Figure 1-11: Paint a selection with the Selection Brush.

If you painted the selection in Mask mode, the selection border is around what you don't want. To switch to what you do want, choose Select⊅Inverse.

The mode you choose is up to you. One advantage of working in Mask mode is that you can partially select areas. By painting with soft brushes, you create soft-edged selections. These soft edges result in partially selected pixels. If you set the overlay opacity to a lower percentage, the pixels are even less opaque or "less selected." If this "partially selected" business sounds vaguely familiar, it's because this is also what happens when you feather selections, as we discuss in the section "Using the Marquee options," earlier in this chapter.

Saving Time with the Quick Selection Tool

No one ever has enough time, so any tool that can shave a few minutes off a selection task is welcome. The Quick Selection tool can do just that. Think of it as a combo Brush/Magic Wand/Lasso tool. Easy to use — and producing surprisingly good results — it's sure to become a favorite part of your collection of selection tools.

To make short work of selecting by using this tool, follow these steps:

1. **Select the Quick Selection tool from the Tools panel.**

   The tool looks like a wand with a marquee around the end. You can also press the A key — or if the tool isn't visible, press A again to cycle through the tools. You can also select the Quick Selection tool in the Tool Options.

   This is one of the few tools that works in either Expert or Quick mode.

2. **Specify the options in the Tool Options.**

   Here's an explanation of the options:

   - *New Selection:* The default option enables you to create a new selection. You also have options to add to and subtract from your selection.
   - *Brush Settings:* Choose your desired brush settings. Specify hardness, spacing, angle, and roundness settings.
   - *Size:* Specify the diameter, from 1 to 2500 pixels.
   - *Sample All Layers:* If the image has layers and you want to make a selection from all the layers, select this option. If this option is left deselected, you can select only from the active layer.
   - *Auto-Enhance:* Select this option to have Elements assist you with automatically refining your selection by implementing an algorithm.

3. **Click and drag over the desired areas of the image.**

   Your selection grows while you drag, as shown in Figure 1-12.

   If you stop dragging and click another portion of the image, your selection includes that clicked area.

4. **Modify your selection, as needed.**

   You have three options to change your selection:

   - *To add to your selection,* press the Shift key while dragging across your desired image areas.

   - *To delete from your selection,* press the Alt key (Option key on the Mac) while dragging across the unwanted image areas.

   - You can also select the Add to Selection or Subtract from Selection options in the Tool Options.

5. **If you need to further fine-tune your selection, click the Refine Edge option in the Tool Options.**

   We explain the Refine Edge settings in detail in the section "Free-Form Selecting with the Lasso Tools," earlier in this chapter. If the object is fairly detailed, you may even need to break out the Lasso or another selection tool to make some final cleanups.

© iStockphoto.com/ABDESIGN Image #209970

Figure 1-12: Drag over your desired selection with the quick-and-easy Quick Selection tool.

Fine-Tuning with the Refine Selection Brush

Being able to make selections quickly and accurately is a valuable skill, and there is a new tool to help you achieve that goal. The Refine Selection Brush helps you add or delete portions of your selection by automatically detecting edges of your desired element.

Here's how to fine-tune your selections with the Refine Selection Brush:

1. **Make your selection using the Quick Selection tool, Selection Brush, or any other selection tool.**

   Don't worry if the selection isn't perfect. That's where the Refine Selection Brush comes in.

2. **Select the Refine Selection Brush.**

   This tool shares a tool slot with the Quick Selection tool, Magic Wand, and Selection Brush.

   Your cursor appears as two concentric circle, as shown in Figure 1-13. The outer circle reflects the tolerance setting to detect an edge. For more on tolerance, see "Talking about tolerance," earlier in this chapter.

© iStockphoto.com/Yuri Image #000015336775

Figure 1-13: Use the new Refine Selection Bruch to fine-tune your selection.

2. **Specify the settings in the Tool Options.**

   Here's a description of the options:

   • *Size:* Use the slider to adjust your brush diameter from 1 to 2,500 pixels.

   • *Snap Strength:* Use the slider to adjust your snap strength from 0% to 100%. Snap is the intensity of the pull.

- *Add/Subtract:* Choose this option to either add to or subtract from your selection.

- *Push:* Place your cursor inside the selection to increase your selection within the diameter of the outer circle of your cursor. It will snap to the edge of the element closest to the cursor. Place your cursor outside the selection to decrease your selection within the diameter of the outer circle.

- *Smooth:* If your selection border looks a little too jagged, use this options to smooth your selection edge.

3. **Continue to use the Refine Selection Brush to perfect your selection until you're happy.**

Resizing Smartly with the Recompose Tool

The Recompose tool is a combination crop-and-transform tool. You can move elements closer together or even change the orientation of a landscape shot from horizontal to vertical without eliminating your most important elements.

Follow these steps to recompose:

1. **In the Photo Editor, in Expert mode, select the Recompose tool from the Tools panel.**

   This tool is just to the right of the Crop tool and looks like a gear in front of a bounding box. You can also press the W key to access the tool.

2. **Using the brushes and erasers in the Tool Options, mark the areas you want to protect and eliminate.**

   Although this step isn't mandatory, it yields better results.

   Here's a description of these options, located at the far-left end of the Tool Options:

   - *Mark for Protection brush:* Brush over the areas of the image you want to protect, or retain (strokes are green). You don't have to be super-precise — just provide Elements with an idea of what you want to keep (or remove, in the case of the next brush).

   - *Mark for Removal brush:* Brush over those areas you want to remove first (strokes are red). Make sure to choose the area you don't mind deleting, as shown in Figure 1-14.

   - *Erase Highlights Marked for Protection:* Use this tool to erase any area you mistakenly marked to retain.

- *Erase Highlights Marked for Removal:* Use this tool to erase any area you mistakenly marked to remove.

© iStockphoto.com/ABDESIGN Image #209970

Figure 1-14: Mark areas to retain or remove.

3. **Specify the other options in the Tool Options.**

   Here's a description of those options:

   - *Size:* Adjust the brush size by clicking the down arrow and dragging the slider to make the brush diameter smaller or larger.

   - *Highlight Skin Tone (green man/brush icon):* Select this option to prevent skin tones from being distorted when scaled.

   - *Preset:* Use a preset ratio or size to which to recompose your image, or leave on the No Restriction default setting.

   - *Width and Height:* Enter width and height scale percentages, if you want.

   - *Threshold:* Set a recomposition threshold to help minimize distortion. Start with a higher percentage and then adjust as needed.

4. **Grab the image handle and resize your image.**

   As you drag, the red areas are removed first, and the green areas remain intact. After all the red areas have been removed, Elements begins to "carve" out areas you didn't indicate to protect.

5. **After you recompose the image, click the Commit (green) check-mark icon to accept the composition.**

   Retouch any areas as needed with the Clone Stamp or Healing tools. For our example, shown in Figure 1-15, we retouched some of the water and sky.

Figure 1-15: A recomposed image.

Chapter 2: Modifying and Transforming Selections

For most people, getting the perfect, pristine selection on the first attempt is difficult. A little too much caffeine or not enough shut-eye, and that once-steady hand is no longer so. Fortunately, Elements, compassionate digital-imaging friend that it is, understands this difficulty and doesn't make you settle for inaccurate selections. You have many ways to modify and transform selections to refine them to the point of near-perfect accuracy. You can add or remove pixels from your selection, scale the selection outline, smooth jagged edges, or switch what's selected for what isn't. In this chapter, we show you how to clean up and modify your selections and enable you to nail an element with precision.

If you haven't already checked out the first chapter of this minibook and gotten a good grasp on how to create selections in the first place, you may want to start there.

When modifying selections, be sure that you're working in the Photo Editor in Expert mode (not in Quick or Guided mode, or in the Organizer). For more on various modes in Elements, see Book I, Chapter 1.

Modifying Selections

Although the selection tools, such as the Lasso, Quick Selection, and Magic Wand, usually do a fair job of capturing most of a selection, making an extremely accurate selection often requires a degree of modification and cleanup. If you give the selection a little extra TLC, you're rewarded with more accuracy and precision. By adding and subtracting from the selection, you can refine it and ensure that you capture only what you want.

With the multitude of tools and features in Elements, you can usually execute the task in more than one way. In the following sections, we show you how to use keyboard operations (along with your mouse) to modify selections. But note that you can also use the four selection option buttons on the left side of the Tool Options to create a new selection, add to a selection, subtract from a selection, or intersect one selection with another. You just choose the selection tool, click the selection option button you want, and drag (or click and release, if you're using the Magic Wand or Polygonal Lasso tool). When you're using the Selection Brush, the Add to Selection and Subtract from Selection buttons are also available.

Adding to a selection

If your selection doesn't contain all the elements you want to capture, you need to add those portions to your current selection.

To add to a current selection, simply hold down the Shift key and click and drag around the pixels you want to include when using the regular Lasso or the Rectangular or Elliptical Marquee tool. If you're using the Polygonal Lasso, click and release around the area. (We wouldn't use the Magnetic Lasso tool to add to a selection; it's way too cumbersome.)

You can also hold down the Shift key and click the area you want when using the Magic Wand tool, or drag on the area you want when using the Quick Selection tool.

After your first drag with the Quick Selection tool, your selection option button should convert to the Add to Selection button automatically. When using the Selection Brush in Selection mode, the selection option button is also set automatically to the Add to Selection button.

You don't have to use the same tool to add to your selection that you used to create the original selection. Feel free to use whatever selection tool you think can get the job done. For example, it's common to start off with the Magic Wand and clean up your selection with the Lasso tool.

Follow these steps to add to a circular selection, such as the one shown in Figure 2-1:

1. **Make your first elliptical selection with the Elliptical Marquee tool, as shown in the left example in Figure 2-1.**

   Be sure to hold down the Alt key (Option on the Mac) to draw from the center out. Also, press the Shift key if you want to constrain your selection to a circle.

2. **To add to your initial selection, hold down two keys at once: First hold down the Shift key to add to the selection and then hold down the Alt (or Option) key to draw from the center out.**

   You must press and hold the keys in this order.

   Note that if you also need to constrain your selection to a perfect circle, you have a dilemma because the Shift key is already being used to add to the selection. See the later section "Avoiding Keyboard Collisions" for a solution.

3. **Drag around the second selection by using the Elliptical Marquee tool.**

   You would have to repeat Steps 2 and 3 several times to select all the tennis balls. Figure 2-1 shows the steps repeated so that a second tennis ball is selected.

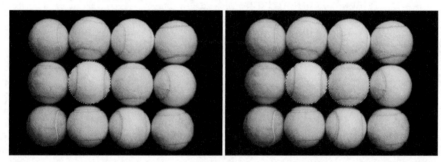

© iStockphoto.com/nico_blue Image #01390580

Figure 2-1: The original selection (left) is increased after including additional pixels (right).

Subtracting from a selection

Just as you can add to a selection marquee, you can subtract from a selection. Here's how to subtract from a current selection using the following tools:

- ✔ **Using the Lasso or the Rectangular or Elliptical Marquee tool:** Hold down the Alt key (Option key on the Mac) and drag around the pixels you want to subtract.

- ✔ **Using the Magic Wand and Quick Selection tools:** Hold down the Alt key (Option key) and click the area you want to remove.

- ✔ **Using the Polygonal Lasso tool:** To subtract a straight-sided area, hold down the Alt key (Option key) and click and release around the area.

- ✔ **Using the Selection Brush tool:** Hold down the Alt key (Option key) and drag.

In Figure 2-2, we first selected the frame by using the Polygonal Lasso tool. We didn't use the obvious tool of choice — the Rectangular Marquee tool — because the frame wasn't completely straight. To deselect the inside of the frame from the selection, we again used the Polygonal Lasso tool, holding down the Alt key (Option key) and clicking at each corner of the inside of the frame to produce the selection that's shown.

© iStockphoto.com/leezsnow Image #4643106 and shauni Image #2008511

Figure 2-2: Press the Alt (or Option) key to delete from the existing selection.

Intersecting two selections

What happens when you hold down Shift+Alt (Shift+Option on the Mac) together? An *intersection,* that's what happens. Holding down both keys while dragging with the Lasso and Marquee tools, clicking and releasing with the Polygonal Lasso tool, or clicking with the Magic Wand tool all create the intersection of the original selection with the second selection.

Avoiding Keyboard Collisions

Elements has a little conflict in its methods. With so many ways of doing things, sometimes you may have to fiddle with Elements to get it to do what you want. For example, when you press the Shift key, how does Elements know whether you want to create a perfect square or add to a selection? Or what if you want to delete part of a selection while also drawing from the center outward? Both actions require the use of the Alt key (Option key on the Mac). You have a way out of this keyboard madness, and the following sections help you find it.

Adding a perfectly square or circular selection

To add a perfectly square or round selection to an existing selection, follow these steps:

1. **Hold down the Shift key and drag when using the Rectangular or Elliptical Marquee tool.**

   Your selection is unconstrained.

2. **While you drag, keeping your mouse button pressed, release the Shift key for just a moment and then press and hold it again.**

   Your unconstrained selection suddenly snaps into a constrained square or circle.

3. **Release the mouse button before you release the Shift key.**

   If you don't release the mouse button before you release the Shift key, the selection shape reverts to its unconstrained form.

You can bypass the keyboard shortcuts in the preceding steps list by using the various selection buttons on the left side of the Tool Options to add, subtract, or intersect to and from your selections.

Deleting from an existing selection while drawing from the center out

To delete part of a selection while drawing from the center out, as shown in Figure 2-3, follow these steps:

1. **Position your mouse cursor in the center of a selection; hold down the Alt key (Option key on the Mac) and drag when using the Rectangular or Elliptical Marquee tool.**

2. **While you drag, keeping your mouse button pressed, release the Alt key (Option key) for just a moment and then press and hold it again.**

   You're now drawing from the center outward.

3. **Release the mouse button before you release the Alt key (Option key).**

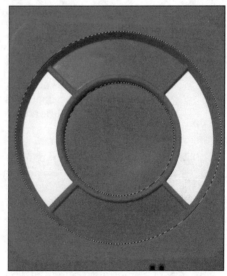

© iStockphoto.com/ericmichaud Image #3920691

Figure 2-3: You can delete from an existing selection and draw from the center outward simultaneously.

Using the Select Menu

Although you can add, subtract, and intersect selections by using the Shift and Alt keys (Option key on the Mac) and the selection option buttons in the Tool Options, you can do even more with the commands on the Select menu. On this menu, you find ways to expand, contract, smooth, and soften your selection and even turn your selection inside out. You can also use this menu to automatically select similar colors. If you use the Select menu, your selections should be ready and rarin' for action.

Selecting all or nothing

The All and Deselect commands are self-explanatory. To select everything in an image or, if it has layers, everything in the chosen layer, choose Select⇨ All or press Ctrl+A (⌘+A on the Mac). To deselect everything, choose Select⇨ Deselect, Ctrl+D (⌘+D on the Mac).

You rarely have to use All. If you don't have a selection border in the image, Elements assumes that you want to apply whatever command you execute to the entire image (or layer).

Reselecting a selection

If you've taken some valuable time to carefully lasso a spiky iguana from its perch on a mangrove tree, the last thing you want is to lose your hard-earned selection border. But that's what happens if you inadvertently click the image when you have an active selection border — it disappears.

Yes, technically, you can choose Edit⇨Undo if you catch your error right away. And you can access the History panel to recover your selection. But a much easier solution is to choose Select⇨Reselect, which retrieves your last selection.

The Reselect command works for only the last selection you made, so don't plan to reselect a selection you made last Wednesday — or even two minutes ago — if you've selected something else after that selection. If you want to reuse a selection for the long term, save it, as we explain in the section "Saving and loading selections," later in this chapter.

Inversing a selection

Sometimes, selecting what you don't want is easier than selecting what you do want. For example, if you're trying to select your cat Princess, photographed against a neutral background, why spend valuable time meticulously selecting her with the Lasso tool when you can just click the background with the Magic Wand tool?

After you select the background, as shown in Figure 2-4, just choose Select⇨ Inverse. *Voilà.* Princess is selected and obediently awaiting your next command.

Feathering a selection

In Chapter 1 of this minibook, we describe how to feather (soften or blur the edges of) a selection when using the Lasso and Marquee tools by entering a value in the Feather option in the Tool Options. This method of feathering requires that you set the Feather radius *before* you create your selection.

A problem may arise with feathering before you make your selection, if later you want to modify your initial selection. When you make a selection with a feather, the selection border adjusts to take into account the amount of the feather. So, the resulting marquee outline doesn't resemble your precise mouse movement. As a result, modifying, adding, or subtracting from your original selection is difficult.

© iStockphoto.com/
SchulteProductions Image #4615709

Figure 2-4: Sometimes, you want to select what you don't want and then inverse your selection.

A much better way to feather a selection is to make your initial selection without a feather, as shown in the left image of Figure 2-5. Clean up your selection as necessary and then apply your feather by choosing Select⇨Feather. In the dialog box, enter a radius value from 0.2 to 250 pixels and click OK. The resulting selection appears in the image on the right in Figure 2-5.

 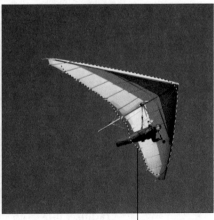

Original selection border   Border after feathering 20 pixels

© iStockphoto.com/Hanis Image #2054524

Figure 2-5: You can more easily clean up your selection before applying a feather.

The *radius* is how far out in all directions the feather extends. A radius of 8 means that the feather extends 4 pixels inward and 4 pixels outward from the selection outline. A large feather radius makes the image appear to fade out.

The Refine Edge command, which appears right after Feather on the Select menu, enables you to fine-tune selection edges by using various options. For full details on this option, see the section on free-form selecting with the Lasso tools in Chapter 1 of this minibook.

Using the Modify commands

The Select⇨Modify menu contains a group of modification commands that are lumped together categorically. You probably don't use these options every day, but sometimes they can come in handy. Here's the lowdown on each command:

- **Border:** Selects the area around the edge of the selection. You specify the width of the area from 1 to 200 pixels, and you create a border outline, as shown on the left in Figure 2-6. Choose Edit⇨Fill Selection and fill the border with color, as shown in the image on the right in Figure 2-6.

© iStockphoto.com/imv Image #2053920

Figure 2-6: The Border command creates a selection outline, which you can then fill with color.

- **Smooth:** Rounds off the nooks, crannies, and jagged edges. Enter a radius value from 1 to 100 pixels, and Elements looks at each selected pixel and then includes or deselects the pixels based on the radius value. If most pixels are selected, Elements includes the strays; if most pixels are deselected, Elements removes these pixels. Start with 2 pixels or so — and if that doesn't seem like enough, increase it by a few pixels.

Use this command with great caution. It's just too easy to produce mushy, inaccurate selections.

✔ **Expand:** Increases the size of your selection by a specified number of pixels, from 1 to 100. This command comes in handy if you just miss the edge of an elliptical selection and want to enlarge it a tad.

✔ **Contract:** Shrinks your selection by 1 to 100 pixels. When you're compositing multiple images, you can benefit by slightly contracting your selection if you plan to apply a feather. You can then avoid picking up a fringe of background pixels around your selection.

After you make a selection, contract it and then feather it before you drag it onto the canvas. This technique helps to create a natural-looking transition between the images in your composite. The amount you decide to contract and feather varies according to the resolution of the images. For example, if you're using low-resolution (72 pixels per inch, or *ppi*) images, you may want to use 1 pixel for the Contract amount and 0.5 pixels for the Feather amount; higher-resolution images may warrant 2 to 3 pixels for the Contract amount and 1 to 2 pixels for the Feather amount. If the word *resolution* makes you scratch your head, see Book III, Chapter 2.

Applying the Grow and Similar commands

The Grow and Similar commands are often mentioned in the same breath with the Magic Wand tool. If you didn't get the perfect selection on the first click — quite a common occurrence, unfortunately — you can use the Grow command. For example, to include more in your selection, you increase the Tolerance setting and try again: Hold down the Shift key and click the area to include. Or you can choose Select➪Grow. The Grow command increases the size of the selection by including adjacent pixels that fall within the range of tolerance.

The Similar command is like Grow, only the pixels don't have to be adjacent to be selected. The command searches throughout the image and picks up pixels within the tolerance range.

Both commands use the Tolerance value that's displayed in the Tool Options when you have the Magic Wand tool selected. Adjust the Tolerance setting to include more or fewer colors by increasing or decreasing the setting, respectively.

Saving and loading selections

If you've invested valuable time perfecting a complex selection, we highly recommend that you save it for future use. It's extremely easy to do and will prevent you from having to start from square one again. Here's what you do:

1. **After you make your selection, choose Select⇨Save Selection.**

2. **In the Save Selection dialog box, leave the Selection option set to New and enter a name for your selection, as shown in Figure 2-7.**

    The option defaults to New Selection.

© Kylie Obermeier

Figure 2-7: Save your selection to load for later use.

3. **Click OK.**

4. **When you want to access the selection again, choose Select⇨Load Selection and choose a selection from the Selection drop-down menu.**

    To inverse your selection, click the Invert box. Note that you also have options to add to, subtract from, or intersect with your selection. These options can come in handy if you want to modify your existing selection. For example, you may select just the head of a person and not the full body. You later decide that you need the whole person. Rather than make a whole new selection, you can select just the body and then choose Add to Selection, and you have your whole person. If you want, you can then save the whole person as a new selection for later use.

Moving and Cloning Selections

When you have your selection modified to perfection, you may then want to move it or clone it. To move a selection, simply grab the Move tool (the four-headed arrow) in the Tools panel and then drag the selection.

Sounds easy enough, right? When you move the selection, however, be warned that the area where the selection used to reside is now filled with the background color, as shown in Figure 2-8. It turns out, though, that the background color appears only if you decide to move both the selection outline and the image pixels. But you don't *have* to move both; you can move just the selection outline (without the pixels), as we explain in the section "Moving the selection outline, but not the pixels," later in this chapter. Also, if you're moving a selection on a layer, you're left with transparent pixels (see Book V).

Cloning

If you don't want to leave a hole in your image, you can copy and move the selection, leaving the original image intact, as shown in Figure 2-9. Just hold down the Alt key (Option key on the Mac) and drag when using the Move tool. This action is often referred to as *cloning* because you're essentially making a duplicate of a selected area and then moving that duplicate elsewhere.

Note that moving and cloning are considered the "old school" way to eliminate an element from your image. If you want to do it the newfangled way, be sure to check out the Content Aware option for the Spot Healing Brush and the Content-Aware Move tool, both described in Book VIII, Chapter 1. But just in case you don't get the results you want with those tools, you now know to use the tried-and-true tools as well.

Moving the selection outline, but not the pixels

If all you want to do is move the selection outline without moving the pixels underneath (for example, to better center an elliptical selection around whatever you want), avoid using the Move tool. Instead, choose any selection tool — a Marquee or Lasso tool — and then click anywhere inside the selection and just drag. That way, you move only the outline of the selection, not the pixels of the selection itself.

© iStockphoto.com/karma_pema
Image #2570387

Figure 2-8: When you move a selection by using the Move tool, you leave a hole that reveals the background color.

© iStockphoto.com/karma_pema
Image #2570387

Figure 2-9: Hold down the Alt (or Option) key while dragging to clone a selection without leaving a hole.

**Book IV
Chapter 2**

Modifying and Transforming Selections

Transforming Pixels

After you select an element, you may find that you need to resize or reorient it. *Transforming* involves scaling, rotating, skewing, distorting, flipping, or adjusting the perspective of your pixels. Although you may consider these types of transformations somewhat pedestrian, we're sure you'll find them practical and useful in your daily digital-imaging chores.

Follow these steps to transform a selection:

1. **Create your selection.**

   We leave this task up to you; just use your selection expertise (or refer to Chapter 1 of this minibook for assistance).

   You can also apply transformations to a layer or to multiple layers. (For more on this topic, see Book VI.)

2. **If you need to rotate the selection, choose Image⇨Rotate and then choose your desired rotation from the submenu:**

   - *Free Rotate Selection:* Enables you to manually rotate the selection.

   - *Rotate Selection 180°, 90° Left, or 90° Right:* Rotates the selection by the specified amounts.

   - *Flip Selection Horizontal or Vertical:* Flips your selection along the vertical or horizontal axis, respectively.

   The other rotate commands have to do with layers.

3. **To scale the selection, choose Image⇨Resize⇨Scale.**

4. **To freely transform, skew, distort, or adjust the perspective of a section, choose Image⇨Transform and then choose a transformation type from the submenu:**

   - *Free Transform:* Enables you to rotate, resize, skew, distort, and adjust perspective all within a single command.

   - *Skew:* Distorts your selection on a given axis.

   - *Distort:* Distorts your selection with no restrictions on an axis.

   - *Perspective:* Applies a one-point perspective to your selection.

   As soon as you select a distortion and release the mouse button, a *bounding box* or *transform box* surrounds your selection, complete with handles on the sides and corners. You don't get a bounding box when you select the Flip or Rotate (by degrees) transformations. (These commands are just applied to your image.)

5. **Depending on which transformation type you choose in Steps 2, 3, or 4, drag the appropriate handle:**

   - *Free Rotate:* Move the cursor outside the bounding box. When the cursor becomes a curved arrow, drag clockwise or counterclockwise. Hold down the Shift key to rotate in 15-degree increments.

     Remember that choosing Rotate 180°, 90° CW, or 90° CCW or Flip Horizontal or Vertical executes the command. Handle-dragging isn't necessary.

   - *Scale:* Corner handles work best for this transformation. Hold down the Shift key to scale proportionately. Hold down the Alt key (Option key on the Mac) to scale from the center.

   - *Skew:* Drag a side handle.

   - *Distort:* Drag a corner handle.

   - *Perspective:* Drag a corner handle.

   Elements executes all the transformations around a *reference point.* The reference point appears in the center of the transform box by default. You can move the reference point anywhere you want, even outside the bounding box. In addition, you can set your own reference point for the transformation by clicking a square on the reference point locator in the Tool Options. Each square corresponds to a point on the bounding box.

   You can also use the fields in the Tool Options to perform most of your transformations. After choosing any of the transformation commands from the menu, fields for a numeric entry to scale, rotate, and skew appear in the Tool Options.

   Execute all your transformations in one fell swoop, as shown in Figure 2-10, if possible. In other words, don't scale a selection now and then five minutes later rotate it, and then five minutes after that distort it. With the exception of flipping or rotating in 90-degree increments, every transformation you apply to an image results in a resampling. You should limit the number of times you resample an image, because it has a degrading effect — your image starts to appear soft and mushy.

6. **After you transform the selection to your liking, double-click inside the bounding box or click the Commit button next to the bounding box.**

   To cancel the transformation, press Esc or click the Cancel button next to the bounding box.

   Your selection is now magically transformed. If your image isn't on a layer, you can end up with a hole filled with the background color after your image is transformed. Check out Book VI on layers to avoid this calamity.

Book IV
Chapter 2

Modifying and Transforming Selections

Handle   Bounding box

Figure 2-10: Apply all transformations at the same time to minimize interpolation.

When the Move tool is active, you can transform a layer without choosing a command. Select the Show Bounding Box option in the Tool Options. This option surrounds the layer or selection with a box that has handles. Drag the handles to transform the layer or selection.

An efficient way to apply multiple transformations is to use the Free Transform command, which enables you to scale, rotate, skew, distort, or apply perspective within a single bounding box.

Book V
Painting, Drawing, and Typing

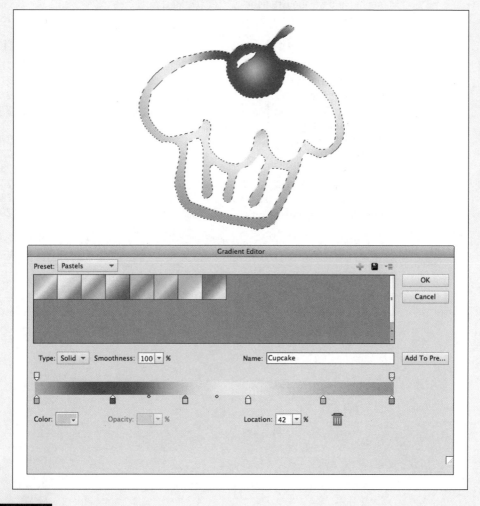

Contents at a Glance

Chapter 1: Painting and Drawing with Elements

In This Chapter

✓ **Making pencil sketches and brush strokes**

✓ **Using Brush presets**

✓ **Creating basic and custom shapes**

✓ **Editing shapes**

Feel free to keep on your street clothes for this chapter on drawing and painting. The tools you work with in Elements are self-cleaning and don't require that you wear a smock. Painting is a basic skill that you need to have down pat in Elements. After you get familiar with the technique of painting strokes and working with brushes, you're well on your way to mastering more advanced skills, such as retouching, which come easier to you if you already have some strong painting skills under your belt.

In tandem with painting, of course, comes drawing. The Elements shape tools add an important dimension to your drawing capabilities. This chapter introduces you to a plethora of tools and techniques. We start with painting and then move on to drawing. Master both, and they can serve you well.

Introducing the Pencil and Brush Tools

The Pencil and Brush tools are like chocolate and mint: They not only work well together but also share many important attributes. Just as important, however, are their differences. You can access these tools in the Tools panel. Press the B key to make the Brush tool appear by default. By pressing the B key again, you can toggle among the Brush tool, the Impressionist Brush, and the Color Replacement tools. You can also select the companion brush tools in the Tool Options. To access the Pencil, press the N key.

Drawing with the Pencil tool

The Pencil and Brush tools are similar, except that the Pencil tool has hard edges whereas the Brush tool can have soft, feathered edges. In fact, the edges of a pencil stroke can't even be *anti-aliased.* Keep in mind that if you draw anything other than vertical or horizontal lines, the lines have some jaggies when they're viewed up close. But hey, don't dismiss the Pencil. Those hard strokes can work great for web graphics because they lend themselves to producing crisp-edged images for display in a browser window. What's more, the Pencil tool can erase itself, and it's helpful for digital sketches, as shown in Figure 1-1.

© iStockphoto.com/Lok Fung Image #18537999

Figure 1-1: The Pencil tool draws hard-edged strokes and is used for digital sketches.

You can do all the following with the Pencil tool:

✏ Drag the mouse to draw freehand lines.

✏ Click at one point, release the mouse button, and then Shift-click at a second point to draw a straight line between the points. As long as you hold down the Shift key, you can keep clicking to draw straight lines between the last clicked point and the current click.

✏ Press the Alt key (the Option key on the Mac) and click any area of color in the drawing to switch the foreground color to that color.

To try out the Pencil tool, follow these steps:

1. **Select the Pencil tool from the Tools panel.**

   You can press the N key to access the tool.

2. **In the Tool Options, choose your pencil settings.**

   Options are

   • *Brush Preset Picker:* By default, the Pencil tool's brush tip is the 1-pixel brush. Click the arrow and select a brush from the Brush Preset Picker drop-down panel that appears. To load another preset library, click the Brush drop-down menu at the top of the panel. You also find options to save, rename, or delete individual brushes and also save, load, and reset brush libraries from the panel menu.

- *Size:* A preset brush's pixel diameters are shown as text below a thumbnail image of the brush shape. If you want to change the size of that brush tip, drag the Size slider or enter a value.

3. **If you want to draw using anything other than Normal mode, select a mode from the Mode drop-down menu in the Tool Options.**

   Blend modes alter the interaction of the color you're applying with the color on your canvas. See more on Blend modes in Book VI, Chapter 3.

4. **In the Tool Options, specify an Opacity percentage for your pencil strokes.**

   If you want your background to show partially through your strokes, select an opacity of less than 100 percent by using the slider or by typing an opacity percentage directly into the text box. The lower the percentage, the more the background images show through.

   Your strokes must be on a separate layer above your images for you to be able to adjust the opacity and Blend modes after you draw them. For more on layers, see Book VI, Chapter 1.

5. **Select Auto Erase to enable that option.**

   This option erases portions of your pencil strokes. For example, the foreground color might be black and the background color white, and you might apply some black strokes. With Auto Erase enabled, you apply white if you drag back over the black strokes. If you drag over the white background, you apply black.

6. **Click and drag with the mouse to create your pencil lines.**

Painting with the Brush tool

The Brush tool is a popular tool used throughout Elements in various incarnations, so getting to know this tool and how it operates is a good idea.

The most important difference between the Brush and the Pencil tools is that, by default, the Brush tool produces soft-edged lines, as shown in Figure 1-2. How soft those strokes are depends on which brush you use. By default, even the hardest brush has a slightly soft edge because it's anti-aliased. *Anti-aliasing*

Pencil stroke

Anti-aliased
brush stroke

Feathered
brush stroke

Figure 1-2: Strokes from the Pencil and Brush tools vary in the softness of their edges.

creates a single row of partially filled pixels along the edges to produce the illusion of a smooth edge. You can also get even softer brushes, which employ feathering.

Although jagged edges are most apparent in diagonal lines, Elements applies anti-aliasing to brush-stroke edges, even in horizontal and vertical lines.

The Brush tool shares most of the basic options found in the Pencil tool, except that the Auto Erase feature isn't available.

Here are a few tips on working with the Brush tool and its unique options:

- Select the Brush tool from the Tools panel or press the B key until you get the Brush.

- In the Tool Options, click the arrow and select a brush tip from the Brush Preset Picker drop-down panel that appears.

- Select a mode and opacity from the options in the Tool Options.

- Drag to paint, click and Shift-click to paint straight lines, and hold down the Shift key while dragging to constrain the Brush tool to horizontal or vertical lines.

- Press the Alt key (the Option key on the Mac) and click any area of color to switch the foreground color to that color.

The Brush tool has several other options:

- **Airbrush Mode:** Click the Airbrush button in the Tool Options to apply the Airbrush mode. This mode produces the spray effect you see with a traditional airbrush. The longer you hold down the mouse button, the more paint pumps out of the tool and the wider the airbrush effect spreads, as shown in Figure 1-3.

- **Tablet Settings:** If you're using a pressure-sensitive digital drawing tablet, check the settings you want the tablet to control, including size, scatter, opacity, roundness, and *hue jitter* (switching between foreground and background colors). The harder you press with the stylus, the greater the effect of these options.

© iStockphoto.com/Beano5 Image #14501558

Figure 1-3: Using the Airbrush mode with the Brush tool enables you to create varied strokes.

✓ **Brush Settings:** In the Tool Options, click Brush Settings to access additional options that enable you to change the brush strokes as you apply them. Here's a quick lowdown on each option (and the way they impact the brush effect, as shown in Figure 1-4):

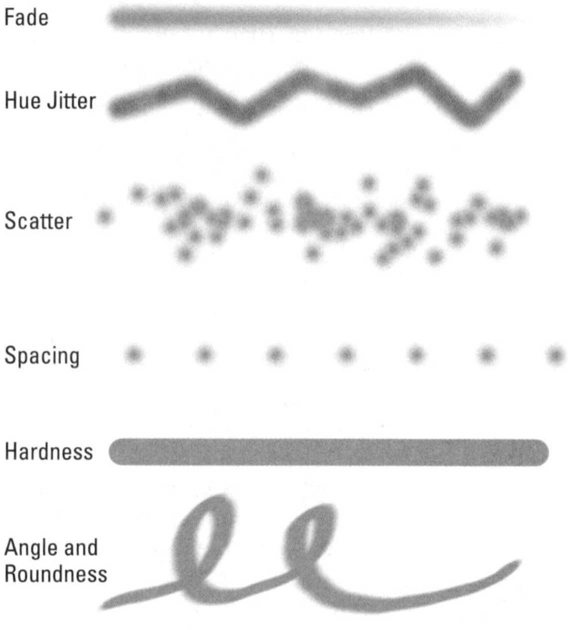

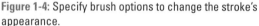

- *Fade:* The lower the value, the quicker the stroke fades. Zero, however, creates no fade.

- *Hue Jitter:* This option varies the stroke between the foreground and background colors. The higher the value, the more frequent the variation.

- *Scatter:* The higher the value, the higher the number of brush marks and the farther apart they are.

Figure 1-4: Specify brush options to change the stroke's appearance.

- *Spacing:* The higher the number, the more space between marks.

- *Hardness:* The higher the value, the harder the brush.

- *Roundness:* A setting of 100 percent is totally circular. The lower the percentage, the more elliptical your brush becomes.

- *Angle:* If you create an oval brush by adjusting the roundness, this option controls the angle of that oval brush stroke. You can more easily drag the points and the arrow on the diagram than "guesstimate" values in the text boxes.

- *Set this as a default:* You can lock in these brush options by selecting this check box, ensuring that every brush you select adopts these settings.

Just as they do for the Pencil tool, more features for the Brush tool appear on the Brush Preset Picker panel menu. (Click the arrow at the top of the panel.) Here's a quick explanation of what you can do with each one:

- ✔ **Save Brush:** Save a custom brush as a preset. See the following section for details.

- ✔ **Rename Brush:** Don't like the name of your brush? Give it a new one with this option.

- ✔ **Delete Brush:** Eliminate an unwanted brush with this option.

- ✔ **Reset Brushes:** Revert your current brush library to the default.

- ✔ **Load Brushes:** Load a preset or custom brush library. They have names such as Special Effect Brushes and Faux Finish Brushes. Select one to append the brushes to your current set or to replace the current set with the library you select. (The dialog box that appears offers a choice of either action.)

- ✔ **Save Brushes:** Save custom brushes in a separate library.

- ✔ **The display options:** A set of commands that enables you to change the way your brush tips are displayed in the drop-down panel. The default view is Stroke Thumbnail, which displays the appearance of the stroke. Other commands include Text Only (text names of brush tips), Small and Large Thumbnail (thumbnail images with diameter in pixels), and Small and Large List (thumbnail images with text names).

You can also manage brush tip libraries by using the Preset Manager option available from the panel menu or by choosing Edit⇨Preset Manager.

Getting artsy with the Impressionist Brush

The Impressionist Brush is designed to paint over photos in a way that makes them look like fine-art paintings. The best way to get familiar with the Impressionist Brush is to open your favorite image and experiment with the tool. You can set various options that change the style of the brush strokes.

Here's how to use this artistic brush:

1. **Select the Impressionist Brush from the Tools panel.**

   It looks like a brush with a curlicue next to it. You can also press the B key to cycle through the various brushes.

2. **Set the brush options.**

   The Brushes Presets, Size, Mode, and Opacity options are identical to those for the Brush tool, described in the previous section. You can also find some unique options on the Advanced panel:

- *Style:* This drop-down list contains various brush stroke styles, such as Dab and Tight Curl.

- *Area:* Control the size of your brush stroke. The larger the value, the larger the area covered.

- *Tolerance:* Control how similar color pixels have to be before they're changed by the brush stroke.

© iStockphoto.com/t-lorien Image #5272702

Figure 1-5: The Impressionist Brush transforms your photo into a painting.

3. **Drag on your image and paint with your brush strokes, as shown in Figure 1-5.**

Creating a custom brush

After playing with the various options, if you like the personalized brush you've created, save it as a preset so that you can access it again and again. Click the arrow at the top of the Brush Preset Picker panel and choose Save Brush from the menu. Name the brush and click OK. Your new, custom brush shows up at the bottom of the Brush Preset Picker drop-down panel.

You have one other way to create a brush. Elements enables you to create a brush from all or part of your image. The image can be a photograph or something you've painted or drawn.

Here's how to create a brush from your image:

1. **Select part of an image with any of the selection tools.**

   If you want to use the entire image or entire layer, deselect everything. (For more on selections, see Book IV, Chapter 1.)

2. **Choose Edit⇨Define Brush or Edit⇨Define Brush from Selection.**

   You see one command or the other, depending on what you do in Step 1.

3. **Name the brush and click OK in the dialog box.**

   The new brush shows up at the bottom of the Brush Preset Picker drop-down panel. Note that your brush is only a grayscale version of your image. When you use the brush, it automatically applies the color you've selected as the foreground color, as shown in Figure 1-6.

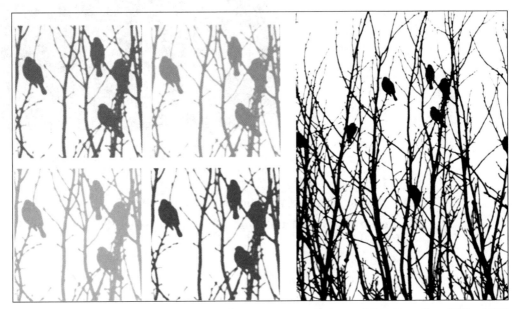

© iStockphoto.com/Flutter_97321 Image #40880

Figure 1-6: Create a custom brush from a portion of your image.

Creating Shapes

Although we're big fans of photos and pixels, sometimes you have the need for a vector shape or two. Maybe you need to create a button for a web page or a simple logo for a poster. In these instances, drawing a vector shape with one of the shape tools does the job.

Before we discuss the ins and outs of creating shapes, here's a little overview that explains the difference between pixels and vectors (both types are shown in Figure 1-7):

✔ **Pixel images describe a shape in terms of a grid of pixels.** When you increase the size of a pixel-based image, it loses quality and begins to look blocky, mushy, and otherwise nasty. For more details on resizing pixel-based images and the ramifications of doing so, see Book III, Chapter 2.

✔ **Vectors describe a shape mathematically.** The shapes comprise paths made up of lines, curves, and anchor points. Because vector shapes are math based, you can resize them with no loss of quality.

When you create a shape in Elements, you're creating a vector-based element. Shapes reside on a special kind of layer called, not surprisingly, a shape layer.

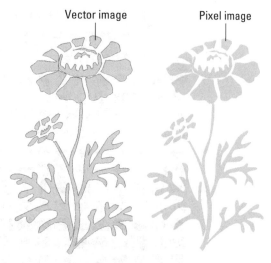

Vector image　　　　Pixel image

Figure 1-7: Elements images fall into one of two camps: vector or pixel.

Drawing a shape

Elements offers an assortment of shape tools for you to choose from. Follow these steps to draw a shape in your document:

1. **Select a shape tool from the Tools panel.**

   You can also press the U key to cycle through the tools. You can select from the following shape tools, shown in Figure 1-8:

   - *Rectangle/Ellipse:* The Rectangle and Ellipse shapes have no special parameters in the Tool Options; however, they both behave much like their counterparts among the selection tools. Hold down the Shift key while dragging a shape to produce a perfect square or circle; hold down Shift+Alt (Shift+Option on the Mac) to additionally draw the shape outward from the center.

   - *Rounded Rectangle:* This shape has the same options as the Rectangle, with the addition of a radius value used to round off the corners of the rectangle.

   - *Polygon and Star:* This tool creates a polygon with a specified number of sides, from 3 to 100. You can also create a star with the same possible number of convex vertices (or corners).

   - *Line:* Creates a line with a width from 1 to 1000 pixels. You can also add an arrowhead at either end or both ends.

   - *Custom Shape:* You can find numerous preset custom shapes to choose from, as shown in Figure 1-8. As with any shape, hold down the Shift key to constrain proportions or the Alt key (Option key on the Mac) to draw from the center out.

   - *Shape Selection:* Use this tool to select and move your shapes.

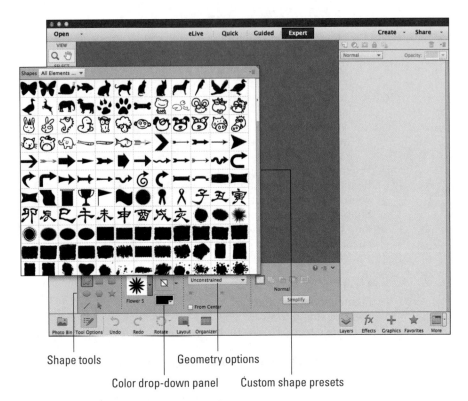

Shape tools   Geometry options

Color drop-down panel   Custom shape presets

Figure 1-8: The shape tools and Tool Options give you all you need to make shapes, from the simple to the ornate.

2. **In the Tool Options, click the down arrow above the (W) and (H) fields to specify Geometry options.**

   Each shape has its own options. For a detailed explanation, see the section "Specifying Geometry options," later in this chapter.

   If you chose the Custom Shape tool in Step 1, click the down arrow to access the drop-down Custom Shapes panel, shown in Figure 1-8, and choose a shape. You can access more preset shape libraries via the drop-down menu at the top of the panel.

3. **Select a color from the Color drop-down panel in the Tool Options.**

   Click the color wheel icon at the bottom of the panel to access the Color Picker for additional color choices.

4. **Select a style from the Style Picker drop-down panel.**

   To spice up the shape with bevels and interesting edges, choose a style from the panel. For more on styles, see Book VII, Chapter 3.

5. **Drag in the document to draw the shape you've defined.**

   The shape appears in the Image window on its own shape layer. Check out the Layers panel to see this phenomenon. Figure 1-9 shows our shape, an Elvis 'do.

Drawing multiple shapes on a shape layer

Figure 1-9: Custom shapes run the gamut from the ordinary to the exotic.

After you create a shape layer, you can draw additional shapes on that layer. You can add, subtract, exclude overlapping, and intersect shapes in exactly the same way you do with selections, as described in Book IV, Chapter 2. Follow these steps:

1. **After you create the first shape, as we explain in the preceding section, select a state button in the Tool Options:**

   • *Add to Shape Area:* Combines and joins two or more shapes.

   • *Subtract from Shape Area:* Subtracts one shape from another shape.

   • *Intersect Shape Areas:* Creates a shape only from the areas that overlap.

   • *Exclude Overlapping Shape Areas:* Creates a shape from only the areas that don't overlap.

2. **Choose a shape tool and draw the next shape.**

   We finished our drawing, as shown in Figure 1-10, by adding a face to our Elvis impersonator.

   You can also hold down the Shift key to temporarily switch to Add to Shape Area while drawing a new shape. Hold down the Alt key (Option key on the Mac) to temporarily switch to Subtract from Shape Area. It works just like adding or subtracting selections.

Figure 1-10: Add to your shape layer.

Specifying Geometry options

Geometry options for your shapes help define how the shapes look. Click the down arrow at the end of the row of Shape tools in the Tool Options to access the Geometry options described in the following sections.

Rectangle and Rounded Rectangle Geometry options

Here's what the Geometry options for the Rectangle and Rounded Rectangle shapes let you do:

- ✔ **Unconstrained:** Freely draw a rectangle of any shape or size.

- ✔ **Square:** Constrain the shape to a perfect square. (You can also hold down the Shift key to do the same thing on the fly.)

- ✔ **Fixed Size:** Draw rectangles only in fixed sizes. Specify the exact size by entering a width and height.

- ✔ **Proportional:** Define an aspect ratio, or proportion, for the rectangle. Type 3 into the W box and 4 into the H box to constrain yourself to drawing any rectangle size with fixed proportions in a 3:4 ratio.

- ✔ **From Center:** Draw the shape from the center outward.

- ✔ **Snap:** Align the edges of a rectangle or rounded rectangle to the pixels on your screen.

- ✔ **Radius:** For rounded rectangles, use an inscribed circle of the given radius to round off the corners of a rectangle.

Elliptical-shape Geometry options

The Ellipse shape has many of the same options available for rectangles. Of course, rather than being able to create a perfect square, you can constrain the shape to be a perfect circle. Also, the Snap to Pixels option (available for rectangles) doesn't exist for ellipses.

Polygon and Star Geometry options

These are the Geometry options for the polygon and star:

- ✔ **Sides:** Lets you indicate the number of sides for the polygon or points for a star.

- ✔ **Smooth: Corners:** Rounds off the corners.

- ✔ **Indent:** Determines the amount the sides of the star indent inward.

- ✔ **Smooth: Indents:** Rounds off the indents of the star.

Line Geometry options

The Line shape's Geometry settings include whether to put arrowheads at the start or end of the line, neither, or both. You can also specify the width, length, and concavity settings, which affect the arrowhead shapes.

Custom Shape Geometry options

The Custom Shape options are similar to those you can find for the other shapes — with a couple of additions:

- ✔ **Defined Proportions:** Draws a shape based on the original proportions you used when you created it.

- ✔ **Defined Size:** Draws a shape based on its original size when you created it.

Editing shapes

You can edit shapes you create by using a variety of tools and techniques. Here's a list of the things you can do to modify your shapes:

- **Select:** Choose the Shape Selection tool in the Tool Options to move one or more shapes in their layers.

- **Move:** Choose the Move tool (press the V key) to move the entire contents of the shape layer.

- **Delete:** Select a shape and press Delete to remove it.

- **Transform shapes:** Choose the Shape Selection tool and select your shape. Choose Image➪Transform Shape and then choose your transformation.

- **Change the color:** Double-click the thumbnail of the shape layer on the Layers panel. This action takes you to the Color Picker, where you can choose a new color.

- **Clone a shape:** Hold down the Alt key (Option key on the Mac) and move the shape with the Move tool.

To convert your vector-based shape into a pixel-based shape, click the Simplify button in the Tool Options or choose Layer➪Simplify Layer. Note that you can't edit a shape after you simplify it, except to modify the pixels. But you can now apply filters to the layer. See Book VII, Chapter 1 for more on fun with filters.

Chapter 2: Filling and Stroking

In This Chapter

🖙 **Adding color to a selection**

🖙 **Filling with the Paint Bucket tool**

🖙 **Adding a stroke around a selection**

🖙 **Working with gradients**

🖙 **Creating and applying patterns**

*E*lements offers several ways to create things like geometric shapes out of pixels. Filling and stroking such elements are two of the most popular commands at your disposal. The Fill command adds a color or a pattern to the entire selection, whereas the Stroke command applies the color to only the selection border.

This chapter shows you how to fill and stroke your selections. If filling and stroking with a solid color is just too mundane for you, we also show you how to create and apply multicolored gradient blends as well as the best ways to make and use patterns. After reading this chapter, you'll have your "fill" of different fills and strokes.

Open the Photo Editor in Expert mode for your filling, stroking, gradient, and pattern activities.

Filling a Selection with a Solid Color

You won't find a Fill tool in the Tools panel. Elements avoids the crowded panel and places the Fill and Stroke commands on the Edit menu. When you want to fill your selection with just a solid color, you can use either the foreground or the background color, among other options. (These colors appear at the bottom of the Tools panel, as we explain in Book III, Chapter 4.)

The following steps show you the basics of filling a selection with either the foreground or background color:

1. **Choose the selection tool of your choice and create your selection on a layer.**

Although you don't have to create a new layer, we recommend it. That way, if you don't like the filled selection, you can delete the layer, and the image or background below it remains safe. See Book IV for all you need to know about selections and Book VI for the scoop on layers.

2. **In the Tools panel, select either the foreground or the background color and then choose a fill color.**

3. **Choose Edit⇨Fill Selection.**

   Note that if you don't have an active selection border in your image, the command says Fill Layer and the entire layer is filled with your color or pattern.

   The Fill Layer dialog box, appears.

4. **Choose a fill from the Use drop-down menu.**

   You can select whether to fill with the foreground or background color.

   You also can choose Color, Black, 50% Gray, White, or Pattern. If you select Color or Pattern, you must complete a couple additional steps, described in the next section.

   You can now also fill your selection using the Content-Aware option which fills your selection with pixels sampled from content nearby. For more details on this new option, see Book VII, Chapter 1.

5. **In the Blending area, specify whether to preserve transparency.**

   This option enables you to fill only the portions of the selection that contain pixels (the nontransparent areas).

   Although you can also choose a *blend mode* (how the fill color interacts with colors below it) as well as an opacity percentage in the Fill Layer dialog box, we don't recommend doing so. Making adjustments on your layer later using the Layers panel commands gives you more flexibility for editing.

6. **Click OK.**

   The color or pattern you chose fills the selection.

Filling Options and Tips

After you make a selection, you're ready to use one of the fill options. You can use the Fill Layer dialog box (as described in the preceding section) to fill the selection with the foreground or background color; you can also choose to fill the selection with color, black, white, or gray. Elements is full of shortcuts and options.

Here are just a few. With the selection active, you can do any of the following:

🖛 Press Alt+Backspace (Option+Delete on the Mac) to fill the selection with the foreground color. All areas within the selection, including transparent areas, fill with the color.

🖛 Press Alt+Shift+Backspace (or Option+Shift+Delete on the Mac) to fill only the pixels in a selection with the foreground color, leaving any transparent pixels untouched.

🖛 If you're working on the Background layer, you can also fill the selection with the background color by pressing the Backspace (Delete on the Mac) key.

🖛 By selecting the Color option from the Use drop-down menu in the Fill Layer dialog box, you access the Color Picker, where you can select any color your heart desires to fill your selection.

🖛 Select the Pattern option from the Use drop-down menu in the Fill Layer dialog box to fill the selection with a pattern. Click the arrow next to the pattern swatch and select a pattern from the drop-down panel. Click OK. To access additional pattern libraries, click the Pattern panel menu to select more pattern libraries.

🖛 Paint part or the entire interior of the selection by using a Pencil or Brush tool. This option lets you partially fill a selection using a bit of flexibility and creativity. When you paint a selection using Brush tools, Elements confines the paint inside the boundaries of your selection, as shown in Figure 2-1. For more on painting, see Chapter 1 in this minibook.

🖛 Pour color from the Paint Bucket tool into the selection. (See more details in the next section.)

Figure 2-1: The Marquee confines your brush strokes to the selected area.

Pouring with the Paint Bucket Tool

The Paint Bucket tool operates much like a combination of the Fill command tool and the Magic Wand tool. It makes a selection based on similarly colored pixels and then immediately fills that selection with color or a pattern. Just like the Magic Wand tool, this tool is used most successfully when you have a limited number of colors, as shown in Figure 2-2.

© iStockphoto.com/Liliboas Image #8559596

Figure 2-2: Select and fill your background simultaneously with the Paint Bucket tool.

To use the Paint Bucket tool, select it and click the area you want to fill with color. If you want a more precise fill, first make a selection and then click inside the selection border. It's as simple as that. Before you click, however, specify your options, which are all in the Tool Options:

- ✐ **Paint:** Select whether to fill with the Foreground color or a Pattern.

- ✐ **Pattern:** If you select Pattern, select a preset pattern from the drop-down panel. You can also load patterns from pattern libraries or create a pattern of your own. Find more information on patterns in the section "Working with Patterns," later in this chapter.

- ✐ **Opacity:** Adjust this value to make the fill more or less transparent.

- ✐ **Tolerance:** Just as you did with the Magic Wand tool, choose a tolerance level (from 0 to 255) that specifies how similar in color a pixel must be before it's selected and then filled. For more on tolerance, see Book IV, Chapter 1.

✔ **Mode:** Select a blending mode to change how the fill color interacts with the color below it. Find details on these modes in Book VI, Chapter 3.

✔ **All Layers:** This option selects and fills pixels within the selection in all layers that are within the tolerance range.

✔ **Contiguous:** If selected, this option selects and fills only pixels that are touching within your selection. If the option is deselected, pixels are selected and filled wherever they lie within your selection and within your tolerance range.

✔ **Anti-aliasing:** Choose this option to smooth the edges between the filled and unfilled areas.

As with other tools that fill, you can prevent the Paint Bucket tool from filling the transparent pixels. Just select the Lock Transparent Pixels icon (lock and checkerboard icon) at the top of the Layers panel.

Stroking a Selection

Stroking enables you to create colored outlines, or borders, of selections or layers. It's up to you to decide whether to put the border inside, outside, or centered on the selection.

To stroke a selection, follow these steps:

1. **In the Tools panel, choose a foreground color.**

2. **In the image, make a selection on a layer using the selection tool of your choice.**

   Although you don't have to create a new layer to stroke a selection, we recommend it. That way, if you don't like the stroked selection, you can just delete the layer and your document remains unadulterated.

3. **Choose Edit⇨Stroke (Outline) Selection.**

4. **In the Stroke dialog box, specify options, as shown in Figure 2-3:**

   • *Width:* Enter a width of 1 to 250 pixels.

   • *Color:* Click in the Color box to select the hue that you want from the Color Picker.

   • *Location:* Specify how Elements should apply the stroke in relation to your selection border. Note that the Inside option always gives you sharp corners on a rectangle. The Center and Outside options can result in blunt corners.

   • *Mode:* Determine how the stroke color interacts with other colors on the same layer.

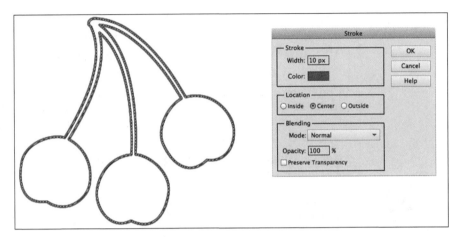

Figure 2-3: Apply strokes up to 250 pixels wide to your selection.

- *Opacity:* The default value is 100%. If you want the stroke to be semi-transparent, enter a lower value.

- *Preserve Transparency:* Select this option to apply the stroke to only nontransparent pixels. Note that if you choose this option on a new, blank layer, nothing is stroked.

5. **Click OK to apply the stroke.**

   We gave a 10-pixel centered stroke to our selection (see Figure 2-4).

Rather than use the Stroke dialog box to adjust the Mode and Opacity settings, we recommend creating a new layer for the stroke and then choosing different Mode and Opacity settings in the Layers panel. This approach gives you better flexibility in editing.

Working with Multicolored Gradients

If one color just doesn't get you fired up, you'll be happy to know that Elements enables you to fill a selection or layer with a *gradient,* a blend of one or more colors that gradually dissolves from one into another or into transparency. Elements provides numerous preset gradients. But creating your own custom gradient is also fun and simple.

You can create the following gradient effects:

- **Foreground to background:** A transition from the current foreground color to the background color

- **Foreground to transparent:** A transition from the current foreground color to transparent, allowing whatever's under the transparent portion to show through

✔ **Black to white:** A transition from black to white

✔ **An array of colorful selections:** A transition including rainbows, coppery sheens, and other effects

You can load other libraries of gradients from those found on the menu of the Gradient panel. They have names such as Color Harmonies, Metals, and Special Effects.

In addition to being able to control the appearance and application of a gradient, you can also specify various Gradient options, which are all in the Tool Options:

✔ **Mode:** Select a blending mode to change how the color of the gradient interacts with the colors below it.

✔ **Opacity:** Select how opaque or transparent the gradient is.

✔ **Reverse:** Reverse the order in which the colors are applied.

✔ **Transparency:** Deselect this option to make Elements ignore any transparent areas in the gradient, making them opaque instead.

✔ **Dither:** Add *noise,* or random information, to produce a smoother gradient that prints with less *banding* (color stripes caused by the limitations of the printing process to reproduce a full range of colors).

Applying a preset gradient to a selection

Here's how to apply a preset gradient:

1. **Select the layer from the Layers panel.**

   If you want the gradient to fill only a portion of that layer, make your selection.

   We recommend making the selection on a new layer so that you can edit the gradient later without harming the underlying image.

   If you don't make a selection, the gradient is applied to the entire layer or background.

2. **Select the Gradient tool from the Tools panel or press the G key.**

3. **Select one of the preset gradients from the Gradient Picker drop-down menu in the Tool Options.**

   Remember that you can find other preset libraries by clicking the Gradient menu at the top of the Gradient Picker panel. Libraries, such as Color Harmonies and Metals, contain interesting presets.

4. **Select the gradient type by clicking an icon in the Tool Options.**

   Figure 2-4 illustrates each gradient type:

- *Linear:* Blends the colors of the gradient in a straight line.

- *Radial:* Blends the colors outward in a circular pattern.

- *Angle:* Creates a counterclockwise sweep around the starting point, resembling a radar screen.

- *Reflected:* Blends the colors by using symmetrical linear gradients on either side of the starting point.

- *Diamond:* Blends the colors outward in a diamond pattern.

5. **Choose any other options you want from the Tool Options.**

   We explain these options earlier in this section.

6. **Place the cursor at the position in the layer or selection where you want to place the starting color of the gradient.**

7. **Drag in any direction to the end point for the gradient.**

   Longer drags result in a more subtle transition between colors, whereas shorter drags result in a more abrupt transition. Hold down the Shift key while dragging to constrain the direction of the gradient so that it's perfectly horizontal or vertical or at an exact 45-degree angle.

8. **Release the mouse button to apply the gradient.**

   We applied a pastel radial gradient to a selection of an abstract symbol in Figure 2-5.

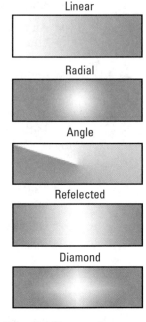

Linear

Radial

Angle

Refelected

Diamond

Figure 2-4: You can choose from five gradient types.

Figure 2-5: Fill your selection with a multicolored gradient.

Customizing and editing gradients

Although Elements includes dozens of gradient presets, you may want to create your own. The Gradient Editor makes that task an easy one by letting you create a custom gradient with as many colors as you want, which you can then save as a preset and reuse at any time.

The Gradient Editor has many options, but it's easy to use when you know what the controls and options do. Follow these steps to create a simple, smooth gradient:

1. **Select the Gradient tool from the Tools panel or press the G key.**

2. **Click the Edit button in the Tool Options.**

   The Gradient Editor dialog box opens, as shown in Figure 2-6.

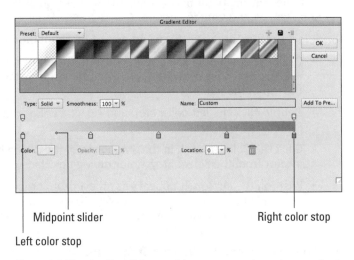

Midpoint slider   Right color stop

Left color stop

Figure 2-6: The Gradient Editor enables you to create custom gradients.

3. **Pick an existing gradient preset from the Presets area to use as the basis for your new gradient.**

4. **Choose Solid or Noise from the Type drop-down menu.**

   As soon as you start to edit the existing gradient, the name of the gradient changes to Custom. A noise gradient is one containing random colors. Because the colors are random, each time you create a noise gradient, the result is different.

5. **If you chose a Solid gradient in Step 4, adjust the Smoothness percentage to determine how smoothly one color blends into another.**

6. **If you chose a Noise gradient in Step 4, specify the options that follow and then skip to Step 15 to finish the gradient.**

   - *Roughness:* Adjust this slider to determine how smoothly or abruptly the colors transition from one stop to another.

   - *Color Model:* Select the color model to set the range of color and get the corresponding color sliders to adjust, if desired.

   - *Restrict Colors:* Select this option to avoid oversaturated colors.

- *Add Transparency:* Select this option to include transparency in your gradient, if desired.

- *Randomize:* Use this option to change the colors in the gradient. Each time you click Randomize, you see a new set of colors.

7. **If you're creating a solid gradient, define the color of the starting point for your gradient; click the left color stop under the gradient bar.**

   The triangle above the stop turns black to indicate that you're working with the starting point of the gradient. Because Noise gradients are random, you can't define the colors.

8. **Select the starting color by using one of these methods:**

   - Click the down-pointing arrow to access the Color menu. You can also access other color libraries from the Color Swatches menu at the top of the panel.

   - Double-click the left color stop and select a color from the Color Picker that appears.

   - Click the Color swatch in the Stops area of the dialog box and choose a color from the Select Stop Color dialog box that opens.

   - Position the cursor (it appears as an eyedropper icon) anywhere on the gradient bar to select a start color from the bar, or position the cursor anywhere within an image on your screen and then click to select the color under the cursor.

9. **Click the end-point color stop at the right side of the gradient bar and use any of the methods described in Step 8 to choose the end color of the gradient.**

10. **Change the percentage of the amount of one color versus the other by moving the starting and ending points to the left or right; drag the midpoint slider (a diamond icon that appears when you click an adjacent color stop) to adjust where the colors mix equally, 50–50.**

    You can also change the position of the midpoint by selecting it and typing a value into the Location box. The position of the color stops can also be changed this way.

11. **(Optional) To add another color, click below the gradient bar at the position you want to add the color and define a color using the new color stop as you did in Step 8.**

12. **(Optional) Repeat Step 11 for additional colors.**

13. **For additional color stops, move the stops to the left or right to adjust the location of the start and end points for each color; adjust the midpoint sliders between the colors.**

14. **If you change your mind, redefine the color of the color stop or remove a color stop altogether by dragging it down or up from its position on the gradient bar.**

15. **After your edits are complete, enter a name for your gradient in the Name field and then click the New button.**

    Your gradient is added to the Presets menu. Figure 2-7 shows an example of a unique gradient that we created in the Gradient Editor.

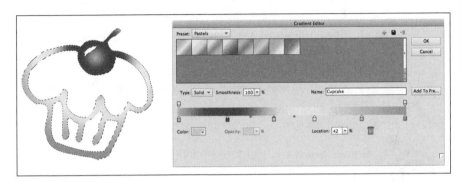

Figure 2-7: The Gradient Editor gives you more creative license than the presets.

Adding transparency to a gradient

By default, a gradient has 100 percent opacity in the start color and progresses to 100 percent opacity in the end color. If you like, you can have the gradient fade out to transparency so that the portion of the image under the gradient shows through. To add transparency to a gradient, follow these steps:

1. **Create a gradient, as described in the preceding section.**

2. **Select the left opacity stop.**

   This stop is located just above the gradient bar, as shown in Figure 2-8.

3. **Use the Opacity slider to specify the amount of transparency for the gradient at its start point.**

   You can also type a value into the Opacity box.

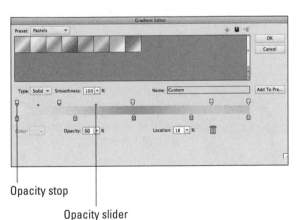

Opacity stop

Opacity slider

Figure 2-8: Add transparency to your gradients by adjusting the opacity of your colors.

4. **Select the right opacity stop and then slide the Opacity slider, or enter a percentage in the text box to specify transparency for the gradient at its end point.**

   The lower the percentage, the less opaque the color.

5. **Move the opacity stops to the right or left to adjust the location where Elements applies each stop's opacity setting.**

6. **Move the midpoint slider (diamond icon) to adjust how the color and the transparency blend.**

7. **Click above the gradient bar to add more opacity stops if you want to vary the transparency of the gradient at different points.**

   For example, you can fade transparency from 100 percent to 50 percent and back to 100 percent to produce a particular effect.

Gradients ordinarily proceed smoothly from one color to another. If you want a less homogeneous appearance, adjust the Smoothness slider to a value of less than 100 percent. (Click the right-pointing arrow to access the slider.)

Managing and Saving Gradients

After taking the time to create custom gradients, store them so that you can use or edit them again later. Before you save them, however, be sure to add them to the gradient presets. (See the section "Customizing and editing gradients," earlier in this chapter.) Here are some tips for managing gradients:

- **To save your set of gradients,** click the Save button (disk icon) in the Gradient Editor dialog box. You save the current presets, including your new gradient, under the current library's name or another one you choose.

- **To load gradient presets into the Gradient Editor,** click the Load button (green plus sign icon) and select the name of the gradient library you want to add to the Presets list.

- **To add to the current presets,** click the Add to Preset/Create a New Gradient Preset button.

Working with Patterns

You may have spotted someone on the golf course with plaid shorts and a striped polo shirt. If so, you've been introduced to the power of patterns. Not always a pretty sight when used with abandon, patterns can be used to fill selections or layers. You can also stamp your image with the Pattern Stamp tool and retouch using a pattern with the Healing Brush tool. Elements offers several preset patterns to keep you happy. But you can create your own, of course.

You select patterns from panels that appear in the Tool Options for many of the tools just mentioned, just as you do with brush tips and gradients. You also manage them in much the same way using the Preset Manager. The following sections show you how to apply a preset pattern and create your own.

Applying a preset pattern

Although you can apply patterns by using many different tools, this chapter sticks with applying patterns as fills. To fill a layer or selection with a preset pattern, follow these steps:

1. **Choose the layer from the Layers panel and/or make the selection you want to fill with a pattern.**

   We recommend making your selection on a new layer above the image for more flexible editing later.

2. **Choose Edit⇨Fill Selection or Fill Layer and then select Pattern from the Use drop-down menu, as shown in Figure 2-9.**

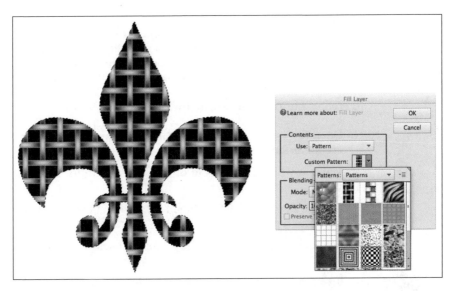

Figure 2-9: Fill the selection with one of the many other preset patterns.

3. **Click the arrow next to the Custom Pattern swatch, and then from the Custom Pattern drop-down panel, select your pattern.**

4. **Choose any other fill options you want to apply, such as Mode, Opacity, or Preserve Transparency.**

   The Preserve Transparency option prevents Elements from filling the transparent areas on your layer with a pattern.

If you choose this option on a new, blank layer, nothing is filled. (For details on the other options, see the section "Filling a Selection with a Solid Color," earlier in this chapter.)

We recommend adjusting the Mode and Opacity settings in the Layers panel rather than in the Fill Layer dialog box. This approach allows you maximum flexibility if you want to make edits later.

5. **Click OK to fill the layer or selection with the chosen pattern.**

Here are a few other tips for working with preset patterns:

- Replace the current patterns with new patterns by selecting Replace Patterns from the panel menu. (Click the right-pointing arrow on the right side of the panel.) Then select the new pattern library from the dialog box that appears.

- Append new patterns to the current set by selecting Load Patterns from the panel menu. Note that any patterns you add must have a .pat file extension.

Creating a new pattern

You can create your own pattern, basing it on an existing image or one you create yourself. Select a small portion of an image to build an abstract pattern or use a recognizable object to define that object as a pattern stamp. You can use anything, from a logo to your signature, as a pattern.

To create your own pattern, follow these steps:

1. **Open the image that contains the area you want to use as a pattern or create an image from scratch.**

2. **Make any modifications to the image to produce the exact pattern you want.**

3. **Use the Rectangular Marquee tool to select the area you want to convert into a pattern.**

   If you don't make a selection, Elements uses your entire image as a basis for the pattern.

   If you're using a selection to define your pattern, you must use a rectangular selection. And you can't use a feathered selection of any kind.

4. **Choose Edit⇨Define Pattern from Selection or Edit⇨Define Pattern.**

5. **Enter a name for your pattern in the Pattern Name dialog box.**

   Your new pattern appears in the Pattern panel for use.

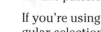

In addition to filling your selection with a pattern, you can stamp on a pattern using the Pattern Stamp tool. For details, see Book I, Chapter 2.

Chapter 3: Working with Type

In This Chapter

⌐ **Understanding type basics**

⌐ **Getting to know the Type tools and modes**

⌐ **Entering and editing text**

⌐ **Simplifying a type layer**

⌐ **Exploring masking, shaping, and warping effects**

*Y*es, images are powerful. But so are words. In fact, humans tend to remember images better when they're combined with words. This is why we don't recall our dreams well — no words are paired with the images. Enough psychobabble. You may never need to pick up a Type tool. But, just in case you need to add a caption, headline, or short paragraph, we want you to be comfortable using the Type tools.

Elements allows you to create, edit, stylize, and even distort type. Keep in mind that this capability is no substitute for a hard-core page layout or word processing program. But for small chunks of text here and there, it's surprisingly effective. This chapter is all about adding great-looking snippets of text to great-looking images — an unbeatable combo.

Understanding Type Modes

The text you create in Elements can be categorized in several different ways, but ultimately, you're either adding just a little text (such as a word or single line) or a lot (a paragraph or so). Accordingly, Elements can create type in three modes:

⌐ **Point type:** Use this mode to create a headline or label. You can create point type by clicking in your image and typing; the line appears while you type and grows to whatever length you need. In fact, it even continues past the boundary of your image! Point type never wraps around to a new line. To wrap to the next line, you must press Enter (Return on the Mac).

⌐ **Paragraph type:** Use this mode to enter longer blocks of text on an image. It's similar to the kind of type you're accustomed to working with in word processing programs. In paragraph type mode, all the text goes into a resizable bounding box; if a line is too long, Photoshop automatically wraps it around to the next line.

✔ **Path type:** Elements also allows you to apply text along a path via three special Type tools. Double-click the path and enter type. The text appears and adheres to the shape of the path.

The various type modes each operate a bit differently, although they share many features and options. We explain each of them separately in the sections "Entering Point Type," "Entering Paragraph Type," and "Creating Path Type," later in this chapter.

Understanding Different Kinds of Type

In addition to the three Type modes Elements offers (see point type, paragraph type, and path type modes in the preceding section), Elements can also display and print type in two different formats. Each format has its pros and cons, and which format you use depends on your needs. Here's a description of each one:

✔ **Vector type:** All text in Elements is initially created as vector type. *Vector* type provides scalable outlines that you can resize without producing jagged edges in the diagonal strokes. You can edit type in this mode, adding or subtracting characters or adjusting attributes, such as kerning and tracking. Vector type is always of optimum quality and appears crisp and clean. (See Book III, Chapter 1, for more details on vector and rasterized images.)

✔ **Raster type:** When Elements converts vector type into pixels, that text is rasterized. Elements refers to this rasterization process as *simplifying.* When text is simplified, it's no longer editable, but is converted into a raster image. In essence, it's a frozen graphic of the text. You usually simplify vector type when you want to apply filters to produce a special effect or when you want to merge the type with the image. You can't resize simplified type without losing some quality or risking jagged edges. For more details, see the section "Rasterizing the Type Layer," later in this chapter.

Exploring the Type Tools

Elements has seven Type tools (found in the Tools panel), but two of them are simply vertically oriented versions of the main two text implements, as shown in Figure 3-1. Don't worry about the Vertical Type tools. Although you can use them, they're designed for the Asian market, to enter Chinese and

Japanese characters. The Horizontal and Vertical Type tools are identical in their attributes, so we cover only the two Horizontal Type tools here, and for the sake of simplicity, we

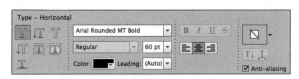

Figure 3-1: Elements offers seven Type tools.

call them the Type tool and the Type Mask tool. The last three Type tools all create text on a path in various ways.

You can use the paragraph or point type mode with the Type and Type Mask tools:

✒ **Type tool:** Use this tool to enter point or paragraph type. This tool creates the type on its own type layer, except when used in Bitmap or Indexed Color modes, neither of which supports layers. For more on layers, see Book VI.

✒ **Type Mask tool:** This tool doesn't create actual type; instead, it creates a selection border in the shape of the type you want to enter. The selection border is added to the active layer. You can do anything with a type selection that you can do with any other selection. For details on selections, see Book IV.

To create a path type, you must use the Text on Selection, Shape, or Custom Path tools:

✒ **Text on Selection tool:** This tool enables you to draw on your image to create a selection. (For more on selections, see Book IV, Chapter 1.) The selection then converts into a path, upon which you can then enter text, which flows along the path.

✒ **Text on Shape tool:** The second tool allows you to create any desired shape from your shapes drop-down list. You can then apply your text on that shape.

✒ **Text on Custom Path tool:** The last tool lets you draw any custom path you want on your image. Enter text on that custom path, and it adheres to that path.

A path is composed of three elements — anchor points, straight segments, and curved segments. The path essentially hovers on the image in its own "space," thereby not altering or marking the image in any way. The path in this context is merely a track upon which the text can flow. You can alter the path as you desire by using the Refine Path option. Find out more about this option in the section "Using the Text on Custom Path tool," later in this chapter.

Entering Point Type

Most of the type you add to Elements will probably consist of point type. Point type is useful for headlines, captions, labels, and similar small amounts of text. You can also use it to create logos and headings for web pages. *Point type* is so named because a single anchor point, which marks the starting point of the line of type, precedes it. Remember that point-type lines don't wrap automatically, as shown in Figure 3-2.

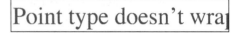

Figure 3-2: Point type doesn't automatically wrap, but can actually run off your image.

To enter point type, just follow these steps:

1. **In the Photo Editor, in Expert mode, open an image or create a new, blank document (or choose File⇨New⇨Blank File).**

   You can also enter type in Quick mode, but we recommend doing it in Expert mode where you have Elements' full arsenal of tools at your disposal.

2. **Select either the Type tool from the Tools panel or press the T key to select it.**

   If the Type tool isn't visible, press T to cycle through the Type tools. You can also select the particular Type tool you want from the Tool Options. Your cursor looks like an I-beam, similar to the one you see in a word processing program.

3. **Click the area of the image where you want to insert the text.**

   For horizontal type, a small, horizontal line about one-third of the way up the I-beam shows the location of the baseline (on which the line of text rests).

4. **Specify type options from the Tool Options.**

   All the options are described in the later section "Using the Tool Options."

5. **Type some text and press Enter (or Return on the Mac) to begin a new line.**

   When you press Enter (or Return), you insert a hard return that doesn't move. You have to remove hard returns if you want to change the length of the lines you type.

6. **When you finish entering the text, click the Commit (the green check-mark icon) button near your text.**

   You can also commit the type by pressing the Enter key on the numeric keypad or by clicking any other tool in the Tools panel. A new type layer containing your text — indicated by the T icon — is created and appears in your Layers panel.

Entering Paragraph Type

If you have larger chunks of text, entering the text as paragraph type is the most practical option. *Paragraph type* is similar to the text you enter in a word processing program, except that it's contained inside a text box or a *bounding box.* While you type into a text box, the lines of text wrap around to fit the dimensions of the box. If you resize the box, Elements adjusts the wrapped ends to account for the new size.

You can type multiple paragraphs, use typographical controls, and rotate or scale the type. You can easily resize paragraph type (and point type, too) by entering a new point size value in the Tool Options without having to reselect all the text. Just make sure that the text layer is selected in the Layers panel and that the Text tool is active. This approach works for all other text characteristics as well.

To enter paragraph type, follow these steps:

1. **Open a saved image or create a new, blank Elements document in the Photo Editor in Expert mode.**

2. **Select either the Horizontal Type tool from the Tools panel or press the T key to select it.**

   If it isn't visible, press T to cycle through the Type tools. You can also select the particular Type tool you want from the Tool Options.

   The cursor looks like an I-beam, similar to the one you see in a word processing program.

3. **On the image, insert and size the text box by using one of the following methods:**

   - *Drag to create a text box close to the size you want.* After you release the mouse button, you can drag any of the handles at the corners and sides of the box to resize the box.

   - *Hold down the Alt (Option on the Mac) key and click the image.* The Paragraph Text Size dialog box appears. Enter the exact dimensions of a bounding box. When you click OK, the specified box appears, complete with handles for resizing the box later.

4. **Select Type options from the Tool Options.**

   Options are described in detail in the later section "Using the Tool Options."

5. **Enter the text.**

   To start a new paragraph, press Enter (Return on the Mac).

   Each line wraps around to fit inside the bounding box, as shown in Figure 3-3.

If you type more text than fits in the text box, an overflow icon (plus sign) appears in the lower-right handle. You can resize the text box by dragging any of the bounding box handles.

6. **Click the Commit button (green check-mark icon) near the text (or press the Enter key on the numeric keypad).**

Elements creates a new type layer, as indicated by the T icon displayed in the Layers panel.

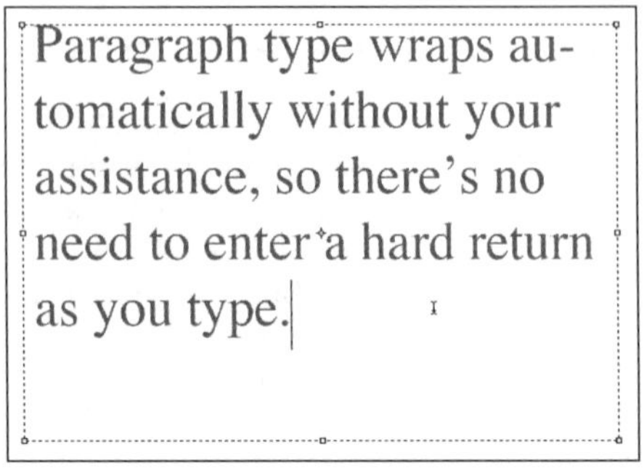

Paragraph type wraps automatically without your assistance, so there's no need to enter a hard return as you type.

Figure 3-3: Paragraph text automatically wraps to conform to the bounding box.

Creating Path Type

If you have a need to have your type flow in a circle, wave, stair step, or any other shape, you're now in luck. Elements provides three Type tools that enable you to do just that. The great thing is that you can easily create totally editable type that resides on its very own layer.

Using the Text on Selection tool

You can create path type by first creating a selection of your image, similarly to how you create a selection with the Quick Selection tool. Here's how:

1. **Open a saved image or create a new, blank Elements document in the Photo Editor in Expert mode.**

2. **Select the Text on Selection tool from the Tools panel or press the T key to cycle through the various Type tools.**

   You can also select the particular Type tool you want from the Tool Options.

3. **On the image, "paint" (drag) over your desired selection.**

4. **Refine your selection by adding or subtracting from your selection in one of two ways.**

   By dragging: Press the Shift key and drag around the additional area that you want to include in your selection.

   • Press the Alt (Option on the Mac) key and drag around the additional area that you want to subtract from your selection.

   • Select the Add to Selection or Subtract from Selection buttons in the Tool Options and drag around your desired areas.

With the Offset slider: Drag the Offset slider right to expand, or left to contract, your selection.

The additional options you can use to refine your selection, common to all the Type tools, are described in detail in the following section.

5. **When your selection is complete, click the Commit check mark icon to convert your selection to a path.**

   If you want to start over, click the red Cancel (slashed circle) icon.

6. **Position your mouse over the path; when the cursor icon changes to an I-beam (capital letter I with a crooked line crossing over), click the path and type your text.**

   The text wraps along the path. If you type more text than can fit on the path, an overflow icon appears. You can move the text around the path or to the outside or inside of the path by holding Ctrl (⌘ on the Mac) while clicking and dragging the mouse around the path or to the outside or inside of the path.

7. **When you finish entering your text, click the Commit icon.**

   Elements creates a new type layer. You can edit any attributes, such as font size, just as you can with point or paragraph text. See the upcoming section "Editing Text" for details.

Using the Text on Shape tool

This tool enables you to create type that flows along the perimeter of any shape. To do so, follow these steps:

1. **Open a saved image or create a new, blank Elements document in the Photo Editor in Expert mode.**

2. **Select the Text on Shape tool from the Tools panel or press the T key to cycle through the various Type tools.**

   You can also select the particular Type tool you want from the Tool Options.

3. **Select your desired shape in the Tool Options.**

4. **Drag your tool over the image to create the shape.**

   - To constrain your proportions, hold the Shift key down while dragging.

   - To draw from the center outward, hold down the Alt (Option on the Mac) key while dragging.

5. **Transform your shape by choosing Image⇨Transform Shape and then your desired transformation from the submenu.**

   For details on transformations, see the upcoming "Editing Text" section.

The additional options you can use to refine your shape, common to all the Type tools, are described in detail in the following section.

6. **Position your mouse over the path; when the cursor icon changes to an I-beam (capital letter I with a crooked line crossing over), click the path and type your text.**

The text wraps along the shape's path, as shown in Figure 3-4. Note that for some shapes, the text wraps inside the shape. You can move the text around or to the inside or outside of the custom path by holding Ctrl (⌘ on the Mac) while clicking and dragging the mouse around the shape or to outside or inside of the path.

© iStockphoto.com/ILLYCH Image #1731516

Figure 3-4: Elements enables you to apply text to a shape's path.

If you type more text than can fit on the path, an overflow icon appears.

7. **When you finish entering your text, click the Commit icon.**

Elements creates a new type layer. You can edit any attributes, such as font size, just as you can with point or paragraph text. See the upcoming section "Editing Text" for details.

You can also refine your shape path by using the Refine Path tool that appears in the Tool Options when the Text on Custom Path tool is selected. Just be sure that you have your type layer selected before working with this option.

Using the Text on Custom Path tool

If you want to create your own path or shape as the basis for your type, the Text on Custom Path tool is the tool for you. Here's what you do:

1. **Open a saved image or create a new, blank Elements document in the Photo Editor in Expert mode.**

2. **Select the Text on Custom tool from the Tools panel or press the T key to cycle through the various Type tools.**

You can also select the particular Type tool you want from the Tool Options.

3. **Drag your tool over the image to create the custom path of your choice.**

4. **Refine your path by selecting the Refine Path option in the Tool Options; drag the anchor points or path segments with the tool to get your desired shape.**

   You can also transform your custom path by choosing Image➪Transform Shape. For details on transformations, see the upcoming "Editing Text" section.

   The additional options to specify your path, common to all the Type tools, are described in detail in the following section.

5. **Position your mouse over the path; when the cursor icon changes to an I-beam (capital letter I with a crooked line crossing over), click the path and type your text.**

   The text wraps along the shape's path. If you type more text than can fit on the path, an overflow icon appears.

   You can move the text around or to the inside or outside of the custom path by holding Ctrl (⌘ on the Mac) while clicking and dragging the mouse around the shape or to outside or inside of the path.

6. **When you finish entering your text, click the Commit icon.**

   Elements creates a new type layer. You can edit any attributes, such as font size, just as you can with point or paragraph text. See the upcoming section "Editing Text" for details.

7. **To create a new custom path, select the background layer and begin again.**

Using the Tool Options

Several character and paragraph type settings are located in the Tool Options, shown in Figure 3-5. These options enable you to specify the type and pair it with your images.

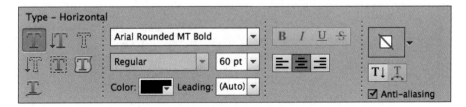

Figure 3-5: The Type options in the Tool Options.

Here's an explanation of each option:

✔ **Font Family:** Select the font or typeface you want from the drop-down list. Elements provides you with a What You See Is What You Get (WYSIWYG) font menu. After the font name, the word *sample* is rendered in the actual font. You also find one of these abbreviations before the font name to let you know what type of font it is:

- a: Adobe Type 1 (PostScript) fonts
- TT: TrueType fonts
- O: OpenType fonts

Fonts with no abbreviation are bitmapped fonts.

✔ **Font Style:** Some font families have additional styles, such as light or semi-bold. And other styles are assigned as separate typefaces. Only the styles available for a particular font appear in the list. The font style also supports a WYSIWYG menu.

If a font you want to use doesn't offer bold or italic styles, you can simulate either (or both) by selecting a faux style in the Tool Options (T icons). But keep in mind the key word here is "faux." The faux bold and italic styles are somewhat crude approximations; if possible, avoid them.

✔ **Font Size:** Select your type size from the drop-down list or just type a size in the text box. Generally, text sizes are shown in points, with 72 points equaling approximately 1 inch.

The Font Size setting now has a scrubby slider, enabling you to change the font quickly. Hover your mouse over the word *Size.* When the mouse icon changes shape, left-click and drag to the left to decrease the font size or to the right to increase the font size.

If you don't like points, you can switch to millimeters or pixels by choosing Edit➪Preferences➪Units and Rulers (or Adobe Photoshop Elements Editor➪Preferences➪Units & Rulers on the Mac).

✔ **Text Color:** Click the color swatch to select a color for your type from the Color Picker. You can also choose a color from the Swatches panel.

✔ **Leading:** *Leading* (pronounced "ledding") is the amount of space between the baselines of lines of type, usually measured in points. The *baseline* is the imaginary line on which a line of type rests. You can select a specific amount of leading or allow Elements to determine the amount automatically by choosing Auto. When you select Auto Leading, Elements multiplies the type size by a value of 120 percent to calculate the leading size. Therefore, Elements spaces the baselines of 10-point type 12 points apart. Elements adds that extra 20 percent so that the bottoms of the lowest letters don't "hook" onto the tops of the tallest letters on the line below them.

Wider line spacing can make text easier to read (as long as you don't go overboard!) or provide an artistic effect. Tighter line spacing makes for more compact text but can decrease readability if the tightening goes too far.

✔ **Text Alignment:** Choose an option to align horizontal text on the left, center, or right. Left-aligned text is even with the left margin and allowed to be ragged on the right side of the column. Centered text is evenly centered in its column and ragged on both right and left edges. Right-aligned text is even with the right margin and allowed to be ragged on the left side.

If you happen to have vertical text, these options rotate 90 degrees clockwise and change into top, bottom, and center vertical settings.

✔ **Anti-aliasing:** Select Anti-aliasing to smooth the edges of your text slightly. Anti-aliasing softens that edge by 1 pixel, as shown in Figure 3-6. For the most part, you should keep this option turned on. The only occasion when you may want to have it turned off is when you're creating small type to display onscreen, such as on web pages. The soft edges can sometimes be tough to read easily.

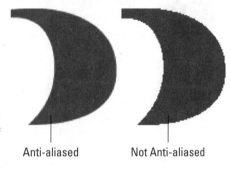

Anti-aliased   Not Anti-aliased

Figure 3-6: Anti-aliasing softens the edges of your type.

✔ **Faux Bold:** Use this option to create a fake bold style when a real bold style (which you'd choose under Font Style) doesn't exist. Be aware that applying faux styles can distort the proportions of a font. You should try to use fonts with real styles, and if they don't exist — oh, well.

✔ **Faux Italic:** This option creates a phony oblique style and carries the same warning as the Faux Bold option.

✔ **Underline:** This setting obviously underlines your type, like <u>this</u>.

✔ **Strikethrough:** Choose this option to apply a ~~strikethrough~~ style to your text. In legal applications, strikethrough is widely used to show sections that have been removed, in their original context.

✔ **Style:** Select a type layer in the Layers panel and then choose a style from the Style picker drop-down list. Choose from simple styles (such as shadows and bevels) to complex ones (such as glass and plastic effects). Note that this option is accessible after you have committed your type.

✔ **Change the Text Orientation:** Select your type layer in the Layers panel and then click this option to switch between vertical and horizontal type orientations.

✔ **Create Warped Text:** This option lets you warp and bend text by using 15 different types of distortion.

Editing Text

You can apply all options described in this chapter while you enter text, or later, when you're rearranging words or fixing typos and other errors. To make changes to the text itself, just follow these steps:

1. **Open your image in the Photo Editor in Expert mode.**

2. **Select the Type tool from the Tools panel.**

3. **In the Layers panel, select the existing type layer you want to modify or click within the text to automatically select the type layer.**

   Double-click the T icon in the Layers panel to simultaneously select all the text in that layer and make the Type tool active.

4. **After selecting some text, use the Tool Options to make changes:**

   • *Change the font family, size, color, or other type option:* If you want to change all the text, simply select that type layer in the Layers panel. To select only portions of the text, highlight the text by dragging across it with the I-beam of the Type tool, as shown in Figure 3-7.

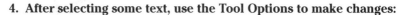

   Figure 3-7: Highlight selected text to modify attributes.

   • *Delete text:* Highlight the text by dragging across it with the I-beam of the Type tool. Then press the Backspace key (Delete on the Mac).

   • *Add text:* Make an insertion point by clicking the I-beam within the line of text. Then type new text.

   Note that these editing steps apply to all the types of text — point, paragraph, and path.

5. **When you finish modifying the text, click the Commit button.**

Occasionally, you may want to transform your text. To do so, make sure that the type layer is selected in the Layers panel. Then choose Image➪Transform➪ Free Transform. Grab a handle on the bounding box and drag to rotate or scale. Press Ctrl (⌘ on the Mac) and drag a handle to distort. After you finish, double-click inside the bounding box to commit the transformation. For more details on transformations, see Book VI, Chapter 2.

For path type, applying the transformation command will enable you to change the shape of your path, but not the actual type itself. Upon double-clicking the bounding box, the type will then rewrap along the transformed path.

Rasterizing the Type Layer

The Type tool creates editable type layers. You can change the wording, spacing, font, font size, and other factors as much as you want as long as the type remains in a type layer, which retains a vector format. (See the section "Understanding Different Kinds of Type," earlier in this chapter, for details.)

However, after you make all the changes you want, you may need to convert your vector type layer to pixels as rasterized type. In Elements, this raster-ization process is referred to as *simplifying.* After the type is simplified, you can apply filters, paint on the type, and apply gradients and patterns.

If you're working with layers and *flatten* your image (merge layers into a single background image), the type layers are also simplified and merged with the other pixels in the image. By the way, if you try to apply a filter to a vector type layer, Elements barks at you that the type layer must be simplified before con-tinuing and gives you the opportu-nity to click OK (if you want to simplify) or Cancel.

Simplified raster type

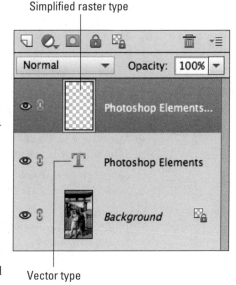

To simplify your type, select the type layer in the Layers panel and choose Layer⇨Simplify Layer. Your type layer is then converted (the T icon disappears) into a regular layer on which your type is now displayed as pixels against a transparent back-ground, as shown in Figure 3-8.

Vector type

Figure 3-8: Simplifying your type layer converts vector type into pixels.

After you simplify your type, you can no longer edit the text, nor can you resize the text without risking jag-gies. Simplify your type only when you're certain that you no longer need to edit or resize it. Another thing to remember about simplified type is that although it looks identical to vector type onscreen, it may not print as crisply and cleanly as vector type. So, if you're experimenting with painting or filters on type, just make a duplicate of the type layer before simplifying it and then hide that layer in the Layers panel. For details on working with layers, see Book VI.

Masking with Type

In addition to its Vertical and Horizontal Type tools that we discuss in the section "Exploring the Type Tools," earlier in this chapter, Elements includes Vertical and Horizontal Type Mask tools. These tools function almost identically to their conventional counterparts, with one important exception: Type Mask tools don't create a new layer. Instead, they create a selection on the active layer, like the one shown in Figure 3-9.

© iStockphoto.com/ ermingut Image #18951814

Figure 3-9: Type Mask tools create selection borders from the letter shapes.

You can treat the selections created with the Type Mask tools just as you would any other selection. Try the following:

- ✔ Move type mask selections around your document when any of the selection tools are active.

- ✔ Store type mask selections for later use by choosing Select⇨Save Selection. See Book IV for details on selections.

- ✔ Use the selection to cut or copy portions of an image in text-shaped chunks, as shown in Figure 3-10. You can find out how this last technique works by following the steps in the upcoming Putting It Together project, "Carving Your Type Out of Stone," in which you find out how to digitally carve your words in stone.

© iStockphoto.com/ermingut Image #18951814

Figure 3-10: Use a Type Mask to create type from an image.

- ✔ On a separate layer, fill the selection with a Foreground to Transparent gradient to have your type gradually fade out over the image, as shown in Figure 3-11. For details on gradients, see Chapter 2 of this minibook.

© iiStockphoto.com/kerkla Image #4504296

Figure 3-11: Gradually fade out type using a Foreground to Transparent gradient.

Putting It Together

Carving Your Type Out of Stone

You can use a Type tool to create selections shaped like text and then use images themselves as fills for the type. For example, if you're creating a floral-themed web page, you can use pictures of flowers as the fill for the text. A type selection can cut out any part of a picture for use in any way you want.

Follow these steps to create letters made from stone:

1. **In the Photo Editor, in Expert mode, open the stone texture image you want to use.**

We're using a sandstone wall, but you can use other kinds of stone or wood or any texture that interests you.

2. **Convert your background into a layer by double-clicking the word *Background* in the Layers panel and then click OK.**

This step enables you to stylize the type later.

3. **Select the Horizontal Type Mask tool from the Tools panel and then click the area where you want to enter text; press the T key to cycle through the various Type tools.**

You can also select the particular Type tool you want from the Tool Options.

4. **Select the font, font style, font size, and other text attributes from the drop-down lists in the Tool Options.**

continued

continued

5. **Click the image and type the text; click the Commit button (the check-mark icon) next to your text.**

    A selection border in the shape of the text appears on your image, as shown in the figure.

6. **Choose Select⇨Inverse, which deselects letter selections and selects everything else.**

7. **Press the Backspace (Delete on the Mac) key to delete everything outside your selection border and choose Select⇨Deselect.**

    Your type is now filled with your stone texture.

8. **Choose Window⇨Effects and select the Styles tab at the top of the Effects panel.**

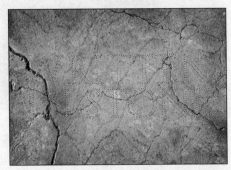

© iStockphoto.com/Lord Runar Image #5498150

9. **Select the Bevels styles library from the drop-down menu on the Styles panel. Double-click a bevel.**

10. **Select the Drop Shadow styles library from the drop-down menu in the upper-right area of the Styles panel and double-click a shadow.**

We selected a Simple Inner bevel and Soft Edge drop shadow to produce our stone letters, as shown in the figure.

To get all the details on how to use the other options in the

© iStockphoto.com/Lord Runar Image #5498150

Layer Style dialog box, check out Book VII, Chapter 3.

 TIP

If you want to admire your type against a solid background, create a new layer and then choose Edit⇨Fill Layer and choose a color from the Use drop-down menu.

Stylizing and Warping Type

You can do a lot more with type than create conventional labels, captions, or paragraphs of text. Type can become an interesting part of your image, especially when you stylize, warp, or otherwise transform it in interesting ways.

Your Elements text can help enhance the impact of your image. The text of a beach scene can appear to be wavy, or watery and translucent. Halloween type can take on a ghostly or spooky appearance. Text on a wedding photo can be elegant and romantic. It all depends on how you create and apply various effects.

The following sections show you some of the tricks you can perform by stylizing and warping your type so that your words come to life and add something special to your images.

Playing with type opacity

Layers are a digital version of the old analog transparency, or acetate, sheets. (Check out Book VI, Chapter 1, for the scoop on layers.) You can change the transparency of a type layer — just as you can with any other layer in Elements — by reducing the *opacity* (transparency) of the type so that it enables the underlying layer to show through. Take a peek at Figure 3-12, which shows type at varying levels of opacity over an image.

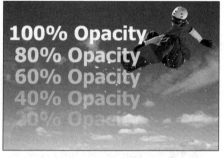

© iStockphoto.com/LUGO Image #4570165

Figure 3-12: Varying the opacity of type allows the underlying image to show through.

Applying filters to type

One of the most interesting things you can do with type in Elements that you can't do in a word processing or page layout program is apply special effects, such as filters. You can make type look as though it's under water or on the move, as shown in Figure 3-13, where we applied a motion blur. The only caveat is that type has to be simplified before you can apply a filter. Be sure to do all your text editing before you reach the filtering stage. Applying the filter is as easy as selecting the simplified type layer

© iStockphoto.com/Pojbic Image #2156292

Figure 3-13: Applying a motion blur to type can make it appear as fast as the car.

in the Layers panel and choosing a filter from the Filter menu. For more on filters, see Book VII, Chapter 1.

Painting over type with color

Changing the color of text is as easy as highlighting it and selecting a color from the Color Picker. But what if you want to do something a little more unconventional, such as apply brush strokes of paint randomly across the type, as we did in the top image shown in Figure 3-14? Honestly, it's easier than it looks. Again, as with applying filters to text, the only criterion is that the type has to be simplified first. After that's done, select a color, grab the Brush tool with settings of your choice, and paint. In our exam-

Figure 3-14: Add visual interest to type with color (top) or a gradient (bottom).

ple, we used a rough, dry brush found in the Brushes presets. We used diameters of 39, 15, and 6 pixels and just clicked the type a few times.

If you want the color or gradient to be confined to only the type area, you can select the text by either Ctrl-clicking (⌘-clicking on the Mac) the layer containing the text or locking the transparency of the layer in the Layers panel.

You can also apply a gradient to your type. Here are the steps to follow after simplifying your type:

1. **In the Photo Editor in Expert mode, select the Gradient tool from the Tools panel.**

2. **In the Tool Options, click the down arrow next to the Gradient Picker to access the Gradient Picker drop-down panel.**

3. **Choose a gradient.**

   If you want to create a custom gradient, find out how in Chapter 2 of this minibook.

4. **Position the gradient cursor on the text where you want the gradient to start and drag to where you want the gradient to end.**

   If you're not happy, drag again until you get the look you want. Remember that you can drag at any angle and to any length, even outside your type. In the bottom image shown in Figure 3-14, we used the copper gradient and just dragged from the top of the letters to the bottom. We also locked the transparent pixels on the layer to confine the gradient to just the type area.

Warping your type

The great automated Elements Warp feature can twist your type in a variety of ways (see Figure 3-15) that are not only repeatable but also, thanks to the controls in their dialog boxes, customizable. The cool part is that even though type has been warped, it remains fully editable until you simplify it.

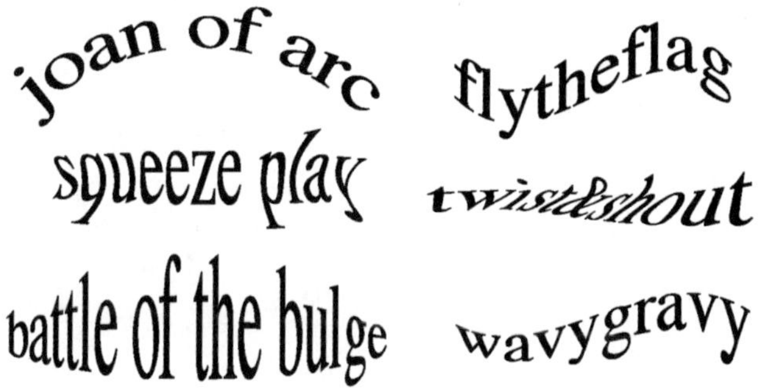

Figure 3-15: Choose from a number of warp styles.

Type-warping is fun and easy to do. Select the Type tool in the Tools panel and then click the Create Warped Text button in the Tool Options. (It's the T with a curved line below it.) This action opens the Warp Text dialog box, where you find a vast array of distortions on the Style pop-up menu with descriptive names such as Bulge, Inflate, and Squeeze. You can adjust the orientation, amount of bend, and degree of distortion by dragging the sliders. The Bend setting affects the amount of warp, and the Horizontal and Vertical Distortions apply perspective to that warp. Luckily, you can preview the results while you adjust. We could give you technical explanations of these adjustments, but the best way to see what they do is to just play with them. Figure 3-15 shows some of the warp styles. The names speak for themselves.

Web designers take note: You can't warp text that has a Faux Bold style applied.

Book VI

Working with Layers and Masks

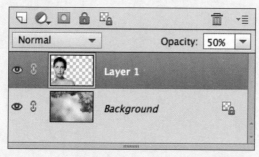

For more details and projects about Photoshop Elements, visit www.dummies.com/extras/photoshopelementsaio.

Contents at a Glance

Chapter 1: Creating Layers

In This Chapter

✐ **Comparing backgrounds versus layers**

✐ **Taking a look at the types of layers**

✐ **Working with the Layers panel**

✐ **Commanding the Layer and Select menus**

✐ **Creating layers**

✐ **Compositing with layers**

*U*sing Elements without the assistance of layers would be like trying to wash your car with a toothbrush and a pail of water instead of with a hose and a power-scrubber brush. Yes, it can be done, but it takes a lot longer and is downright tedious. The benefit to using layers is that you have tremendous flexibility. You can make endless edits as long as those layers exist. You can rearrange their order, and if you decide that you no longer want them, you simply delete them. Layers make working in Elements a lot more forgiving, allowing you to make changes quickly and productively.

But hey, it's not just the technical and practical aspects that make layers awesome. Layers also allow you to express your creative side: You can composite several images into one with just a drag of the mouse or a swipe on the trackpad, for example. This chapter gives you the basics on working with layers. Chapter 2 of this minibook fills in the rest of the details. After you give layers a try, you'll find that they make your image-editing life much easier. Now, if only they would go out and wash the car.

Getting Familiar with Layers

In terms of a real-world analogy, think of layers as sheets of acetate or transparency film, similar to those clear plastic sheets used with overhead projectors. You have drawings, photos, or type on the individual sheets. What you place on one sheet doesn't affect the other sheets. You can show just one sheet, or you can stack several on top of one another to create a combination image, or *composite* (or *collage*). You can reshuffle the order of the sheets, add sheets, or delete sheets. Any space on the sheet that doesn't have an image, a drawing, or some type on it is transparent.

That's how layers work in Elements. You can place elements on separate layers yet show them together to create a composite. You can also add, delete, or rearrange layers. And, unlike using real sheets of acetate, you can adjust an element's *opacity,* or how opaque or transparent the element is on the layer. You can also change the way the colors between layers interact by using Blend modes. Both opacity and Blend modes are covered in Chapter 3 of this minibook.

When you create a new image with a white or colored background, scan an image into Elements, or open a file from a CD or your digital camera, you basically have a file with just a *Background.* You have no layers yet.

At this basic level, an image contains only the single Background, and you can't do much to it besides paint on it and make basic adjustments. You can't rearrange the Background in the stack of layers (after you have some) — it's always on the bottom of the Layers panel. Nor can you change the opacity or Blend mode of a Background. What you can do is convert a Background to a layer, making it possible to shuffle, change the opacity, and change the Blend modes of your newly formed layer.

To work with layers, you must be in the Photo Editor in Expert mode.

To convert a background into a layer, follow these steps:

1. **In the Photo Editor, in Expert mode, choose Window⇨Layers to display the Layers panel.**

   The Layers panel is explained in the later section "Getting to Know the Layers Panel."

2. **Double-click *Background* in the Layers panel.**

   You can also choose Layer⇨New⇨Layer from Background. Note that the name *Background* is italicized in the Layers panel, as shown in Figure 1-1.

   The New Layer dialog box appears.

3. **Name the layer or leave it at the default name Layer 0.**

   Note that you can also adjust the Blend mode and opacity of the layer in the New Layer dialog box. However, you shouldn't do it here. Instead, you should make those adjustments by using the Layers panel commands where you have more editing flexibility. We cover these techniques in Chapter 3 of this minibook.

4. **Click OK.**

   Elements converts the background into a layer, also known as an *image layer.* Note that the layer name is no longer italicized nor is it locked.

Figure 1-1: A newly opened image in Elements contains only a background.

When you create a new image with transparent content for the background, the image doesn't contain a Background; it's created with a single layer. You can convert a layer into a Background by selecting it and then choosing Layer➪New➪Background from Layer, which moves the background to the bottom of the stack. Note that this option is available only when no Background exists.

Introducing Different Types of Layers

Although turning the Background into a layer (discussed in the preceding section) is a popular activity, Elements refers to plural *layers* for a reason. You'll probably create image layers most of the time, but other types exist. Elements offers *five* types of layers. Some you may never use, and some you may use only occasionally, but you should be familiar with them all.

Working with image layers

The image layer is the one that most closely matches the acetate analogy (discussed in the section "Getting Familiar with Layers," earlier in this chapter). You put various elements on separate layers to create a composite image. You can create blank layers and add images to them, or you can create layers from images themselves. You can create as many layers as your computer's memory allows.

Because each layer in an image is a separate entity, you can edit, paint, transform, mask (described in Chapter 4 of this minibook), or apply a filter to a layer without affecting the other layers or the background. And, after an element is on a layer, you no longer have to make a selection to select it. (See Book IV for details on selections.) Just drag the element with the Move tool. The element freely floats in a sea of transparency.

Because showing *clear* areas, or transparency, is impossible on a computer monitor, Elements uses a gray-and-white checkerboard by default to represent the transparent areas of a layer.

Using Adjustment layers

An *Adjustment layer* is a special kind of layer used mostly for color and contrast correction. The helpful aspect of Adjustment layers is that you can apply those corrections without permanently affecting any pixels on your other layers. Adjustment layers are nondestructive. They project the correction to all layers below them without affecting any layers above them.

Because the adjustment resides on a layer, you can edit, delete, duplicate, merge, or rearrange the Adjustment layer at any time. You have more flexibility in your image-editing chores and more freedom for experimentation. Additionally, none of this experimentation harms your image because it takes place above the image on an Adjustment layer.

Another unique feature of Adjustment layers is that when you create one, you also create a layer mask on that layer. A *layer mask* is sort of a second sheet of acetate that hovers on the underlying layers. You use the layer mask to selectively apply the adjustment to the layers below it by applying shades of gray — from white to black — on the mask. For example, because the mask is, by default, completely white, you can fully

Figure 1-2: Layer masks are added when creating an adjustment layer.

apply the adjustment to the layers. If you paint on a layer mask with black, as shown in Figure 1-2, the areas under those black areas don't show the adjustment. If you paint with a shade of gray, those areas partially show the adjustment. The darker the shade of gray, the less these areas show the adjustment. Note that if your image has an active selection border in it before you add an adjustment layer, the adjustment is applied to only the area within the selection border. The resulting layer mask also reflects that selection: The selected areas are white, and the deselected areas are black.

You can also apply a layer mask at will and use it to creatively blend two or more layers. Be sure to see Chapter 4 of this minibook to find out how. It's definitely worth your while.

Elements has eight kinds of Adjustment layers, and you can use as many as your heart desires. The adjustments offered are, for the most part, the same ones you find on the Enhance⇨Adjust Lighting and Enhance⇨Adjust Color submenus. For specifics on each adjustment and the problems it corrects or the enhancement it makes, see Book VIII, Chapters 1 and 2.

Here's how to create an Adjustment layer:

1. **In the Photo Editor, in Expert mode, open an image of your choice.**

   Because you're applying an Adjustment layer, you may want to use an image that's in need of some color adjustment. Note that when you use Adjustment layers, you don't need to convert the Background into a layer.

2. **Click the Create Adjustment Layer icon in the Layers panel.**

   The Adjustment Layer drop-down menu appears.

   You can also choose Layer⇨New Adjustment Layer and then choose an adjustment layer type from the submenu. Name the layer, leave the other options at their defaults, and click OK.

3. **From the drop-down menu, choose an adjustment.**

   The dialog box pertaining to your adjustment appears in the Adjustments panel.

4. **Make the necessary adjustments in the particular Adjustments panel.**

   The Adjustment layer appears in the Layers panel, shown in Figure 1-3. The Adjustment Layer icon (sporting a few gears) and a thumbnail (representing a layer mask) appear on the Adjustment layer.

When you first apply the Adjustment layer, the mask will appear white, enabling your adjustment to be applied at full strength over the entire image. However, in our example, the layer mask of the Levels adjustment layer (refer to Figure 1-2) is black and white. Where the mask is white, the adjustment shows up over the image at full strength; where the mask is black, the adjustment doesn't appear at all. We achieved this by painting on the layer mask to allow only portions of our image to receive the adjustment. We also did this to our Hue/Saturation adjustment layer in Figure 1-3. Use the Brush or Pencil tool to paint. Or, you can also make a selection and fill it with any shade of gray, from white to black. Finally, you can use the Gradient tool on the mask to create a gradual application of the adjustment.

Book VI
Chapter I

Creating Layers

Image layer   Create Adjustment layer   Adjustment layer

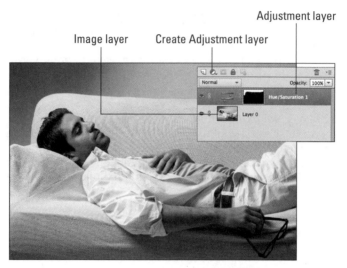

© iStockphoto.com/Tempura Image #13332733

Figure 1-3: Applying corrections with an Adjustment layer, rather than directly on the image, allows for more editing flexibility.

You can also adjust the opacity and Blend modes of an adjustment layer, just as with image layers. Reducing the opacity of an adjustment layer reduces the effect of the adjustment on the underlying layers.

Viewing and deleting Adjustment layers

If you want to view your image without the adjustment, click the eye icon in the left column of the Layers panel to hide the adjustment layer.

If you want to delete the adjustment layer, simply drag it to the Trash icon in the Layers panel or choose Layer➪Delete Layer from the Layer menu or the Layers panel menu. (Click the down-pointing arrow in the upper-right corner of the Layers panel to access the menu.)

Editing Adjustment layers

After you create an adjustment layer, you can easily edit it. Simply double-click the Adjustment Layer icon in the Layers panel. You can also choose Layer➪Layer Content Options. In the adjustment's dialog box, make any edits and then click OK.

The only Adjustment layer you can't edit is the Invert adjustment layer. It's either totally on or totally off.

Using the Adjustments panel controls

Click an icon at the bottom of the Adjustments panel. From left to right, here's what the icons do:

✔ Clip the Adjustment layer to the layer below it (affects only the layer directly beneath it, not all underlying layers in the stack).

✔ Toggle the Adjustment layer visibility on and off.

✔ Reset the Adjustment layer settings to their defaults.

Isolating your adjustments

If you don't use an Adjustment layer when you make color corrections, the correction you apply affects only the *active layer* (the layer highlighted in the Layers panel). The correction doesn't affect all layers below it, as it would if you used an Adjustment layer. But you can also isolate the Adjustment layer to a single layer or a portion of a single layer by clipping.

Here are some tips for using and isolating Adjustment layers:

✔ **Correct part (but not all) of a layer.** To enable the Adjustment layer to correct only a portion of a layer, make a selection before you create the adjustment layer. The adjustment affects only the pixels within the selection outline. The adjustment affects the pixels within the selection outline *on each layer that resides below the Adjustment layer.*

Another way to correct part of a layer is to paint on the Adjustment layer mask. Painting with black hides the adjustment, and painting with various levels of gray partially hides the adjustment. For more on masks, see Chapter 4 of this minibook.

✔ **Clip to the layer.** If you want the Adjustment layer to affect only the immediate underlying layer and not those below that layer, you can create a clipping group. To do so, press the Alt key (Option on the Mac) and click the line between the Adjustment layer and the immediate, underlying image layer. For details on clipping groups, see Chapter 4 of this minibook.

Taking advantage of Fill layers

A *Fill layer* lets you add a layer of solid color, a gradient, or a pattern. Like Adjustment layers, Fill layers also have layer masks, as indicated by the Mask icon thumbnail image in the Layers panel.

Just as with image layers and Adjustment layers, you can create as many Fill layers as you want. You can also edit, rearrange, duplicate, delete, and merge Fill layers. Additionally, you can blend Fill layers with other layers by using the opacity and Blend mode options in the Layers panel.

You can confine the effects of a Fill layer, as you can with an Adjustment layer, to a portion of the image. Make a selection before you create the Fill layer (see Book IV for more on selections) or paint on the mask later (described in the previous section). Editing a Fill layer is similar to editing an adjustment layer. To edit a Fill layer, double-click the Fill Layer thumbnail in the Layers panel.

Here's how to create a Fill layer:

1. **In the Photo Editor, in Expert mode, open an image.**

   In this case, open an image that would look good with a frame or border or even some type. If you don't have an active selection, the Fill layer encompasses your entire layer.

2. **Click the Create Adjustment Layer icon in the Layers panel; from the drop-down menu, choose a fill of a solid color, gradient, or pattern.**

   You can also choose Layer⇨New Fill Layer and then choose a Fill layer from the submenu. In the New Layer dialog box, name the layer, leave the other options at their defaults, and click OK. Specify options such as Mode and Opacity within the Layers panel, where you have more editing flexibility.

   The dialog box specific to your type of fill appears.

3. **Specify your options, depending on the fill type you chose in Step 2:**

   - *Solid Color:* Select a color from the Color Picker.

   - *Gradient:* Click the down arrow to choose a preset gradient from the drop-down panel or click the Gradient preview to display the Gradient Editor and create your own gradient. For details on gradients, see Book V, Chapter 2.

   - *Pattern:* Select a pattern from the drop-down panel, as shown in Figure 1-4. Choose a value from the Scale drop-down menu, if you want. Click Snap to Origin to make the origin of the pattern the same as the origin of the document. Select the Link with Layer option to specify that the pattern moves with the fill layer if you move the layer.

4. **Click OK.**

   The Fill layer appears in the Layers panel. Similar to what happens in Adjustment layers, a layer mask is created on the Fill layer. In our example, in Figure 1-5, the words *DOGGIE daycare* appear in white on the layer mask, thereby allowing our pattern to show through. The remaining areas are black, hiding the pattern. We also added some layer styles (bevel and drop shadow) to jazz up our type. For more on layer styles, see Book VII, Chapter 3.

   If you want to delete the Fill layer, first select the layer in the Layers panel and drag it to the Trash icon in the Layers panel.

You can simplify a fill layer to convert it to a regular image layer. Choose Layer⇨Simplify. By doing so, you can use painting tools or filters on that layer. For more on simplifying layers, see Chapter 2 of this minibook.

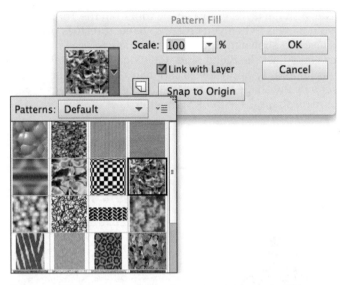

Figure 1-4: Choose from a variety of preset patterns for the fill layer.

Figure 1-5: Your chosen fill shows through your selected areas.

Making use of shape layers

Believe it or not, Elements isn't just about photos and painting. It also has a set of shape-drawing tools — six, to be exact. You can fill those shapes with solid color, gradients, or patterns. When you create a shape, you're creating a *vector-based* object: The shapes are defined by mathematical equations, which create points and paths, rather than by pixels. The advantage of using vector-based objects is that you can freely size these objects without causing degradation. Additionally, they're always printed with smooth edges, not with the familiar jaggies you see in pixel-based elements.

To create a shape layer, grab a shape tool from the Tools panel and drag it onto your canvas. When you create a shape, it resides on its own, unique shape layer, as shown in Figure 1-6. Although you can move and transform shapes and adjust the Blend modes and opacity, your ability to edit shape layers is limited. To apply filters and many other special effects, you must first *simplify* the shape layers — that is, convert the vector paths to pixels. For more on shapes, see Book V, Chapter 1.

Figure 1-6: A shape layer is a vector-based object.

Using type layers

To create type, such as the type shown in Figure 1-7, click the canvas with the Type tool and type some text. After you commit your text by pressing Enter on the numeric keypad, clicking the Commit button (the check mark icon) in the Tool Options, or pressing Ctrl+Enter (⌘+Return on the Mac), you've created a type layer. In the Layers panel, you see a layer with a T icon, indicating that it's a type layer. Initially, the name of the type layer corresponds to the text you typed. (You can change the layer name, if you want.) Like shapes, the text in Elements is vector-based type and, if left in that format, always prints smoothly and without the jaggies. For more information on vector images, see Book III, Chapter 1.

Another useful aspect of type in Elements is that it's *live:* You can edit the text at any time. Besides being able to change the font and size, you can change the orientation, apply anti-aliasing (softening of the edges), and even warp it into various distortions. You can transform, move, rearrange, copy, and change the layer options (opacity and mode) of a type layer just as you can for image layers. If, however, you want to apply filters, you must first *simplify* (convert into pixels) the text. For everything you need to know about type, see Book V, Chapter 3.

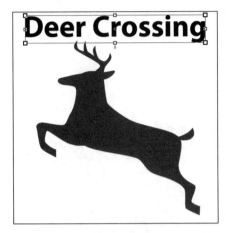

Figure 1-7: Type layers automatically appear when you create and commit type.

Getting to Know the Layers Panel

Just like every other important aspect of Elements, layers are controlled in their very own panel. You may have seen bits and pieces of the Layers panel throughout this chapter, but now it's time for a full-blown discussion of its capabilities. To display the Layers panel, shown in Figure 1-8, choose Window➪Layers in the Photo Editor, in Expert mode.

The order of the layers in the Layers panel represents the order in the image. We refer to this concept as the *stacking order*. The top layer in the panel is the top layer in your image, and so on.

For some tasks, you can work on only one layer at a time. For other tasks, you can work on multiple layers simultaneously.

Here's the lowdown on how to work with the Layers panel:

✒ **Select a layer.** Click a layer name or thumbnail. Elements then highlights the *active layer* in the panel.

✒ **Select multiple contiguous layers.** Click your first layer and then Shift-click your last layer.

✓ **Select multiple noncontiguous layers.** Ctrl-click (⌘-click on the Mac) some layers.

Only visible layers are printed. This limitation can be useful if you want to have several versions of an image (each on a separate layer) for a project within the same file. Click the eye icon to show and hide a layer.

Active layer

Create a New layer   Delete layer

Type layer   Image layer

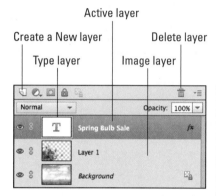

© iStockphoto.com/Liliboas Image #2819705 and kertlis Image #6565377

Figure 1-8: The Layers panel is Control Central for your layers.

✓ **Select the actual element (the nontransparent pixels) on the layer.** Ctrl-click (⌘-click on the Mac) the layer's thumbnail in the panel.

✓ **Create a new, blank layer.** Click the Create a New Layer icon (a dog-eared page) at the top of the panel.

✓ **Add a layer mask.** Click the Add Layer Mask icon at the top of the panel. A *layer mask* enables you to selectively show and hide elements or adjustments on your layer as well as creatively blend layers. For more details, see Chapter 4 of this minibook.

✓ **Create an Adjustment or Fill layer.** Click the Create a New Fill or Adjustment Layer icon (the black-and-white circle) at the top of the panel. See the earlier sections "Using Adjustment layers" and "Taking advantage of Fill layers" for more on these types of layers.

✔ **Duplicate an existing layer.** Drag the layer to the Create a New Layer icon at the top of the panel.

✔ **Rename a layer.** When you create a new layer, Elements provides default layer names (Layer 1, Layer 2, and so on). To rename a layer, double-click the layer name (the name, not the thumbnail) in the Layers panel, enter the name directly in the Layers panel, and press Enter (Return on the Mac). Although giving layers meaningful names may seem tedious, doing so can increase your productivity, especially when the number of layers in your file increases.

✔ **Adjust the interaction between colors on layers and adjust the transparency of layers.** You can use the Blend modes and the Opacity drop-down menus at the top of the panel to mix the colors between layers and adjust the transparency of the layers. (Take a look at Figure 1-9, where we set the opacity at 50%) For details, see Chapter 3 of this minibook.

Figure 1-9: Control opacity and blending with the Layers panel.

✔ **Delete a layer.** Drag a layer to the Trash icon at the top of the Layers panel. You can also choose Layer⇨Delete Layer or choose Delete Layer from the Layers panel menus.

You use the remaining icons at the top of the Layers panel to link layers and lock layers. Both actions warrant sections of their own. Additionally, you can view, hide, rearrange, merge, and flatten layers. See Chapter 2 of this minibook for more details on all these features.

Using the Layer and Select Menus

As with many features in Elements, you usually have more than one way to do something, especially when working with layers. Besides the commands in the Layers panel, you have two layer menus — the Layer menu and the Select menu — both of which you can find on the main Menu bar at the top of the Application window on a PC or at the top of the screen on a Mac.

The Layer menu

Much of what you can do with the Layers panel icons, you can also do by using the Layer menu on the Menu bar and the Layers panel menu. (Click the down arrow in the upper-right corner.) Commands such as New, Duplicate, Delete, and Rename are omnipresent throughout. But you also find commands that are exclusive to the panel, the main Layer menu, and the Layers panel menu. So, if you can't find what you're looking for in one area, just go to another. Some commands require an expanded explanation and are described in other sections of this and other minibooks.

Here's a quick description of most of the commands:

- **Delete Linked Layers and Delete Hidden Layers:** These commands delete only those layers that have been linked or hidden from display in the Layers panel.

- **Layer Style:** These commands manage the styles or special effects you apply to your layers.

- **Arrange:** You use this command to shuffle the layer-stacking order.

- **Group with Previous and Ungroup:** The Group command creates a *clipping group*, in which a group of layers is constrained to the boundaries of a base layer. Find more details in Chapter 4 of this minibook.

- **Type:** The commands on the Type submenu control the display of type layers.

- **Rename Layer:** You use this option to give a layer a new name. You can also simply double-click the name in the Layers panel.

- **Simplify:** This command converts a type layer, shape layer, or fill layer into a regular image layer. In other words, it converts vector-based type and images to pixel-based type and images.

- **Merge and Flatten:** The various Merge and Flatten commands combine multiple layers into a single layer or, in the case of flattening, combine all layers into a single background.

- **Flattened copy on a layer:** This command doesn't appear on the menu but is accessible via the keyboard shortcut of Ctrl+Alt+Shift+E (⌘+Option+Shift+E on the Mac). This command makes a flattened copy on a layer that sits above all the visible layers.

✔ **Panel Options:** Choose Panel Options from the Layers panel menu and select a thumbnail size. You can also choose whether to display just the boundary of the layer contents or the whole document in the thumbnail.

The Select menu

Although the Select menu's main duty is to assist you in making and refining your selections, it offers a few handy layer commands. Here's a quick introduction to each command:

✔ **Select All Layers:** If you want to select all the elements in your file quickly, choose Select➪All Layers. Note that this command doesn't select the background.

✔ **Select Layers of Similar Type:** This command is helpful if you have different types of layers in your document — such as regular layers, type layers, shape layers, and adjustment layers — and you want to select just one type. Select a layer and then choose Select➪Similar Layers.

✔ **Deselect All Layers:** Choose Select➪Deselect Layers.

Making Layers

Good old-fashioned image layers are the backbone of the world of layers. You can create multiple image layers within a single document. Even more fun is creating a composite from several images. The creative possibilities are endless. The following sections look at the various ways to create these layers.

Creating a new layer

You can create a layer in a new file or an existing one. To go the new-file route, choose File➪New in the Photo Editor, in Expert mode. Then, in the New dialog box that appears, select Transparent for the Background Contents option. (*Note:* Your new file appears labeled as `Layer 1` rather than as `Background`.)

If you have an open image and you want to create a new, blank layer, you can use any of the following methods to do so:

✔ In the Photo Editor, in Expert mode, click the Create New Layer icon at the top of the Layers panel. A layer with the default name of *Layer 1* appears in the Layers panel.

✔ In the Photo Editor, in Expert mode, select New Layer from the Layers panel menu (click the down-pointing arrow in the upper-right area of the panel).

✔ Choose Layer➪New➪Layer.

If you create a layer by using either the second or third method in this list, you open a dialog box in which you name your layer and can specify other options for blending and opacity. Provide a name for your layer and click OK. You should specify the other options directly in the Layers panel later.

After your new transparent layer is ready to go, you can put content on the new layer in one of several ways:

- **Paint directly on the layer.** Use one of the painting tools, such as the Brush or Pencil.

- **Copy and paste a selection to your layer.** Make a selection on another layer or on the background within the same document or from another image entirely. Then choose Edit⇔Copy. Select your new, blank layer in the Layers panel and choose Edit⇔Paste.

- **Cut and paste a selection to your layer.** Make a selection on another layer (or on the background) within the same document or from another image and then choose Edit⇔Cut. Select a new, blank layer and choose Edit⇔Paste. Just remember that Elements deletes the selection from the source and adds it to your new layer, as shown in Figure 1-10.

- **Transfer an entire image to your new layer.** Choose Select⇔All and then either Edit⇔Copy or Edit⇔Cut. Select a new, blank layer and choose Edit⇔Paste.

Using Layer via Copy and Layer via Cut

Another way to create a layer is to use the Layer via Copy command on the Layer menu. Make a selection on a layer or background and choose Layer⇔New⇔Layer via Copy. The copied selection is placed on a new layer with the default name of *Layer 1.* You can do the same with the Layer via Cut command, but in this case, Elements cuts, or deletes, the selected area from the source layer or background and places it on the new layer. The source layer is left with a transparent or background-colored hole (refer to Figure 1-10).

You can use these two commands only within the same image. You can't use them between images.

Duplicating layers

If you want to duplicate an existing layer, first select it in the Layers panel. Then drag the layer to the Create New Layer icon at the top of the Layers panel. You can also duplicate a layer by selecting Duplicate Layer from the Layers panel menu or by choosing Layer⇔Duplicate Layer. As when you create a new layer, both menu methods prompt you with a dialog box to name your layer and specify other options. Provide a name for your layer and click OK. If you choose the first method, Elements provides the default name of the original layer with the word *Copy* appended to the name.

© *iStockphoto.com/steps Image #859410*

Figure 1-10: Cutting and pasting a selection from one layer to another leaves a transparent hole on the original layer.

Duplicating layers can be especially handy when you want to experiment with a special effect but don't want to harm your original image.

Compositing with Multiple Images

Often, when working with layers, you're not using just a single image. Face it: You can do only so much to that family portrait taken down at the local photo studio. But pluck your family out of that stale studio and put them in front of the ruins at Pompeii or the summit at K2, and you have endless hours of fun. When you get the hang of working with several images, you find that it opens up a completely new realm of creative possibilities. And, you're not limited to snapshots. You can incorporate type, shapes, and scans of just about anything you can place on a scanning bed. Apply some effects, maybe a filter or two, and you have an image worthy of some major wall space.

Copying and pasting images

In the earlier "Making Layers" section, we explain how to use the Copy, Cut, and Paste commands within the same image or between two images when you want to fill a new, blank layer with content. You can also use the Copy and Paste commands without having a blank layer ready. When you copy and paste a selection without a blank layer, Elements automatically creates a new layer from the pasted selection. You can go on your merry way and perform all your layer creations by using only those commands. However, we rarely use them when working with multiple images. We prefer the drag-and-drop method, which we describe in the following section.

The Copy Merged command on the Edit menu creates a merged, or *joined,* copy of all visible layers within the selection.

Rather than cut, and or copy, and paste a layer from one image to another, we prefer to drag and drop. By dragging and dropping, you bypass the temporary storage area for copied and stored data — the *Clipboard.* Storing images on the Clipboard can slow your system. Keeping your Clipboard clear of data ensures that Elements is running more efficiently. If you want to perform a little spring cleaning on your Clipboard, choose Edit⇨Clear⇨Clipboard Contents, which empties it of any stored data.

Dragging and dropping layers

Follow these steps to drag and drop layers from one file to another:

1. **In the Photo Editor, in Expert mode, open two or more images.**

2. **In one of your images, select a layer in the Layers panel.**

3. **Grab the Move tool (the four-headed arrow) from the Tools panel.**

4. **Position the Move tool within an image and click it; then drag and drop the layer onto your destination file.**

   The dropped layer pops in as a new layer above the active layer in the image, as shown in Figure 1-11. You don't need to have a selection border to copy the entire layer. But, if you want to copy just a portion of the layer, make your selection with one of the many selection tools, such as the Lasso or Quick Selection tools, before you drag and drop with the Move tool. If you want the selected element centered on the destination file, press the Shift key while you drag and drop. Flip to Book IV, Chapter 1 for help with making selections.

Figure 1-11: Dragging and dropping a selection keeps the Clipboard lean and mean.

Be sure to check out the new Photomerge Compose command (described in Book VIII, Chapter 3), which enables you to select elements in your image and combine them with other images quickly and easily.

Using the Paste into Selection command

The Edit⇨Paste into Selection command lets you paste one selection into another. For example, if you want to make it appear as though a snake is poking its head out of the opening of a cave or a paintbrush is poking out of a can, Paste into Selection is your command (see Figure 1-12).

Follow these steps to insert a copied or cut selected image into a selection outline:

1. **In the Photo Editor, in Expert mode, make the selection on the layer that you want the image to fill.**

   It's the *destination* layer.

2. **Select the image that will fill that selection.**

   This *source* image can be within the same file or from another file.

3. **Choose Edit⇨Copy.**

4. **Return to the destination image layer and choose Edit⇨Paste into Selection.**

   The pasted selection is visible only inside the selection outline. (Refer to Figure 1-12.) If necessary, reposition your pasted selection with the Move tool. If you need to scale the pasted selection, choose Image⇨ Transform⇨Free Transform. For more on transformations, see Chapter 2 of this minibook. In our example, our bottle is showing only inside our selection. The bottom of the bottle is hidden, making it look as though it's sitting inside the ice bucket.

© iStockphoto.com/joxsxxjo Image #2466705 and Bedolaga Image #18359494

Figure 1-12: Use the Paste into Selection command to make one layer appear as though it's emerging from another.

Putting It Together

Creating Layers and Using the Paste into Selection Command to Make a Collage

You probably remember from elementary school cutting out a bunch of pictures from magazines and pasting them on a piece of construction paper. Well, with Elements, the idea of a collage isn't much different, though the activity is a little more refined.

Maybe you want to unleash your artistic side. Or, maybe you need to combine several images into one as part of a job. Whatever your reason, you can use the steps here to get started on your first collage. And, if *collage* is too prissy a word for you, you can substitute it with *composite* — which has the definition "derived from many components." We usually do.

Creating a collage takes many steps. Throughout this minibook, you can find a couple of ongoing Putting It Together projects, all of which build on each other and lead you to a finished collage. Be sure to save your collage file so that you can work on it while you make your way through this minibook, if you like.

To create the first layer of your collage, follow these steps:

1. **Decide on two images to use in your collage and open them in the Photo Editor, in Expert mode, by choosing File⇨Open.**

   © *iStockphoto.com/PIKSEL Image #2300338*

   You can pick an image to use as your main canvas, as shown in the figure, and then open a supporting image that you can select and then drag onto that main image. However, if you want, you can also start with just a blank document, which is what we've done. We then filled the blank image with light green. See Book V, Chapter 2 for details on filling with color.

2. **Choose Window⇨Layers to open the Layers panel if it isn't already open.**

   Always be sure that the Layers panel is visible whenever you're creating a composite from multiple images. You need to see what's happening while you drag and drop, and you need to be aware, at all times, of which layer you're working on.

continued

continued

3. **Select an element in the supporting image.**

Feel free to use whichever selection method suits your fancy, but remember that the finished collage will look only as good as its individual selections. For more on making selections, see Book IV.

We used the Quick Selection tool to select the girl, as shown in the figure. We then used the Lasso tool and cleaned up our selection border.

4. **Choose Select⇨Modify⇨Contract and, in the Contract Selection dialog box, enter a value; choose Select⇨Feather and enter a value in the Feather Selection dialog box.**

Contract the selections slightly (we chose a value of 1 pixel) before you apply a feather (we chose a 0.5-pixel value) to avoid picking up some of the background during the feathering process. Note

© iStockphoto.com/PIKSEL Image #2300338

that the values you choose depend on the resolution of your images; the lower the resolution, the smaller the value needed.

Using a small feather helps to avoid the harsh, I cut it out-with-a-pair-of-pinking-shears look.

5. **With the Move tool, drag and drop the selection onto the background image.**

The Layers panel shows that you've produced a layer. Notice that your main image remains as the background below the layer.

Don't worry if your element isn't the right size. You can find a Putting It Together project in Chapter 2 of this minibook that shows you how to scale the layer.

6. **Choose File⇨Save As, and in the Save As dialog box, name the file collage and make sure that the format is Photoshop.**

Keep the file in a handy spot on your hard drive so that you can find it when you're ready to do more with your collage.

In the preceding step list, we show you how to create a layer by dragging and dropping an image onto a background image. The following process shows you how to paste one selection into another:

1. **In the Photo Editor, in Expert mode, choose File⇨Open, select the file you saved from the preceding exercise, and open a new supporting image, as shown in the figure.**

2. **Choose Window⇨Layers to open the Layers panel if it isn't already open.**

Always keep the Layers panel visible whenever you're creating a composite from multiple images.

3. **Select the part of the supporting image you want to use.**

Feel free to use whichever selection method you want, but make the selection as accurate as you can.

We wanted to use the whole image, so we chose Select⇨All.

4. **Contract and feather the selection (as described in Step 4 in the preceding set of steps).**

Unless you're going for a special effect, be consistent with the treatment of the edges of each element in your composite.

We bypassed this step because we're using the entire image.

5. **Choose Edit⇨Copy.**

6. **In your saved collage file, use the Lasso tool (or any other selection tool) to create a selection in which to paste your new supporting image.**

We selected the blank screen of the girl's laptop with the Polygonal Lasso tool.

7. **Choose Edit⇨Paste into Selection.**

Use the Move tool to position the pasted image within the boundaries of the selection outline.

If your image needs to be scaled or rotated, choose Image⇨Transform⇨Free Transform. For details on transforming layers, see Chapter 2 of this minibook.

8. **Choose File⇨Save.**

© iStockphoto.com/PIKSEL Image #2300338

Chapter 2: Managing Layers

In This Chapter

✓ **Viewing, moving, and shuffling layers**

✓ **Rearranging and transforming layers**

✓ **Simplifying and converting layers**

✓ **Aligning layers**

✓ **Linking and locking layers**

✓ **Flattening and combining layers**

We hope that you have the time and inclination to check out the first chapter of this minibook. That's where you find all the basic information on creating layers. In this chapter, you get all the details on how to manage the layers you've created. And, unlike some employees, clients, or children, layers are extremely agreeable to being managed — even micromanaged, for that matter. You can scale and rotate them, hide them, rearrange them, link and lock them, and even condense them into one loving, collective layer. Yes, Elements has a slew of ways to line up your layers in the orderly and organized fashion you deserve.

Viewing Layers

Often, hiding all layers in an image except for the layer you want to edit is useful. You can then focus on the element at hand without the distraction of seeing all other elements of the image. You can hide layers with a single quick click of the mouse button, as we describe in the following list:

✓ **Hide all the layers but selected.** Select the layer(s) you want to display. Alt-click (Option-click on the Mac) the eye icon for that layer in the left column of the Layers panel, and all other layers disappear from view. To redisplay all layers, Alt-click (Option-click on the Mac) the eye icon again.

✓ **Hide an individual layer.** Click the eye icon for that layer. To redisplay the layer, click the blank space in the eye column. Figure 2-1 shows the girl layer hidden in the bottom figure.

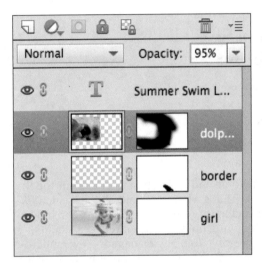

© iStockphoto.com/Yuri_Arcurs Image #18860532 and JohnnyH5 Image #915486

Figure 2-1: You can hide and show individual layers to better focus your tasks.

Only visible layers print. Hiding layers for printing can be useful if you want to have several versions (each on a separate layer) of an image for a project within the same document. You can view selective layers and print them, get approval from the powers that be, and then delete the layers with the scrapped versions. Only one file to manage — even we can handle that.

Rearranging Layers

You can shuffle the order of layers like clear sheets of acetate used with overhead projectors. The *stacking order* of the layers in the Layers panel corresponds to the order of the layers in the document. If you want to move a layer to another position in the stacking order, drag the layer up or down in the Layers panel. While you drag, you see a fist icon. Release the mouse button when a highlighted line appears where you want to insert the layer.

Alternatively, you can change the order by selecting the layer and then choosing Layer⇨Arrange. Then select one of the following commands from the submenu:

✔ **Bring to Front** *or* **Send to Back:** Send the layer to the top or bottom of the stacking order.

✔ **Bring Forward** *or* **Send Backward:** Move the layer one level up or down.

✔ **Reverse:** Switch the order of your layer stack when you have two or more layers selected.

If your image has a background, it always remains the bottommost layer. If you need to move the background, first convert it to a layer by double-clicking the name in the Layers panel. Enter a new name for the layer and then click OK.

Moving Layer Elements

Rearranging layers is different from moving the content on the layer. Because the elements on a layer are free-floating on a bed of transparency, you can easily move the element whenever necessary. Moving the element(s) on one layer has no effect on any other layer and doesn't harm the image.

To move an image on a layer, first select the layer in the Layers panel. Then position the Move tool (the four-headed arrow in the Tools panel) anywhere on the image and drag it to the position you want. It doesn't get any simpler than that.

Here are a few more handy tips for moving an image and using the Move tool:

✔ **Move the image on the layer in 1-pixel increments.** Press an arrow key when you have the Move tool selected. To move the layer in 10-pixel increments, press Shift when you press the arrow key.

✔ **Find out which layer holds the image you want to move or edit.** If you have the Auto-Select Layer option selected in the Tool Options, select the Move tool and click the element. Elements automatically activates the layer that the element resides on. If you don't have this option selected, Ctrl-click (⌘-click on the Mac) the element.

✔ **Switch to a layer when you click with the Move tool on any part of a layer.** To perform this trick, select the Auto-Select Layer option in the Tool Options. *Be careful* when using this option, especially if you have a lot of overlapping elements — you may inadvertently select a layer when you don't want to.

✔ **Display a *bounding box* (a rectangle that encloses a selection or an image on a layer) that has handles around the elements on your layer.** To do this one, select the Show Bounding Box check box in the Tool Options. This box can be useful if all your elements are melting into one another in an indistinguishable conglomeration.

We recommend keeping this option selected so that you have essentially the same controls (scale, rotate, and so on) as when you choose Image⇨Transform⇨Free Transform.

✔ **Show Highlight on Rollover.** Hover the mouse cursor on any element found on the canvas, and an outline magically appears around the element on your layer. Click the highlighted layer to select it and then move it.

Transforming Layers

When working with multiple images, you no doubt have to scale, or even rotate, some images to fit them into your composite. Fortunately, Elements makes scaling an easy chore by providing you with the Transform and Free Transform commands on the Image menu. When it comes to transforming layers and transforming selections, the methods are identical. After an element is on a layer, you can just choose the appropriate transformation command, and off you go. In addition, you can apply a transformation to multiple layers simultaneously if you select the various layers first.

Here's how to transform a layer:

1. **In the Photo Editor, in Expert mode, select a layer in the Layers panel.**

   You can also apply a transformation to multiple layers simultaneously by linking the layers first. For details, see the section "Linking Layers," later in this chapter.

2. **Choose Image⇨Transform⇨Free Transform.**

   A bounding box surrounds the contents of your layer, as shown in Figure 2-2. (In our example, the bounding box surrounds the dolphin layer.)

3. **Transform your layer as you want.**

   You have several options:

   - *Resize the contents:* Drag a corner or side handle to size the contents. Press Shift while dragging to constrain the proportions. You can also click the link icon between the W and H fields to do the same.

   - *Rotate the contents:* Move the mouse cursor just outside a corner handle until the cursor turns into a curved arrow and then drag.

   - *Distort, skew, or apply perspective to the contents:* Right-click and choose a command from the context menu that appears. You can also click the Rotate, Scale, and Skew icons in the Tool Options as well as enter Transform values numerically in the fields.

4. **When your layer is transformed to your liking, double-click inside the bounding box.**

The bounding box disappears, leaving behind your transformed layer.

© iStockphoto.com/Yuri_Arcurs Image #18860532 and JohnnyH5 Image #915486

Figure 2-2: Transform your layers.

Try to perform all transformations in one execution. Don't go back numerous times to apply various transformations. With the exception of rotations in multiples of 90 degrees, every time you transform pixels, you put your image through the *interpolation* process (increasing, decreasing, or remapping pixels). Done repeatedly, this process can degrade the quality of your image, which is why you're prudent to use the Transform⇨Free Transform command rather than individual commands — so that all transformations are executed in one fell swoop. Note that the above doesn't apply to shape or type layers.

Simplifying Layers

When you *simplify* a layer, you're simply converting a type layer, shape layer, or fill layer into a regular image layer. You want to do this to apply filters or to edit the layers with painting tools. However, simplifying comes with a price: After you simplify a shape layer, for example, you no longer have access to the shape-editing options — only the editing options available to a regular image layer. And, when you simplify a type layer, your text is converted to pixels, so you can no longer edit the text. The moral of the story? Be sure that your type is spelled and formatted to your liking before simplifying.

Putting It Together

Transforming and Moving Layers in a Collage

When you have a couple of images in your collage (see the Putting It Together project in Chapter 1 of this minibook), you can start transforming them to your liking. Moving and scaling are the manipulations you'll probably perform the most. Elements enables you to transform layers without affecting any other layer within the image. To transform and move images in a collage, follow these steps:

1. **In the Photo Editor, in Expert mode, choose File⇨Open. Select your saved collage file in the dialog box that opens.**

2. **Choose Window⇨Layers to open the Layers panel.**

3. **In the Layers panel, select the layer (or layers) you want to transform.**

   In our example, we chose the layer that has the girl and her laptop.

4. **Choose Image⇨ Transform⇨Free Transform.**

   The Free Transform bounding box appears around your layer. By choosing Free Transform, you interpolate the image only once rather than multiple times.

© iStockphoto.com/PIKSEL Image #2300338

5. **Shift-drag a corner transformation handle to scale the image down to the size you want but maintain its proportions, which reduces the amount of distortion.**

   We reduced the girl's size by about 20 percent.

6. **Position the cursor just outside the handle until a curved arrow appears. Rotate the image the desired amount.**

   Our layer didn't need any rotation.

7. **After you scale and rotate your image, place the cursor inside the Free Transform bounding box and position your layer elements by dragging them to your desired location.**

   We positioned our layer at the bottom of the Image window.

8. **When you transform the selection to your liking, double-click inside the Free Transform bounding box or press Enter (Return on the Mac).**

9. **Transform any remaining layers, by following Steps 3 through 8.**

If you're transforming a layer with a layer mask, be sure to choose the layer's thumbnail and not the layer mask thumbnail. Otherwise, you transform the layer mask rather than the layer.

10. **As always, when you transform a selection to your liking, double-click inside the Free Transform bounding box.**

11. **Choose File⇨Save.**

You probably already have a good sense of the possibilities (which are infinite) available to you when you create and change collages. Of course, you can always add more stuff to a collage and rearrange its layers, as needed. Just follow these steps:

1. **In the Photo Editor, in Expert mode, choose File⇨Open, select a collage file, and open another image.**

   We chose an image of a temple in Kyoto.

2. **Choose Window⇨Layers to open the Layers panel if it isn't already visible.**

3. **Select an element in the new image you open.**

   It goes without saying that making the selection accurate can only enhance your composite. We want to use our whole image, so we didn't need to make a selection.

4. **Contract and feather the image's edges (as described in the Putting It Together project in Chapter 1 of this minibook) and use the Move tool to drag the selection into the collage file.**

   For the most consistent appearance possible, use consistent values for modifying and feathering all selections in this composite.

5. **Position and transform the selection, as needed.**

   Follow the directions provided in the preceding step list. In our example, we scaled the temple image about 50 percent smaller and positioned it in the upper-right corner.

6. **In the Layers panel, rearrange your layers, if needed, by selecting a layer and dragging it above another layer.**

   In our image, we dragged the temple layer below the girl layer, as shown in the figure.

   Because layers are independent entities, you can shuffle them indefinitely, like a deck of cards.

7. **Choose File⇨Save.**

© iStockphoto.com/PIKSEL Image #2300338

Here's how to simplify a layer:

1. **In the Photo Editor, in Expert mode, select a layer in the Layers panel.**

2. **Choose Layer➪Simplify Layer.**

   You can also choose the command from the Layers panel menu (click the down arrow in the upper-right corner of the panel). If you select a shape layer, you can also click the Simplify command in the Tool Options.

Aligning and Distributing Layers

If you're a precision junkie, like we are, you'll appreciate Elements' capability to align and distribute your layers. These commands can be especially useful when you need to align such items as navigation buttons on a web page mock-up or a row of head shots for a corporate publication.

Follow these steps to align and distribute your layers:

1. **In the Photo Editor, in Expert mode, select the layers you want to align in the Layers panel.**

   Select your first layer and then Ctrl-click (⌘-click on the Mac) to select more layers.

2. **With the Move tool selected from the Tools panel, click the Align option in the Tool Options and choose an alignment option.**

   Elements provides you with handy little icons that illustrate the various alignment types, as shown in Figure 2-3.

   Note that, depending on which alignment type you choose, Elements aligns to the layer element that's the farthest from the top, bottom, left, or right. If you align to the center, Elements splits the difference among the various layers.

3. **In the Layers panel, select three or more layers that you want to distribute evenly.**

4. **With the Move tool selected from the Tools panel, click the Distribute option in the Tool Options and choose a distribution option.**

   The Distribute commands evenly space the layers between the first and last elements in either the row or column.

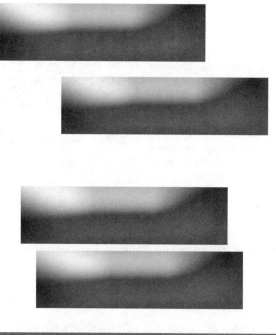

Figure 2-3: The Tool Options offers different alignment buttons.

As with aligning, you find an icon illustrating the distribution types. You can see the buttons from Figure 2-3 precisely aligned and evenly distributed in Figure 2-4.

Linking Layers

You'll probably find that you don't need to link layers in most cases. You can simply select multiple layers and apply your command — moving, scaling, or rotating, for example. Occasionally, however, you may want to link layers so that they stay grouped as a unit until you decide otherwise.

Figure 2-4: The aligned and evenly distributed buttons.

To link layers, follow these short steps:

1. **In the Photo Editor, in Expert mode, select your first layer in the Layers panel. Ctrl-click (⌘-click on the Mac) to select your additional layers.**

2. **Click the Link/Unlink layers icon just to the left of the layer thumbnail in the Layers panel, as shown in Figure 2-5.**

The Link/Unlink layers icon appears highlighted in the Layers panel.

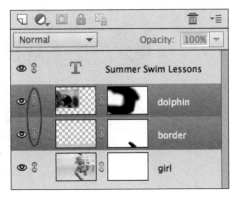

Figure 2-5: Use the Link Layers command to group layers.

To remove a link, click the Link/Unlink layers icon again.

Locking Layers

When you have your layers how you want them, you may want to lock them to prevent them from being changed, as shown in Figure 2-6. To lock a layer, select it in the Layers panel and select one of the two lock options at the top of the Layers panel. The checkerboard square icon locks all transparent areas of your layers: You're prevented from painting or editing any transparent areas on the layers. The lock icon locks the entire layer and prevents it from being changed in any way, including moving or transforming the elements on the layer. You can, however, still make selections on the layer. To unlock the layer, simply click the icon again to toggle off the lock.

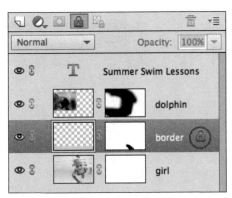

Figure 2-6: Locking prevents unwanted edits.

By default, the Background is locked and can't be unlocked until you convert the Background into a layer by choosing Layer⇨New⇨Layer from Background. You can also just double-click Background in the Layers panel. In addition, by default, type and shape layers have the Lock Transparent Pixels option selected. These options are grayed out and can't be deselected. However, if you need to paint on the type or shape layer, you can always simplify it (as described in the section "Simplifying Layers," earlier in this chapter), thereby removing the locked option.

Flattening and Merging Layers

True layers evangelists that we are, we tout the glories of layers in the first chapter of this minibook. And, although layers are wonderful, they have a dark side: They can make your file go from slim and trim to bulky and bloated. You not only create a larger file size that slows your computer system's performance, but you're also limited to the file formats that allow you to save layers: the native Photoshop format (.psd), TIFF (.tif), and PDF (.pdf). If you save your file in any other format, Elements smushes your layers into a background. This file limitation often forces users to save two versions of every layered file — one as a native Photoshop file and one as something else, such as EPS or JPEG, to import into another program. (For more on file formats, see Book III, Chapter 3.)

Book VI
Chapter 2

To curb large file sizes or to use your image in a nonlayer supporting format, you have a couple of options:

- ✔ **Merge layers:** Combines visible, linked, or adjacent layers into a single layer (not a background). The intersection of all transparent areas is retained. You can also merge adjustment or fill layers, although they can't act as the target layer for the merge. Merging layers can help decrease file size and make your documents more manageable. You're still restricted to the layer-friendly file formats, however.

- ✔ **Flatten an image:** Combines all visible layers into a background. Elements deletes hidden layers and fills any transparent areas with white. Flattening is usually reserved for when you're finished editing your image. We recommend, however, that before you flatten an image, you make a copy of the file with all its layers intact and save it as a native Photoshop file. That way, if you ever need to make any edits, you have the added flexibility of having your layers.

Merging layers

You can merge layers in several ways. First, simply select the layers you want to merge in the Layers panel and choose Merge Layers from the panel menu or the Layer menu.

You can also merge just visible layers by following these steps:

1. **In the Photo Editor, in Expert mode, ensure that all the layers you want to merge are visible in the Layers panel, as shown in Figure 2-7.**

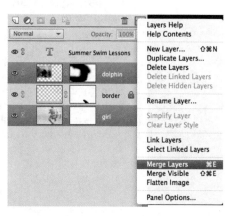

Figure 2-7: Merging layers can make your file size a lot smaller.

2. **Choose Merge Visible from the Layers panel menu or the Layer menu.**

   All visible layers merge into a single Background layer.

Hold down Alt (Option on the Mac) when choosing Layer⇨Merge Visible. Elements merges those layers onto a new layer.

You can also merge layers by following these steps:

1. **Position the layers that you want to merge adjacent to each other in the Layers panel.**

2. **Select the top layer of the ones you want to be merged.**

3. **Choose Merge Down from the Layers panel drop-down menu or the Layer menu.**

   Note that Merge Down merges your active layer with the layer directly below it.

One last merge command doesn't appear in the menu but is accessible via the key command of Ctrl+Alt+Shift+E (⌘+Opt+Shift+E on the Mac). This command creates a merged copy of your layers on a layer that sits above all the visible layers.

Flattening layers

To flatten an image into a single background, follow these steps:

1. **In the Photo Editor, in Expert mode, ensure that all layers you want to retain are visible in the Layers panel.**

   Elements discards all hidden layers.

2. **Choose Layer⇨Flatten Image or choose Flatten Image from the Layers panel menu.**

   The transparent areas of flattened images fill with the background color and appear as a background in the Layers panel.

   If you mistakenly flatten an image, you can undo the command immediately by choosing Edit⇨Undo. If you go ahead and perform another action, undo your mistake by using the Undo History panel. However, note that if the flattening step is no longer in the Undo History panel, you have no way to undo the flattening.

Putting It Together

Checking Your Collage for Flaws and Consolidating Layers

When you begin a project, you may think that you know what you want the result to look like. But when your creative juices start flowing, you may decide that something doesn't look right. For example, while we were working on our collage, we felt that our green background was a little boring, so we followed these steps to add a pattern to the existing background:

Book VI
Chapter 2

Managing Layers

1. **In the Photo Editor, in Expert mode, open the saved collage file and open a new image that you want to incorporate into the collage.**

   In our example, we thought the green background needed some texture, so we opened an image that contained some Japanese characters we like.

2. **Select the part of the image that you want to add to your collage, as shown in the figure.**

   We wanted the whole image, so we didn't need to make a selection.

3. **With the Move tool, drag and drop your new selection, or the entire image, onto your collage image.**

4. **Choose Image⇨ Transform⇨Free Transform.**

   Transform and position your new layer, as described in the earlier Putting It Together project in this chapter.

When you're close to finalizing your collage, you may want to consolidate layers. Minimizing the number of layers

© iStockphoto.com/PIKSEL Image #2300338

makes projects easier to manage and the file size smaller, which is helpful when you get ready to add the finishing touches to your collage.

continued

continued

Before you merge your layers, be certain that you'll never have to manipulate them separately again, especially if the elements on the layer overlap each other, as ours do.

To consolidate two layers, follow these steps:

1. **In the Photo Editor, in Expert mode, select the layers in the Layers panel.**
2. **Choose Merge Layers from the Layers panel drop-down menu.**

   The two layers merge and become one.
3. **Choose File⇨Save.**

Chapter 3: Playing with Opacity and Blend Modes

In This Chapter

✔ **Adjusting opacity**

✔ **Applying Blend modes for effects**

✔ **Setting the blend options**

In this chapter, we show you how to have a little fun and get those creative juices flowing. This chapter, along with Chapters 1 and 3 in Book VII, gives you a few ways to tweak the layers you've so diligently created. Maybe you want to make one of your layers semitransparent so that you can see the layer beneath it. Or perhaps you want to try blending the colors between a couple layers in a way that's slightly offbeat. Look no further.

Take these techniques as far as you want. ***Remember:*** There's no substitute for good old experimentation. Before you jump into these techniques, you should have a handle on the methods of layer creation and management that we explain in Chapters 1 and 2 of this minibook.

Adjusting Layer Opacity

One of the easiest ways by far to make your image look interesting is to have one image ghosted over another, as shown in Figure 3-1. Creating this effect is an easy task with the Opacity option in the Layers panel. You adjust the opacity by selecting a layer in the Layers panel. Then either access the slider by clicking the right arrow or enter a percentage value in the Opacity text box.

The Opacity setting allows you to mix the active layer with the layers below it in varying percentages from 100% (completely opaque) to 0% (completely transparent). Remember that you can adjust the opacity only on a layer, not on the Background.

You can also use the scrubby slider by pressing and dragging your mouse over the word *Opacity* in the Layers panel.

© iStockphoto.com/babyblueut and Image#4266855 and muratkoc Image #3357562

Figure 3-1: Adjusting the opacity enables one image to ghost over another.

Creatively Mixing with Blend Modes

Elements sports an impressive 25 Blend modes. *Blend modes* affect how colors interact between layers and how colors interact when you apply paint to a layer. Blend modes can produce a multitude of interesting, sometimes even bizarre, effects. What's more, you can easily apply, edit, or discard Blend modes without modifying your image pixels one iota.

Blend modes are located on a drop-down menu at the top of the Layers panel in Expert mode. The best way to get a feel for the effect of Blend modes isn't to memorize the descriptions we give you in the following sections. Instead, grab an image with some layers and apply each Blend mode to one or more of the layers to see what happens. In fact, try a few different images because the effects may be subtle or intense, depending on the colors in the image and the colors with which they're blending. Throw in some different opacity percentages, and you're on your way to endless hours of creative fun.

You see Blend modes called *Painting modes, Brush modes, Layer modes, calculations,* or just plain *modes.* They're usually referred to as *Blend modes* or *Layer modes* when used with layers and painting modes, and as *Brush modes* when used in conjunction with a painting or an editing tool.

General Blend modes

Normal Blend mode doesn't require an explanation. It's the one you probably use the most. Dissolve is the next one on the list and, ironically, is probably the one you use the least. (You can see both at work in Figure 3-2.)

- ✔ **Normal:** The default mode displays each pixel, unadjusted. Note that you can't see the underlying layer at all with the Normal blend mode.

- ✔ **Dissolve:** You can see this mode only on a layer with an opacity setting of less than 100%. The lower the opacity, the more intense the effect. Dissolve allows some pixels from lower layers, which are randomized, to show through the target (selected) layer.

**Book VI
Chapter 3**

**Playing with
Opacity and Blend
Modes**

Normal　　　　　　　　　Dissolve

Figure 3-2: The Dissolve Blend mode enables pixels from one layer to peek randomly through another layer.

Blend modes that darken

Overall, all the Blend modes we cover in this section produce effects that darken an image, as shown in Figure 3-3.

Here's one of our favorite uses for the Darken Blend mode. Scan a handwritten letter or sheet of music and layer it over an image. Apply the Darken Blend mode to the letter or sheet music layer. The white areas of the paper become transparent, and only the letters or musical notes display, creating a nice composite image.

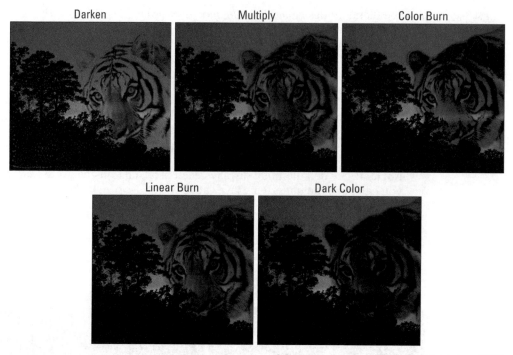

© iStockphoto.com/dlewis33 Image #2434140 and PhotoInc Image #464286

Figure 3-3: These Blend modes darken, or burn, your layers.

Here are the Blend modes that darken your image in some way:

- **Darken:** Turns lighter pixels transparent if the pixels on the target layer are lighter than those on layers below. If the pixels are darker, they're unchanged.

- **Multiply:** Burns the target layer onto the layers underneath, thereby darkening all colors where they mix. When you're painting with the Brush or Pencil tool, each stroke creates a darker color, as though you're drawing with markers.

- **Color Burn:** Darkens the layers underneath the target layer and burns them with color, creating an increased contrast effect, like applying a dark dye to an image. Blending with white pixels has no effect.

- **Linear Burn:** Darkens the layers underneath the target layer by decreasing the brightness. This effect is similar to Multiply but often makes portions of an image black. Blending with white has no effect.

- **Dark Color:** When blending two layers, the darker color of the two colors is visible. This mode comes in handy when you overlay elements like scanned sheets of music, handwritten letters, or logos over your images and you want the white portions to appear transparent.

Blend modes that lighten

If you have Blend modes that darken, well, having modes that lighten just makes good sense. So, if you have the need to throw some digital bleach on your brightly colored pixels, try a couple of these Blend modes, as shown in Figure 3-4.

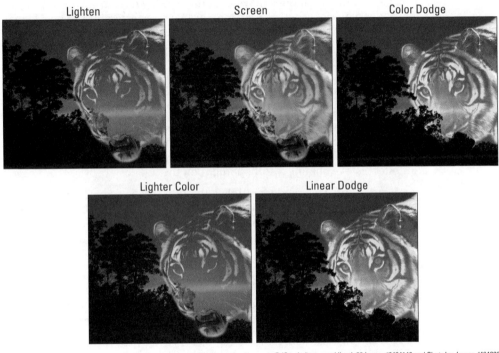

© iStockphoto.com/dlewis33 Image #2434140 and PhotoInc Image #464286

Figure 3-4: These Blend modes lighten, or dodge, your layers.

- ✔ **Lighten:** Turns darker pixels transparent if the pixels on the target layer are darker than those on layers below. If the pixels are lighter, they're unchanged. This effect is the opposite of Darken.

- ✔ **Screen:** Lightens the target layer where it mixes with the layers underneath. Blending with black has no effect. This effect is the opposite of Multiply.

- ✔ **Color Dodge:** Lightens the pixels in the layers underneath the target layer and infuses them with colors from the top layer. Blending with black has no effect. This effect is similar to applying a bleach to an image.

- ✔ **Lighter Color:** When you're blending two layers, the lighter color of the two colors is visible.

✔ **Linear Dodge:** Lightens the layers underneath the target layer by increasing the brightness. This effect is similar to Screen but often makes parts of an image pure white. Blending with black pixels has no effect.

Lighting or Contrast Blend modes

This group of Blend modes plays with the lighting in your layers. Some of these Blend modes, such as Pin Light, are best reserved for the occasional wacky special effect. See these Blend modes in action in Figure 3-5.

✔ **Overlay:** Multiplies the dark pixels in the target layer and screens the light pixels in the underlying layers. Enhances the contrast and saturation of colors.

✔ **Soft Light:** Darkens the dark pixels (greater than 50% gray) and lightens the light pixels (less than 50% gray). Blending with black or white results in darker or lighter pixels but doesn't make parts of your image pure black or pure white. It's similar to Overlay, but is softer and subtler. The effect is like shining a soft spotlight on the image.

✔ **Hard Light:** This mode multiplies the dark pixels (greater than 50% gray) and screens the light pixels (less than 50% gray). It can be used to add highlights and shadows to an image. Blending with black or white gives you black and white. The effect is similar to shining a bright, hard spotlight on the image.

✔ **Vivid Light:** If the pixels on the top layer are darker than 50% gray, this mode darkens the colors by increasing the contrast. If the pixels on the top layer are lighter than 50% gray, the mode lightens the colors by decreasing the contrast. It's a combination of Color Burn and Color Dodge.

✔ **Linear Light:** If the pixels on the top layer are darker than 50% gray, the mode darkens the colors by decreasing the brightness. If the pixels on the top layer are lighter than 50% gray, the mode lightens the colors by increasing the brightness. It's a combination of Linear Burn and Linear Dodge.

✔ **Pin Light:** Replaces the colors of pixels, depending on the colors in the top layer. If the pixels on the top layer are darker than 50% gray, the mode replaces the pixels that are darker than those on the top layer and doesn't change pixels that are lighter. If the pixels on the top layer are lighter than 50% gray, the mode replaces the pixels that are lighter than those pixels on the top layer and doesn't change pixels that are darker. It's a combination of Darken and Lighten; useful for special effects.

✔ **Hard Mix:** Similar to Vivid Light but reduces the colors to a total of eight: cyan, magenta, yellow, black, red, green, blue, and white. Although the results depend on the mix of existing colors on the top and bottom layers, this mode usually creates a highly posterized (a cartoon or flat illustration) effect.

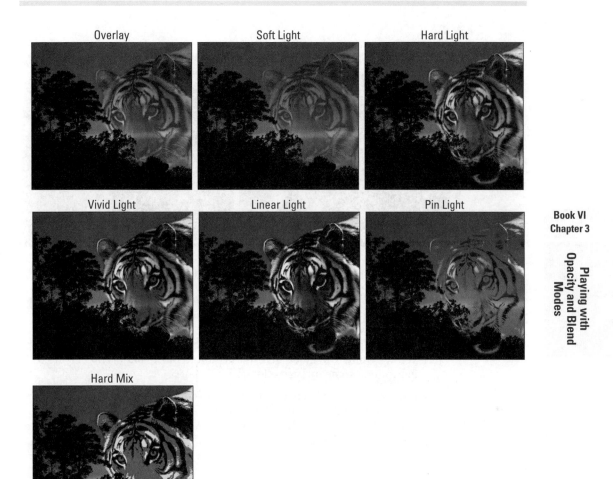

Figure 3-5: These Blend modes adjust the lighting between image layers.

Blend modes that invert

If the Blend modes discussed in the preceding sections are a little too sedate for you, you may want to experiment with the inverters — Difference and Exclusion. These Blend modes, also referred to as Comparative blend modes, invert your colors and can produce some interesting special effects, as shown in Figure 3-6.

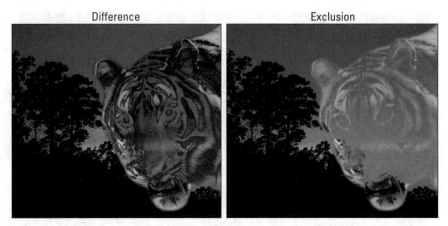

© iStockphoto.com/dlewis33 Image #2434140 and PhotoInc Image #464286

Figure 3-6: The Difference and Exclusion Blend modes invert colors.

✔ **Difference:** Produces a negative, or inverted, effect according to the brightness values on the top layers. If the pixels on the top layer are black, no change occurs in the underlying layers. If the pixels on the top layer are white, the mode inverts the colors of the underlying layers. It can produce some intense effects.

✔ **Exclusion:** Like Difference, but with less contrast and saturation. If the pixels on the top layer are black, no change occurs in the underlying layers. If the pixels on the top layer are white, this mode inverts the colors of the underlying layers. Medium colors blend to create shades of gray.

HSL color model Blend modes

These Blend modes, sometimes referred to as the Comparative blend modes, use the HSL (Hue, Saturation, Luminosity) color model to mix colors, as shown in Figure 3-7.

✔ **Hue:** Blends the *luminance* (brightness) and *saturation* (intensity of the color) of the underlying layers with the *hue* (color) of the top layer.

✔ **Saturation:** Blends the luminance and hue of the underlying layers with the saturation of the top layer.

✔ **Color:** Blends the luminance of the underlying layers with the saturation and hue of the top layer. This mode enables you to paint color while preserving the shadows, highlights, and details of the underlying layers.

Hue   Saturation

Color   Luminosity

© iStockphoto.com/dlewis33 Image #2434140 and PhotoInc Image #464286

Figure 3-7: These Blend modes use the Hue, Saturation, Luminosity color model to mix colors.

Our favorite Blend mode in this group is Color; you use it to apply color to images without obscuring the tonality. Color mode is helpful for "hand painting" grayscale images. If you've ever admired those hand-tinted, black-and-white photos used in greeting cards and posters, you can create the same effect fairly easily. First, make sure that your black-and-white image is in RGB (red, green, blue) mode so that it can accept color. Create a new layer in the Layers panel and set it to the Color Blend mode. Grab the Brush tool (with a soft-edged tip), choose a color, and paint over the image. Adjust the opacity to less than 100% to create a softer effect.

✔ **Luminosity:** The opposite of Color, this mode blends the hue and saturation of the underlying layers with the luminance of the top layer. This mode also preserves the shadows, highlights, and details from the top layer and mixes them with the colors of the underlying layers.

Putting It Together

Adjusting Opacity Settings in a Collage

If you've followed along with the Putting It Together projects we discuss in Chapters 1 and 2 of this minibook, you may have a collage that you're satisfied with. You just need to make the final tweaks to get it to the state of perfection.

One of the most important tweaks you can make concerns opacity. Follow these steps to adjust the opacity settings on some of the layers:

1. **In the Photo Editor, in Expert mode, open your saved collage file.**

2. **If the Layers panel isn't already visible, choose Window⇨Layers to open it.**

3. **Select a layer in the collage and move the Opacity slider, located at the top of the Layers panel, to the left or right.**

   If you want the layer to be more opaque, move the slider to the right. If you're interested in making the layer more transparent, move the slider to the left.

   We chose our Japanese-characters layer and adjusted the opacity to 10%. We wanted the characters to create just a subtle texture, not to appear in full strength.

4. **Save the file and then move to the next layer you want to adjust.**

   If you have more complicated opacity settings to adjust, keep reading.

5. **Select another layer, choose Duplicate Layer from the Layers panel menu, and click OK to close the Duplicate Layer dialog box.**

   Making a copy of a layer is useful because you can add a Blend mode and then adjust it to create just the right amount of the effect.

   For example, if you want to define an element in your collage but applying it directly on the layer makes the effect too intense, make a copy of the layer. We made a copy of our temple layer.

6. **Select the duplicated layer and choose a mode (such as Soft Light) from the Blend Mode drop-down menu in the Layers panel.**

   Leaving our duplicated and blended layer at 100% opacity is a little too garish.

7. **Adjust the opacity to tone it down as much as you want.**

   We brought ours down to 25%.

8. **When you're satisfied with the opacity and contrast, save the collage file.**

Oh, by the way, we added a dark green background box and a lucky cat to our collage.

**Book VI
Chapter 3**

**Playing with
Opacity and Blend
Modes**

Chapter 4: Cutting, Erasing, and Masking

In This Chapter

- ✓ **Using the Cookie Cutter tool**
- ✓ **Getting rid of items with the eraser tools**
- ✓ **Using layer masks**
- ✓ **Adding clipping masks**

*I*n Book IV, we present you with lots of information about making selections with the many tools that Elements provides for that very purpose, such as the Marquee and Lasso tools, the Magic Wand, the Quick Selection tool, and the Selection Brush. But we left the discussion of a few tools until this chapter. The tools in Book IV involve making selections by dragging around, clicking, or painting over. And, though the result is similar — selecting what you want or don't want in an image — the tools in this chapter are a little different in their methodology. They involve cutting out, masking from, and erasing around.

To add to your selection repertoire, we give you details on layer masking, a feature that is the most versatile way to get what you want out of an image. Layer masking is essentially just another way of making a selection. Rather than define your selection with a selection outline or by erasing away what you don't want, you can use masks to define the selection with up to 256 levels of gray. This gives you varying levels of selection. You can choose to fully show your layer, partially show it, or hide (or *mask*) certain areas. The nice thing about layer masks is that you can creatively blend one layer into another in a multitude of ways.

We round out this chapter by showing you how to create a clipping group, yet another way to blend your layers by masking them to the opaque areas of a base layer. Don't worry: It may sound complicated, but it's a piece of cake.

Working with the Cookie Cutter Tool

The Cookie Cutter tool is a cute name for a powerful tool. Think of it as a Custom Shape tool for images. But, whereas the Custom Shape tool creates a mask and only hides everything outside the shape, the Cookie Cutter cuts away everything outside the shape, much like a traditional cookie cutter does with dough. The preset libraries provide you with a variety of shapes, from animals and flowers to symbols and faces.

Here's how to use the Cookie Cutter:

1. **In the Photo Editor, in Expert mode, choose the Cookie Cutter tool from the Tools panel.**

    The tool icon looks like a flower. You can also press the C key.

2. **Specify the following options in the Tool Options:**

    - *Shape:* Click the down arrow and choose a shape from the Custom Shape picker preset library. To load other libraries, click the panel drop-down menu and choose one from the submenu.

    - *Geometry Options:* Draw your shape using certain parameters:

        Unconstrained: Draw freely using the default, Unconstrained.

        Defined Proportions: Keep the height and width proportional.

        Defined Size: Crop the image to the original, fixed size of the shape you choose. You can't make it bigger or smaller.

        Fixed Size: Enter a width and height in the W and H fields.

        From Center: Draw the shape from the center outward.

    - *Feather:* Create a soft-edged selection.

    - *Crop:* Crop the image into the shape. The shape cuts the canvas to the edges of the bounding box of the shape.

3. **Click and drag the mouse on the image to create your desired shape and then size and position the shape.**

    You can size the shape by dragging one handle of the bounding box. You can then position the shape by placing the mouse cursor inside the box and dragging.

    You can also perform other types of transformations, such as rotating and skewing, manually or via the options in the Tool Options.

    Take a gander at the Layers panel. Notice the temporary creation of a Layer Mask icon, as shown in Figure 4-1. See the section "Working with Layer Masks," later in this chapter, for details on layer masks.

4. **Click the Commit button (green check mark) near the Cookie Cutter bounding box, press Enter, or double-click inside the bounding box to complete the cut.**

   Figure 4-1 shows our image cut into a flower. If you change your mind and don't want the cut, click the Cancel button (red slashed circle) near the bounding box or press Esc.

© iStockphoto.com/Maria Pavlova Image #13009049

Figure 4-1: Cut your photo into an interesting shape.

Selective Erasing with the Eraser Tools

The eraser tools let you erase portions of an image. The three eraser tools are the regular Eraser, the Magic Eraser, and the Background Eraser, which all share a flyout menu in the Tools panel.

The eraser tools look like real erasers, so you can't miss them. But just in case you do, press E to cycle through the three tools.

When you erase pixels, those pixels are gone — for good. Before using the eraser tools, make a backup of your image. You can save the image as either a separate file or another layer. That way, if things run amok, you have some cheap insurance.

Using the Eraser tool

The Eraser tool allows you to erase areas on your image. If the image contains just a background, you erase to the background color. If the image is on a layer, you erase to transparency. Both instances are shown in Figure 4-2.

To use this tool, simply select the image and then click and drag through your desired area on it, and you're done. Because it isn't the most accurate tool on the planet, remember to zoom way in and use smaller brush tips to erase accurately.

These options in the Tool Options control the Eraser tool:

✔ **Brush Presets Picker:** Click the drop-down panel to access the Brush presets. Choose the brush you want. Again, additional brush libraries are available from the Brush panel menu.

✔ **Size:** Slide the Size slider and choose a brush size between 1 and 2500 pixels.

✔ **Opacity:** Specify a percentage of transparency for the erased areas. The lower the Opacity setting, the less it erases. This option isn't available for Block mode.

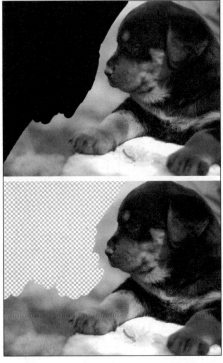

© iStockphoto.com/gmutlu Image #4440145

Figure 4-2: The Eraser tool erases to either the background color (top) or, if you're on a layer, transparency (bottom).

✔ **Type:** Select from Brush, Pencil, and Block. When you select Brush or Pencil, you have access to the Brush Preset Picker panel in the Tool Options. When you select Block, you're stuck with one size (a 16-x-16-pixel square tip). But because the block size remains constant, if you zoom way in, you can perform some detailed erasing.

Selecting and erasing by color

The Magic Eraser tool works like a combination Eraser and Magic Wand tool. It selects and erases similarly colored pixels simultaneously. Here's how it works:

✔ **When you click a layer:** The Magic Eraser tool erases pixels of a similar color based on a specified range and leaves the area transparent, as shown in Figure 4-3.

✔ **When you click the background:** The Magic Eraser tool automatically converts the background to a layer and then does the same pixel-erasing thing.

✔ **When you click a layer with locked transparency:** The Magic Eraser tool erases the pixels and replaces the area with the background color.

Here are the options for using the Magic Eraser tool:

✔ **Tolerance:** Defines the range of colors that Elements erases, just as it does with the Magic Wand tool. The value determines how similar a neighboring color has to be to the color you click. A higher value picks up more colors, whereas a lower value picks up fewer colors.

✔ **Anti-aliasing:** Creates a slightly soft edge around the transparent area.

✔ **Contiguous:** Selects only similar colors that are adjacent to each other. Deselect this option to select and then delete similarly colored pixels wherever they appear in your image.

✔ **Sample All Layers:** Samples colors using data from all visible layers, but erases pixels on only the *active* layer.

✔ **Opacity:** Works like it does for the regular Eraser tool, described in the previous section.

© Bob Woerner

Figure 4-3: Clicking with the Magic Eraser simultaneously selects and erases similarly colored pixels.

Removing the background from an image

The Background Eraser tool is probably the most sophisticated of the Eraser-tool lot. It erases the background from an image and should leave the foreground untouched. But if you're not careful in using the Background Eraser tool, it can erase the foreground and anything else in its path.

Like the Magic Eraser tool, the Background Eraser tool erases to transparency on a layer. If you drag on the background, Elements converts the background into a layer.

To use the Background Eraser tool successfully, carefully keep the crosshair, or *hot spot,* which appears in the center of the cursor, on the background pixels while you drag. The hot spot samples the color of the pixels and deletes pixels of that color wherever they fall under the brush circumference. But, if you get close to a foreground pixel with the hot spot, that pixel is gobbled up as well. This tool works better with images that have good contrast in color between the background and foreground objects, as shown in Figure 4-4. Also, if your image has very detailed or wispy edges (such as

© Bob Woerner

Figure 4-4: Be careful when using the Background Eraser because you can inadvertently eat up pixels.

hair or fur), you're better off using a layer mask, which we describe next.

Here's the rundown on the options, found in the Tool Options, for the Background Eraser:

- ✓ **Brush Settings:** Click the Brush Settings button to bring up the settings to customize the size, hardness, spacing, roundness, and angle of your brush tip. The Size and Tolerance settings at the bottom are for pressure-sensitive drawing tablets. You can base the size and tolerance on the pen pressure or position of the thumbwheel.

- ✓ **Limits:** The Contiguous sampling setting erases similar colors that are adjacent to one another under the brush circumference. The Discontiguous sampling setting erases similar colors whenever they're under the brush circumference, regardless of whether they're adjacent.

- ✓ **Tolerance:** Works just like the Magic Eraser Tolerance setting, described in the previous section.

Working with Layer Masks

A layer mask is one of the most helpful and powerful creative tools at your disposal. But before we get ahead of ourselves and tell you how to create a layer mask, you may want to know what one is and why in the world you would ever need one.

A *layer mask* is similar to a second sheet of acetate that hovers over a layer. You can use layer masks with image layers and adjustment layers, as follows:

✔ For an image layer, the layer mask allows you to selectively show, hide, or partially show portions of your image.

✔ With adjustment layers, the layer mask lets you selectively apply the adjustment to the layers below it.

You do this by painting on a layer mask with black and white and various shades of gray. Any black areas on the mask hide the image or the adjustment; any white areas show the image or adjustment; and anything between them (gray) partially shows the image or adjustment, as shown in Figure 4-5, where we hid the background of the girl image so that the image of the balloons would show through. The darker the shade of gray, the less it shows the image or adjustment.

© iStockphoto.com/Zennie Image #478144 and kaisersosa67 Image #186601

Figure 4-5: A layer mask uses varying shades of gray to selectively show and hide the underlying layer.

Note that if you have an active selection border in your image before you add an adjustment layer, the adjustment is applied to only that area within the selection border. The resulting layer mask also reflects that selection: The selected areas are white, and the unselected areas are black. By default, the mask is completely white. This allows the image or adjustment to be fully applied to the layers.

Layer masks are excellent for blending layers of images and creating soft transitions between elements. You can gradually brush in transparency and opacity on a selective-pixel basis. You can even apply gradients and filters to your layer masks to create interesting special effects.

Masking is just another way of making a selection. Rather than make a selection with a single selection outline (it's either selected or it isn't), masks let you create a selection with up to 256 levels of gray — from white to black.

Now, for the fun part. Follow these steps to create a layer mask:

1. **In the Photo Editor, in Expert mode, open or create a layered image.**

2. **In the Layers panel, select the layer that you want to hide portions of.**

   In our case, we want to hide the background of the little girl (refer to Figure 4-5) so that the balloons layer underneath could show through instead.

3. **In the Layers panel, click the Add Layer Mask icon (circle on a square) at the top of the panel.**

   You see the appearance of a second thumbnail, directly to the right of your image thumbnail, in the Layers panel.

4. **With the painting tool of your choice (we recommend the Brush tool), paint on your layer mask.**

   Make sure that the mask is selected, not the actual layer. You see black brackets around the thumbnail in the Layers panel.

   a. *Apply a foreground color of black where you want to hide the portions of the layer.* Leave the mask white where you want the layer to show.

   b. *Adjust the Opacity setting in the Tool Options to paint with a less-opaque black, which is essentially like painting with gray.* The higher the opacity, the darker the gray and the more it partially hides the layer. If you want subtle blending between layers, use a large, feathered brush tip and vary your opacity settings accordingly.

   If things start to run amok, just choose Edit⇨Fill and fill the entire layer mask with white to start again. As you can see from the figure, we painted some of the background of the girl with black. We used a large feathered brush to create soft edges around the girl and her smaller balloons.

You can also use the Gradient tool on the layer mask. Using foreground and background colors of white and black, you can create a nice transition from showing and hiding the layer, as shown in Figure 4-6. The darker areas of the gradient gradually hide the image, whereas the lighter areas gradually show the image. This is a helpful way to creatively and subtly blend one layer into another. For more on gradients, see Book V, Chapter 2.

You can also use layer masks to selectively show and hide the effects of an Adjustment layer. (See Chapter 1 of this minibook for more on Adjustment layers.)

Here are some other things to remember when using layer masks:

© iStockphoto.com/najin Image #13699329 and shaunl Image #2008511

Figure 4-6: Layer masks enable you to also softly blend two layers.

✔ You can't add a layer mask to a background layer. You must convert the background into a layer first.

✔ Feel free to edit your layer mask at will. Unlike simply making a feathered selection, you can continue adjusting how much of the current layer or underlying images show — or how gradually one image blends into another. Just change the areas of white, black, and gray on the layer mask by painting with any of the painting tools.

✔ To load the mask as a selection outline, Ctrl-click (⌘-click on the Mac) the layer mask thumbnail in the Layers panel.

✔ To temporarily hide a mask, Shift-click the layer mask thumbnail in the Layers panel. Repeat to show the mask.

✔ To view the mask without seeing the image, Alt-click (Option-click on the Mac) the Layer Mask thumbnail in the Layers panel. This action can be helpful when editing a layer mask.

✔ You can unlink a layer from its layer mask. By default, Elements links a layer mask to the contents of the layer. This link enables them to move together. To unlink a layer from its mask, click the link icon on the layer in the Layers panel. Click again to reestablish the link.

✔ To delete a layer mask, drag the layer mask thumbnail to the trash icon in the Layers panel and click Delete in the dialog box.

✔ To apply a layer mask so that it's fused to the layer and can no longer be edited, drag the mask thumbnail to the Trash icon in the Layers panel and click Apply in the dialog box.

✔ Try applying a filter to your layer mask to create an interesting special effect.

Note that many of these commands are also available from the Layer➪Layer Mask submenu.

Creating Clipping Masks

In a *clipping mask,* the bottommost layer (also known as the *base layer*) acts as a mask for the layers above it. The layer or layers above clip to the opaque areas of the base layer and don't show over the transparent areas of the base layer.

Creating a clipping mask works well if you want to fill a shape or some type with different images on multiple layers.

Using the steps that follow, we opened our image and converted the Background to a layer. We then used the Custom Shape tool to create a shape of an alarm clock on another layer and put that layer underneath the layer of the actor. We then created a clipping mask between the actor and the shape of the alarm clock. We then added a new layer, filled it with white, and made it the bottom-most layer.

Follow these steps to create your own clipping mask:

1. **In the Photo Editor, in Expert mode, open or create an image that has several layers.**

    To best see how this technique works, try creating a shape layer for your base layer. For more on shape layers, see Book V, Chapter 1.

2. **Arrange your layers so that your base layer is the bottommost layer.**

    See Chapter 2 of this minibook for more on rearranging layers.

3. **Hold down Alt (Option on the Mac) and, in the Layers panel, position the mouse cursor over the line dividing the base layer and the layer above it.**

    The cursor changes to two overlapping circles with a small arrow icon. You can also choose Layer➪Create Clipping Mask.

4. **Click the mouse button.**

5. **Repeat Steps 3 and 4 for any remaining layers you want to have clipped to the base layer.**

    Notice how our actor image clips to the base layer (the alarm clock shape) in the Layers panel (appears indented).

    Nothing outside the boundaries of the clock shape is visible on the layer in the clipping mask, as shown in Figure 4-7. The down-arrow icon beside the layer in the Layers panel indicates that the layer is clipped. The clipped layers take on the opacity and Blend mode of the base layer.

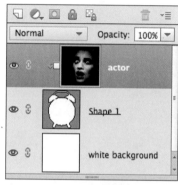

Figure 4-7: In a clipping mask, layers mask to the opaque areas of a base layer.

Keep these additional tips in mind when working with clipping masks:

- **Remove a layer from the clipping mask.** Alt-click (Option-click on the Mac) the line between the two layers in the Layers panel. Or you can select the layer and choose Layer⇨Release Clipping Mask. Both commands remove from the clipping group the selected layer and any layers above it.

- **You can also apply clipping masks to adjustment and fill layers.** If you clip between a regular layer and an adjustment layer, or between a regular layer and a fill layer, the adjustment or fill layer affects only the pixels of the adjacent underlying layer rather than all the underlying layers.

Book VII
Filters, Effects, Styles, and Distortions

For more details and projects about Photoshop Elements, visit www.dummies.com/extras/photoshopelementsaio.

Contents at a Glance

Chapter 1: Making Corrections and Having Fun with Filters

In This Chapter

- Figuring out how filters work
- Applying filters repeatedly or selectively
- Fading a filter's effects
- Working in the Filter Gallery
- Getting creative with filters

Filters have a long and glorious history, ranging from performing essential tasks (such as removing abrasive particles from the oil in your car's engine) to even more important tasks involving the pixels in your images in Elements. In both cases, filters (also called *plug-ins* because they can be installed and removed independently) manipulate pixels in useful and simply frivolous and fun ways. They can correct less-than-perfect images by making them appear sharper or by covering flaws. Or they can enhance your images by making them appear as though they're painted, tiled, photocopied, or lit by spotlights. The result of this effort can be something to be admired.

This chapter introduces you to the basics of the Photoshop Elements filter facilities and starts you on the road to filter proficiency.

Understanding Filter Basics

All filters do a simple task in a seemingly complicated way. Deep within a filter's innards is a set of instructions that tells Elements what to do with a particular pixel in an image or a selection. Elements applies these instructions to every pixel in the relevant area by using a process that pixelheads call *convolution* (creating a form or shape that's folded or curved in tortuous windings), which we normal humans refer to as simply *applying a filter*.

You can apply a filter in three ways:

- ✔ **From the Filter menu (in either Expert or Quick mode):** Choose a filter category and then select a specific filter.

- ✔ **From the Effects panel (in Expert mode only):** Choose Window➪Effects, or click the Effects icon in the lower right of the workspace, to open the Effects panel. Click the Filters button at the top of the panel. Select a filter category from the drop-down menu in the upper-right corner of the panel. Double-click the thumbnail of your chosen filter or drag the filter onto the Image window.

- ✔ **From the Filter Gallery (in either Expert or Quick mode):** Choose Filter➪Filter Gallery to apply one or more filters in a flexible editing environment. The Filter Gallery is described in the section "Working in the Filter Gallery," later in this chapter.

You can't apply filters to images that are in Bitmap mode or Indexed Color mode. Neither can you apply them to type or shape layers. And some filters don't work on images in Grayscale mode. For a refresher on color modes, see Book III, Chapter 3.

Corrective and destructive filters

Most digital imagers classify filters into two basic categories:

- ✔ **Corrective filters** are usually used to fix problems in an image. These filters fine-tune color, add blur, improve sharpness, or remove such nastiness as dust and artifacts. Remember that pixels are still being modified; it's just that these filters don't change the basic look of an image. They're just intended to enhance its good points and hide the bad.

  Be sure to check out the important techniques of sharpening and blurring, covered in Book VIII, Chapter 2. Sharpening and blurring are the king and queen of the corrective filters.

- ✔ **Destructive filters** tend to obliterate at least some detail in an original image while they add special effects. They may overlay an image with an interesting texture; move around pixels to create brush strokes; or distort an image with twists, waves, or zigzags. You can often tell at a glance that a destructive filter has been applied to an image: The special effect often looks like nothing that exists in real life.

An unaltered image (such as the image on the left in Figure 1-1) can be improved by using a corrective filter such as Unsharp Mask (center) or changed dramatically with a destructive filter such as Rough Pastels (right).

Original   Unsharp Mask   Rough Pastels

© iStockphoto.com/-IB-Image #10778734

Figure 1-1: Filters come in a wide variety from the corrective (center) to the destructive (right).

Single-step and multistep filters

Whether a filter is corrective or destructive, it falls into one of these two camps:

- **Single-step filters:** The easiest filters to use, single-step filters have no options and use no dialog boxes. Just choose the filter from the menu and watch it do its stuff on your image or selection.

- **Multistep filters:** Most filters come complete with at least one dialog box, along with (per-haps) a few lists, buttons, and check boxes. And, almost every multistep filter has sliders you can use to adjust the intensity of an effect (see Figure 1-2). These filters are marked on the menus with an *ellipsis* (a series of dots) following their names.

© iStockphoto.com/RedBarnStudio Image #127608

Figure 1-2: Multistep filters require you to specify various settings before applying a filter.

The controls themselves are easy to master. The tricky part is figuring out what the various parameters you're using *do*. How does changing the brush size affect an image when you're using a brush-stroke filter? What happens when you select a particular pattern with a texturizing filter? You can read descriptions of how various filter controls affect an image, but your best bet is to simply experiment until you discover the effects and parameters that work best for you.

Save a copy of the original image before you start experimenting with filters. Filters do permanent damage to files — by modifying, adding, and deleting pixels.

Reapplying a filter

You can reapply the last filter you worked with — using the same settings — by pressing Ctrl+F (⌘+F on the Mac). (It's also the first command on the Filter menu.) You might want to do this to strengthen the effect of a filter on a particular image, layer, or selection. Or you may simply want to apply the same filter to a succession of images or selections.

To bring up the dialog box for the last filter you applied, press Ctrl+Alt+F (⌘+Option+F on the Mac). This shortcut can be quite useful when you apply a filter and then decide that you don't like the results and want to go back and try different settings. After applying the filter, press Ctrl+Z (⌘+Z on the Mac) to undo and then press Ctrl+Alt+F (⌘+Option+F on the Mac) to bring up the filter's dialog box. The dialog box opens with the settings you used last time, allowing you to make adjustments and then reapply the filter.

Fading a filter

Sometimes, you don't want the full effect of a filter applied to an image. Sometimes, fading a filter a bit softens the effect and makes it look less "digitized," as shown in Figure 1-3.

Here's what you can do to dial down a filter:

1. **In Expert mode, choose Layer⇨Duplicate Layer and then click OK when the dialog box appears.**

   Creating a duplicate layer enables you to blend the original image and filtered layer together as desired.

2. **Make sure that your duplicated layer is selected in the Layers panel and then apply your chosen filter to the duplicate layer.**

   We applied a Palette Knife filter. (You can find it in the Artistic category.)

Figure 1-3: Fading a filter allows you to mix the filtered and unfiltered images.

3. **Use the Blend modes and Opacity settings located in the Layers panel to merge the filtered layer with the original unfiltered image.**

   We brought the opacity of our image down to 65%. If you need more details on working with layers, see Book VI.

4. **(Optional) With the Eraser tool, selectively erase portions of your filtered image to enable the unfiltered image to show through.**

   For example, if you applied a Gaussian Blur filter to soften a harshly lit portrait, try erasing the blurred portion that covers the subject's eyes to let the unblurred eyes of the layer below show through. The sharply focused eyes provide a natural focal point.

Rather than erase, you can also apply a layer mask to selectively show and hide portions of your filtered image. For details on layer masks, see Book VI, Chapter 4.

Selectively applying a filter

You don't need to apply filters to an entire image or an entire layer. You can achieve some of the best effects when you apply a filter to only a portion of an image — say, to an object in the foreground, but not on the background. For example, you can blur a distracting background so that the person in your image gets due attention. Or, as shown in Figure 1-4, we applied a Twirl filter to the water, leaving the surfer unfiltered to avoid that overly "Photoshopped" effect. (Not surprisingly, you find Twirl in the Distort category.)

© iStockphoto.com/schutzphoto Image #9642901

Figure 1-4: Selectively applying a filter can prevent an image from looking overly manipulated.

Working in the Filter Gallery

When you apply a filter, you may be presented with a huge dialog box. This editing window is officially named Filter Gallery. You can also access it by choosing Filter⇨Filter Gallery. In the flexible Filter Gallery, you can apply multiple filters, delete them, and edit them to your heart's content. This feature has made filters more flexible, more user-friendly, and easier to apply.

Even when you're using the Filter Gallery, make a backup copy of the image —
or at least create a duplicate layer — *before* you apply filters. Filters change
the pixels of an image permanently, and when you exit the Filter Gallery, you
can't remove the filters that you applied.

Follow these steps to get up and running in the Filter Gallery:

1. **In either Expert or Quick mode, choose Filter⇨Filter Gallery.**

   The Filter Gallery dialog box appears, as shown in Figure 1-5.

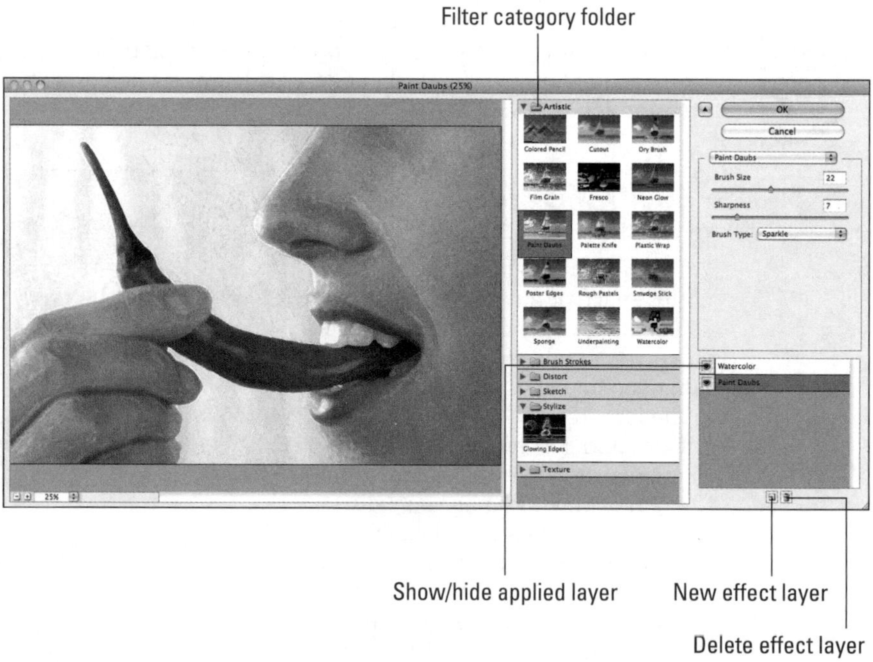

Filter category folder

Show/hide applied layer   New effect layer

Delete effect layer

Figure 1-5: Use the Filter Gallery to apply and edit multiple filters within a single dialog box.

2. **In the center of the editing window, click the folder for the desired filter category.**

   The folder expands and displays the filters in that category. A thumbnail
   illustrating the filter's effect accompanies each filter. To collapse the filter category folder, simply click the folder again.

3. **Select a filter.**

   You see a large preview of your image in the left side of the dialog box.
   Use the magnification controls to zoom in and out of the preview. To preview a different filter, simply select that filter.

4. **In the rightmost section, specify any settings associated with the filter.**

   The preview is updated accordingly.

5. **When you're happy with the filter, click OK in the upper-right corner of the dialog box to apply the filter and exit; if you want to apply another filter, leave the dialog box open and proceed to Steps 6 through 8.**

6. **If you want to apply another filter, click the New Effect Layer button at the bottom of the dialog box.**

   Clicking this button duplicates the existing filter.

7. **Select a new filter, which then replaces the duplicate in the Applied Filters area of the dialog box.**

   Elements lists each of the filters you apply to the image in the lower-right area of the dialog box.

8. **When you're done, click OK to apply the second filter and exit the dialog box.**

   You can apply as many filters as you want to your image. But often, less is more.

Here are some other helpful tips to keep in mind when you're using the Filter Gallery:

- **Delete an applied filter:** Select it in the list in the lower-right area of the dialog box and click the Delete Effect Layer button (the trash can icon) at the bottom of the dialog box.

- **Edit an applied filter's settings:** Select it from the list and make any necessary changes. Click OK to reapply. Although you can edit a particular filter's settings, that edit affects any subsequent filters you've added after applying that particular filter.

- **Rearrange the order of the applied filters:** Simply select and drag the filter up or down within the list.

   Rearranging the order of the filters you're using changes the results of applying the filters.

- **Resize the Filter Gallery dialog box:** Drag the lower-right corner.

- **Hide the Filter menu and provide the maximum real estate for the preview box:** Click the arrow to the left of the OK button.

- **Choose any of the filters found in the Filter Gallery from the Filter menu itself:** Choosing a Filter menu filter launches the Filter Gallery automatically — but not all filters are available in the Filter Gallery. You have to access some of them individually from the Filter menu.

Book VII Chapter 1

Making Corrections and Having Fun with Filters

Filters change the pixels of an image permanently, and after you apply one, you can't remove it. Be sure that you truly like what you've done and that you have a backup copy of that precious family photo or critical project image.

Having Fun with Filters

After you get familiar with what filters are, how you can apply them, and how you can modify and tone them down, it's time to experiment and have some fun. Experimenting is something you can do on your own when you have an hour or so and some willing images lying around. Create a composite with multiple layers and apply some filters. Add some different opacity settings and Blend modes, and you have yourself a party.

To get your party started, we give you a few tips on a few of our favorite filters.

Correcting camera distortion

If you've ever tried to capture a skyscraper or another imposing piece of architecture in the lens of your camera, you know that it often involves tilting your camera and putting your neck in an uncomfortable position. And then, after all that, what you end up with is a distorted view of what was an impressive building. The Correct Camera Distortion filter fixes the distorted perspective created by both vertical and horizontal tilting of the camera. As a bonus, this filter also corrects other kinds of distortions caused by lens flaws.

Here's how to fix those lens issues:

1. **Choose Filter⇨Correct Camera Distortion in either Expert or Quick mode.**

2. **In the Correct Camera Distortion dialog box, select the Preview option, as shown in Figure 1-6.**

3. **Specify your correction options:**

   - *Remove Distortion:* Corrects *lens barrel,* which causes images to appear spherized or bloated. This distortion can occur when you're using wide-angle lenses. It also corrects *pincushion* distortion, which creates images that appear to be pinched in at the center, a flaw that's found when using telephoto or zoom lenses. Slide the slider while keeping an eye on the preview. Use the grid as your guide for proper alignment.

   - *Vignette:* Adjusts the amount of lightening or darkening around the edges of your photo that can sometimes be created from incorrect lens shading. Change the width of the adjustment by specifying a Midpoint value. A lower Midpoint value affects more of the image. Then move the Amount slider while viewing the preview.

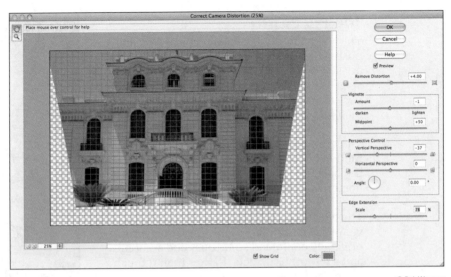

Figure 1-6: The Correct Camera Distortion filter fixes distortions caused by camera tilt and lens flaws.

- *Vertical Perspective:* Corrects the distorted perspective created by tilting the camera up or down. Again, use the grid to assist in your correction. We used the Vertical Perspective option to correct the church. (Refer to Figure 1-6.)

- *Horizontal Perspective:* Corrects halos and blurs caused by moving the camera (or if your subject can't sit still). For better results, set the angle of movement under the Angle option.

- *Angle:* Enables you to rotate the image to compensate for tilting the camera. You may also need to tweak the angle slightly after correcting the vertical or horizontal perspective.

- *Edge Extension:* When you correct the perspective on an image, blank areas may remain on your canvas. You can scale the image up or down to crop into the image and eliminate these "holes." Note that scaling up results in interpolating your image up to its original pixel dimensions. Therefore, if you do this, be sure to start with an image that has a pixel dimension or resolution high enough to avoid severe degradation.

- *Show Grid:* Shows and hides the grid, as needed. Choose the color of your grid lines.

- *Zoom:* Zooms in and out for the view you want.

4. **Click OK to apply the correction and close the dialog box.**

The Facet filter

The Facet filter breaks up an image by using a posterizing effect. It gathers blocks of pixels that are similar in brightness and converts them to a single value, using geometric shapes. (When you *posterize* an image, you reduce it to a very small number of tones.)

The geometric shapes make the image look more randomly produced while eliminating much of the banding effect you see with conventional posterizing filters.

The effects of the Facet filter are subtle and best viewed at close range. The image in Figure 1-7 originally contained some dust and scratches and a few other defects. Rather than retouch them one by one, we used Facet.

Facet is a single-step filter, so you don't need to adjust any controls. Just choose Filter⇔Pixelate⇔ Facet and evaluate your results. You can apply the filter multiple times. However, even one application smoothes out the picture and eliminates the worst of the artifacts.

Figure 1-7: The Facet filter can simply eliminate annoying artifacts or convert an image into a "painted" piece.

If you apply the Facet filter multiple times, the image takes on a kind of pointillist, stroked look that becomes more and more obvious. Using the filter repeatedly on the same image can yield interesting special effects.

Getting artsy

Several filters produce great artistic effects. You can find a large collection of them on the Artistic, Sketch, and Stylize submenus.

Many users employ these filters to create images that look as though they were painted. What those users may not tell you, unless pressed, is that filters can make photos of less than the best quality look better. These filters can disguise a multitude of photographic sins, turning shoebox rejects into decent digital transformations.

Try any of the following artistic filters:

- **Poster Edges:** This filter gives the picture an artsy, poster-like look but also enhances the edges to make the outline of the object appear sharper, as shown in Figure 1-8.

✔ **Rough Pastels:** This filter gives the look of a fine-art piece created with oil pastels.

✔ **Dry Brush:** This filter can add an even more stylistic effect, reducing details to a series of broad strokes.

✔ **Colored Pencil:** This filter crosshatches the edges of an image to create a pencil-like effect.

✔ **Cutout:** This effect assembles an image from what looks like cut-out paper shapes, which resemble a kid's art project.

Figure 1-8: Making a mediocre image more interesting with artistic filters.

✔ **Film Grain:** This photographic effect diffuses an image with thousands of tiny dots that simulate clumps of film grain. (If you're old enough, think of old home movies.)

✔ **Fresco:** This effect looks (supposedly) like pigments applied to fresh, wet plaster. Okay, we guess — if you squint.

✔ **Paint Daubs:** This effect uses smears of color from your choice of a half-dozen different brush types — very Jackson Pollock.

✔ **Plastic Wrap:** This filter can produce a wet look, particularly when you apply it to a selection and then fade the filter so that it doesn't overpower the detail in the image.

✔ **Watercolor:** This nice pastel effect diffuses an image while adding an interesting, watery texture.

Stroking your image

The filters on the Brush Strokes submenu try to mimic the appearance of art created with pen, brush, airbrush, ink, and paint. Here are a few of our favorites:

✔ **Ink Outlines:** Adobe describes this filter as producing the look of a corroded ink drawing.

✔ **Spatter:** This filter generates the look you might see from a sputtering airbrush.

✔ **Accented Edges:** Use this filter to make a subject jump out from its background by emphasizing the edges of all objects in the picture.

✔ **Sprayed Strokes:** This filter creates a textured, painted brush stroke effect, as shown in Figure 1-9.

Distorting for fun

With a couple exceptions, the Elements Distortion filters twist, turn, and bend images in surprising ways, turning ordinary objects into wavy images, pinched shapes, and bloated spheres.

Figure 1-9: Brush Stroke filters mimic effects created with analog tools such as paint brushes.

The first exception? The Diffuse Glow filter distorts images only to the extent that it imbues them with a soft, romantic, fuzzy look that can make the sharpest image look positively ethereal, as shown in Figure 1-10.

The Glass filter can add a glass-block texture or a frosted-glasslike fuzziness to an image. Other filters on this submenu produce wavy images, add pond ripples, pinch images, or transform images into spheres.

Getting noisy

Noise in images consists of any graininess or texture that occurs because of either the inherent quality of the image or the editing process. Noise filters, such as Add Noise, produce random texture and grain in an image. If you're new to image editing, you might wonder why you'd want to add noise to an image in the first place. Wouldn't it be smarter to remove it? Well, sometimes. In practice, you can find a lot of applications that call for a little noise here and there:

Figure 1-10: Give your photo a heavenly aura with the Diffuse Glow filter.

- ✔ **Add texture:** Objects that become too smooth, because of either blurring or another type of image editing you may have done, often look better when you add some noise to give them a texture, as shown in Figure 1-11. This technique is particularly useful if one object in an image has been edited, smoothed, or blurred more than the other objects in the image.

- ✔ **Blend foreign objects into a scene:** When you drop a new object into the middle of an existing scene, the amount of grain or noise in the new object is often quite different from the objects it's joining.

Say that you've decided to take a photo of your house and want to insert a certain luxury car in your driveway. Unfortunately, the photo of your in-laws' car is a lot sharper than the picture of your house. Adding a little noise can help the two objects blend more realistically. You may even forget that the car isn't yours.

✔ **Improve printed image quality:** Images that contain smooth gradients often don't print well because some printers can't reproduce the subtle blend of colors from one hue to another. The result is *objectionable banding* in the printed image: You can see distinct stripes where

Figure 1-11: Adding some noise can give an image some needed texture.

the colors progress from one to another. Adding a little noise can break up the gradient enough that your printer can reproduce the blend of colors, and the noise/grain itself is virtually invisible on the printed sheet.

The other filters on the Noise submenu don't add noise; instead, they make noise and *artifacts* (flaws, such as the dust and scratches on old film) less noticeable.

Breaking your image into pieces

The Pixelate filters break up images into bits and pieces, providing more of the painterly effects that you can create with brush strokes and artistic filters. The Pixelate submenu includes the Crystallize filter, shown in Figure 1-12, as well as filters that produce color halftone effects, fragmented images, and a pointillism effect.

Rendering

In computer lingo, *rendering* means creating something from a set of instructions, in a way. That's why all rendering filters produce special effects by creating a look, an object, or a lighting effect that's melded with your original image. Here are a few of our favorite render filters and what you can do with them:

© iStockphoto.com/Snapphoto
Image #338432

Figure 1-12: The Crystallize filter breaks an image into polygonal shapes.

✔ **Clouds:** Create a sky full of clouds using random values taken from a range between the foreground and background colors, as shown in Figure 1-13. To create a cloud effect with more contrast, hold down the Alt key (Option key on the Mac) quickly when choosing the command. If you don't like the first set of clouds you see, apply the filter repeatedly until you do. If you want a more "realistic" sky, try using a dark sky blue for the foreground color and a very light blue or white color for the background color.

✔ **Difference Clouds:** Create puffy objects in the sky (or foggy clouds at lower levels). The Difference Clouds filter uses image information to calculate the difference in pixel values between the new clouds and the image they're joining. The result is a unique cloud effect. Try applying the filter repeatedly to create a marbleized effect.

© iStockphoto.com/skodonnell
Image #1217074

Figure 1-13: Make your own clouds.

✔ **Lens Flare:** Create the reflection effect that plagues photographers when they point their cameras toward a strong light source, such as the sun. The filter mimics several kinds of photographic lenses, giving you useful flares that can spice up concert photos and add a sunset where none existed. Specify a location for the center of the flare by clicking the image thumbnail or by dragging the crosshair.

✔ **Fibers:** Adjust variance and strength settings to create a hairy, fibrous effect.

Getting organic with the Sketch filters

If you've ever envied people who can crank out a beautiful pen sketch in a matter of minutes, this filter menu is the one for you. The Sketch submenu includes plenty of traditional media artistic effects, such as Graphic Pen, Conté Crayon, Note Paper, Chalk, and Charcoal. Here's a brief rundown of a few effects that aren't quite so traditional:

✔ **Photocopy:** Gives that infamous, anachronistic look dating back to the days when photocopiers didn't reproduce halftone images. This filter creates areas of black and white with little gray value when the default foreground and background colors of black and white are selected.

✔ **Plaster:** Creates a look that resembles molten plastic more than it looks like plaster. The filter uses the foreground and background values to color the image.

✔ **Stamp:** Mimics a rubber or wooden-block stamp.

✔ **Reticulation:** Adds texture by reproducing a veritable photographic disaster — the wrinkling of film emulsion that occurs when you move film from one developing chemical to another that has an extremely different temperature. The highlights look grainy; the shadow areas look thick and goopy.

✔ **Torn Edges:** Creates the look of ragged paper and colorizes the image using the foreground and background colors.

✔ **Water Paper:** Creates the look of paint-like daubs on fibrous, wet paper.

No matter which Sketch filter you're using, if you want to reset your sliders to the default values for the preset, press the Alt (Option on the Mac) key, and the Cancel button will change to Reset.

Creating a comic

The Comic filter takes your photo and converts it into a cartoon or comic-like illustration. This filter is easy to use with great results for most photos. Follow these steps to apply the new Comic filter:

1. **In either Expert or Quick mode, choose Filter⇨Sketch⇨Comic.**

2. **In the filter dialog box, choose from four presets, as shown in Figure 1-14.**

Figure 1-14: The Comic filter creates a comic-like illustration from a photograph.

3. **From here you can adjust the default setting of the sliders for the various settings for the Color and Outline areas of the filtered image:**

   - *Soften:* Creates rounder or rougher areas of colors.

   - *Shades:* Use a higher value to add more tonal levels.

   - *Steepness:* Use a higher value to make the colored areas more defined and contrasting.

   - *Vibrance:* Brightens the overall color of the image.

   - *Thickness:* Affects the thickness and blackness of the outlined strokes.

   - *Smoothness:* Fine-tunes your edges and enhances the overall filter effect.

4. **Adjust your view as needed by using the following controls:**

   - *Zoom:* Zoom in and out for your desired view. You can also use the 1:1 view (recommended) or Fit in Window view.

   - *Hand tool:* Moves you around the image window when you are zoomed in.

5. **Click OK to apply the filter and close the dialog box.**

Getting graphic

The Graphic Novel filter takes a bit of experimentation to get the effect you want. But after you get your settings established, the look is quite interesting. It creates an illustrative look as if done with pen or graphite, as shown in Figure 1-15.

Here are the steps to apply the Graphic Novel filter on a photo:

1. **In either Expert or Quick mode, choose Filter⇨Sketch⇨Graphic Novel.**

2. **In the filter dialog box, choose from four presets, as shown in Figure 1-15.**

3. **From here, you can adjust the default setting of the sliders for the various settings for the filtered image:**

   - *Darkness:* A higher value creates more areas of lightness.

   - *Clean Look:* A higher value makes smoother, more refined strokes.

   - *Contrast:* The higher the value, the more contrast and darker overall an image appears. A lower value will produce a lower-contrast, light gray image.

   - *Thickness:* Affects the thickness and blackness of the outlined strokes. A higher value produces a "goopier" stroke appearance.

   - *Smoothness:* Fine-tunes your edges and enhances the overall filter effect.

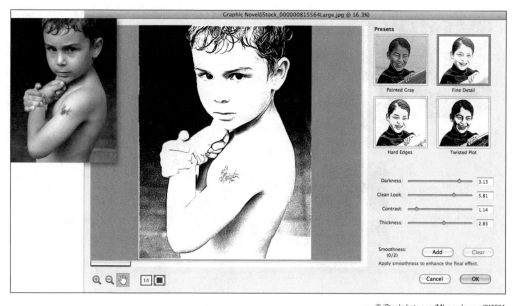

Figure 1-15: Create an illustration for a graphic novel.

4. **Adjust your view as needed by using the following controls.**

   • *Zoom:* Zoom in and out for your desired view. You can also use the 1:1 view (recommended) or the Fit in Window view.

   • *Hand tool:* Moves you around the image window when you are zoomed in.

5. **Click OK to apply the filter and close the dialog box.**

Using the Pen & Ink filter

This filter, similar to the Graphic Novel filter, gives your photo more of an illustrative look, as if created with a pen and colored or black ink.

Here are these steps to apply the Pen & Ink filter on your photo:

1. **In either Expert or Quick mode, choose Filter⇨Sketch⇨Pen & Ink.**

2. **In the filter dialog box, choose from four presets, as shown in Figure 1-16.**

3. **From here you can adjust the default setting of the sliders for the various settings for the Ink and Pen areas of the filtered image:**

   • *Detail:* A higher value creates finer, crisper edges.

   • *Width:* A higher value creates thicker, goopier strokes, while a lower value creates crisper strokes.

Figure 1-16: Use the Pen & Ink filter to create an inked, illustrative image.

- *Darkness:* A higher value creates more areas of darkness.

- *Contrast:* The higher the value, the more contrast the image has and the more dark ink strokes are applied.

- *Hue:* Adjust the slider to select your desired color along the color ramp.

- *Contrast:* A higher value adds more contrast, darkness, and colored areas.

- *Fill:* Fills the image with more areas of color and less white.

4. **Adjust your view as needed by using the following controls:**

- *Zoom:* Zoom in and out for your desired view. You can also use the 1:1 view (recommended) or the Fit in Window view.

- *Hand tool:* Moves you around the image window when you're zoomed in.

5. **Click OK to apply the filter and close the dialog box.**

Adding texture

Elements lets you add a lot of interesting textures to your image, such as the cracked canvas effect generated by the Craquelure filter (see Figure 1-17) or the pixel effect produced by the Patchwork filter.

© *iStockphoto.com/stphillips Image #2405095*

Figure 1-17: The Craquelure filter gives an Old World–painting feel to your image.

You can find other filters on this menu to help you create mosaic effects, add another kind of film grain, and create stained-glass effects in images. But the most versatile filter in this set is surely the Texturizer, which enables you to apply various kinds of textures to your images or selections, including Brick, Burlap, Canvas, or Sandstone.

You can select the relative size of the texture compared with the rest of your image by using the Scaling slider. You can even select the direction of the light source that produces the 3-D look, selecting from top or bottom, either side, or any of the four corners of the image.

Chapter 2: Distorting with the Liquify Command

In This Chapter

☞ **Checking out the Liquify window**

☞ **Understanding the options**

☞ **Liquifying an image**

*L*iquify is the only Elements filter that garners a chapter of its own. That's because Liquify is not your run-of-the-mill filter. Truth be told, it's the ultimate distortin' fool, with a bevy of tools, modes, and options that make it a good deal more complex than most of its kin on the Filter menu.

The Liquify filter lets you push and pull on parts of an image; twist, turn, and pinch other parts; and bloat and reflect others. You can basically manipulate an image as though it were pliable saltwater taffy. And, although these actions would create worthwhile entertainment on their own, you can use the Liquify filter to perform some productive tasks.

If you pick up any fashion magazine, we guarantee you that many of the images of models and celebrities you see there have made their way through the Liquify filter for nips and tucks and overall body sculpting. Yes, even people blessed with natural beauty are given a dose of digital beautification for good measure.

Exploring the Liquify Window

At first glance, the Liquify window is a little daunting. It's a little daunting on second, third, and fourth glances, too. But when you quit glancing and dive into using this versatile filter, you find that the tools and options make a lot of sense.

Open the Liquify window by choosing Filter⇨Distort⇨Liquify. The Liquify Tools panel appears on the left, as shown in Figure 2-1. The other options available with Liquify appear on the right side of the window. The Tools panel includes tools that you can use to paint and distort an image.

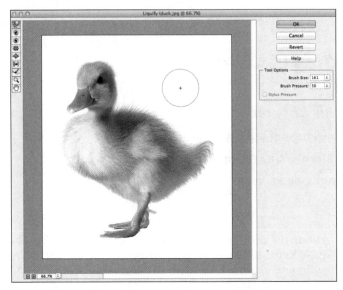

Figure 2-1: The Liquify window is quite user-friendly after you become familiar with its tools and settings.

As on the main Elements Tools panel, you can activate each tool by pressing a keyboard shortcut letter associated with its name.

The distortion painting tools

You use the first group of tools in the Tools panel to paint distortions on an image. The following list describes each tool, with its keyboard shortcut in parentheses. To see what the tool icon looks like, refer to Figure 2-1. To see what each tool does to pixels, check out Figure 2-2.

- ✔ **Warp (W):** This tool is faintly reminiscent of the Smudge tool but doesn't obliterate details in the pixels quite as much as it pushes them forward while you drag, creating a stretched effect. Use the Warp tool to push pixels where you want them to go, using short strokes or long pushes. This tool is the main one to use when you want to body-sculpt the person in an image.

- ✔ **Twirl Clockwise (R) and Twirl Counterclockwise (L):** Place the cursor in one spot, press the mouse button, and watch the pixels under your brush rotate like a satellite photo of a tropical storm. Or drag the cursor to create a moving twirl effect. Pixels move faster in the center than along the edges of the brush.

  Try this technique with the other tools we describe in this list. (With some tools, the effect is more obvious than with others.) Simply hold down the mouse button. The longer you hold it down, the more prominent the effect becomes.

✔ **Pucker (P):** This tool is the equivalent of the Pinch filter, squishing pixels toward the center of the area covered by the brush while you hold down the mouse button or drag. To reverse the pucker direction, which essentially applies a bloat, hold down the Alt key (Option key on the Mac) while you hold down the mouse button or drag.

 ✔ **Bloat (B):** Think of this tool as a kind of Spherize filter, pushing pixels toward the edge of the brush area while you hold down the mouse button or drag the mouse. To reverse the bloat direction — doing so applies a pucker — hold down the Alt key (Option key on the Mac) while you hold down the mouse button or drag.

 ✔ **Shift Pixels (S):** This odd tool moves pixels to the left when you drag the tool straight up. Drag down to move pixels to the right. When you drag right, pixels move up; when you drag left, pixels move down. Drag clockwise to increase the size of the object being distorted. Drag counter-clockwise to decrease the size. To reverse any of the directions, hold down the Alt key (Option key on the Mac) while you hold down the mouse button or drag.

**Book VII
Chapter 2**

Distorting with the
Liquify Command

© iStockphoto.com/svera Image #2741294

Figure 2-2: The tools in the Liquify filter transform the ordinary into the extraordinary.

The other tools

Three tools in the Liquify Tools panel help with undoing distortions you may no longer want and also help with navigation. These tools (shown here with their keyboard shortcuts) are:

✔ **Reconstruct (R):** This tool is a variation on the old standby, Undo. It lets you reverse or alter — completely or partially — the distortions you've made. You can retrace your steps if you went overboard in your distortion activities.

✔ **Hand (H):** The Hand tool works exactly like the standard Elements Hand tool. Click and drag the image to move it around within the Preview window. You can find more about the Hand tool in Book I, Chapter 2.

✔ **Zoom (Z):** This tool works exactly like the Elements Zoom tool, which zooms images in and out. Just click the image to zoom in. Hold down the Alt key (Option key on the Mac) and click to zoom out. You can also zoom by selecting a magnification percentage (from 6 to 1,600 percent) from the pop-up menu in the lower-left corner of the dialog box. Or, if you like buttons, click your way to magnification by using the +/– zoom control buttons. See Book I, Chapter 2, for more on using the Zoom tool.

The Options Area

On the right side of the Liquify window (refer to Figure 2-1), you can find some menus and buttons that let you specify options for the tools. We point them out to you here and cover how to use them in the rest of this chapter:

✔ **Brush Size:** Specifies the width of the brush.

✔ **Brush Pressure:** Specifies the speed at which you distort while you drag. The lower the value, the slower the distortion is applied.

✔ **Stylus Pressure:** Selects the pressure of the stylus when you click it, if you have a graphics tablet and stylus. Clicking this option then controls the width of your brush stroke.

Distorting an Image with Liquify

Liquify is as easy to apply as finger paint after you play with it a little. Here's a step-by-step scenario of the things you might do to apply some distortion to an image of your own:

1. **Select and open in the Photo Editor an image that you want to distort, in either Expert or Quick mode.**

2. **In the Layers panel, select a layer.**

TIP

If you don't want to distort the whole layer, you can select part of it. For more on selections, see Book IV. For information on layers, see Book VI.

3. Choose Filter➪Distort➪Liquify.

The Liquify dialog box appears with the image in the preview area, as shown in Figure 2-3.

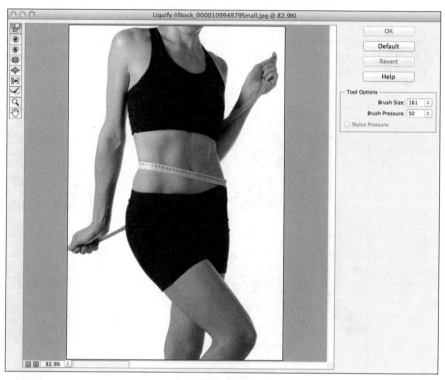

© *iStockphoto.com/deliormanli Image #10994979*

Figure 2-3: The Liquify dialog box is where the magic happens.

**Book VII
Chapter 2**

Distorting with the
Liquify Command

4. Choose a distortion weapon of choice.

For a detailed description of each tool, see the earlier section "The distortion painting tools." To see what each tool does, take another gander at Figure 2-2.

5. Specify options in the Tool Options area.

Remember to adjust the brush size and pressure to get the exact coverage you want. For a description of each option, see the previous section.

6. **If you take the distortions a little too far, select the Reconstruct tool to partially or fully reverse or modify your distortions.**

   Note that the reconstruction occurs faster at the center of the brush's diameter. To partially reconstruct an image, set a low brush pressure and watch closely while the mouse drags across the distorted areas.

7. **Apply the distortion to the image by clicking OK and exiting the Liquify dialog box.**

If you mucked up and want to start again, click the Revert button to return to the original, unaltered image. This action also resets the tools to their previous settings. Figure 2-4 shows the Before (and the Extreme After) of our image.

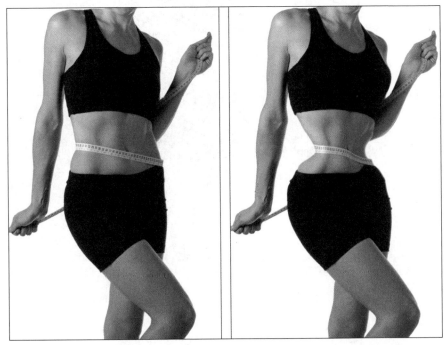

© iStockphoto.com/deliormanli Image #10994979

Figure 2-4: Perform a digital nip and tuck using Liquify.

Chapter 3: Adding Pizzazz with Styles and Effects

In This Chapter

✔ **Working with the Effects panel**

✔ **Taking photo effects for a spin**

✔ **Stylizing layers**

✔ **Tweaking layer styles**

*A*fter you have all the basic elements lined up in your layered composite image, you may want to give it a little pizzazz. Elements provides a lot of different effects that you can apply to enhance your images. Maybe a headline would pop out a little more if you beveled the edge, or maybe that silhouetted image would take on a little more dimension if you placed a drop shadow behind it. In this chapter, you find out how to do all these things.

Seeing What the Effects Panel Can Do

Elements has organized all its various effects in one neat panel. In the Photo Editor in Expert mode, choose Window➪Effects, or click the Effects icon in the lower right of the workspace. On the right side of the Elements workspace, you see the Effects panel, shown in Figure 3-1. Buttons for the various categories of effects — Filters, Styles, and Effects — are at the top of the panel. Subcategories (or *libraries*) of Filters, Styles, and Effects are just underneath, accessible via a drop-down menu. Individual effects, styles, and filters are located in the bottom portion of the panel and are displayed by thumbnail or name.

You can also apply effects in Quick mode.

Click the down arrow in the upper-right corner of the Effects panel to change the view of your effects, filters, and styles as thumbnails or as names. You also find a fast track to Effects help, if you need it.

Later sections of this chapter explain how to apply effects and styles. We go into a hefty discussion about filters in Book VII, Chapter 1.

Enhancing with Effects

Elements provides a variety of effects that you can apply to your photos. Some effects automatically create a duplicate of the selected layer, whereas other effects work only on flattened images. You can't preview how the effect will look on your image or type, as you can when you apply filters. Also, you have no options to specify.

Here are the steps to follow when applying a photo effect:

1. **In the Photo Editor, in Expert mode, select an image layer in the Layers panel.**

   Or, if you're applying the effect to only a single selection, make the selection before applying the effect.

   For applying effects in Quick mode, see the section "Adding Effects, Textures, and Frames in Quick Mode," later in this chapter. You may also want to check out the interesting effects found in Guided mode.

2. **Choose Window⇨Effects.**

   You can also click the Effects icon (fx symbol) in the lower right of the workspace.

3. **In the Effects panel, click the Effects tab at the top of the panel.**

   Refer to Figure 3-1.

Drop-down menu of libraries

Individual Effects

Figure 3-1: Add effects, styles, and filters via the Effects panel.

4. **Select a subcategory, or library, of Effects from the drop-down menu at the top of the panel:**

   Elements 13 reorganizes the categories of the effects and adds about 20 new effects (as of the writing of this book):

   - *Faded Photo, Monotone Color, and Vintage:* Makes your image fade from color to grayscale, appear as a single color, or look like an old pencil sketch or a photo on old paper.

   - *Glow:* Creates a soft focus and/or a white glow to your images.

   - *Painting:* Makes your images look like paintings or chalk illustrations.

   - *Panels:* These effects divide your image into paneled sections

   - *Seasons:* Includes effects that make your photo appear snowy, rainy, sunny (bright and yellow), or wintery (white and overexposed).

   - *Textures:* Creates a lizard skin or rubber-stamped appearance.

   - *Show All:* Shows all effects described in this list.

5. **In the Effects panel, double-click an effect or drag the effect onto the image.**

   In our example, in Figure 3-2, we applied the Oil Pastel effect to our image and the Fluorescent Chalk effect to our type layer, both from the Painting library.

© iStockphoto.com/Beano5 Image #17899613

Figure 3-2: Enhance images by adding effects to your image and type layers.

You can also apply an effect to type. Select a type layer in the Layers panel and follow Steps 2 through 5 in the preceding list. Note that a dialog box alerts you that the type layer must be simplified before you can apply the effect. If you simplify the layer, you can no longer edit the text, so be sure that your type is exactly as you want it. For more on working with type layers, see Book V, Chapter 3.

Unlike styles (described in the following section), you can't edit effects. Effects automatically creates another layer, so if you don't care for the effect, simply delete that layer by dragging it to the trash can at the top of the Layers panel.

Working with Layer Styles

Layer styles (also referred to as just *styles*) range from simple shadows and bevels to more complex designs, such as buttons and patterns. The wonderful characteristic of layer styles is that they're completely nondestructive. Unlike filters, layer styles don't change your pixel data. You can edit them or even delete them if you're unhappy with the results, so feel free to use them with abandon.

Getting the scoop on layer styles

Here are a few fun facts about layer styles:

- **You can apply layer styles only to layers.** Therefore, if all you have in your image is a background, be sure to convert it to a layer first. See Book VI for details on working with layers.

- **Layer styles are dynamically linked to the contents of a layer.** If you move or edit the contents of the layers, the results are updated.

- **When you apply a layer style to a layer, an fx icon appears next to the layer's name in the Layers panel.** Double-click the fx icon to open the Styles Settings dialog box and make any adjustments that are necessary to create the look you want.

- **Layer styles are stored in different libraries.** You can add shadows, glows, beveled and embossed edges, and more complex appearances, such as neon, plastic, chrome, and other man-made textures. See Figure 3-3 for a layer style sampler.

- **Delete a layer style or styles.** Choose Layer⇨Layer Style⇨Clear Layer Style or drag the fx icon in the Layers panel to the trash can in the panel.

- **Copy and paste layer styles onto other layers.** Select the layer containing the layer style and choose Layer⇨Layer Style⇨Copy Layer Style. Select the layer or layers on which you want to apply the effect and choose Layer⇨Layer Style⇨Paste Layer Style. You can also just drag and drop an effect from one layer to another while holding down the Alt key (the Option key on the Mac). Note that if you drag and drop an effect without holding down the Alt or Option key, you move the layer style from one layer to another.

- **Hide or show layer styles.** Choose Layer⇨Layer Style⇨Hide All Effects or Show All Effects.

| Drop Shadow | Original | Bevel |

| Inner Glow | Wow Neon | Wow Plastic |

© iStockphoto.com/TimAbramowitz Image #9234104

Figure 3-3: Add dimension by applying styles such as shadows, glows, and bevels to an object or some type.

> ✔ **Scale a layer style.** Choose Layer⇨Layer Style⇨Scale Effects. Select Preview and enter a value between 1 and 1,000 percent. Then you can scale the style without scaling the element.

Applying a layer style

Here are the steps to apply a style and a description of each of the style libraries:

1. **In the Photo Editor, in Expert mode, select an image or type layer in the Layers panel.**

2. **Choose Window⇨Effects.**

   You can also click the Effects icon (fx symbol) in the lower right of the workspace.

3. **Select the Styles tab at the top of the Effects panel.**

   Refer to Figure 3-1.

4. **Select a library of styles from the drop-down menu at the top of the panel:**

   - *Bevels:* Adds a three-dimensional edge on the outside or inside edges of the contents of a layer, giving the element some dimension. Embossed styles make elements appear as though they're raised off or punched into the page. You can change the appearance of these styles, depending on the type of bevel chosen. Adjust attributes, such as the lighting angle, distance (how close the shadow is to the layer contents), size, bevel direction, and opacity.

   - *Drop and Inner Shadows:* Add a soft drop or an inner shadow to a layer. Choose from an ordinary shadow or one that includes noise, neon, or outlines. You can adjust the lighting angle, distance, size, and opacity.

   - *Outer and Inner Glows:* Add a soft halo that appears on the outside or inside edges of your layer contents. Adjust the appearance of the glow by changing the lighting angle, size, and opacity of the glow.

   - *Visibility:* Click Show, Hide, or Ghosted to display, hide, or partially show the layer contents. The layer style remains fully displayed.

   - *Complex and others:* The remaining layer styles are a group of different effects ranging from simple glass buttons to the more exotic effects, such as Tie-Dyed Silk and Abstract Fire. You can customize all these layer styles somewhat by adjusting the various settings, which are similar to those for other styles in this list.

5. **In the Effects panel, double-click a style or drag the style onto the image.**

   The style, with its default settings, is applied to the layer. Note that styles are cumulative. You can apply multiple styles — specifically, one style from each library — to a single layer.

   You can also apply styles to type layers, and the type layer doesn't need to be simplified. This is an advantage over Effects because you can retain the type's editability, as shown in Figure 3-4.

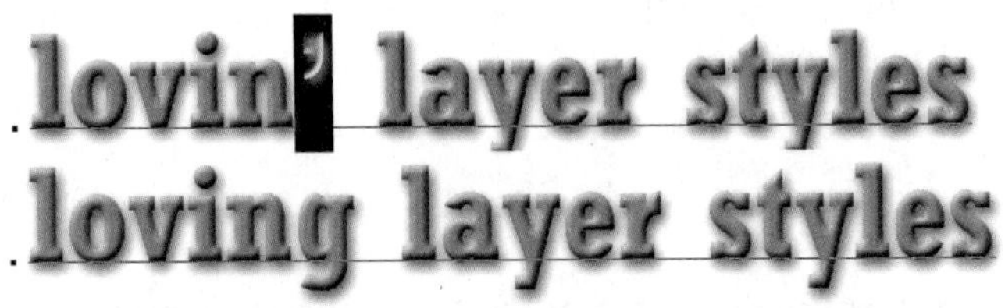

Figure 3-4: Styles are advantageous because they don't alter your pixels.

Editing Layer Styles

Layer styles are quite agreeable. They're not only easy to apply but also equally easy to edit. Here's how:

1. **In the Photo Editor in Expert mode in the Layers panel, double-click the fx icon on the layer.**

   The Style Settings dialog box opens, as shown in Figure 3-5.

2. **Be sure to select Preview so that you can view how your edits are affecting the layer style.**

3. **Expand the options for any layer style category by clicking the arrow (referred to as a *disclosure triangle*) just to the left of the layer style name.**

   You can toggle the layer style on and off by selecting and deselecting the style.

4. **Depending on which layer style category you use, specify the options.**

   Here's a rundown:

   • *Lighting Angle:* Specify the angle of your light source. If you've decided to put together a realistic composite of multiple images, make sure that all the shadows and highlights of all the different elements are consistent. You don't want one layer to look like it's 6 a.m. and another to look like it's 2 p.m.

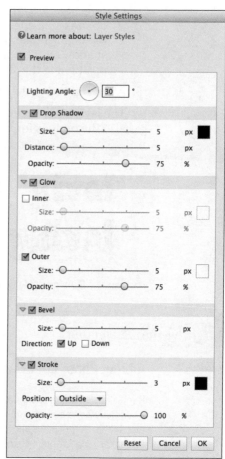

Figure 3-5: Layer styles, such as shadows, are live, enabling you to edit them at any time.

Book VII Chapter 3

Adding Pizzazz with Styles and Effects

   • *Size:* Specify the size of your shadow, glow, bevel, or stroke from 0 to 250 pixels.

   • *Distance:* Adjust how far the shadow or glow is offset (from 0 to 30000 pixels) from your element.

- *Opacity:* Adjust the Opacity setting to change how transparent the shadow, glow, or stroke appears — from 0% to 100%.

- *Glows - Inner/Outer:* Specify whether your glow is an inner or outer glow.

- *Color:* Click the color swatch and choose a glow color from the Color Picker. Click OK to close the Color Picker dialog box.

- *Direction Up/Direction Down:* Specify whether the bevel (the raised or sunken-in edge) direction is up or down. Direction Up positions the highlight along the edge closest to the light source and the shadow on the opposite edge. Direction Down does the opposite, positioning the shadow near the light source.

5. **After you refine the layer style settings, click OK.**

   The layer style is edited and ready to go, as shown in Figure 3-6. Note also the options for *Reset,* to start over, or *Cancel,* to bail out entirely.

lovin' layer styles
loving layer styles

Figure 3-6: An original and an edited layer style.

Putting It Together

Adding Photo Effects and Layer Styles to a Collage

If you like your images and text simple and unadorned, more power to you. But if you feel a sudden urge to add an embellishment or two, make sure that you're prepared to do that. In this exercise, we show you how to add some type to a collage and apply effects and styles to the various elements. Just follow these simple steps:

1. **In the Photo Editor, in Expert mode, open a previously created and saved collage file.**

   Make sure that the Layers panel is also open. Our image is a collage made up of four images, each residing on its own layer — the blue background, the butterfly, the gardening tools, and the flower/watering can/sky/grass image. For details on creating collages from multiple images, see Book VI.

2. **Select the Eyedropper tool from the Tools panel and click in the collage on a color you like.**

   The color you sampled is now the foreground color, as you can see from your swatches at the bottom of the Tools panel. We sampled one of the light blue clouds.

3. **Select the Type tool and then select a font, style, and point size and other formatting options from the Tool Options.**

   We recommend choosing an easy-to-read font and applying a bold style to it. We're using Times New Roman Bold, and we set the point size to 30 and the leading to 24 points.

   We selected the Anti-aliasing option so that our text transitions nicely with the image elements.

4. **Click inside the image and type some text.**

   We typed *Organic Gardening* for our garden collage. We also added a second line of text with the day and time.

5. **Select the Move tool from the Tools panel and position the type in the collage.**

   We put the text in the lower-right corner.

© iStockphoto.com/YinYang Image #9046002, imv Image #2053920 and 101cats Image #6401174

© iStockphoto.com/YinYang Image #9046002, imv Image #2053920 and 101cats Image #6401174

Book VII Chapter 3

Adding Pizzazz with Styles and Effects

6. **With the type layer selected in the Layers panel, click the Effects icon. In the Effects panel, click the Styles tab at the top and choose Drop Shadows from the library drop-down menu. Double-click the Low drop shadow.**

continued

continued

If you need to edit the layer style, double-click the fx icon in the Layers panel and specify settings. For details on how to do this, see the previous section. We edited the drop shadow to make it a little smaller, less opaque, and closer to the type.

7. **Next, choose Bevels from the library drop-down menu. Double-click the Simple Inner bevel. Make any necessary edits to the bevel layer style.**

We reduced the size of our bevel to make the effect crisper, as shown in the figure.

8. **Repeat Step 6 or 7, or both, on any other of your layers, if desired.**

We added a Low drop shadow to our gardening tools layer.

9. **To add an effect, in the Effects panel, click the Effects tab at the top, choose Glow from the library drop-down menu, and double-click the Soft Flat Color effect.**

We added a Soft Flat Color effect to each of our image layers.

10. **Choose File⇨Save.**

You're all done. If you feel like it, keep adding to or refining the collage as you discover new tricks.

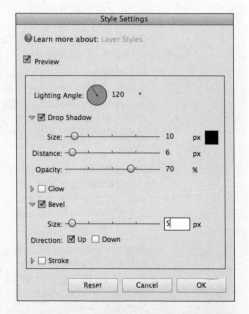

© iStockphoto.com/YinYang
Image #9046002, imv Image #2053920 and
101cats Image #6401174

Adding Content from the Graphics Panel

If you aren't the artistic type or need a quick graphic in a pinch, check out the Graphics panel.

Here's how to add a graphic from the Graphics panel:

1. **In the Photo Editor, in Expert mode, choose Window⇨Graphics, or click the Graphics icon in the lower right of the workspace.**

2. **From the drop-down menu at the top of the Graphics panel, select the search criteria by category for your desired graphic.**

   Choices include categories, such as seasons, mood, and activity.

3. **From the drop-down menu just to the right of the search categories, select the specific season, mood, activity, or other effect.**

4. **From the graphics drop-down menu below the categories, continue to filter your results.**

   Choose from Backgrounds, Frames, Graphics, Shapes, and Text.

5. **After you select your graphic, double-click the graphic thumbnail in the panel or drag the thumbnail onto your image window.**

   The graphic is added to your image as a Smart Object layer, as indicated by the white square/black page icon on your layer in the Layers panel. Smart Objects are special kinds of layers that enable you to repeatedly size and transform your layer without the fear of degradation. For more on Smart Objects, see Book III, Chapter 1.

   To remove the content, simply delete the layer.

Adding Effects, Textures, and Frames in Quick Mode

To apply an effect in Quick mode, first click the Effects icon in the lower-right corner of the workspace. In the Effects panel, double-click your desired effect or drag it onto your image. One of the great things about the Effects panel is the live previews that give you an idea of what the effect will look like before you even apply it. After it is applied, if you aren't happy, click the Reset button (the curved arrow) in the upper right of the panel. Note that effects are applied as a new layer with a layer mask that can be edited in Expert mode. For example, if you applied an effect to a portrait, but don't want the effect to cover the person's face, you can edit the layer mask to hide the effect over the face. For more on editing layer masks, see Book VI, Chapter 4. We applied the Vintage effect to our image.

To apply a texture to an image in Quick mode, click the Textures icon in the lower-right corner of the workspace. In the Textures panel, click your desired texture. After it's applied, if you aren't satisfied, click the Reset button in the upper right of the panel. Like effects, textures are also applied as a new layer with a layer mask that can be edited in Expert mode. We applied the Old Canvas texture to our photo.

Here's how to add a frame to an image in Quick mode:

1. **In the Photo Editor, in Quick mode, click the Frames icon in the lower right of the workspace.**

2. **In the Frames panel, shown in Figure 3-7, click your desired frame style.**

   We chose the Basic Black frame. Elements automatically fits your image into the frame the best way possible.

3. **Using the bounding box that appears, drag any handle to size and otherwise transform your image within the frame.**

   Note that you can also use the onscreen controls that appear near the bounding box. Drag the slider to size your image. Click the Rotate icon to rotate your image's orientation.

4. **After you're satisfied with the results, click the Commit icon (the green check mark) or double-click inside the bounding box.**

5. **If you need to further tweak your framed image, go to Expert mode, where you will see that your framed image is on its own image layer. In addition, the background of the frame is also on its own Fill layer.**

   To change the color of your frame's background (not the frame itself), double-click the fill icon on the Fill layer in the Layers panel. In the Color dialog box, click your desired color in the Color field or enter your desired color formula values and click OK.

Figure 3-7: An image with an effect, texture, and frame applied in Quick mode.

Book VIII
Retouching and Enhancing

For more details and projects about Photoshop Elements, visit `www.dummies.com/extras/photoshopelementsaio`.

Contents at a Glance

Chapter 1: Quick Image Makeovers

In This Chapter

✔ Using one-step auto-fixes

✔ Editing in Quick mode

✔ Cloning realistically

✔ Healing wrinkles, spots, and blemishes

✔ Fixing small flaws

One of Elements' strongest assets is its ability to fix images quickly, painlessly, and effectively. When you work with digital imaging, cloning an image with a shadow, adjusting the color or contrast of a photo, or eliminating flaws from that otherwise perfect portrait are all fixes that you can do successfully, whatever your skill level. With these simple image-makeover tools, Elements makes these tasks as easy to perform as clicking a button or making a few swipes with a brush.

But before you dive into this chapter of fixer-uppers, be sure to size, crop, and straighten your image to its final desired dimensions and resolution. To find out how, check out Book III, Chapter 2.

Applying One-Step Auto-fixes

Elements has seven automatic lighting-, contrast-, and color-correction tools that can quickly improve the look of your images with a single menu command. These commands are available in either Expert or Quick mode, and they're all on the Enhance menu.

What's great about these auto-fixes is that they're very easy to use. You don't need to know a heck of a lot about color or contrast to use them. The not-so-good news is that the result of these auto-fixes often isn't as good as you could get via a manual color-correction method. And sometimes these fixes may even make your image look worse than before by giving you strange shifts in color. But, because these correctors are quick and easy — and easily undone — they're worth a try. Usually, you don't want to apply more than one of the auto-fixes. If one doesn't work on your image, just remember that you can undo the fix and try another. If you still don't like the result, move on to one of the manual methods that we describe in Chapter 2 of this minibook.

Auto Smart Tone

This auto-fix is designed to adjust the tonal values (the range of tones or shades from black to white) in your image.

Follow these steps to check out this new command:

1. **In either Expert or Quick mode, with your image open, select Enhance⇨ Auto Smart Tone.**

   Elements automatically applies a default correction.

2. **Moving the controller *joystick,* the small double circle icon, as shown in Figure 1-1, fine-tune your correction.**

   The thumbnail previews in each corner give you an idea of how the image will look when you move the joystick in that particular direction.

The joystick

Figure 1-1: Apply the Auto Smart Tone command to quickly improve an image's tones.

3. **Select the Learn from This Correction option (the arrow with lines icon) in the lower left of the dialog box to have Elements "learn" from this editing session.**

If you select this option, Elements remembers what corrections you made on this image and positions the joystick on the basis of that correction on the next image you open and correct. The more images that are corrected, the smarter the Auto Smart Tone corrections become. This intelligent algorithm is able to distinguish between various types (based on the tonal characteristics) of images and remembers the adjustment for that particular type of image.

Move the Before and After toggle to see the before and after of the adjustment previews.

If your adjustments are starting to get way out of whack and you feel that you need to reset the learning archive, choose Edit⇨Preferences⇨ General⇨Reset Auto Smart Tone Learning (Adobe Photoshop Elements Editor⇨Preferences⇨General⇨Reset Auto Smart Tone Learning on the Mac).

4. **When you're satisfied with the adjustment, click OK.**

   If you want to start over, click the Reset button.

Auto Smart Fix

This all-in-one command attempts to adjust it all. Auto Smart Fix is designed to improve lighting, improve the details in shadow and highlight areas, and correct the color balance, as shown in Figure 1-2. The overexposed image on the left was improved with the Auto Smart Fix command.

Figure 1-2: Apply the Auto Smart Fix command to quickly improve an image overall.

 The Auto Smart Fix command, as well as the Auto Color, Auto Levels, Auto Contrast, Auto Sharpen, and Auto Red Eye Fix commands, are available in the Organizer in the panel on the right, where you can apply the commands to several selected images simultaneously.

If Auto Smart Fix didn't quite cut it, you can ramp it up and try Adjust Smart Fix. This command is similar to Auto Smart Fix, but it gives you a slider that allows you to control the amount of correction applied to the image.

Auto Levels

The Auto Levels command adjusts the overall contrast of an image. This command works best on images that have pretty good contrast (detail in the shadow, highlight, and midtone areas) to begin with and just need a little adjustment, but it can also work wonders for seemingly unsalvageable images, as shown in Figure 1-3. Auto Levels works by *mapping,* or converting, the lightest and darkest pixels in your image to white and black, which makes highlights appear lighter and shadows appear darker.

Figure 1-3: Auto Levels adjusts the overall contrast of an image.

Although Auto Levels can improve your contrast, it may also produce an unwanted *color cast* (a slight trace of color). If a color cast happens, undo the command and try the Auto Contrast command instead. If that still doesn't improve the contrast, try the Levels command that we describe in Chapter 2 of this minibook.

Auto Contrast

The Auto Contrast command is designed to adjust the overall contrast in an image without adjusting its color. This command may not do as good a job of improving contrast as the Auto Levels command, but it does a better job of retaining the color balance of an image. Auto Contrast usually doesn't cause the strange color casts that can occur when you're using Auto Levels. This command works really well on images with a haze, as shown in Figure 1-4.

Auto Color Correction

The Auto Color Correction command adjusts both the color and contrast of an image, based on the shadows, midtones, and highlights it finds in the image and a default set of values. These values adjust the number of black and white pixels that Elements removes from the darkest and lightest areas of the image. You usually use this command to remove a color cast or to balance the color in your image, as shown in Figure 1-5. Sometimes this command can be useful in correcting oversaturated or undersaturated colors.

Figure 1-4: The Auto Contrast command clears up hazy images.

Figure 1-5: Use Auto Color Correction to remove a color cast.

Auto Sharpen

Sometimes photos taken with a digital camera or scanned on a flatbed scanner can appear *soft,* meaning slightly out of focus. Sharpening gives the illusion of increased focus by increasing the contrast between pixels. Auto Sharpen attempts to improve the focus, as shown in Figure 1-6, without going too far. What happens when you oversharpen? Your images go from soft to grainy and noisy.

Figure 1-6: Use Auto Sharpen to improve focus.

 Always make sharpening the last fix after you make all other fixes and enhancements. You don't want to sharpen nasty flaws and make them even more noticeable than they already are. For more accurate sharpening methods, see the Unsharp Mask and Adjust Sharpness features discussed in Chapter 2 of this minibook.

Auto Red Eye Fix

The Auto Red Eye Fix command automatically detects and eliminates red-eye in an image. *Red-eye* occurs when a person or an animal (where a red-eye can also be a yellow, green, or even blue eye) looks directly into the flash.

Many cameras have a red-eye prevention mode, which is a pre-flash that causes the subjects' pupils to contract when the real flash goes off. Other cameras mount the flash high or to the side of the lens, which also minimizes the chance of red-eye. However, these preventive measures are of little solace when you have a great picture that features bright red pupils as its dominant feature.

Using the Red Eye Removal tool

If, for some reason, the Auto Red Eye Fix command doesn't correct the problem, you can always try the Red Eye Removal tool in the Tools panel. Here's how to remove red-eye manually:

 1. **Select the Red Eye Removal tool from the Tools panel in the Photo Editor in Expert mode.**

    Note that this tool is also available in Quick mode.

2. **Using the default settings, click the red portion of the eye in your image.**

   This one-click tool darkens the pupil while retaining the tonality and texture of the rest of the eye, as shown in Figure 1-7.

Figure 1-7: The Auto Red Eye Fix and the Red Eye Removal tools detect and destroy the dreaded red-eye.

3. **If you're unhappy with the fix, adjust one or both of these options in the Tool Options:**

   - *Pupil Size:* Use the slider to increase or decrease the size of the pupil.

   - *Darken Pupil:* Use the slider to darken or lighten the color of the pupil.

Pets can get white, green, blue, or yellow eyes from the flash. Elements provides a Pet Eye option. If this option still doesn't fix the problem, your best bet is to use the Color Replacement tool. See the section "Colorizing with the Color Replacement Tool," later in this chapter. If all goes well, your image is now cured of the dreaded red-eye. (Refer to the image on the right in Figure 1-7.)

You can also use the Brush tool with a Color blend mode and paint away the red. Or you can use the Color Replacement tool with a black foreground to color away the crimson. If you're trying to fix green-eye in animals, your best bet is to use the Color Replacement tool.

Editing in Quick Mode

If you get the results you want with the auto-fixes we cover in the previous sections while working in Quick mode, you may already have all the tools you need to repair and enhance your images. This means that you may not have to visit Expert mode at all.

As you've probably already figured out by now, Quick mode is a pared-down version of Expert mode that provides basic image-correcting tools and throws in a few dedicated features — such as a before-and-after

**Book VIII
Chapter 1**

**Quick Image
Makeovers**

preview of your image — for good measure. To get a general idea of how Quick mode works, take a look at the following step-by-step workflow, which shows you how you'd put Quick mode to use to fix your photos:

1. **Open a photo.**

   You can open a photo in one of three ways from within Elements:

   - In the Organizer, select one or more photos. Click the Photo Editor button at the bottom of the workspace and then click the Quick button at the top of the workspace.

   - In Expert mode, select your desired image(s) from the Photo Bin. Click the Quick button at the top of the workspace.

   - In Expert mode, open your desired images by choosing File⇨Open. Click the Quick button at the top of the workspace.

2. **Specify your preview preference from the View drop-down menu at the top of the workspace.**

   You can choose to view just your original image (Before Only), your fixed image (After Only), or both images side by side (Before & After) in either portrait (Vertical) or landscape (Horizontal) orientation, as shown in Figure 1-8.

Figure 1-8: Quick mode enables you to view before-and-after previews of your image.

3. **Use the Zoom and Hand tools to magnify and navigate around your image.**

You can also specify the Zoom percentage by using the Zoom slider in the Tool Options or in the upper right of the workspace.

4. **Crop your image by using the Crop tool in the Tools panel.**

5. **To rotate the image in 90-degree increments, click the Rotate Left or Rotate Right (accessed via the arrow next to Rotate Left) button in the left side of the workspace.**

6. **Remove the red from your subjects' eyes.**

   Automatically fix red-eye by selecting the Red Eye Removal tool from the Tools panel and clicking the Auto Correct button in the Tool Options. If that doesn't work, try clicking the red-eye in your image with the Red Eye Removal tool itself.

7. **Apply any necessary auto-fixes, such as Auto Smart Fix, Auto Levels, Auto Contrast, and Auto Color Correction.**

   All these commands are on the Enhance menu or under Smart Fix, Lighting, and Color in the right Adjustments pane of the workspace. Click a down-pointing arrow to access the various commands. If the commands aren't visible, click the Adjustments button in the lower-right corner of the workspace.

   Each of these fixes is described in the section "Applying One-Step Auto-fixes," earlier in this chapter.

   Usually one of the fixes is enough. Don't stack them on top of each other. If one doesn't work, click the Reset button in the upper right of the image preview and try another. If you're not happy, go to Step 8. If you are happy, skip to Step 9.

8. **If the auto-fixes don't quite cut it, gain more control by using the sliders, or clicking the thumbnails, that are available for Smart Fix, Exposure, Lighting, Color, and Balance.**

   Here's a brief description of each available adjustment:

   - *Exposure:* Adjusts the brightness or darkness of an image. Move the slider left to darken and right to lighten. The values are in increments of f-stops and range from –4 to 4.

   - *Shadows:* When you drag the slider to the right, the darker areas of your image lighten without adjusting the highlights.

     For all adjustments, you can now hover your cursor over any of the thumbnails in the pane to get a dynamic preview of that particular adjustment. The slider will automatically move accordingly.

   - *Midtones:* Adjusts the contrast of the middle (gray) values and leaves the highlights and shadows as they are.

   - *Highlights:* When you drag the slider to the right, the lighter areas of your image darken without adjusting the shadows.

- *Saturation:* Adjusts the intensity of the colors.

- *Hue:* Changes all colors in an image. Make a selection first to change the color of just one or more elements. Otherwise, use restraint with this adjustment.

- *Vibrance:* Adjusts the saturation of an image by increasing the saturation of less saturated colors more than those that are already saturated. Tries to minimize clipping (loss of color) as it increases saturation and preserves skin tones. Move the slider right to increase saturation. The values are in increments of F-stops and range from –1 to 1.

- *Temperature:* Adjusts the colors to make them warmer (red) or cooler (blue). You can use this adjustment to correct skin tones or to correct overly cool images (such as snowy winter photos) or overly warm images (such as photos shot at sunset or sunrise).

- *Tint:* Adjusts the tint after you adjust temperature to make the color more green or magenta.

If you still don't get the results you need, move on to one of the more manual adjustments that we describe in Chapter 2 of this minibook.

You can always apply fixes to just selected portions of your image. Quick mode offers the Quick Selection tool for your selection tasks. For details on using this tool, see Book IV, Chapter 1.

9. **Add final fixes by using the remaining tools in the Tools panel.**

Here's a quick description of each tool you'll need from the Tools panel:

- *Whiten Teeth:* This digital fix whitens teeth at a fraction of the cost of the real analog procedure. Choose an appropriate brush size from the Tool Options before whitening. (For more on brush options, see Book V, Chapter 1.) Using a brush diameter that's larger than the area of the teeth also whitens or brightens whatever else it touches — lips, chin, and so on. Click the Brush Settings option to specify Hardness, Spacing, Roundness, and Angle of the brush tip. Click the teeth. Note that this tool makes a selection and whitens simultaneously. After your initial click, your selection option converts from New Selection to Add to Selection in the Tool Options. If you pick up too much in your dental selection, click the Subtract from Selection option and click the area you want to eliminate. When you're happy with the results of your whitening session, choose Select➪Deselect or press Ctrl+D (⌘+D on the Mac).

- *Spot Healing Brush/Healing Brush:* These tools are great for fixing flaws, both big (Healing Brush) and small (Spot Healing Brush). For a detailed explanation on using these tools, see the upcoming sections, "Performing Cosmetic Surgery with the Healing Brush Tool" and "Zeroing In with the Spot Healing Brush."

You can find these same fixes (and many more) in Expert mode, under the Smart Brush and Detail Smart Brush tools.

10. **You can add any desired text by clicking your image with the Text tool. See Book V, Chapter 3, for details on working with text.**

    You can now use the Move tool in Quick mode to fine-tune the positioning of your text.

11. **Sharpen your image either automatically (by clicking the Auto button under Sharpen in the right pane) or manually (by dragging the Sharpen slider).**

    This fix should always be the last adjustment you make on your image. Sharpening increases contrast, so you want to fix the flaws first so that you don't exacerbate them by making them more noticeable.

In Quick mode, click the Effects icon in the lower-right corner of the workspace, and you'll find various effects, such as Toy Camera and Cross Process, to apply to your image. Click the Frames icon and you can apply borders, such as Scalloped and Scrapbook, to the perimeter of your photo. Finally, click the Texture icon to access textures, such as Blue Wash and Old Canvas. Click the Adjustments icon to return to your default panel settings. To apply an Effect, Texture, or Frame, simply click the thumbnail in the pane.

Cloning with the Clone Stamp Tool

Say that you want to duplicate an element in your image. That's easy enough, right? Make a selection and copy and paste it into the new location. That works fine most of the time. But what if the element has a shadow behind it, next to it, above it, or below it? You face the dilemma of having a hard edge on the copied element because the shadow (called a *cast shadow*) is cut off by the selection outline. You could feather the selection, but then you have to make sure that the copied element blends realistically with the background. What a pain. The better method is to clone the element by using the Clone Stamp tool. It's quick and easy, and no one will know that only one element was there originally.

Believe it or not, you can also reach for this tool when retouching imperfections, such as scratches, scars, bruises, date/time stamp imprints from cameras, and other minor flaws. In fact, that used to be one of its major functions. In some retouching instances, it does a decent job, although the arrival of the Healing Brush and Spot Healing tools has relegated the Clone Stamp tool more to the pure cloning functions and less to the hard-core retouching jobs.

The Clone Stamp tool works by taking sampled pixels from one area and *cloning* (or copying) them onto another area. Follow these steps to clone an element without any genetic engineering:

**Book VIII
Chapter 1**

**Quick Image
Makeovers**

1. **Open an image and choose the Clone Stamp tool from the Tools panel in Expert mode.**

2. **In the Tool Options, choose a brush from the Brush Preset drop-down panel and then use the brush as is or adjust its size with the Size slider.**

3. **Select the Blend mode of your choice in the Tool Options.**

   Selecting a mode such as Difference, Multiply, or Color can produce some interesting special effects. For info on Blend modes, see Book VI, Chapter 3.

4. **To make the clone more or less opaque, use the Opacity slider or text box in the Tool Options.**

   To make your cloned image appear ghosted, use an opacity setting of less than 100%.

5. **Select or deselect the Aligned option, depending on your preference.**

   With Aligned selected, the clone source moves when you move your cursor to a different location. If you want to clone multiple times from the same location, deselect the Aligned option.

6. **Select or deselect the Sample All Layers option.**

   This option enables you to sample pixels from all visible layers for the clone. If this option is deselected, the Clone Stamp tool clones from only the active layer. Check out Book VI for details about working with layers.

7. **Optionally, click the Clone Overlay button.**

   Select the Show Overlay option, if desired. Applying an overlay can be useful when cloning subjects that need to be in alignment with the underlying image. Adjust the Opacity to your desired percentage. Select Clipped to have the overlay clipped, or contained, only within the boundaries of your brush. In our opinion, this makes it a lot easier to clone exactly what you want. Select the Auto-Hide option, which, when you release your mouse button, will display a ghosted preview of how your cloned pixels will appear on the image. While you're painting, however, the overlay will be hidden. Select Invert Overlay to reverse the colors and tones in your overlay. This setting can also assist you in aligning areas.

8. **Alt-click (Option-click on the Mac) the area of your image that you want to clone to define the source of the clone.**

9. **Click or drag along the area where you want the clone to appear, as shown in Figure 1-9.**

   While you drag, Elements displays a crosshair cursor along with the Clone Stamp cursor. The crosshair represents the source you're cloning from, and the Clone Stamp cursor shows where the clone is being applied. While you move the mouse, the crosshair moves as well. This provides a continuous reference to the area of your image that you're cloning. Keep an eye on the crosshair, or you may clone something you don't want.

© iStockphoto.com/Pinnacle Marketing Image #1426264

Figure 1-9: When using the Clone Stamp tool, drag along the area where you want the clone to appear.

When you successfully complete the cloning process, you have two identical objects.

If you're cloning an element, try to clone it without lifting your mouse. Also, when you're retouching a flaw, try not to overdo it. Clicking once or twice on each flaw is usually plenty. If you're heavy-handed with the Clone Stamp, you get a blotchy effect that's a telltale sign something has been retouched.

10. Save the image and close it.

Here are a few additional tidbits regarding the Clone Stamp tool:

- ✔ **Use the Clone Stamp tool to fix simple flaws.** To clean up a flaw that's pretty straight, such as a stray hair or scratch, Alt-click (Option-click on the Mac) with the tool to define the source. Then click at one end of the straight flaw and Shift-click at the other end. The cloned source pixels cover up the flaw.

- ✔ **Pay attention to the origin point for sampling.** Depending on what you're cloning (for example, when covering up a flaw), if you keep sampling from the same point without ever varying it, the area you're cloning starts to look like ugly shag carpeting. Or, at best, it starts to appear blotchy and over-retouched.

- ✔ **Zoom out once in a while to check how your image looks overall.** Doing so helps you avoid those funky clone-stamp repetitive patterns and blotches.

Performing Cosmetic Surgery with the Healing Brush Tool

The Healing Brush tool is similar to the Clone Stamp tool (see the preceding section). Both tools let you clone pixels from one area and apply them to another area. But that's where the similarities end, and the Healing Brush leaves the Clone Stamp tool in the dust.

The problem with the Clone Stamp tool is that it doesn't take the tonality of the flawed area — the shadows, midtones, and highlights — into consideration. So, if the pixels you're sampling from aren't shaded and lit exactly like the ones you're covering, you have a mismatch in color, which makes seamless and indecipherable repairs hard to achieve.

That's where the Healing Brush tool comes in. This very intelligent tool clones by using the *texture* from the sampled area (the source) and then using the *colors* around the brush stroke when you paint over the flawed area (the destination). The highlights, midtones, and shadows remain intact, and the result of the repair is more realistic and natural — not blotchy, miscolored, and screaming "retouched."

Follow these steps to heal your favorite, but imperfect, photo:

1. **Open an image in need of a makeover and select the Healing Brush tool from the Tools panel in the Photo Editor in Expert mode.**

   Our guy, shown in Figure 1-10, looks like he could stand to get some "work done," as they say in Hollywood. Note that you can also heal between two images. Just make sure that they have the same color mode — for example, both RGB (red, green, blue).

2. **In the Tool Options, specify a size for the Healing Brush tool.**

   Click the Brush Settings button to select your desired diameter and hardness, as well as spacing, angle, and roundness if you want, for your brush tip. You'll most

© iStockphoto.com/twohumans Image #1426264

Figure 1-10: Getting ready for a digital makeover.

likely specify your brush settings several times while retouching your image. Using the appropriate brush size for the flaw you're repairing is important.

3. **Choose your desired Blend mode.**

   You can change your Blend mode, if necessary. The Replace mode preserves textures, such as noise or film grain, around the edges of your strokes when you're using a soft brush. For most simple retouching jobs, such as this one, you can leave it set at Normal.

4. **Choose one of these Source options:**

   You have a choice between Sampled and Pattern:

   - *Sampled:* Uses the pixels from the image. You'll probably use this option 99.9 percent of the time.

   - *Pattern:* Uses pixels from a pattern that you select from the Pattern Picker drop-down panel.

   For our example, we're sticking with Sampled because we don't think our guy would look that good with a Tie-Dye pattern across his face.

5. **Select or deselect the Aligned option in the Tool Options.**

   For most retouching tasks, you probably should leave Aligned selected. Here are the details on each option:

   - *With Aligned selected:* When you click or drag with the Healing Brush, Elements displays a crosshair along with the Healing Brush cursor. The crosshair represents the sampling point, also known as the *source.* When you move the Healing Brush tool, the crosshair also moves, providing a constant reference to the area you're sampling. (We left the Aligned option selected in our example.)

   - *With Aligned deselected:* Elements applies the source pixels from your initial sampling point, no matter how many times you stop and start dragging.

6. **Select the Sample All Layers option to heal an image by using all visible layers.**

   If this option is deselected, you heal from only the active layer.

   To ensure maximum editing flexibility later, select the Sample All Layers option and add a new, blank layer above the image you want to heal. When you heal the image, the pixels appear on the new layer and not on the image itself. You can then adjust opacity, adjust Blend modes, and make other tweaks to the "healed" pixels.

7. **Optionally, click the Clone Overlay button.**

   For details on all the Clone Overlay options, see the preceding section.

Book VIII
Chapter 1

Quick Image
Makeovers

8. **Establish the sampling point by Alt-clicking (Option-clicking on the Mac).**

   Make sure to click the area of your image you want to clone *from.*

   In our example, we clicked the smooth area on the cheek and portions of the forehead.

9. **Release the Alt (Option on the Mac) key and click or drag over a flawed area of your image.**

   Pay attention to where the crosshair is located because that's the area you're healing from. We brushed over the wrinkles under and around the eyes and on the forehead. This guy never looked so good, as shown in Figure 1-11, and he experienced absolutely no recovery time.

© iStockphoto.com/twohumans Image #1426264

Figure 1-11: In just five or ten minutes, this gentleman lost about ten years.

Zeroing In with the Spot Healing Brush

Whereas the Healing Brush is designed to fix larger flawed areas, the Spot Healing Brush is designed for smaller blemishes and little imperfections, with the exception of the Content-Aware option, which we explain in a moment. The biggest difference between the Healing Brush and the Spot Healing Brush is that the Spot Healing Brush doesn't require you to specify a sampling source. It automatically takes a sample from around the area to be retouched. The good news is that it's quick and easy. The downside is that it doesn't give you as much control over the sampling source. Consequently, reserve this tool for small and simple flaws.

Follow these steps to quickly fix imperfections with the Spot Healing Brush tool:

1. **In the Photo Editor, in Expert mode, open your image and grab the Spot Healing Brush tool from the Tools panel.**

   The diamond nose ring on this lovely hip senior, as shown in Figure 1-12 on the left, is no match for the power of the Spot Healing Brush.

© iStockphoto.com/VikramRaghuvanshi Image #5791196

Figure 1-12: Watch the nose ring (left) disappear (right).

2. **In the Tool Options, click the Brush Presets Picker and select a brush tip. Adjust the size as needed with the Size slider.**

   Try to select a brush that's a little larger than the flawed area you want to fix.

3. **Select a Blend mode in the Tool Options.**

   Just as with the Healing Brush, you can select the Replace mode. Most likely, the Normal mode works the best.

4. **Select a type in the Tool Options:**

   - *Proximity Match:* Samples the pixels around the edge of the selection to fix the flawed area.

   - *Create Texture:* Uses all the pixels in the selection to create a texture to fix the flaw.

   - *Content-Aware:* If you want to eliminate something larger or more substantial than a nose ring, mole, or freckle, this is the option to use. This option takes actual content from the image and uses it as a kind of patch for the flawed area. You can delete large objects with the Content-Aware option, as shown in Figure 1-13, where we eliminated the 21st-century signs from the front of the 17th-century barn.

   You may have to paint over the offending object a couple times to get your desired result. Also keep in mind that you may need to do some touching up with the Clone Stamp or other healing tools. Ours is a little smudgy in parts and could use a bit of touching up.

**Book VIII
Chapter 1**

**Quick Image
Makeovers**

Try Proximity Match first, and if it doesn't work, undo and try Create Texture or Content-Aware.

Figure 1-13: Eliminate distracting objects with the Content-Aware option.

5. **Choose Sample All Layers to heal an image by using all visible layers.**

   If you leave this option deselected, you heal from only the active layer.

6. **Click, or click and drag, the area that you want to fix.**

   In Figure 1-12, we used the Spot Healing Brush for the nose ring.

Repositioning with the Content-Aware Move tool

The Content-Aware Move tool allows you to select and move a portion of an image. What's great is that when you move that portion, the hole left behind is miraculously filled using content-aware technology. In other words, Elements analyzes the area surrounding the selected portion you're moving and then fills the "hole" with matched content.

Here's how to use this great editing tool:

1. **In Expert mode, open your image and select the Content-Aware Move tool.**

   It's the tool that looks like two arrows. You can also press the Q key.

2. **Choose your Mode, either Move or Extend.**

   When you choose Move, Elements moves your selection to a new location and then fills in the remaining "hole" with content-aware pixels. The

Move mode works well when you need to move an object, or objects, in your image for a more desirable composition. Keep in mind that this technique works best when the background of the new location of the object is similar to the background from which it was extracted.

When you choose Extend, Elements attempts to extend your selected area, while maintaining any lines and structural elements and blending them into the existing object. This option works great for expanding or contracting objects such as hair, fur, trees, buildings, and so on.

For my example, I chose the Move mode because I wanted to bring my yogis closer together, as shown in Figure 1-14.

3. **Choose your desired Healing setting.**

   Healing controls the amount of flexibility that Elements uses in determining how to shift pixels around and how strictly regions are preserved when determining the content-aware fill. The default setting is smack dab in the middle, which is what we stuck with.

© iStockphoto.com/motionstock Image #11837058

Figure 1-14: Two yogis who need to get closer.

You can also choose Sample All Layers to use content from all your layers. If you leave this check box deselected, you will only use content from the active layer.

4. **Drag around the area of your image that you want to move or extend.**

   If you need to fine-tune your selection, you can use the Path Operations options on the Options bar. Or, you can press the Shift key to add to your selected area or press Alt (Option on the Mac) to delete from your selection.

5. **Move your selection to your desired location, as shown in Figure 1-15.**

6. **Touch up any areas that require it.**

   You can break out any of the healing tools or the Clone Stamp tool to fix any mismatches or remaining flaws.

© iStockphoto.com/motionstock Image #11837058

Figure 1-15: Two yogis recomposed using the Content-Aware Move tool.

Note that you now also have the option of filling any selected area with a Content-Aware option. Make a selection and choose Edit⇨Fill. Under Contents, choose Content-Aware from the Use pop-up menu.

Colorizing with the Color Replacement Tool

The Color Replacement tool allows you to replace the original color of an image with the foreground color. You can use this tool in a variety of ways. Create the look of a hand-painted photo by colorizing a grayscale image. Or maybe you just want to change the color of an object or two, such as a couple of flowers in a bouquet. And even though Elements has a bona fide Red Eye tool, you can also use the Color Replacement tool to eliminate red- (or yellow- or green-) eye in people and animals.

The great thing about the Color Replacement tool is that, like the other healing tools, it completely preserves the tonality of the image. The color that you apply doesn't obliterate the midtones, shadows, and highlights as it would if you were applying color with the regular Brush tool. The Color Replacement tool works by first sampling the original colors in the image and then replacing those colors with the foreground color. By specifying different sampling methods, limits, and tolerance settings, you can control the range of colors that Elements replaces.

Follow these steps to replace existing color with your foreground color:

1. **In the Photo Editor, in Expert mode, open your image and select the Color Replacement tool from the Tools panel.**

   You can also press the B key to cycle through all the Brush tools.

2. **In the Tool Options, select your desired brush tip from the Brush Preset Picker drop-down panel and further adjust your brush size as needed.**

3. **Adjust the hardness, spacing, roundness, and angle under Brush Settings.**

4. **In the Tool Options, select your desired Blend mode:**

   - *Color:* This default mode works well for most colorizing jobs. It changes the color without changing the brightness levels, thereby retaining your tonal range. Use this mode if you're trying to get rid of red-eye.

   - *Hue:* This mode is similar to color, but less intense, providing a subtler effect.

   - *Saturation:* This mode is the one to use to convert the color in your image to grayscale. Set your foreground color to Black in the Tools panel.

   - *Luminosity:* This mode is the opposite of the Color mode. It changes the brightness levels, with no regard to color. Although this Blend mode can create a beautiful effect between two image layers, it doesn't tend to provide that great an effect in other circumstances.

5. **Select your sampling Limits mode:**

   - *Contiguous:* The default setting replaces the color of pixels containing the sampled color that are adjacent to each other directly under the brush.

   - *Discontiguous:* Replaces the color of the pixels containing the sampled color wherever it occurs under your brush.

6. **Specify your Tolerance percentage.**

   Tolerance refers to a range of color. A high tolerance lets you replace a broad range of color. A low tolerance limits the replacement of color to only the areas that are very similar to the sampled color.

7. **Choose whether you want anti-aliasing.**

   Remember, anti-aliasing slightly softens and smoothes the edge of the sampled areas.

8. **After you establish your settings, click or drag in your image.**

   Notice how the color, which in our example is purple, replaces the original colors of the sampled areas, which is dark pink (see Figure 1-16). Of course, the exact effect you get depends on your settings.

© iStockphoto.com/courtneyk Image #15324176

Figure 1-16: The Color Replacement tool replaces the original color in your image with the current foreground color.

TIP

If you want to be more accurate, make a selection before you replace your color so that you can avoid coloring elements that you don't want to color.

Lightening and Darkening with Dodge and Burn Tools

Dodging and burning originated in the darkroom, where photographers would salvage negatives containing areas that were too dark or too light by adding or subtracting exposure as an enlarger made the prints.

Lucky for us, the digital Dodge and Burn tools are a great deal more flexible and precise. With the Elements Dodge and Burn tools, you can specify the size of the tool and its softness by selecting one of the many brush tips available.

You can also limit the correction to a specific tonal range in your image — shadows, midtones, or highlights. You can adjust the degree of lightening and darkening applied by specifying an exposure percentage, too.

The Dodge (used to lighten) and Burn (used to darken) tools can be very effective, but you can't add detail that isn't there. Keep the following in mind:

- ✔ When you lighten very dark shadows that contain little detail, you end up with grayish shadows.

- ✔ Darkening very light areas that are completely washed out doesn't make your image look very good, either. You'll end up with white patches.

In either case, you want to use the Dodge and Burn tools in moderation and work only with small areas. To dodge or burn a portion of an image, just follow these steps:

1. **In the Photo Editor, in Expert mode, open an image with underexposed or overexposed areas and select the Dodge or Burn tool from the Tools panel.**

   Press the O key to cycle among the Dodge, Burn, and Sponge tools. (See the next section for details.)

2. **In the Tool Options, select a brush from the Brush Presets Picker drop-down panel and also adjust the brush size, if necessary.**

   Larger, softer brushes spread the dodging-and-burning effect over a larger area, making blending with the surrounding area easier, creating a more realistic, natural appearance.

3. **In the Tool Options, under the Range drop-down menu, select Shadows, Midtones, or Highlights.**

   Select Shadows to lighten or darken detail in the darker areas of your image. Choose Midtones to adjust the tones of average darkness. And select Highlights to make the brightest areas even lighter or darker.

   In Figure 1-17, the original image had mostly dark areas, so we dodged the shadows. Note the increased detail in the eyes, teeth, and hair. We also gave a couple swipes to the highlight areas with the Burn tool.

4. **In the Tool Options, select the amount of correction you want to apply with each stroke by using the Exposure slider or text box.**

   Exposure is similar to the Opacity setting that you use with the regular Brush tool. Start with a lower percentage to better control the amount of darkening or lightening. High exposure values can overcorrect and produce unnatural-looking, obviously dodged or burned areas in your images. (We used a setting of 10%.)

Figure 1-17: The Dodge and Burn tools are effective when touching up smaller dark and light areas.

5. **Drag or "paint" over the areas that you want to lighten or darken, gradually building up the desired effect.**

   You can make a selection prior to your dragging to make certain that the adjustment is applied only to that specific area.

6. **If you go too far, press Ctrl+Z (⌘+Z on the Mac) to reverse your most recent stroke.**

7. **When you finish, choose File⇨Save to store the image.**

Turning Color Up or Down with the Sponge Tool

The Sponge tool soaks up or squeezes out color. It can reduce the richness or intensity (or saturation) of a color in applied areas. It can also perform the reverse, giving a specific area richer, more vibrant colors.

Surprisingly, the Sponge tool also works in grayscale mode by darkening or lightening the pixels. Unlike the Hue/Saturation command (under Enhance⇨ Adjust Color), which works only on layers or selections, you can use the Sponge tool on any area that you can paint with a brush.

You can use the Sponge tool on an image in subtle ways to reduce the saturation in selected areas for an interesting effect. For example, you may have an object that's the center of attention in your picture simply because the colors are very bright. The Sponge tool lets you reduce the color saturation of that area (and only that area) to allow another section of your image to become the focal point. You can also use the Sponge tool to make an artistic statement: You could reduce or increase the saturation of a single person in a group shot to give that person more attention (perhaps as being more colorful than the rest).

To use the Sponge tool, just follow these steps:

1. **In the Photo Editor, in Expert mode, open an image and select the Sponge tool from the Tools panel.**

   Press the O key to cycle among the Dodge, Burn, and Sponge tools.

2. **In the Tool Options, select a brush from the Brush Preset Picker drop-down panel and further adjust the size of the brush tip, if needed.**

   Use large, soft brushes to saturate/desaturate a larger area. Smaller brushes are useful mostly to change the saturation of a specific small object in an image.

3. **In the Tool Options, select either Desaturate (reduce saturation) or Saturate (increase saturation) from the Mode drop-down menu.**

4. **In the Tool Options, select a flow rate with the Flow slider or text box.**

   The *flow rate* is the speed with which the saturation/desaturation effect builds while you brush.

5. **Paint carefully over the areas you want to saturate or desaturate with color.**

   In Figure 1-18, we saturated the birthday boy to make him more of a focal point and desaturated the other partygoers and the background.

Figure 1-18: The Sponge tool saturates (increases color intensity) and desaturates (decreases color intensity).

Smoothing with the Smudge Tool

The Smudge tool performs a kind of warping effect by pushing your pixels around as if they consisted of wet paint, using the color that's under the cursor when you start to stroke. However, don't view the Smudge tool as a simple distortion tool that produces only comical effects. We use it on tiny areas of an image to soften the edges of objects in a way that often looks more natural than when we use the Blur tool. You can also use the Smudge tool to create a soft, almost-painted look, as shown in Figure 1-19. Just don't get too carried away, or you may obliterate detail that you want to preserve.

© *iStockphoto.com/agmit Image #1725665*

Figure 1-19: The Smudge tool can give your objects a soft, painted look.

Smudged areas may be obvious because of their smooth appearance. Adding a little texture by using the Noise filter after you smudge is often a good idea if you want to blend a smudged section in with its surroundings. You can find tips on applying the Noise filter in Book VII, Chapter 1.

To apply the Smudge tool, just follow these steps:

1. **In the Photo Editor, in Expert mode, open the image and select the Smudge tool from the Tools panel.**

   Press R to cycle through the Smudge, Blur, and Sharpen tools.

2. **In the Tool Options, select a brush from the Brush Preset Picker drop-down panel and use the Size slider to specify your desired brush diameter.**

   Use a small brush for smudging tiny areas, such as edges. Larger brushes produce drastic effects, so use them with care.

3. **In the Tool Options, select a blending mode from the Mode drop-down menu.**

4. **In the Tool Options, select the strength of the smudging effect with the Strength slider or text box.**

   Low values produce a lighter effect; high values really push your pixels around.

5. **If your image has multiple layers, skip to Step 6. If your image has multiple layers, select the Sample All Layers option to make Elements use pixels from all visible layers when it produces the effect.**

   The smudge still appears only on the active layer, but the look is a bit different depending on the contents of the underlying layers.

6. **Use the Finger Painting option to begin the smudge by using the foreground color.**

   You can create interesting effects with this option. Rather than using the color under your cursor, this option smears your foreground color at the start of each stroke.

   You can switch the Smudge tool into Finger Painting mode temporarily by holding down the Alt key (the Option key on the Mac) while you drag. Release Alt (Option) to go back to Normal mode.

7. **Paint over the areas you want to smudge.**

   Pay attention to your strokes because this tool can radically change your image. If you don't like the results, press Ctrl+Z (⌘+Z on the Mac) to undo the changes and then lower the Strength percentage (discussed in Step 4) even more.

   This tool can be a little destructive. If you're looking to preserve reality, use it with restraint. If you want to get wild, go crazy.

8. **When you finish, choose File⇨Save to store your image.**

Softening with the Blur Tool

The Blur tool can repair an image, or you can use it for more creative tasks. Adding a little blur here and there can save an image with a few defects. Blurring can also be used for artistic effect — say, to add a little motion to a soccer ball frozen in time by a too-fast shutter speed. You can also blur portions of your image to emphasize and focus on a particular element, as shown in Figure 1-20, where we blurred the classroom background a bit to draw attention to the teacher and students. The Blur tool makes it easy to paint your blur effects exactly where you want them. This tool works by decreasing the contrast among adjacent pixels in the painted area. The mechanics of using the Blur tool and several of its options are similar to those of the Smudge tool. Just follow these steps:

© iStockphoto.com/ matka_Wariatka Image #4248830

Figure 1-20: Use the Blur tool to soften a rough edge or emphasize a focal point.

1. **In the Photo Editor, in Expert mode, open an image and select the Blur tool from the Tools panel.**

2. **In the Tool Options, select a brush from the Brushes Presets drop-down panel.**

   Use a small brush for applying small areas of blur.

   Use larger brushes with caution. For example, if your goal is to blur the entire background to make a foreground object appear sharper in comparison, it's better to make a selection and apply the Blur filter, as described in Book VII, Chapter 1.

3. **In the Tool Options, select a blending mode from the Mode drop-down menu.**

4. **In the Tool Options, select the strength of the blurring effect with the Strength slider or text box.**

5. **If your image has multiple layers, select the Sample All Layers option to make Elements use pixels from all visible layers when it produces the effect.**

   Selecting this option can produce a smoother blur when you merge the layers later. See Book VI for more info on layers.

6. **Paint over the areas you want to blur.**

7. **When you finish, choose File⇨Save to store your image.**

Focusing with the Sharpen Tool

In theory, the Sharpen tool is nothing more than the Blur tool in reverse — instead of decreasing contrast among pixels, the Sharpen tool increases the contrast. In practice, however, use this tool with a bit more care than the Blur tool. Whereas blurred areas tend to fade from a viewer's notice (at least, in terms of how his or her eyes perceive them), sharpened areas of an image jump out at people. Even a small area that's been oversharpened can quickly lead to overly grainy and noisy images.

You can often successfully sharpen small areas with the Sharpen tool. Sometimes, the eyes in a portrait can benefit from a little sharpening, as shown in Figure 1-21. Or you may want to sharpen an area to make it stand out more distinctly against a slightly blurred background.

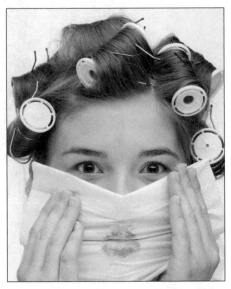

© iStockphoto.com/Thomas_EyeDesign Image #1194770

Figure 1-21: Use the Sharpen tool sparingly and in small areas, such as in the eyes of this portrait.

Follow these simple steps to use the Sharpen tool:

1. **In the Photo Editor, in Expert mode, open an image and select the Sharpen tool from the Tools panel.**

2. **In the Tool Options, select a brush from the Brushes Presets drop-down panel.**

   Use a small brush for applying small areas of sharpening.

3. **In the Tool Options, select a blending mode from the Mode drop-down menu.**

4. **In the Tool Options, select the strength of the sharpening effect with the Strength slider or text box.**

   Using a fairly low value (say, 25% or less) is a good idea because you can build up sharpness slowly, being careful not to overdo it.

   You know you've gone too far with the sharpness when the pixels start to look noisy and grainy.

5. **If your image has multiple layers, select the Sample All Layers option to make Elements use pixels from all visible layers when it produces the effect.**

6. **Select the Protect Detail option to enhance the details in the image and minimize artifacts.**

    If you leave this option deselected, your sharpening is more pronounced.

7. **Paint over the areas you want to sharpen.**

8. **When you finish, choose File⇨Save to store your image.**

Sharpening increases contrast, so be careful when using the Sharpen tool if you plan to also adjust the Levels or Curves controls. Any change that increases contrast in the whole image also boosts the contrast of an area you've sharpened.

The Unsharp Mask and Smart Sharpen filters offer more options and better overall control, so unless you really need to use the sharpening effect, you're usually better off using a filter.

 Putting It Together

Fixing a Photo

Even if you're a highly skilled photographer, you probably have a few photos that require a number of digital fixes. Certainly, we both do. Although it may seem like fixing them is too much trouble or will take too long, you'll find how easy it is after you practice the techniques a few times. After a while, you may even get into the habit of running through your personal quick-editing workflow before you organize and archive your images in the Organizer. If you have more time to burn, you can also add a few artistic touches to further enhance those shots.

Note that most of the details for executing these steps are described in this chapter. When they aren't, we give you the book and chapter where you can find further explanations. If these steps are too tedious for you, you can always follow the Quick mode route we describe earlier, in the section "Editing in Quick Mode."

1. **In the Photo Editor, in Expert mode, open any image in need of repair.**

The image of our two girls is in pretty bad shape — horrible contrast, bad color cast, soft focus, and in need of some healing, as shown in the figure.

continued

**Book VIII
Chapter 1**

Quick Image
Makeovers

continued

2. If you need to rotate the image, choose Image➪Rotate and select a rotation amount.

3. Crop the image using the Crop tool in the Tools panel.

4. To allow for maximum flexibility in editing, convert your background to a layer by double-clicking *Background* in the Layers panel; click OK in the New Layer dialog box.

   For details on working with layers, see Book VI.

5. Adjust the contrast of your image, if needed.

   Try choosing Enhance➪Auto Contrast. If that doesn't work well, undo it by pressing Ctrl+Z (⌘+Z on the Mac) and choose Enhance➪Adjust Lighting➪Shadows/Highlights or Levels.

   Make sure that you have good tones in the shadows (dark areas), midtones (middle-toned areas), and highlights (light areas). Also ensure that you can see details in all the tonal ranges, as shown in the figure. For details on using the Shadows/Highlights and Levels commands, see Chapter 2 of this minibook. For our girls, we broke out the big guns — Levels.

6. Adjust the color of your image, if needed. If you didn't use an auto-fix in Step 5, you can try the Auto Color command on the Enhance submenu. Or choose Enhance➪Adjust Color and select one of the color-adjustment commands described in Chapter 2 of this minibook.

   If you need to adjust the skin tones of your people, you can try the Adjust Color for Skin Tone command. We recommend using the Adjust Color Curves command for overall color adjustment, as we did for our girls in the figure. Usually working with this curve will do the trick, no matter what your color issues are.

Note that you can fix just selected portions of your image. Make a selection first and then apply the adjustment. For details on making selections, see Book IV, Chapter 1.

7. **If you have any people or animals with nasty red-eye, use the Red Eye Removal or Color Replacement tool.**

   Remember to use the Zoom and Hand tools to magnify and navigate around your image, as needed.

8. **If you need to whiten the teeth of any of your people, click Quick at the top of the workspace and use the Whiten Teeth tool in the Tools panel.**

   Although our girls have pretty white teeth, we gave a swipe or two with the Whiten Teeth tool.

   Click Expert at the top of the workspace to return to Expert mode.

9. **Perform any additional repair or healing tasks by using the Healing Brush, Spot Healing Brush, and Clone Stamp tools.**

   Our girls are quite gorgeous as they are, but we broke out the Spot Healing Brush and got rid of a mole and blemish here and there.

10. **Sharpen your image.**

    You can return to Quick mode and either click the Auto button or drag the Sharpen slider under Sharpen in the right pane. Or, for more precise control, in Expert mode, choose Enhance⇨Adjust Sharpness, as described in Chapter 2 of this minibook.

    This fix should always be the last adjustment you make on your image. You want to make sure that all your contrast, color, and flaws are fixed before sharpening. The reason is that the sharpening process increases contrast, so you don't want to exacerbate any problems that may exist. Our "fixed" girls are shown in the final figure.

**Book VIII
Chapter 1**

**Quick Image
Makeovers**

Chapter 2: Correcting Lighting, Color, and Clarity

In This Chapter

✔ Navigating the Histogram panel

✔ Adjusting lighting, color, and clarity

✔ Working with the Smart Brush tools

*I*f you've tried the quick automatic fixes on your photos but they didn't correct the photos to your satisfaction, this chapter should be of some help. Fortunately, Elements offers multiple ways and multiple levels of correcting and enhancing your images. If an auto-fix doesn't work, elevate to a manual fix. Chances are good that if you can't find the tools to correct and repair your images in Elements, those images are probably beyond salvaging.

Correcting Your Images the Logical Way

Using this chapter and the information provided in Chapter 1 of this minibook as your jumping-off points, try to employ some kind of logical workflow when you tackle the correction and repair of your images. Personally, we're partial to the following series of steps:

1. **Crop, straighten, and resize your images, if necessary.**

2. **When you have the images in their proper physical state, correct the lighting and establish good tonal range for your shadows, highlights, and midtones to display the greatest detail possible.**

   Often, just correcting the lighting solves minor color problems. If not, move on to adjusting the color balance.

3. **Eliminate any color casts and adjust the saturation, if necessary.**

4. **Grab the retouching tools, such as the healing tools and filters, to retouch any flaws.**

5. **Apply any desired enhancements or special effects.**

6. **Sharpen your image if you feel that it could use a boost in clarity and sharpness.**

By following these steps, in this order, you should be able to get all your images in shape to print, post, and share with family and friends.

Understanding the Histogram Panel

One of the first things you want to do before you make any color or tonal adjustments to your image is to take a good look at the quality and distribution of the tones throughout your image. We don't mean just eyeballing the composite image on your screen. We're talking about getting inside your image and looking at its guts with the Histogram panel — and keeping it onscreen so that you can see its constant feedback on your image adjustments.

A *histogram* displays the tonal range of an image, as shown in Figure 2-1. It shows how the pixels are distributed by graphing the number of pixels at each of the 256 brightness levels in an image. On this graph, pixels with the same brightness level are stacked in bars along a vertical axis. The higher the line from this axis, the greater the number of pixels at that brightness level. You can view the distribution for the entire image, a selected layer, or an adjustment composite.

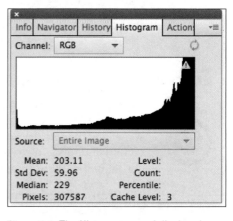

Figure 2-1: The Histogram panel displays how pixels are distributed at each of the 256 brightness levels.

From this graph, you can determine whether the image contains enough detail in the shadow, midtone, and highlight areas. This information helps you determine what image adjustments you may need to make. The following steps walk you through the basics of using the panel and understanding the information you find there:

1. **Choose Window⇨Histogram to bring up the panel.**

2. **Select your desired source of the histogram's display from the Source drop-down menu:**

   - *Entire Image:* Displays a histogram of the entire image.

   - *Selected Layer:* Displays a histogram of just the selected layers in the Layers panel.

   - *Adjustment Composite:* Displays a histogram of a selected adjustment layer and all the layers below it.

3. **Select an option to view isolated portions of your image by choosing an option from the Channel drop-down menu:**

   - *RGB:* Displays a composite image of all color channels — red, green, and blue.

   - *Red, Green and Blue:* Displays the histogram of each individual color channel.

   - *Luminosity:* Displays the luminance, or intensity, of the RGB composite image.

   - *Colors:* Displays the composite RGB histogram by color. Red, green, and blue represent the pixels in each of those channels. Gray represents the area where all three channels overlap.

4. **Examine the tonal range in the histogram.**

   An image with good tonal range displays pixels in all areas. An image with poor tonal range has gaps or slopes that lean heavily toward the right or left sides in the histogram, as shown in Figure 2-2.

   The rest of this chapter explains ways that you can correct contrast and color problems that you find.

5. **(Optional) If you're into numbers, check the statistics to evaluate your image.**

   Drag your cursor within the histogram to see the statistics about a range of values. Or position the cursor within a specific area of the histogram that interests you.

Adjusting Lighting

Elements has several simple, manual tools you can use to fix lighting if the Auto tools (see Chapter 1 of this minibook) don't cut the mustard. The manual tools offer more control for adjusting overall contrast, as well as bringing out details in shadow, midtones, and highlight areas of your images. You can find all lighting adjustments in both Expert and Quick modes.

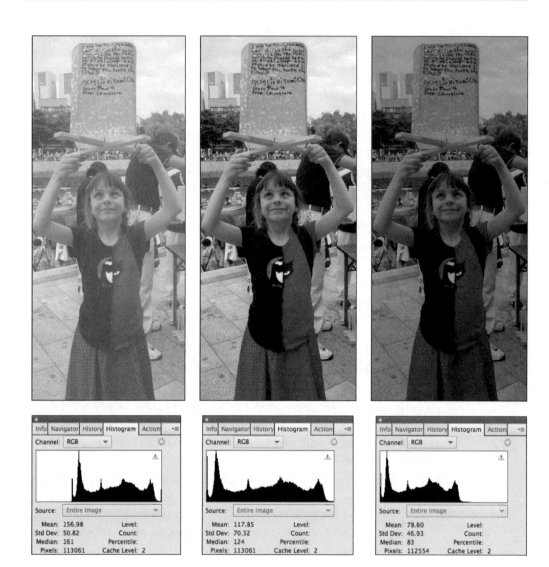

Figure 2-2: Images with poor tonal range have noticeable gaps in the histogram.

Fixing lighting with Shadows/Highlights

The Shadows/Highlights command offers a quick-and-easy method of correcting overexposed and underexposed areas. This feature works especially well with images shot in bright, overhead light or in light coming from the back (backlit). These images usually suffer from having the subject partially or completely surrounded in shadows, such as the original image (left) in Figure 2-3.

Before   After Adjusted with Shadows/
Highlights Command

Figure 2-3: Correct the lighting in your images with the Shadows/
Highlights command.

To use the Shadows/Highlights command, follow these steps:

1. **In Expert or Quick mode, choose Enhance⇨Adjust Lighting⇨Shadows/
   Highlights and make sure that the Preview check box is selected.**

   When the Shadows/Highlights dialog box appears, the default correction
   is applied automatically in your preview.

2. **If the default adjustment doesn't fix the problem, move the sliders (or
   enter a value) to adjust the amount of correction for your shadows
   (dark areas), highlights (light areas), and midtones (middle-toned
   areas).**

   Try to reveal more detail in the dark and light areas of your image. If,
   after you do so, your image still seems to need more correction, add or
   delete contrast in your midtone areas.

3. **If you need to start over, press the Alt key (Option on the Mac) and
   the Cancel button becomes Reset; click Reset to start again.**

4. **Click OK to apply the adjustment and close the dialog box.**

Using Brightness/Contrast

Despite its very descriptive name, the Brightness/Contrast command doesn't
do a great job of either brightening (making an image darker or lighter) or
adjusting contrast. Initially, users tend to be drawn to this command because
of its logical name and ease of use. But, after users realize its limitations,
they move on to better tools with more controls, such as Shadows/Highlights
and Levels.

The problem with the Brightness/Contrast command is that it applies the adjustment equally to all areas of the image. For example, you may have a photo that has some highlights that need darkening, but all the midtones and shadows are okay. The Brightness slider isn't adept enough to recognize that, so when you start to darken the highlights in your image, the midtones and shadows also become darker. To compensate for the unwanted darkening, you try to adjust the Contrast slider, which doesn't fix the problem.

The moral is, if you want to use the Brightness/Contrast command, select only the areas that need the correction, as shown in Figure 2-4. After you make your selection, choose Enhance⇨Adjust Lighting⇨Brightness/Contrast.

Figure 2-4: The Brightness/Contrast command is best reserved for correcting selected areas (left) rather than the entire image (right).

Nailing proper contrast with Levels

If you want the real deal when it comes to correcting the brightness and contrast (and even the color) in your image, look no further than the Levels command. Granted, the dialog box is a tad more complex than those for the other lighting and color-adjustment commands, but when you understand how it works, the payoff is well worth the effort.

You can get a taste of what Levels can do by using Auto Levels, explained in Chapter 1 of this minibook. However, the Levels command offers much more control. And, unlike the rudimentary Brightness/Contrast command, Levels enables you to darken or lighten 256 different tones. Keep in mind that you can use Levels on your entire image, a single layer, or a selected area. You can also apply the Levels command by using an adjustment layer, a recommended method, as we describe in Book VI, Chapter 1.

If you're serious about image editing, the Levels command is one tool you want to master. Here's how it works:

1. **In Expert or Quick mode, choose Enhance⇨Adjust Lighting⇨Levels.**

   We recommend using Expert mode for this command because you have access to the Info panel needed in Step 2. If you're in Quick mode, skip to Step 3.

The Levels dialog box appears, displaying its own histogram. This graph displays how the pixels of the image are distributed at each of the 256 available brightness levels. Shadows are shown on the left side of the histogram, midtones are in the middle, and highlights are on the right. For details on histograms, see the first section of this chapter.

Although you generally make changes to the entire document by using the RGB channel, you can apply changes to any one of an image's component color channels by selecting the specific channel on the Channel drop-down menu. You can also make adjustments to just selected areas, which can be helpful when one area of your image needs adjusting and others don't.

2. **In Expert mode, choose Window⇨Info to open the Info panel.**

3. **Set the black and white points manually by using the eyedroppers in the dialog box.**

   To do so, first select the White Eyedropper tool and then move the cursor over the image.

4. **Look at the Info panel, try to find the lightest white in the image, and then select that point by clicking it.**

   The lightest white has the highest RGB values.

5. **Repeat Steps 3 and 4, using the Black Eyedropper tool and trying to find the darkest black in the image.**

   The darkest black has the lowest RGB values.

   When you set the pure black and pure white points, the remaining pixels are redistributed between those two points.

   You can also reset the white and black points by moving the position of the white and black triangles on the input sliders (just below the histogram). Or, you can enter values in the Input Levels boxes. The three boxes represent the black, gray, and white triangles, respectively. Use the numbers 0 to 255 in the white and black boxes.

6. **Use the Gray Eyedropper tool to remove any color casts by selecting a neutral gray portion of your image, one in which the Info panel shows equal values of red, green, and blue.**

   If your image is grayscale, you can't use the Gray Eyedropper tool.

   If you're not sure where you have a neutral gray, you can also remove a color cast by choosing a color channel from the Channel drop-down menu and doing one of the following:

   • Choose the Red channel and drag the midtone slider to the right to add cyan or to the left to add red.

   • Choose the Green channel and drag the midtone slider to the right to add magenta or to the left to add green.

• Choose the Blue channel and drag the midtone slider to the right to add yellow or to the left to add blue.

7. **If your image has too much contrast, adjust the output sliders at the bottom of the Levels dialog box.**

   Moving the black triangle to the right reduces the contrast in the shadows and lightens the image. Moving the white triangle to the left reduces the contrast in the highlights and darkens the image.

8. **Adjust the midtones (or *gamma values*) with the gray triangle input slider.**

   The default value for gamma is 1.0. Drag the triangle to the left to lighten midtones and drag to the right to darken them. You can also enter a value.

9. **Click OK to apply your settings and close the dialog box.**

   The contrast in your images should be improved, as shown in Figure 2-5.

Figure 2-5: Improve the contrast of an image with the Levels command.

When you click the Auto button, Elements applies the same adjustments as the Auto Levels command, as we explain in Chapter 1 of this minibook. Note the changes and subsequent pixel redistribution shown in the histogram after you click this button.

Adjusting Color

Getting the color you want sometimes seems about as likely as finding a pot of gold at the end of a rainbow. Sometimes, an unexpected *color cast* (a shift in color) is created when photographing, for example, by using (or not using, in some cases) a flash or lens filter or by setting the camera's white balance for lighting conditions that aren't present. After the fact, you can usually do a decent job of correcting the color with one of the many Elements adjustments. Occasionally, you may want to change the color of your image to create a certain special effect. Conversely, you also may want to strip out most of the color from your image to create a vintage feel. Remember that you can apply all these color adjustments to the entire image, to a single layer, or to only a selection. Whatever your color needs, they'll no doubt be met in Elements.

All color adjustments are available in either Expert or Quick mode except for Defringe Layers, which is available only in Expert mode.

Removing color casts automatically

If you ever took a photo in an office or classroom and got a nasty green tint in your image, it was most likely caused by the overhead fluorescent lighting. To eliminate this green tint, or *color cast,* you can apply the Remove Color Cast command. This feature is designed to adjust the image's overall color and remove the cast. Note that it also works with the orange/yellow cast you can get with incandescent lighting.

Follow these short steps to correct your image:

1. **Choose Enhance⇨Adjust Color⇨Remove Color Cast in either Expert or Quick mode.**

   The Remove Color Cast dialog box appears. Move the dialog box to better view your image. Note that this command is also available in Guided mode.

2. **Click an area in your photo that should be white, black, or neutral gray, as shown in Figure 2-6.**

Figure 2-6: Get rid of nasty color shifts with the Remove Color Cast command.

   The colors in the image are adjusted according to the color you choose. Which color should you choose? The answer depends on the subject matter of your image. Feel free to experiment. Your adjustment is merely a preview at this point and isn't applied until you click OK.

3. **If you goof up, click the Reset button.**

   Your image reverts to its unadjusted state.

4. **If you're satisfied with the adjustment, click OK to accept it and close the dialog box.**

If the Remove Color Cast command doesn't fix the problem, try applying a photo filter (as we describe in the section "Adjusting color temperature with photo filters," later in this chapter). For example, if your photo has too much green, try applying a magenta filter.

Adjusting with Hue/Saturation

The Hue/Saturation command enables you to adjust the colors in your image based on their hue, saturation, and lightness. *Hue* is the color in your image. *Saturation* is the intensity, or richness, of that color. And *lightness* controls the brightness value.

Follow these steps to adjust color by using the Hue/Saturation command:

1. **In either Expert or Quick mode, choose Enhance⇨Adjust Color⇨Adjust Hue/Saturation.**

   The Hue/Saturation dialog box appears. Be sure to select the Preview check box so that you can view your adjustments. Note that this command is also available in Guided mode.

2. **Select all the colors (Master) from the dialog box's Edit drop-down menu or choose one color to adjust.**

3. **Drag the slider for one or more of the following attributes to adjust the colors as described:**

   - *Hue:* Shifts all the colors clockwise (drag right) or counterclockwise (drag left) around the color wheel.

   - *Saturation:* Increases (drag right) or decreases (drag left) the richness of the colors. Dragging all the way to the left gives you the appearance of a grayscale image.

   - *Lightness:* Increases the brightness values by adding white (drag right) or decreases the brightness values by adding black (drag left).

     The top color ramp at the bottom of the dialog box represents the colors in their order on the color wheel before you make any changes. The lower color bar displays the colors after you make your adjustments.

When you select an individual color to adjust, sliders appear between the color bars so that you can define the range of color to be adjusted. You can select, add, or subtract colors from the range by choosing one of the Eyedropper tools and clicking in the image.

4. **(Optional) Select the Colorize option to change the colors in your image to a new, single color; drag the Hue slider to change the color to the desired hue.**

   The pure white and black pixels remain unchanged, and the intermediate gray pixels are colorized.

Use the Hue/Saturation command with the Colorize option to create tinted photos, such as the sepia-colored image shown in Figure 2-7. You can also make selections in a grayscale image and apply a different tint to each selection. This can be especially fun with portraits. Tinted images can create a vintage or moody feel and can greatly improve mediocre photos.

Figure 2-7: Colorize your image with the Hue/Saturation command.

Eliminating color with Remove Color

Despite all the talk in this chapter about color, we realize that sometimes you don't want *any* color. With the Remove Color command, you can eliminate all the color from an image, layer, or selection. In Figure 2-8, we selected the background and applied the Remove Color command. To use this one-step command, simply choose Enhance➪Adjust Color➪Remove Color.

TIP

Sometimes, stripping away color with this command can leave your image *flat,* or low in contrast. In this case, adjust the contrast by using one of the many lighting fixes in Elements, such as Auto Levels, Auto Contrast, or Levels.

The Convert to Black and White command (on the Enhance menu) enables you to convert a selection, a layer, or an entire image to grayscale. But, rather than just arbitrarily stripping color (as the Remove Color command does), the Convert to Black and White command enables you to select a conversion method by first choosing an image style. To further refine the results, you can add or subtract colors (red, green, or blue) or contrast by moving the Intensity sliders until your grayscale image looks the way you want. You aren't really adding color; you're simply altering the amount of data in the color channels.

© iStockphoto.com/antares71 Image #14472632

Figure 2-8: Eliminate color with the Remove Color command.

Switching colors with Replace Color

The Replace Color command enables you to replace designated colors in an image with other colors. You first select the colors you want to replace by creating a *mask,* which is a selection made by designating white (selected), black (deselected), and gray (partially selected) areas. (See Book VI, Chapter 4, for more details on working with masks.) You can then adjust the hue and/or saturation of those selected colors.

Follow these steps to replace colors with others:

1. **In Quick or Expert mode, choose Enhance⇨Adjust Color⇨Replace Color.**

   The Replace Color dialog box appears.

2. **Select the Preview check box, if it isn't selected already.**

3. **Choose either Selection or Image:**

   - *Selection:* Shows the mask in the Preview area. The deselected areas are black, partially selected areas are gray, and selected areas are white.

   - *Image:* Shows the actual image in the Preview area.

4. **Click the colors you want to select in either the image or the Preview area.**

5. **Shift-click or use the plus sign (+) Eyedropper tool located in the Replace Color dialog box to add more colors.**

6. **Press the Alt key (Option on the Mac) or use the minus sign (–) Eyedropper tool to delete colors.**

7. **To add colors similar to the ones you select, adjust the Fuzziness slider to fine-tune your selection, adding or deleting from the selection based on the Fuzziness value.**

   To further fine-tune your selection, try using the Localized Color Clusters option. This option lets you select multiple color clusters and can assist in getting a cleaner, more precise selection, especially when you're trying to select more than one color.

8. **Move the Hue and/or Saturation sliders to change the color or color richness, respectively; move the Lightness slider to lighten or darken the image.**

   Go easy with the Lightness slider. You can reduce the tonal range too much and end up with a mess.

9. **View the result in the Image window.**

10. **Click OK to apply the settings and close the dialog box.**

    Figure 2-9 shows how we substituted the color of our tomatoes to change them from red to purple.

Correcting with Color Curves

The most sophisticated of the color correctors is the Color Curves command. This adjustment attempts to improve the tonal range in color images by making adjustments to highlights, shadows, and midtones in each color channel. Try using this command on images in which the foreground elements appear overly dark due to backlighting. Conversely, the adjustment is also designed to correct images that appear overexposed and washed out.

Book VIII Chapter 2

Correcting Lighting, Color, and Clarity

© iStockphoto.com/pixhook Image #2054907

Figure 2-9: The Replace Color command enables you to replace one color with another.

Here's how to use this adjustment on a selection, a layer, or an entire image:

1. **In Quick or Expert mode, choose Enhance⇨Adjust Color⇨Adjust Color Curves.**

   The Adjust Color Curves dialog box appears.

2. **Select the Preview check box, if it isn't selected already.**

   Move the dialog box to the side so that you can view the Image window while making adjustments.

   Various curve adjustments appear in the Select a Style area of the dialog box.

3. **Select a style to make your desired adjustments while viewing your image in the After window.**

4. **(Optional) If you need more precision, use the Adjust Highlights, Midtone Brightness, Midtone Contrast, and Adjust Shadows sliders, as shown in Figure 2-10.**

   The graph on the right represents the distribution of tones in your image. When you first access the Adjust Color Curves dialog box, the tonal range of your image is represented by a straight line. As you drag the sliders, the straight line is altered, and the tonal range is adjusted accordingly.

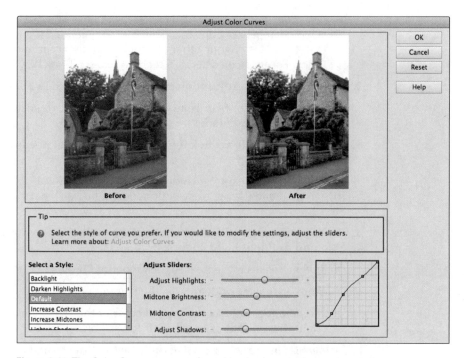

Figure 2-10: The Color Curves command provides basic and advanced controls.

5. **To start over, click the Reset button.**

6. **Click OK when you've adjusted the image satisfactorily.**

   You see before-and-after images in the Adjust Color Curves dialog box.

Adjusting skin tones

Sometimes, the family and friends in your photos appear nauseated (green), sunburned (red), or frigid (blue), or they've taken on some other nonflesh-colored tone. To fix that problem, Elements provides a command that's designed to adjust the overall color in the image and restore skin tones to more natural and attractive shades.

Here's how to fix those skin tones:

1. **Open your image in Quick or Expert mode, select the Preview check box, and do one or both of the following:**

   • *Select the layer that needs to be adjusted.* If you don't have any layers, your entire image is adjusted.

- *Select the desired areas of skin that need to be adjusted.* Only the selected areas are adjusted. This is recommended if you're satisfied with the color of your other elements and just want to fix the skin tones. For more on selection techniques, see Book IV, Chapter 1.

2. **Choose Enhance⇨Adjust Color⇨Adjust Color for Skin Tone.**

   The Adjust Color for Skin Tone dialog box appears. You can also find this command in Guided mode.

3. **In the Image window, click the portion of skin that needs to be corrected.**

   The command adjusts the color of the skin tone, as well as the color in the overall image, layer, or selection, depending on what you selected in Step 1.

4. **If you're unhappy with the results, click another area or adjust the Skin and Ambient Light sliders:**

   - *Tan:* Increases or decreases the amount of brown in the skin.

   - *Blush:* Increases or decreases the amount of red in the skin.

   - *Temperature:* Adjusts the overall color of the skin, making it warmer (right toward red) or cooler (left toward blue).

5. **To start from square one, click the Reset button; to bail out completely, click Cancel.**

6. **When you're satisfied with the correction, click OK to apply the adjustment and close the dialog box.**

   Your improved skin appears, as shown in Figure 2-11.

Figure 2-11: Give your friends and family a complexion makeover with the Adjust Color for Skin Tone command.

Defringing layers

A surefire sign of a sloppily composited image is a selection with a fringe. Don't get us wrong: If the fringe is the kind that is hanging off of your '70s-era buckskin leather jacket, that's fine. You just don't want the fringe that consists of those background pixels surrounding the edges of your selections, as shown in Figure 2-12. Sometimes, when making a selection, you pick up some of the background pixels. These pixels are referred to as a *fringe* or *halo*.

Luckily, the Defringe command replaces the color of the fringe pixels with the colors of neighboring pixels that don't contain the background color. In our example, we plucked the globe out of a white background and placed it on a black background. Some of the background pixels were included in our selection and appear as white fringe. When we apply the Defringe command, those white fringe pixels are changed to colors of nearby pixels (see Figure 2-12).

Fringe

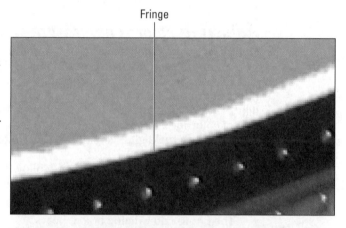

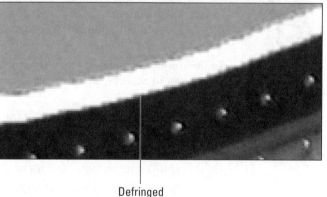

Defringed

Figure 2-12: Remove the colored halo around your selections with the Defringe command.

Book VIII Chapter 2

Correcting Lighting, Color, and Clarity

Follow these steps to defringe your selection:

1. **In Expert mode only, copy and paste a selection onto a new or existing layer, or drag and drop a selection onto a new document.**

   The Defringe Layer command doesn't work in Quick mode.

2. **Choose Enhance⇨Adjust Color⇨Defringe Layer.**

   The Defringe dialog box appears.

3. **Enter a value for the number of pixels that needs to be converted.**

   Try entering 1 or 2 first to see whether that fixes the fringe problem. If not, you may need to enter a slightly higher value.

4. **Click OK to accept the value and close the dialog box.**

Adjusting color temperature with photo filters

Light has its own color temperature. A photo shot in a higher color temperature of light makes an image blue. An image shot in a lower color temperature makes a photo yellow. Photographers sometimes use colored glass filters in front of their camera lenses to adjust the color temperature of the light. They do this to warm up or cool down their photos or just to add a hint of color for subtle special effects. You can, however, mimic this effect in Elements with the digital versions of these filters.

To apply the Photo Filter adjustment, follow these steps:

1. **In Expert mode, choose Filter⇨Adjustments⇨Photo Filter.**

   The Photo Filter dialog box appears.

   You can also apply the photo filter to an individual layer by creating a photo-filter adjustment layer. For details on adjustment layers, see Book VI, Chapter 1.

2. **In the dialog box, select Filter to choose a preset filter from the drop-down list, or select Color to select your own filter color from the Color Picker.**

   Here's a brief description of each of the preset filters:

   - *Warming Filter (85), (81), and (LBA):* Adjust the white balance in an image to make the colors warmer or more yellow. Filter (81) is like (85) and (LBA), but it's best used for minor adjustments.

   - *Cooling Filter (80), (82), and (LBB):* Also adjust the white balance that's shown, but instead of making the colors warmer, they make the colors cooler or bluer. Filter (82) is like (80) and (LBB), but it's designed for slight adjustments.

   - *Red, Orange, Yellow, and so on:* The various color filters adjust the hue, or color, of a photo. Choose a color filter to try to eliminate a color cast or to apply a special effect.

3. **Adjust the Density option to specify the amount of color applied to your image.**

4. **Select Preserve Luminosity to prevent the photo filter from darkening your image.**

5. **Click OK to apply your filter and close the dialog box.**

Figure 2-13 shows the image before and after the application of a photo filter (80) applied to an overly warm image.

Figure 2-13: Photo filters adjust the color temperature of your image.

Mapping your colors

Elements provides commands referred to as *color mappers,* which change the colors in your image by mapping them to other values. You can find the color mappers by choosing Filter⇨Adjustments. Figure 2-14 shows results of using these commands, which we also briefly describe in the following list:

- **Equalize:** This mapper first locates the lightest and darkest pixels in the image and assigns them values of white and black. It then redistributes all the remaining pixels among the grayscale values. The exact effect depends on your individual image.

- **Gradient Map:** This command maps the tonal range of an image to the colors of your chosen gradient. For example, colors (such as orange, green, and purple) are mapped to the shadows, highlight, and midtone areas.

- **Invert:** This command reverses all the colors in your image, creating a kind of negative. Black reverses to white, and colors convert to their complementary hues (blue goes to yellow, red goes to cyan, and so on).

- **Posterize:** This command reduces the number of brightness levels in your image. Choose a value between 2 and 255 levels. Lower values create an illustrative, poster look, and higher values produce a more photorealistic image.

- **Threshold:** Threshold makes your image black and white, with all pixels that are brighter than a value you specify represented as white, and all pixels that are as dark or darker than that value as black. You can change the threshold level to achieve different high-contrast effects.

Equalize   Gradient Map   Invert

Threshold   Posterize

© iStockphoto/szefei Image #6707199

Figure 2-14: Change the colors in your image by remapping them to other values.

The Threshold command can come in handy when you need to clean up scans of line art, such as hand-drawn sketches, people's signatures, pages from a book, or even sheet music. Often, when you scan things on paper, the slight color from the paper appears as a dull gray background in the scan. By applying the Threshold command, you can adjust the tones in your image to black and white and drop out the gray. Simply move the slider to get your desired balance of white and black areas.

Adjusting Clarity

After you've corrected the contrast and color and fixed your major flaws, like scratches, wrinkles, and blemishes (as we describe in Chapter 1 of this minibook), you're ready to finally work on the overall clarity of that image. If your image suffers from an overall problem like dust, scratches, or *artifacts* (blocky pixels or halos), you may need to employ the help of a filter. Then finally, after you totally clean up your image, your last task is to give it a good sharpening. Why wait until the very end to do so? Sometimes, improving the contrast and color and getting rid of flaws can reduce the clarity and sharpness of an image. So you want to be sure that your image is as soft as it's going to get before you dive into sharpening. On the other hand, keep in mind that sharpening increases contrast, so (depending on how much of the image you're sharpening), you may need to go back and fine-tune it by using the lighting adjustments described in the section "Adjusting Lighting," earlier in this chapter.

Finally, we know we've been harping on the value of sharpening, but believe it or not, you may also need to blur an image occasionally. Blurring can eliminate unpleasant patterns that occur during scanning, soften distracting backgrounds to give a better focal point, or even create the illusion of motion.

Removing noise, artifacts, dust, and scratches

We know it sounds ironic, but the tools you use to eliminate unwanted garbage from your images are found on the Filter➪Noise submenu in Expert mode. With the exception of the Add Noise filter, the others actually help to hide noise, dust, scratches, and artifacts. Here's the list of *cleaners:*

- **Despeckle:** Decreases the contrast, without affecting the edges, to make the dust in your image less pronounced. You may notice a slight blurring of your image (that's what's hiding the garbage), but the edges should still be sharp.

- **Dust & Scratches:** Hides, well, dust and scratches by blurring those areas of your image that contain the gunk. (It looks for harsh transitions in tone.) Specify your desired Radius value, which is the size of the area to be blurred. Also, specify the Threshold value, which determines how much contrast between pixels must be present before they're blurred.

  Use restraint with the Dust & Scratches filter. It can wipe out detail and make your image look like mush.

- **Median:** Reduces contrast around dust spots. The process the filter goes through is rather technical, but basically light spots darken, dark spots lighten, and the rest of the image isn't changed. Specify your desired radius, which is the size of the area to be adjusted.

✓ **Reduce Noise:** Designed to remove luminance noise and artifacts from your images. We used this filter to correct the original image (on the left) in Figure 2-15, which had the nasty blockiness caused by JPEG compression. *Luminance noise* is grayscale noise that makes images look overly grainy. Specify these options to reduce the noise in an image:

- *Strength:* Specify the amount of noise reduction.

- *Preserve Details:* A higher percentage preserves edges and details but reduces the amount of noise that's removed.

- *Reduce Color Noise:* Remove random colored pixels.

- *Remove JPEG Artifact:* Remove the blocks and halos that can occur from low-quality JPEG compression.

Figure 2-15: Use the Reduce Noise filter to remove noise and artifacts.

Blurring when you need to

It may sound strange that anyone would intentionally want to blur an image. But, if your photo is overly grainy or suffers from an ugly *moiré* pattern (described in the following list), you may need to blur the image to correct the problem. Also, often, you may even want to blur the background of an image to deemphasize distractions or to make the foreground elements appear sharper and provide a better focal point, as shown in Figure 2-16.

You can access all the blurring tools by choosing Filter➪Blur in Expert or Quick mode. The exception is the Blur tool, which we explain in Chapter 1 of this minibook:

✔ **Average:** This one-step filter calculates the average value of the image or selection and fills the area with that average value. You can use it for smoothing overly noisy areas in your image.

✔ **Blur:** Another one-step filter, this one applies a fixed amount of blurring to the whole image.

✔ **Blur More:** This one-step blur filter gives the same effect as Blur, but more intensely.

✔ **Motion Blur:** This filter mimics the blur given off by moving objects. Specify the angle of motion and the distance of the blur. Make sure to select the Preview check box to see the effect while you enter the values.

Figure 2-16: Blur your image to emphasize a focal point.

✔ **Radial Blur:** This filter produces a circular blur effect.

    a. Specify the amount of blur that you want.

    b. Choose the Spin method to blur along concentric circular lines, as shown in the thumbnail.

    Or choose Zoom to blur along radial lines and mimic the effect of zooming in to your image.

    c. Specify the desired Quality level.

    Because the Radial Blur filter is notoriously slow, Elements gives you the option of Draft (fast but grainy), Good, or Best (slow but smooth). The difference between Good and Best is evident only on large, high-resolution images.

    d. Indicate where you want the center of your blur by moving the blur diagram thumbnail.

✔ **Smart Blur:** This filter provides several options to enable you to specify how the blur is applied.

    a. Specify a value for the radius and threshold, both defined in the following section.

    Start with a lower value for both and adjust from there.

    b. Choose a quality setting from the drop-down menu.

    c. Choose a mode setting.

Normal blurs the entire image or selection. Edge Only blurs only the edges of your elements and uses black and white in the blurred pixels. Overlay Edge also blurs just the edges, but it applies only white to the blurred pixels.

✔ **Surface Blur:** This filter blurs the surface, or interior, of the image, rather than the edges. If you want to preserve your edge details but blur everything else, this is the filter for you.

✔ **Gaussian Blur:** The last Blur filter we discuss is probably the one you'll use most often. It offers a Radius setting to let you adjust the amount of blurring you desire.

Use the Gaussian Blur filter to camouflage moiré patterns on scanned images. A *moiré pattern* is caused when you scan halftone images. A *halftone* is created when a continuous-tone image, such as a photo, is digitized and converted into a screen pattern of repeating lines (usually between 85 and 150 lines per inch) and then printed. When you then scan that halftone, a second pattern results and is overlaid on the original pattern. These two different patterns clash and create an ugly moiré pattern. The Gaussian Blur filter doesn't eliminate the moiré — it just merges the dots and reduces the appearance of the pattern.

If you've ever played with the aperture settings on a camera, you know that you can specify how shallow or deep your depth of field is. Depth of field relates to the *plane of focus* (the areas in a photo that are in front of or behind the focal point and that remain in focus) or how in-focus the foreground elements are when you compare them to the background elements. The Lens Blur filter allows you to give the effect of a shallower depth of field after you have already captured your image. This filter enables you to take a fully focused image and create this type of selective focus. You can also use it to create a kind of dreamy effect, as shown in Figure 2-17.

Follow these steps to use the Lens Blur filter:

1. **Choose Filter⇨Blur⇨Lens Blur.**

2. **In the Lens Blur dialog box, choose your Preview mode.**

   Faster gives you a quick preview, while More Accurate shows you the final rendered image.

3. **Choose a Source from the drop-down menu for your depth map, if you have one.**

   You can choose between a layer mask or transparency. A good way to create an image with this shallow depth of field effect is to create a layer mask on your image layer and fill it with a white-to-black gradient — black where you want the most focus and white where you want the least focus or most blur. Choose Transparency to make an image blurrier and more transparent.

The filter uses a depth map to determine how the blur works.

4. **Drag the Blur Focal Distance slider to specify how blurry or in focus an area of the image is.**

   Alternatively, click the crosshair cursor on the part of the image that you want to be in full focus.

   Dragging the slider enables you to specify a value. You can also select Invert to invert, or reverse, the depth map source.

5. **Choose an Iris shape, such as triangle or octagon, from the Shape drop-down menu.**

   The Iris settings are meant to simulate a camera lens.

Figure 2-17: Use the Lens Blur filter to create a shallow depth of field effect.

6. **Specify the shape of the lens, as well as the radius (size of the iris), blade curvature (how smooth are the iris edges), and rotation of that shape.**

7. **Set the Brightness and Threshold values in the Specular Highlights area.**

   The Lens Blur filter averages the highlights of an image, which, if left uncorrected, cause some highlights to appear grayish. The Specular Highlights controls help to retain specular highlights, or those highlights that should appear very white. Set the Threshold value to specify which highlights should be specular (remain white). Set a Brightness value to specify how much to relighten any blurred areas.

8. **Drag the Amount slider in the Noise area to add noise back into your image; choose monochromatic to add noise without affecting the color.**

   Blurring obliterates any noise (or film grain) that an image may have. This absence of noise can cause the image to appear inconsistent or unrealistic, in many cases.

9. **Click OK to apply the Lens Blur and exit the dialog box.**

Sharpening for better focus

Of course, if your images don't need any contrast-, color-, and flaw-fixing, feel free to move right into sharpening. Sometimes, images captured by a scanner or a digital camera are a little soft, and it's not due to any tonal adjustments. Occasionally, you may even want to sharpen a selected area in your image just so that it becomes a better focal point.

Keep in mind that you can't really improve the focus of an image after capturing it. But you can do a decent job of faking it. All sharpening tools work by increasing the contrast between adjacent pixels. This increased contrast causes the edges to appear more distinct, thereby giving the illusion that the focus is improved, as shown in Figure 2-18. Remember that you can also use the Sharpen tool for very small areas, as described in Chapter 1 of this minibook.

Figure 2-18: Sharpening mimics an increase in focus by increasing contrast between adjacent pixels.

Here's the lowdown on sharpening commands:

- **Unsharp Mask:** Unsharp Mask, on the Enhance menu in Expert or Quick mode, gives you several options that enable you to control the amount of sharpening and the width of the areas to be sharpened. Use them to nail your desired sharpening:

  - *Amount:* Specify an amount (from 1% to 500%) of edge sharpening. The higher the value, the more contrast between pixels around the edges. Start with a value of 100% (or less), which usually gives good contrast without appearing overly grainy.

- *Radius:* Specify the width (from 0.1 to 250 pixels) of the edges that the filter will sharpen. The higher the value, the wider the edge. The value you use is largely based on the resolution of your image. Low-resolution images require a smaller radius value. High-resolution images require a higher value.

Be warned that specifying a value that's too high overemphasizes the edges of your image and makes them appear thick and goopy.

A good rule for selecting a starting radius value is to divide your image's resolution by 150. For example, if you have a 300-ppi (pixels per inch) image, set the radius at 2 and then use your eye to adjust from there.

- *Threshold:* Specify the difference in brightness (from 0 to 255) that must be present between adjacent pixels before the edge is sharpened. A lower value sharpens edges with very little contrast difference. Higher values sharpen only when adjacent pixels are very different in contrast. We recommend leaving Threshold set at 0 unless your image is very grainy. Increasing the value too much can cause unnatural transitions between sharpened and unsharpened areas.

Occasionally, the values you enter for Amount and Radius may sharpen the image effectively but can create excess *grain,* or noise, in your image. You can sometimes reduce this noise by increasing the Threshold value.

- **Adjust Sharpness:** Another sharpening option is the Adjust Sharpness command, as shown in Figure 2-19. This feature enables you to control the amount of sharpening applied to shadow and highlight areas. It also allows you to select from various sharpening algorithms.

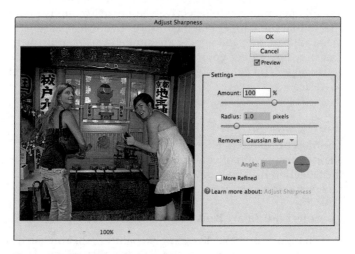

Figure 2-19: The Adjust Sharpness command.

Specify the following options:

- *Amount* and *Radius:* See the two descriptions in the earlier Unsharp Mask bullet.

- *Preset:* You can save your sharpening settings as a preset that you can load and use later.

- *Remove:* Choose your sharpening algorithm. Gaussian Blur is the algorithm used for the Unsharp Mask command. Lens Blur detects detail in the image and attempts to respect the details while reducing the nasty halos that can occur with sharpening. Motion Blur tries to sharpen the blurring that occurs when your camera, or your subject, moves.

- *Angle:* Specify the direction of motion for the Motion Blur algorithm, described in the preceding Remove bullet.

- *Shadows/Highlights:* You can now control the amount of sharpening in the Shadow and Highlight areas of your image. Determine the amount of sharpening with the Fade Amount setting. For the Tonal Width option, specify the range of tones you want to sharpen. Move the slider to the right to sharpen only the darker of the shadow areas and the lighter of the highlight areas. Finally, for the Radius setting, specify the amount of space around a pixel that's used to determine whether a pixel is in the shadow or the highlight area. Move the slider right to specify a greater area.

Working Intelligently with the Smart Brush Tools

The two Smart Brush tools — Smart Brush and Detail Smart Brush — are fun tools that enable you to selectively apply image adjustments or special effects that then appear on all or part of your image. What's great is that these adjustments and effects are applied via an adjustment layer, meaning that they hover over your layers and don't permanently alter the pixels in your image. The adjustments can also be flexibly edited and deleted, if you so desire.

Using the Smart Brush

The Smart Brush tool allows you to paint a variety of image adjustments on all or just a portion of your image. The action of the tool is similar to that of the Selection Brush — as you brush, you make a selection and adjust simultaneously. Follow these steps to use the Smart Brush tool:

1. **Select the Smart Brush tool from the Tools panel in Expert mode.**

   The tool icon looks like a house paintbrush. You can also press the F key to switch between the Smart Brush and Detail Smart Brush tools.

2. **In the Tool Options, choose your desired brush size.**

3. **Choose additional attributes, such as hardness, spacing, and roundness, from the Brush Settings drop-down panel.**

4. **Select your desired adjustment category and then a particular preset adjustment from the Smart Paint Preset Picker drop-down panel in the Tool Options, as shown in Figure 2-20.**

   In the Smart Paint preset panel, choose adjustments ranging from photographic effects, such as a vintage Yellowed Photo, to nature effects, such as Sunset (which gives a warm, orange glow to your image).

5. **Paint an adjustment on a layer in your image, as shown in Figure 2-20, where we painted with the Antique Contrast effect.**

   While you paint, the Smart Brush tool attempts to detect edges in your image and snaps to those edges. In addition, while you brush, a selection border appears.

© iStockphoto.com/billyfoto Image #2758280

Figure 2-20: The Smart Brush enables you to paint on adjustments.

A new adjustment layer is automatically created with your first paint stroke. The accompanying layer mask also appears on that adjustment layer. For more on adjustment layers, see Book VI, Chapter 1.

6. **Using the Add and Subtract Smart Brush modes in the Tool Options, fine-tune your adjusted area by adding and subtracting from it.**

   When you add and subtract from your adjusted area, you're essentially modifying your layer mask. Adding to the adjusted area adds white to the layer mask, and subtracting from an adjusted area adds black to the layer mask. For more on layer masks, see Book VI, Chapter 4.

7. **Select a different preset adjustment for your selected area, if you want.**

   In fact, try them all out before you make your final choice.

8. **If you believe that you need to refine your selected area, choose the Refine Edges option in the Tool Options.**

   For more on Refine Edges, see Book IV, Chapter 2.

   If you'd rather apply the adjustment to your unselected area, select the Inverse option in the Tool Options.

   If you want to modify your adjustment, double-click the Adjustment Layer pin on your image. The pin is annotated by a small, square, black-and-red gear icon. After you double-click the pin, the dialog box corresponding to your particular adjustment appears. For example, if you double-click the Shoe Box Photo adjustment (under Photographic), you access the Hue/Saturation dialog box.

9. **Make your necessary adjustments in the dialog box and click OK.**

   You can also right-click (on the Mac, Control-click if you're using a one-button mouse) and select Change Adjustment Settings from the contextual menu that appears. Or, you can select Delete Adjustment and Hide Selection from the same menu.

10. **After you finish, simply deselect your selection by choosing Select⇨ Deselect.**

You can add multiple Smart Brush adjustments. After you apply one effect, reset the Smart Brush tool and apply additional adjustments.

Getting accurate with the Detail Smart Brush

The Detail Smart Brush tool also enables you to paint various image adjustments on all or part of your image. The action of the tool is similar to the regular Brush tool, enabling finer control than that of the Smart Brush. Follow these steps to use the Detail Smart Brush tool:

1. **Select the Detail Smart Brush tool from the Tools panel in Expert mode.**

   The tool icon looks like an art paintbrush. You can also press the F key to switch between the Smart Brush and Detail Smart Brush tools.

2. **In the Tool Options, choose a brush tip from the Brush Preset Picker drop-down panel and adjust the brush tip size as desired.**

   Feel free to change your brush tip and size as needed to achieve the desired effect. For more on working with brushes, see Book V, Chapter 1.

3. **Select an adjustment category and then your particular preset adjustment from the Smart Paint drop-down panel in the Tool Options.**

   Effects include making your image look like a film negative or an X-ray, as well as more subtle looks, such as creating a vintage photo with the Sepia Duotone effect. Figure 2-21 shows a pencil sketch effect.

4. **Paint an adjustment on the desired layer in your image.**

   A new adjustment layer is automatically created with your first paint stroke, along with an accompanying layer mask.

5. **Follow Steps 6 through 9 in the preceding step list for the Smart Brush tool.**

© iStockphoto.com/WorldWideImages Image #4363392

Figure 2-21: The Detail Smart Brush lets you paint on a variety of special effects.

Chapter 3: Compositing with Photomerge

In This Chapter

- ↗ **Combining multiple images into a single panoramic image**
- ↗ **Getting the hero shot with Group Shot**
- ↗ **Improving an image with Faces**
- ↗ **Cleaning up your images with Scene Cleaner**
- ↗ **Working with Exposure**

Sometimes, working with just a single shot isn't quite enough. Imagine this scenario: As much as you try, you just can't quite squeeze that vacation scenic vista into one photo; in fact, it takes a total of three shots. Or one of your relatives is always blinking or looking the wrong way in your family reunion snapshots, so no single shot ends up being the perfect group photo. Or maybe bystanders or cars keep crossing the path of your camera when you're trying to capture that historic landmark.

Not to worry, because the Elements Photomerge commands are designed to help you fix these types of problems. One command seamlessly stitches multiple shots of your panorama into a single image, while another eliminates distracting elements from your shots, and a third command enables you to combine multiple group shots to get the best composite. And the newest command enables you to more easily extract one image and combine it with another.

 You can access all but one (Photomerge Panorama) of the Photomerge commands in all three Photo Editor modes — Expert, Quick, and Guided — or in the Organizer. Photomerge Panorama is only available in Expert mode and in the Organizer.

Stitching a Scene with Photomerge Panorama

The Photomerge Panorama command enables you to combine multiple images into a single panoramic image. You can take several overlapping photos, from skylines to mountain ranges, and stitch them together into one shot.

If you know your ultimate goal is to create a Photomerge composition, you can make things easier for yourself by making sure that when you shoot your photos, you overlap your individual images by 15 percent to 40 percent, but no more than 50 percent. Adobe recommends that you avoid using distortion lenses (such as a fish-eye) and that you also avoid using your camera's zoom setting. Additionally, try to keep the same exposure settings for even lighting. Finally, try to stay in the same position and keep your camera at the same level for each shot. Using a tripod and rotating the head can help you achieve this consistency. Note, however, that rotating the head may make it difficult to keep even lighting, depending on the angle of your light source relative to the camera. You may also introduce a perspective distortion. To minimize distortion while shooting, try to have your tripod on a level and parallel surface, if possible. If you still get some distortion, you can correct it during the stitching described in the following steps.

Follow these steps to assemble your own Photomerge Panorama composition:

1. **In the Photo Editor, in Expert mode, choose Enhance⇨Photomerge⇨ Photomerge Panorama.**

   This command is the only Photomerge command that is accessible only from the Expert mode or from the Organizer.

2. **In the first Photomerge dialog box, shown in Figure 3-1, select your source files.**

   You can select from Files (which uses individual files you select) or from Folder (which uses all images in a folder) from the Use drop-down list. Click the Add Open Files button to use all currently open files. Or click the Browse button to navigate to certain files or folders.

3. **Under Layout, select a projection mode.**

   The thumbnail illustration visually demonstrates each mode, but we give you a little more description of each here:

   • *Auto:* Using the Auto mode, Elements analyzes your images on its own.

   • *Perspective:* Select this mode if your images have been shot with perspective or at acute angles. This mode is also good to use if you've shot images using the tripod method described earlier in this section.

   • *Cylindrical:* Select this option if you shot images with a wide-angle lens. This mode is also good for those 360-degree, full panoramic shots.

   • *Spherical:* This projection method aligns images by rotating, positioning, and uniformly scaling each image. It may be the best choice for true panoramas, but you may also find it useful for stitching together images based on common features.

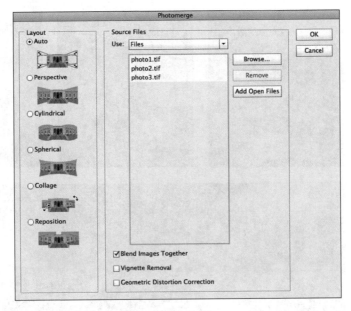

Figure 3-1: Select the source files for your composition.

- *Collage:* This mode is useful when stitching together a 360-degree panorama in which you have a wide field of view, both horizontally and vertically. Use this option for shots taken with a wide-angle lens.

- *Reposition:* When you select this mode, Elements doesn't take into account any distortion but merely scans the images and positions them in what it considers the best position.

4. Select one of the following options:

- *Blend Images Together:* Corrects the color differences that can occur from blending images with different exposures.

- *Vignette Removal:* Corrects exposure problems caused by lens vignetting (when light at the edges of images is reduced and the edges are darkened).

- *Geometric Distortion Correction:* Corrects lens problems such as barrel distortion (bulging out) and pincushion distortion (pinching in), which are both types of radial distortion.

5. Click OK to create the panorama.

Elements opens and automatically assembles the sources files to create the composite panorama, as shown in Figure 3-2.

Figure 3-2: Combine multiple images into a single panoramic shot using Photomerge Panorama.

Note that, with any of the modes, Elements leaves your merged image in layers. Also notice that a layer mask has been added to each layer to better blend the panoramic image. For more on layer masks, see Book VI.

Elements alerts you if it can't composite your source files. If that happens, you may have to composite your images manually by creating a large canvas and dragging and dropping your images onto that canvas.

Getting the Best Shot with Photomerge Group Shot

Getting a group of people to smile, not blink or fidget, and look in the same direction is about as easy as herding cats. With Elements, you no longer have to worry about snapping the perfect group shot anymore. Just take a bunch of shots (on burst mode is a great way to go) and later create the ultimate perfect shot by compositing those shots using Photomerge Group Shot.

Here are the steps to create a Photomerge Group Shot image:

1. **In any of the Photo Editor modes, select two or more photos from your Photo Bin at the bottom of your Image window.**

2. **Choose Enhance⇨Photomerge⇨Photomerge Group Shot.**

   The Photomerge Group Shot dialog box appears.

3. **Take your best overall group shot and drag it from the Photo Bin onto the Final pane.**

4. **Select another photo in the Photo Bin to use as your source image and then drag it to the Source pane.**

5. **With the Pencil tool, draw a line around the portions of the source photo you want to merge into your final photo, as shown in Figure 3-3.**

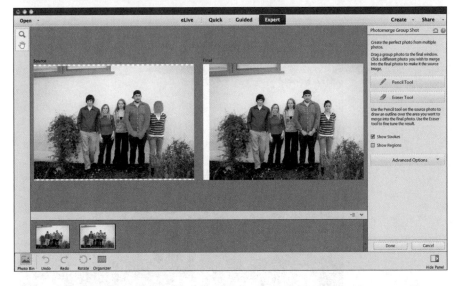

Book VIII
Chapter 3

Compositing with
Photomerge

Figure 3-3: Use Photomerge Group Shot to composite the perfect group shot from several images.

In the Options area on the right side of the dialog box, you can choose to show the yellow pencil strokes (Show Strokes) or show regions (Show Regions), which are then highlighted with a blue overlay. Use the Eraser tool to remove any portions you don't want to be merged onto the final image.

6. **Repeat Steps 4 and 5 with any remaining photos.**

   If your photos aren't aligned, you can use the Alignment tool under Advanced Options.

7. **Using the Alignment tool, click the source image and position the three target markers on three key locations.**

   Do the same on the final image and choose similar locations.

   You can click the Pixel Blending option to better blend pixels.

8. **Click the Align Photos button.**

   Again, as with Photomerge Panorama, the more similar (in framing, size, lighting, and so on) that your source and final images are, the better the merged result.

   Optionally, if you see any noticeable seams on your final image around the copied area, you can click the Pixel Blending button to help smooth over those flaws.

9. **If you make a mess of things, click the Reset button and go back to Step 3.**

10. **When you're satisfied with the result, click Done.**

    The file opens as a new window (save to create a new file) in Elements, as shown in Figure 3-4.

Figure 3-4: The perfect group shot.

Photomerge Faces

Photomerge Faces enables you to create the perfect portrait by compositing several less-than-perfect shots of a person. For example, you can get the smile from one shot, the eyes from another shot, and so on. You can also use this feature in more of a whimsical, fun way to blend features from multiple faces to create sort of a hybrid face. To create a hybrid human, select two or more photos from your Photo Bin and choose File⇨New⇨Photomerge Faces in any of the edit modes. Use the Alignment and Pencil tools to choose how you'd like to merge the photos, similar to the steps described in the section "Getting the Best Shot with Photomerge Group Shot."

Eliminating with Photomerge Scene Cleaner

Photomerge Scene Cleaner sounds like a covert job with the CIA where you spend your days mopping up evidence at crime scenes, but it isn't quite that intriguing. This Photomerge command toolset enables you to create the optimum image by allowing you to eliminate annoying distractions, such as cars, passersby, and so on.

To get the best source images for a "clean scene," be sure to take multiple shots of your scene from the same angle and distance. It also works best when the elements you want to eliminate are moving.

Follow these steps to create a Photomerge Scene Cleaner composite:

1. **Select two or more photos from your Photo Bin.**

2. **Choose Enhance⇨Photomerge⇨Photomerge Scene Cleaner in any of the Photo Editor modes.**

   The Photomerge Scene Cleaner dialog box appears.

   Elements attempts to auto-align your images the best it can.

3. **Take your best overall shot of the scene and drag it from the Photo Bin onto the Final pane.**

4. **Select one of your other photos in the Photo Bin to use as your source image and then drag it to the Source pane.**

5. **With the Pencil tool, draw a line on or around the elements in the final photo that you want to be replaced by content from the source photo, as shown in Figure 3-5.**

6. **Repeat Steps 4 and 5 with the remaining shots of the scene.**

   If your photos aren't aligned, you can use the Alignment tool under the Advanced Options.

Book VIII
Chapter 3

Compositing with
Photomerge

Figure 3-5: Create the ideal photo from multiple shots with Photomerge Scene Cleaner.

7. **Using the Alignment tool, click the source image and position the three target markers on three key locations; do the same on the final image, choosing similar locations.**

8. **Click the Align Photos button.**

   Again, as with the other Photomerge commands, the more similar the starting source images (similar framing, similar angle, similar lighting), the better the merged result will be.

9. **(Optional) If you see any noticeable seams on your final image around the copied area, click the Pixel Blending button to help smooth over those flaws.**

10. **If you make a mess of things, click the Reset button and go back to Step 3.**

11. **When you're satisfied with the result, click Done.**

The cleaned-up image opens as a new file in Elements. You have to admit, for a command that's so easy to use, the results are impressive (see Figure 3-6).

Be sure to check the edges of your composite image carefully for artifacts or blurring caused by the aligning of the multiple images. Execute a quick crop with the Crop tool, and you're good to go.

Figure 3-6: A clean scene, free of any annoying distractions.

Fixing Lighting with Photomerge Exposure

Occasionally, you need to capture a shot that presents an exposure challenge —
your foreground and background require different exposure settings. This challenge often occurs in shots that are backlit. For example, you have a person in
front of an indoor window in the day or someone in front of a lit nighttime
cityscape or sunset. With Photomerge Exposure, you can take photos with two
different exposure settings and let the command blend them together for the
perfect shot.

You can capture your shots using *exposure bracketing* (shooting at consecu-
tive exposure camera settings) or with a flash and then without. Elements
can detect all these camera settings. We recommend that you use a tripod to
keep your shots as aligned as possible. Good alignment helps the blending
algorithm do a better job.

Here's how to use this command:

1. **Select two or more photos from your Photo Bin.**

2. **Choose Enhance⇨Photomerge⇨Photomerge Exposure in any of the
   Photo Editor modes.**

3. **If you've used a tripod or have a done a good job keeping your shots aligned, click the Automatic mode tab and then select a Blend mode:**

   • *Simple Blending:* Select the Simple Blending option, and Elements automatically blends the two images.

   • *Smart Blending:* Select the Smart Blending option to access sliders to adjust the Highlights, Shadows, and Saturation settings for finer tuning of the resulting images.

   If you mess up things, click the Reset button.

4. **If you feel the need for even more control, click the Manual mode tab.**

5. **In Manual mode, choose your first shot from the Photo Bin and drag it to the Final window.**

   If your other image isn't already the source image, drag it from the Photo Bin to the Source window.

6. **With the Pencil tool, draw over the well-exposed areas you want to retain in the source image.**

   As you draw, your final image shows the incorporation of those drawn areas, as shown in Figure 3-7.

7. **If you mistakenly draw over something you didn't want to keep, grab the Eraser tool and erase the Pencil tool marks.**

   Choose to have your preview show strokes and/or regions.

8. **Gain further control of the blending by dragging the Transparency slider.**

   Dragging to the right blends less of the source areas into the final image. Select the Edge blending option to get an even better blend of the two images.

9. **If your photos aren't aligning correctly, grab the Alignment tool under Advanced Options:**

   a. *With the Alignment tool, click your source image and position the three target markers on three key locations.*

   b. *Do the same on the final image, choosing similar locations.*

10. **Click the Align Photos button.**

    Again, as with the other Photomerge commands, the more alike your starting source images are (similar framing, similar angle, and so on), the better the merged result.

11. **If you muck up things too badly, click the Reset button and then start at the appropriate step, depending on your mode.**

    If you're in Automatic mode, start again from Step 3. If you're in Manual mode, start again from Step 5.

Figure 3-7: Get the shot you want by blending two images with two different exposures.

12. **When you're satisfied with the result, click Done.**

The file opens as a new, layered image in Elements. The blended image appears on Layer 1. The background is your starting final image. You can then flatten the layered file, which retains the appearance of Layer 1. Or you can double-click your background to convert it to a layer and then delete it by dragging it to the Trash icon in the Layers panel.

Compositing Multiple Images with Photomerge Compose

Although there are several ways to select and extract portions of images in Elements, the new Compose feature enables you to more easily extract one image and composite it into another.

Here's how to extract an element from one image and combine it with another:

1. **Open two photos in the Photo Bin.**

2. **In any of the edit modes, choose Enhance⇨Photomerge⇨Photomerge Compose.**

3. **From the Photo Bin, drag the image from which you want to extract an element onto the canvas.**

4. **Choose a Selection tool:**

    • *Quick Select:* Brush over to select your desired element, as shown in Figure 3-8. This tool works exactly like the regular Quick Select tool. Choose your selection mode — a new selection or add or subtract from an existing selection. You can also adjust the size of the diameter of your brush.

    • *Outline Select:* Trace around your desired element. After your initial trace, release your mouse. A red overlay appears over the unselected areas. Add or subtract from the red overlay, and then adjust the size of the diameter of your brush as needed.

5. **Further refine your selection using the Selection Edit tool.**

In addition to the options found with the tools earlier, you can specify these additional settings:

    • *Snap:* Use the slider to adjust your snap strength (intensity of the pull) from 0% to 100%.

    • *Push:* Place your cursor inside the selection to increase your selection within the diameter of the outer circle of your cursor. It will snap to the edge of the element closest to the cursor. Place your cursor outside the selection to decrease your selection within the diameter of the outer circle.

Figure 3-8: Select what you want to extract.

- *Smooth:* If your selection border looks a little too jagged, use this option to smooth your selection edge.

6. **Click Advance Edge Refinement.**

   You can choose to set the background — in other words, the unselected portion of your current image — to Source Image (which leaves your image as is) or have it fill with transparency, black, white, or a red overlay.

   You can also access the Refine Edge feature.

7. **Click Next.**

Your extracted image is composited into your second image, as shown in Figure 3-9. Move and size your image as desired.

Figure 3-9: Composite two images realistically.

You can further refine your selection by using the Hide and Reveal tools to either add to or delete from your selection. You can adjust the size, opacity, and hardness of your brush to better fine-tune your extracted element.

Chapter 4: Getting Help in Guided Mode

*W*ouldn't it be nice if a mentor could sit behind you and walk you through the necessary steps every time you encounter a new feature in a program?

Photoshop Elements doesn't provide you with a robot mentor to instruct you on the best way to perform an edit, but it does offer you the next best thing in the form of the Guided panel. In this chapter, we show you how to use the Guided panel and describe all it has to offer you.

Understanding Guided Mode

The Guided panel provides you easy control over important editing tasks that you perform routinely when working on images.

Click the Guided button at the top of the Photo Editor window. The Guided workspace opens and reveals the panel of available guided edits, shown in Figure 4-1.

As shown in Figure 4-1, the Guided panel is divided into four categories. Within each category, you will find edits that relate to the respective category. Here are your choices:

✓ **Touchups:** Here you find the kinds of edits frequently used to fix and retouch photos. Cropping, rotating, correcting contrast and color, fixing flaws, and sharpening photos are part of this group.

✓ **Photo Effects:** With these edits, you can easily apply a variety of different filters that produce many different effects, such as converting color to black and white, line drawings, old-fashioned photos, saturated film, and others. Elements 13 offers a few new edits — B&W Color Pop, B&W Selections, and Black and White.

✔ **Camera Effects:** Elements 13 moves some of the Photo Effects edits, such as Lomo Camera and Zoom Burst effects, into this new category.

✔ **Photo Play:** This category includes edits with several effects that are pure fun, such as taking a photo and creating a puzzle effect, turning your image into pop art, creating a reflection of your image, and having part of a photo appear as if it were jumping out of the frame (out of bounds). Elements 13 moves Recompose from Touchups into this category.

Here are few general tips to keep in mind when working in Guided mode:

✔ In applying any guided edit, choose Unit⇨Undo to undo a particular step.

✔ To reset the particular panel, click the Reset icon (blue curved arrow) in the upper right of the Guided panel.

✔ To view an online video tutorial, click the white arrow on a blue square icon located in the upper right of the Guided panel.

✔ For Help, click the question mark icon located in the upper right of the Guided panel.

Walking through Touchups

The edits in this workflow help you perform the kinds of basic tasks frequently used in most of your Elements editing sessions. When you choose Crop Photo, for example, the Crop instructions and options appear in the Guided panel with the Crop tool selected and a crop frame drawn on the photo. Similar steps are also provided for straightening a photo. You might use this feature frequently when scanning photos. Other frequently used edits include correcting contrast and color and sharpening your images.

Figure 4-1: The Guided panel.

Adjusting contrast and color

Adjusting the contrast and color is among the most important and frequent edits you make on photos.

You'll want to always adjust contrast first and then color. Often, by simply adjusting the contrast of your image, you will also fix some color issues simultaneously.

Under the Touchups workflow are several edits that involve both contrast and color, such as Brightness and Contrast, Lighten and Darken, and Enhance Colors. Selecting one of these edits changes the panel view to one where you can either click an Auto adjustment button or, for more control, move various sliders to make adjustments. The fixes you can perform here are pretty straightforward; with the help offered in the panel, making these kinds of adjustments is intuitive and easy.

Using the Levels adjustment

Things get a bit more complicated when you start using the Levels adjustment. The Levels adjustment is one of the most effective features in correcting the contrast of an image. We go into quite a bit of detail about Levels in Chapter 2 of this minibook. Be sure to read that chapter when you want to figure out more about using this important dialog box.

It's a good idea to use Levels by making an adjustment layers. That way you have maximum editing flexibility later. You can find more information on creating and using adjustment layers in Book VI, Chapter 1.

Creating an adjustment layer and applying settings from the Levels dialog box can be a little confusing. The Guided panel, fortunately, breaks down the complicated steps into easy-to-follow instructions to assist you in making the edits. Here's an overview of how you can edit along with help from the panel:

1. **Select the Levels option in the Guided panel.**

   The panel view changes to the one shown in Figure 4-2. Here you find helpful information explaining how to use the Levels dialog box and what the histograms mean.

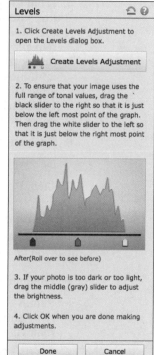

Figure 4-2: The Levels panel.

Book VIII Chapter 4

Getting Help in Guided Mode

2. **Read the information contained in the panel.**

When you start with this edit, we recommend reading all the help information before you make the adjustments.

3. **Click the Create Levels Adjustment button.**

The New Layer dialog box opens.

4. **Type a name for the new adjustment layer and then click OK.**

The Levels dialog box opens, as shown in Figure 4-3.

5. **From the information you obtained in the Guided panel, move the shadows (black triangle), midtones (gray triangle), or highlights (white triangle) sliders in the Levels dialog box to make your corrections.**

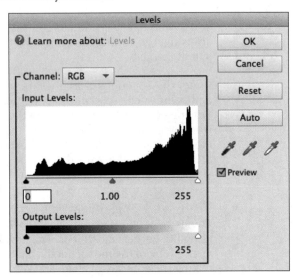

Figure 4-3: The Levels dialog box.

6. **Click OK to accept the corrections and exit the Levels dialog box.**

Or if you've mucked things up, you can click Reset to start again.

7. **Click Done in the Levels panel to get back to the main panel.**

Correcting color in the Guided panel

The three best commands you find for color correction in the Guided panel help you improve the color in your photos:

- ✔ **Enhance Colors:** You get sliders to adjust hue, saturation, and lightness.

- ✔ **Remove a Color Cast:** Use the Eyedropper to sample a medium-gray tone, and Elements corrects color in the image. For more information on removing color casts, see Chapter 2 of this minibook.

- ✔ **Correct Skin Tones:** One of the most important color adjustments you can make is adjusting skin tones. The Correct Skin Tones panel provides you with an Eyedropper tool. Click a person's skin, and the color is adjusted to match that neutral tone for the entire image. You can tweak the color for skin tones by moving the sliders in the panel.

Sharpening a photo

An important edit listed under Touchups is Sharpen. This is another edit you'll make frequently when working on your photos in Elements. To get a feel for using the Sharpen command in Guided mode, do the following:

1. **Open a photo in Guided mode.**

2. **In the Guided panel, in the Touchups workflow, click Sharpen.**

   The panel changes to display the instructions and options you have for sharpening a photo, as shown in Figure 4-4.

Figure 4-4: See a before-and-after display of the original and edited versions beside each other.

3. **Change the view in the Image window.**

   By default, your photo appears in the Image window in a maximized After Only view. You can view your photo with a before-and-after view where the original photo appears unedited on the left side of the window and the edits you apply appear on the right side. To create a before-and-after effect, click the down arrow where you see After Only in the upper left of the panel. You can also choose a vertical orientation.

4. **Click Auto Fix or adjust the Sharpen slider.**

You have the option of clicking the Auto Fix button, and Elements makes a best-guess adjustment to sharpen the image. To manually sharpen the image, move the slider left and right.

5. **Click Done at the bottom of the panel to apply the edits.**

The advantage you have in using the Guided panel is that Elements offers helpful information to guide you through the edits.

The unique Perfect Portrait edit, shown in Figure 4-5, walks you through numerous steps to enhance your portrait. Start with fixing skin texture, adding clarity by increasing contrast, enhancing facial features by using the healing tools, eliminating red-eye, darkening eyebrows, and whitening teeth. You'll end by adding a dewy glow and, if you so desire, putting your portrait on a digital diet by using an edit to slim down the person. The process sounds complicated, but just follow the steps with this guided edit, and it's a no-brainer. You're sure to end up with a beauty, such as our mustachioed hipster shown in Figure 4-5.

© iStockphoto.com/RyanJLane Image #8529161

Figure 4-5: Execute the various steps to create a perfect portrait.

Other commands under the Touchups workflow enable you to perform important tasks, such as fixing flaws (Scratches and Blemishes) to resizing an image without losing vital content (Recompose). You can find detailed information on all these edits throughout the book. This minibook in particular provides detailed explanations on fixing and enhancing images.

The Restore Old Photo edit enables you to restore your image by walking through the steps to remove cracks, fix discoloration, remove dust, and fix contrast and other flaws.

Enhancing with Photo and Camera Effects

Photo and Camera effects work like applying filters, which we cover extensively in Book VII, Chapters 1 and 2. Whereas the Filter Gallery dialog box provides you with many options to apply a filter, the Guided panel offers you filter effects and then takes you through steps for adjusting brightness values, changing hue and saturation, and making other adjustments to perfect the result.

You can choose from these many options:

- **B&W Color Pop** enables you to highlight a desired color, such as blue shown in Figure 4-6, while desaturating the other colors in the image.

- **B&W Selection** desaturates the colors of selected areas of your image.

- **Black and White** converts your color images to black and white. You can choose from crisp or diffused, glowy effects.

- **High Key** creates a light-toned image of mostly white and grays. Click the Diffuse Glow option to create an even more dreamy photo.

- **Line Drawing** converts your photos to a pen-and-ink drawing.

- **Low Key** creates a dramatic, dark toned, chiaroscuro (Italian for "light-dark")–type image, as shown in Figure 4-6.

- **Old Fashioned Photo** gives your images a vintage, sepia appearance.

- **Saturated Slide Film Effect** simulates the colors of saturated film used in film cameras (as opposed to digital cameras).

- **Depth of Field** creates a sharp and blurry lens effect (see the next section).

- **Lomo Camera Effect** creates a cross-processed, vignetted effect.

- **Orton Effect** gives a dreamy quality to your image by softening the focus and overexposing the image. (The upcoming section "Orton Effect" describes it in detail.)

- **Tilt-Shift** effect creates a miniaturized effect by simulating an adjustment of the focal plane.

- ✓ **Vignette Effect** creates a darkening or lightening at the corners and outside edges around an image.

- ✓ **Zoom Burst Effect** creates the illusion of motion with focus on the center of the image.

© iStockphoto.com/alija Image #27630618

Figure 4-6: Apply the new B&W Color Pop effect.

Depth of Field effect

This great edit in the Camera Effects workflow changes the appearance of the *depth of field,* which is defined as the areas of sharpness in relation to the focal point in your image. This edit is useful when your image has an overly busy background and is causing a distraction from your focal point. By making the depth of field shallower (blurring the distracting background), your focal point becomes more prominent.

To apply this edit, follow these steps:

1. **Open a photo in Guided mode.**

2. **In the Guided panel, in the Camera Effects edits, click Depth of Field to open the panel.**

3. **Click either the Simple or Custom method in the panel.**

   Simple adds depth in one step (well, sort of; it consists of three sub-steps), whereas Custom enables you to define the area you want to keep in focus.

   We clicked Custom.

4. **If you chose Custom, define the area you want to keep in focus in the Depth of Field-Custom panel.**

   We used the Quick Selection Tool to select the moody teenager, as shown in Figure 4-7.

Figure 4-7: Create a shallower depth of field to eliminate a distracting background.

**Book VIII
Chapter 4**

Getting Help in
Guided Mode

5. **Click the Add Blur button to blur the unselected areas and create a shallower depth of field; to increase the blur, drag the slider to the right.**

6. **Click Done after you've achieved your desired depth of field.**

Orton Effect

To experiment a little, take a look at the Orton Effect option and follow these steps to produce an image with a dreamy appearance:

1. **Open an image in Guided mode.**

2. **In the Guided panel, in the Photo Effects workflow, click Orton Effect to open the Create Orton Effect panel, as shown in Figure 4-8.**

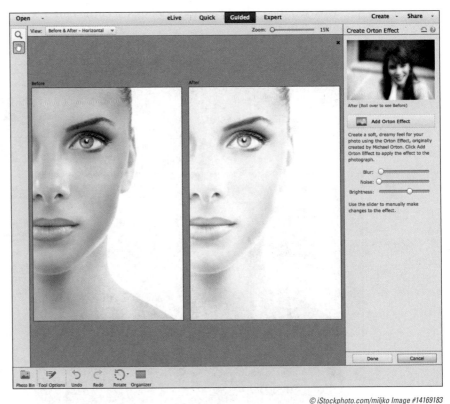

© iStockphoto.com/miljko Image #14169183

Figure 4-8: Apply the Orton Effect in the Guided panel.

3. **Click Add Orton Effect.**

4. **Use the sliders to increase the Blur and/or Noise, as shown in Figure 4-8.**

5. **Make the photo brighter by adjusting the Brightness slider.**

6. **Click Done to accept the effect and return to the main panel.**

Playing with Photos

The Photo Play workflow of edits is just plain fun. To apply any of these edits, simply open a photo in Guided mode and click your desired effect. Then follow the steps explained, and if you like what you see, click Done. If you're just doing a "look and see," click Cancel to bail out and get back to the main Guided panel.

We applied the new Puzzle Effect to our image, as shown in Figure 4-9.

© iStockphoto.com/_IB_ Image #22277564

Figure 4-9: The Puzzle Effect in action.

Book IX

Creating and Sharing with Elements

For more details and projects about Photoshop Elements, visit www.dummies.com/extras/photoshopelementsaio.

Contents at a Glance

Chapter 1: Creating Elements Projects

In This Chapter

- ✓ Understanding creations
- ✓ Creating photo books, greeting cards, and photo calendars
- ✓ Creating photo collages and slideshows
- ✓ Ordering prints
- ✓ Constructing DVDs with menus
- ✓ Sharing creations

*A*dobe Photoshop Elements offers a number of creations that you can share onscreen or in print. From both the Create and Share panels in the Task Pane in the Organizer and from within the Photo Editor Panel Bin (for Create only), you have menu choices for producing creations and sharing your media.

In Chapter 3 of this minibook, we look at sharing files for screen and web viewing. In this chapter, we talk about creations designed for print and sharing.

Getting a Handle on Creations

In Chapter 3 of this minibook, we talk about online albums, attaching files to emails, using photo mail, and using online sharing services. All these creations offer different output options, such as emailing, burning files to a disc (Windows), creating HTML or PDF documents, as well as printing. You create them all using the Share panel.

You create the remaining creations — photo prints, photo books, photo collages, photo calendars, greeting cards, and print labels — via the Create panel. All these creations are designed for output to your printer or for sending files to an online printing service or to friends and family.

When you observe the Create panel in Windows and on the Macintosh, you see identical options listed in the panel, as shown in Figure 1-1.

When you make a creation that will ultimately be sent to an online service or shared with other users, keep in mind that you first must select the photos you want in your creation. For example, before you create a photo book by clicking the Photo Book button in the Create panel, you need to select photos for your book. If you happen to click the Photo Book button and nothing happens, more than likely, you haven't selected any photos.

You can select photos in either the Organizer or the Photo Bin in the Photo Editor. Note that the Instant Movie and DVD with Menu options appear only if you have installed Premiere Elements.

After selecting photos, click the Create button. Elements then opens a drop-down menu where options are listed for the type of creation you want to make. The options for Photo Book, Greeting Card, Photo Calendar, and Photo Collage all use the same wizard when you click one of the respective buttons in the Create panel. The remaining options — Photo Prints, Slideshow, and Facebook Cover — use different wizards where options are selected.

Figure 1-1: The only difference between platforms with the Create options is that the Macintosh has no support for creating slideshows.

Facebook Cover is a new feature in Elements 13. Using this option, you can create images for a Facebook cover image and upload a cover image and profile picture by following some simple guided steps. The magic of it all is that this feature permits you to precisely place the profile picture on top of the cover image, and the files are sized perfectly for display on your Facebook page.

Elements offers you some consistency when creating photo books, greeting cards, photo calendars, and photo collages. If you know how to set attributes for one of these creations, you can easily work with any of the other creation types.

After you make a creation, you can save it as a project that can also be added to the Organizer window. Photoshop Elements projects are saved as Photo Project Format with a .pse extension. If you want to return to a project and make more edits, you can open the .pse file and edit your project. You can add .pse files to the Organizer and view them in the Media Browser so that they're easily accessible if you choose to open a project and perform more edits.

Creating Facebook Cover Images

You can select one or more images in the Organizer and open the files in the Editor. Open the Photo Bin so you can see your open files. To create a Facebook cover and upload the file(s) to your Facebook account, do the following:

1. **Select photos in the Photo Bin.**

2. **Open the Create Panel and choose Facebook Cover (see Figure 1-2).**

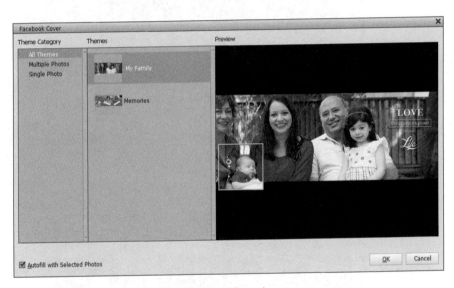

Figure 1-2: Choose a Theme for your Facebook Cover image.

3. **Choose a Theme.**

   The Facebook Cover wizard opens. Click a theme and decide whether you want to use a single photo or multiple photos by clicking the corresponding Theme Category.

4. **Edit the images for position and size.**

   Click the green check mark when you have the image(s) sized to your liking.

5. **(Optional) Click the Save button (shown in Figure 1-3) to save the file as a PSE file that you can reopen and rework if you change your mind.**

6. **Click Next (see Figure 1-4) and proceed through the guided steps in the Facebook wizard to upload the final image to your Facebook account.**

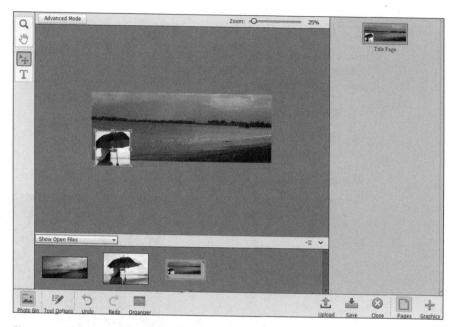

Figure 1-3: Manipulate the image(s) and position as you like.

Figure 1-4: Click Next and proceed through the steps to upload the image.

Creating a Photo Book

You can design the creations you make for printing locally to your desktop printer or for uploading to a professional print service. The professional services offer you choices for covers, assembly, paper stocks, and so on, as

well as opportunities to distribute the printed material to friends and
family.

Photo books follow a sequence of steps that are the same for other creations
you make in Elements. To describe completely the process for making a creation, we start by showing you how to create a photo book.

Follow these steps to create a photo book (the same steps are used for creating greeting cards, photo calendars, and photo collages):

1. **Select files in the Organizer and click the Create tab. Or, open several
   photos in the Photo Editor, select the open files in the Photo Bin, and
   click the Create tab.**

   You begin working with creations following the same procedure. You
   first select files in the Organizer or photos in the Photo Bin in the
   Photo Editor and then click the Create tab in the Organizer Task Pane
   or Photo Editor Panel Bin. Ideally, you might start with an album containing the photos you want to use for your photo book. (See Book II,
   Chapter 3, for more on creating albums.) You can then just click the
   album to display the album photos in the Organizer window and easily
   select all the photos or select an album directly in the Photo Bin in the
   Photo Editor.

   To select all photos shown in the Organizer's Media Browser or the
   Photo Editor Photo Bin, press Ctrl+A (⌘+A on the Mac).

2. **Open the Create drop-down menu and choose Photo Book.**

   Whether you're working in the Organizer or the Photo Editor, the Photo
   Book option is available in the same Create drop-down menu in the
   Panel Bin. When you click the Photo Book menu item, a wizard opens,
   and you can make choices for the output and the design of your creation. The same wizard opens for other creations, such as greeting
   cards, photo calendars, and photo collages.

3. **Choose an option for outputting your creation.**

   In the left pane shown in Figure 1-5, you make a choice for either printing
   your creation or using the Shutterfly online service. For both Print
   Locally and Shutterfly, you have options for choosing the size of your
   output.

4. **Select a theme.**

   In the middle column, choose a theme for the photo book design. When
   you click a theme, the preview pane on the right side of the window displays a preview of the selected theme. Elements uses an Adobe Flash
   interface where you see photo book pages automatically scroll using the
   selected theme.

At this point, click different themes and observe the Preview pane for a dynamic display of the respective theme. Take a little time to look over all the wonderful options you have for a photo book design.

The first time you use a Theme or other asset in the Graphics panel, Elements downloads the Asset to your computer. The assets are stored on Adobe's website. You must wait until the download finishes before you can continue.

Figure 1-5: Select photos and click the Photo Book option to open the Photo Book wizard.

5. Type the number of pages in the Number of Pages text box.

By default, Elements adds a title page and two additional pages no matter how many photos you select for your album. Count the total photos you intend to use and type the number of photos in the text box. You can add or delete pages when you're in the Creation wizard.

6. Click OK and then examine the pages.

When you click OK, the Create panel changes and displays three buttons at the bottom of the panel. As shown in Figure 1-6, the buttons open panes for Pages, Layouts, and Graphics. When you open each pane, you can make additional edits. By default, when creating photo albums, the pane in view is the Pages pane, shown in Figure 1-6. In the Pages pane, look over the total number of pages for your photo book. You can scroll pages by clicking the left/right arrows at the top of the Image window (see Figure 1-6) or by double-clicking pages in the Pages panel.

Switch to Advanced mode

Click the arrows or pages to preview each page

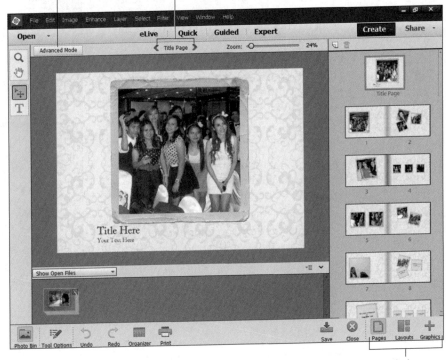

Click a button to switch panes

Figure 1-6: The Create panel has three buttons that are used for changing the Create Panel panes.

7. **Click the Layouts button and choose a layout.**

In the Layouts pane, you find many choices for different layouts. At the top of the panel, a display of different layouts appears, as shown in Figure 1-7. Scroll down the panel to find additional layouts for One, Two, and Three photos per page.

To change a layout, double-click the layout choice in the Create panel. When you change layouts, you need to populate the placeholders. Drag photos from the Photo Bin to a placeholder, and Elements fits the photo in the placeholder frame.

REMEMBER

When you see arrows pointing up or down in any of the panes in the Create panel, you can click them to collapse/expand items in the individual panes.

8. **Adjust a photo in a frame.**

   If you change a layout or add more photos to placeholders, or even if you let Elements populate a layout, you may want to make adjustments for individual photos within placeholders.

   To edit a photo within a placeholder, double-click the photo. A toolbar appears above the photo, as shown in Figure 1-8. From left to right on the toolbar, you can

   • Zoom in or out of the photo by dragging the slider left and right.

   • Rotate the photo by clicking the blue icon. (Each mouse click rotates the photo 90 degrees.)

   • Get a new photo to place in the frame represented by the folder icon.

   • Commit the current operation. You click the green check mark to accept your edits.

   • Cancel the current operation. Click the last icon above the image to cancel your edits.

   You can also size a photo within a frame by clicking one of the handles on the selected image and dragging in to reduce size or out to size up. Move the cursor just outside a corner handle on a selected frame, and you can rotate the image and frame together.

   If you double-click a photo in a frame, you can open a context menu (right-click or Control-click a one-button mouse on a Macintosh) and choose from some transformation options that include scaling, perspective, and distorting the photo. Choose a menu command and drag a handle to perform the operation.

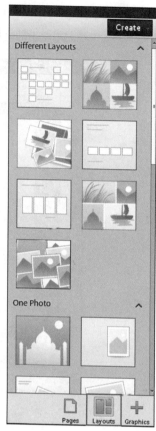

Figure 1-7: The Layouts pane offers many choices for changing the layout design.

Figure 1-8: Double-click an image to open a toolbar above the image.

You can skew an image by pressing Ctrl or Option (Mac) and dragging a corner handle.

9. **Click the Graphics button and use artwork.**

   Click the Graphics button, shown in Figure 1-9. In the Graphics pane, you can change the background design and frames and add graphics.

   To change the background or frames, double-click a background and/or frame in the Graphics pane. To add a graphic, click and drag the graphic to the Image window where a photo page is displayed.

10. **(Optional) Switch to Advanced mode to edit images and the layers.**

    Click the Advanced Mode button (refer to Figure 1-6) to open Advanced mode, where you find more editing options, as shown in Figure 1-10. You can edit the layers for further customization of the photos in your photo book. To do so, you need to know a lot about working with layers, layer styles, and layer effects, as we explain throughout Book VI. Also, you have access to the Expert Photo Editor Tools panel, where you can apply edits to images as well as have full access to menu commands.

11. **Click the Basic Mode button if you're in Advanced mode and look over the project.**

    Now you're ready to take the last steps to finish the project.

12. **When your project is complete, decide what you want to do with it:**

    * *Click the Print button* to open the Photo Prints pane in the Create panel.

    * *Click the Save button* if you want to save your project and return to it later for additional editing. You can also save your creation as an Adobe PDF file. You can then exchange the PDF with friends and family.

    * Click the Close button to close the project.

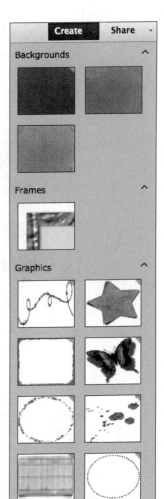

Figure 1-9: Scroll the Artwork tab to find options for Backgrounds, Frames, and Graphics.

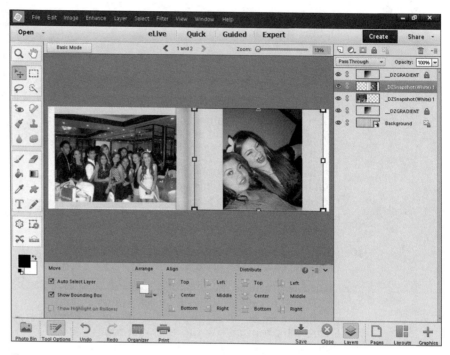

Figure 1-10: Click Advanced Mode to gain access to layers, tools, and menus for full editing operations.

In the Print dialog box, you find options for printing your creation to your local printer as a photo book, as a picture package, or as a contact sheet, as shown in Figure 1-11. For more details on these print settings and complete coverage of all options in the Print dialog box, see Chapter 2 in this minibook.

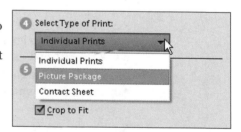

Figure 1-11: Click the Print button at the bottom of the window to open the Print dialog box.

All the steps outlined in this section are the same steps that you use for making greeting cards, photo calendars, and photo collages.

Getting in Touch with Greeting Cards

In Photoshop Elements, creating greeting cards like the one shown in Figure 1-12 is a snap. Here's how to create a card by using the Greeting Card panel:

1. **Open the Organizer and select a photo or open a photo in the Photo Editor.**

2. **Open the Create menu in the Panel Bin and select Greeting Card.**

3. **Follow the same steps as you do when creating photo books, which we cover in the previous section.**

   First choose the output source (local printer or Shutterfly); then choose a theme and click OK. Click the Print button at the bottom of the wizard to open the Print dialog box if printing locally on your printer.

When you make creations and use Vthe templates provided by Elements, your photos automatically are assigned a photo frame. In most cases, you'll want to eliminate the frame and use one of your own choosing. We talk about how to clear photo frames and add new frames in a web extra for creating calendars that you can find at www.dummies.com/extras/photoshopelementsaio.

Top photo courtesy of Leah Valle (www.13thwitch.com)

Figure 1-12: Use the same steps for creating greeting cards as you do for creating photo books.

Making a Photo Calendar

Are you ready to design a personal calendar using your favorite photos? Elements helps you design an attractive calendar of the kids, the girls' soccer team, the Bullhead Moose fraternity, or any other type of activity or event you want to work with. Elements makes it easy to create professional-looking calendars.

There's quite a bit to creating calendars in Elements. For more information on creating calendars and also making your own custom calendars, see our two web extras at www.dummies.com/extras/photoshopelementsaio.

Here's how you create a calendar that can be ordered and professionally printed via an online service:

1. **Select photos in the Organizer. Alternatively, you can open images in the Photo Editor and select the open photos in the Photo Bin.**

For calendars, you might want to select 13 photos — one photo for the calendar cover and one photo for each month. You can also choose 12 photos and use one of the calendar months for the cover photo.

2. **Open the Create drop-down menu in the Panel Bin and click the Photo Calendar option.**

3. **Choose an output source the same as when choosing a source for photo books.**

4. **Follow the same steps that we outline in the section "Creating a Photo Book," earlier in this chapter.**

When saving creations, you have a choice to save as a Photoshop Elements Project (*.pse) or as an Adobe PDF (*.pdf) file. In Figure 1-13, we saved a calendar as a PDF document and opened it in Adobe Reader.

Photos courtesy of Leah Valle (www.13thwitch.com)

Figure 1-13: A photo calendar saved as a PDF file.

Assembling a Photo Collage

To put together a photo collage (see Figure 1-14), you first need to select a few photos in the Organizer or the Photo Bin and then click the Photo Collage option in the Create panel.

The Photo Collage wizard opens, and you follow the same steps that we cover in the earlier section "Creating a Photo Book."

Creating a Slideshow

Photoshop Elements 13 offers you a much more simplified method for creating dynamic slideshows that you can export to H.264 MP4 files that can be viewed on Windows, Macintosh, iOS, and Android devices.

The Slideshow option in the Create panel was previously reserved for Windows. In Elements 13, all the options for creating slideshows are the same for Windows and Mac users.

Creating slideshows follows the same initial steps as you find with other creations. To create a slideshow using the Create panel, follow these steps:

1. **Select the images you want in the Organizer or Photo Bin, click the Create tab, and then click the Slideshow option.**

   The first thing you see is the Choose a Theme panel in the Slideshow wizard, as shown in Figure 1-15.

2. **Click the theme you want to use and click Next.**

   The Slideshow Builder appears when you click the Edit button in the Slideshow preview, as shown in Figure 1-16.

3. **Add or delete media in the Slideshow Builder.**

   Open the Add Media drop down menu and add media from the Organizer or from folders on your hard drive.

4. **Click Export to export your slideshow.**

5. **Choose a preset for your export in the Export dialog box (see Figure 1-17).**

   You can choose between 640x480, 720p HD, or 1080p HD. The file is exported as an MP4 file that can be viewed on multiple devices.

Figure 1-14: Photo collages are a snap to create in Elements.

Figure 1-15: The Slideshow Preferences dialog box.

Figure 1-16: The Slideshow Builder.

Export

Filename

ArnieVideo

Location

C:\Users\Ted\Videos\

Browse

Quality

Preset: 720p HD

OK   Cancel

Figure 1-17: Choose a preset in the Export dialog.

Working with Photo Prints

When you open the Create panel and click the Photo Prints option, you find options for printing files locally on your desktop printer and ordering prints from online services.

Printing to your desktop printer

When you click Photo Prints on the Create drop-down menu, the panel displays options for printing to your local printer or ordering online prints with a professional print service (see Figure 1-18).

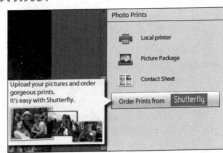

Figure 1-18: The Photo Prints panel.

Click the Local Printer option in the Photo Prints panel and the Print dialog box opens. This action is no different than choosing File⇨Print in the Organizer or in the Photo Editor. In all cases, the Print dialog box opens where you set attributes for the print output.

The other options you have for local printing are Picture Package and Contact Sheet. These options are also available in the Print dialog box.

For local printing and the options you can use, see Chapter 2 of this minibook, where we thoroughly discuss local printing of individual photos, picture packages, and contact sheets.

Ordering prints online

You can order prints online by using only the Shutterfly online service. When you mouse over Shutterfly, a pop-up box provides some information about the service (refer to Figure 1-18).

When you click Order Prints from Shutterfly, a wizard opens and walks you through the steps for setting up an account and ordering prints. You also find options for choosing the address or addresses where you want your prints to be shipped. You can have one set of prints sent to your address and duplicate prints sent to family and friends.

Online print services were once the cat's meow for photo distribution. However, in recent years, sharing photos via social services such as Facebook, Flickr, Myspace, and Adobe Revel has proven to be much faster and much more efficient — and more environmentally conscious. Unless you have a good reason for having photo prints, join us in using one of the many social service networks that we explain in Chapter 3 of this minibook. The social networks are much more efficient and less costly than using a print service.

Printing to Adobe PDF

All the print options you have in Elements can be saved as PDF documents. Rather than collect printed paper documents for items such as calendars, greeting cards, and photo collages, you can make your creations and save to PDF files. You can then share these files on your social network connections.

To output a creation to PDF, you need a little help from another application. You have two choices in Windows:

✓ **Purchase Adobe Acrobat Standard or Pro and use the Adobe PDF printer driver that's installed with your program installation.** Simply choose the Adobe PDF from the Select Printer drop-down menu in the Print dialog box and click OK. Your file is then printed to disk as a PDF file.

✓ **Download a free PDF printer driver, such as pdf995.** You can find several PDF printer drivers available for free download by searching the Internet. After a driver is installed, it appears as a printer. You follow the same steps as for printing to Adobe PDF. Select the printer driver in the Print dialog box and click OK, and the file is then printed in PDF format.

Macintosh users don't need to be concerned with printer drivers. Output to PDF is built into OS X. When you choose File➪Print, click the PDF drop-down menu and select Save as PDF. Your file is saved as a PDF document that can be viewed in the free Adobe Reader software or with OS X's Preview application.

Getting Organized with CD/DVD Labels

Another creation option in Elements is a simple, easy way to create CD and DVD labels. From the Create panel, choose a menu item for CD Jacket, DVD Jacket, or CD/DVD Label from the More Options drop-down list. From templates provided in the panel, Elements offers you an easy method for printing your personalized labels and jackets for CDs and DVDs.

This feature for printing CD/DVD labels is a bit weak in Elements. You may need to fiddle around quite a bit to get the images to fit a label. Using some templates provided by the label developers is often a much better method for printing labels.

Creating a DVD with a Menu

Creating a DVD with a menu is supported in both Windows and on the Macintosh; however, you need to have Adobe Premiere Elements installed to create a DVD with a menu. In Windows, you can create slideshows and use the slideshows when creating a DVD with a menu. On the Macintosh, you need movie files that can be created from still images using Adobe Premiere Elements, Apple's iMovie, or Apple's iPhoto.

Chapter 2: Getting It Printed

In This Chapter

- ✔ Preparing images for printing
- ✔ Adjusting your print settings
- ✔ Printing contact sheets and picture packages
- ✔ Using color profiles
- ✔ Printing color from different printers
- ✔ Taking advantage of online printing services

*W*e live in an ever-changing world when it comes to technology and the way we consume content. When it comes to showing off your photos, you have many alternatives to printing pictures. You can, for example, show slide shows and photo collections on cellphones, tablet devices, laptops, and computer systems. Each of these methods, over time, becomes a low-cost alternative to purchasing printers, papers, and inks.

With the advent of the Apple iPad and many more tablet devices, you can find some superb mechanisms for displaying photo albums, slide shows, and individual pictures. All your data can be stored in the *cloud* (that is, on the Internet by using Facebook, Adobe Revel, Flickr, iCloud, and so on), so you don't need to worry about losing precious photos.

As you review this chapter, think of printing as a last resort for displaying albums of photos. At times, though, you may need to print a picture, and this chapter is designed to inform you of many issues to know if and when you must print a photo.

In this chapter, we talk about options — many options — for setting print attributes for printing to your own color printer. If you need to, reread this chapter a few times just to be certain that you understand the process for printing good-quality images. A little time spent here will, we hope, save you some headaches down the road.

Getting Images Ready for Printing

Perhaps the greatest challenge for individuals using programs such as Photoshop Elements (and even for the professionals who use its grand-daddy, Adobe Photoshop) is turning what they see on the monitor into a reasonable facsimile on a printed page. You can find all sorts of books on color printing — how to get color right, how to calibrate your equipment, and how to create and use color profiles — all for the purpose of getting a good match between your computer monitor and your printer. It's downright discouraging to spend a lot of time tweaking an image so that all the brilliant blue colors jump out on your computer monitor, only to find that all those blues turn to murky purples when the photo is printed.

If you've already read Book III (especially Chapters 2, 3, and 5), you're ahead of the game because you know a little bit about color management, color profiles, and printer resolutions. After you check out those chapters, your next step is to get to know your printer or your print service center and understand how to correctly print your pictures.

The first step toward getting your photos to your desktop printer or to a printing service is to prepare each image for optimum output. You have several considerations when you're preparing files, including the ones in this list:

- **Set resolution and size.** Before you print a file, use the Image Size dialog box (choose Image⇨Resize⇨Image Size) to set your image size and the optimum resolution for your printer. Files that have too much resolution can print images that are inferior to files optimized for a printer. See your printer's documentation for recommendations for resolution. As a general rule, 300 ppi (pixels per inch) works best for most printers printing on high-quality paper. If you print on plain paper, you often find that lower resolutions work just as well or even better.

- **Make all brightness and color corrections before printing.** It stands to reason that you want to ensure that your pictures appear their best before sending them off to your printer. If your monitor is properly calibrated, you should see a fair representation of what your pictures will look like after they're printed.

- **Decide how color will be managed before you print.** You can color-manage output to your printer in three ways, as we discuss in the next section. Know your printer's profiles and how to use them before you start to print your files.

- **Get your printer ready.** Finally, when printing to desktop color printers, always be certain that your ink cartridges have sufficient ink and that the nozzles are clean. Make sure that you use the proper settings for paper and ink when you send a file to your printer. Be sure to review the manual that came with your printer to know how to perform all the steps required to make a quality print.

Setting Print Options

As you might expect, you print files from Elements by choosing File➪Print. Choose the same menu command from either workspace to open the Print dialog box. On the Mac when you choose File➪Print, you are automatically switched to the Photo Editor, where all Mac printing is performed.

You have only one difference between using the Print dialog box from the Organizer and the Print dialog box from the Photo Editor. In the Color Management settings in the More Options dialog box, the Organizer doesn't permit you to manage color like you find when using the Photo Editor's Print dialog box. All other options are identical in both dialog boxes.

You have a number of settings to adjust when printing color photos from the Photo Editor, as we explain a little later in the section "Printing with Color Profiles." For now, take a look at the different options you have in the print dialog boxes that you open from the Organizer and from the Photo Editor.

Printing from the Organizer

You can print photos from either the Organizer or in the Photo Editor in Windows. On the Macintosh, you can choose File➪Print in the Organizer, but Elements redirects your output to the Photo Editor. For the moment, we skip color management and look at settings identical in the Print dialog box from the Organizer and the one from the Photo Editor.

You can select one or more images in the Organizer and then choose File➪ Print. The images selected when you choose the Print command appear in a scrollable list, as shown in Figure 2-1. Likewise, you can select multiple photos in the Photo Bin in the Photo Editor and print them similarly.

Options you have in the Prints dialog box include

A. **Image thumbnails:** When you select multiple images in the Organizer, all the selected images appear in a scrollable window on the left side of the dialog box.

B. **Scroll bar:** When so many photos are selected that they all can't be viewed in the thumbnail list on the left side of the dialog box, you can use the scroll bar to see all images.

C. **Add/Remove:** If the Prints dialog box is open and you want to add more photos to print, click the Add (+) icon and the Add Photos dialog box opens, as shown in Figure 2-2. A list of thumbnails appears, showing all photos in the current open catalog. Select the check boxes adjacent to the thumbnails to indicate the photos you want to add to your print queue. You can also choose an entire catalog, albums, photos marked with keyword tags, photos with a rating, and hidden photos. For more information on albums, keyword tags, and ratings, see Book II, Chapter 3.

A   B

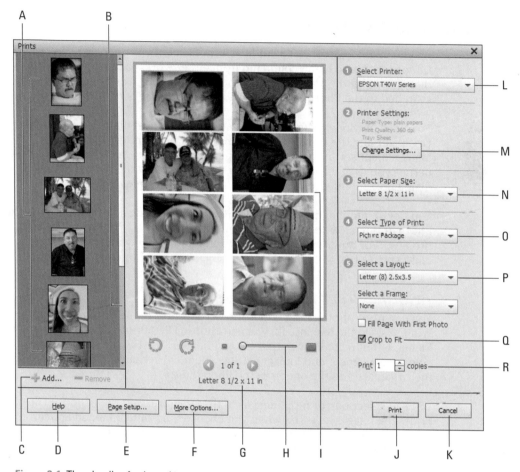

L

M

N

O

P

Q

R

C D   E   F G H I   J K

Figure 2-1: Thumbnails of selected images appear in the Prints dialog box.

If you want to remove photos from the list to be printed, click the photo in the scrollable list in the Prints dialog box and click the Remove (–) icon.

D. Help: Click the Help button to open help information pertaining to printing photos.

E. Page Setup: Click this button to open the Page Setup dialog box. Page Setup is relative to the printer that you have selected in the Select Printer item (L). The Page Setup dialog box changes when you change printers on the Select Printer drop-down menu.

F. More Options: Click the More Options buttons to open another dialog box, which we explain in the section "Using More Options," later in this chapter.

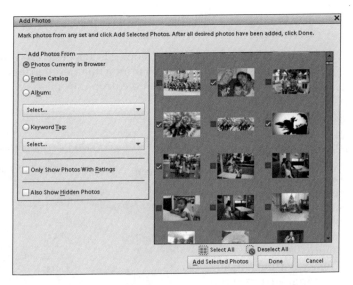

Figure 2-2: Thumbnails of selected images appear in the Add Photos dialog box.

G. Print Page Size: The readout displays the paper size.

H. Zoom image: Move the slider left/right to zoom out/in on the image.

I. Print Preview: This option displays a preview of the image that's to be printed.

J. Print button. Click this button to send the image(s) to your printer after all other options have been selected.

K. Cancel: Clicking Cancel dismisses the dialog box without sending a photo to the printer.

L. Select Printer: Select a target printer from the drop-down menu.

M. Change Settings: Click this button to open properties that are unique to the selected printer.

N. Select Paper Size: Choose from paper sizes that your printer supports. This list may change when you select a different printer from the Select Printer drop-down menu.

O. Select Type of Print: In Windows, you have three options: Individual Prints, Contact Sheets, and Picture Packages. For more information on contact sheets and picture packages, see the "Printing Multiple Images" section, later in this chapter. On the Mac, you can choose Picture Package and Contact Sheet II from the File menu.

P. Select Print Size: Select from the number of options for print sizes that your printer supports.

Q. Crop to Fit: Select this check box to crop an image to fit the selected paper size.

R. Print ___ Copies: By default, 1 copies is selected. If you remove the check mark, you can choose to print a number of prints on the same page by making selections from the drop-down list.

Using Change Settings

When you click the Change Settings button in the Print/Prints dialog box, the Change Settings dialog box opens for the printer you have selected on the Select Printer drop-down menu. In Figure 2-3, we opened the Change Settings dialog box for an Epson Stylus T40W printer. In this dialog box, you can make a few selections for print attributes that may be unique to your printer. However, for most desktop printers, the options you find in the Change Settings dialog box can be controlled in the Print/Prints dialog box.

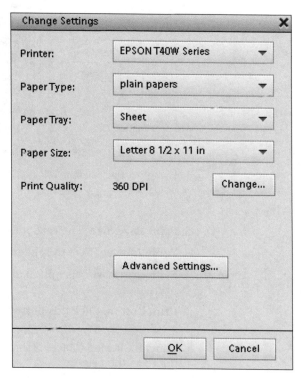

Figure 2-3: The Change Settings dialog box for an Epson Stylus T40W printer.

Using Printer Properties

Click the Advanced Settings button in the Change Settings dialog box and you arrive at various settings for your printer. This dialog box will vary with options and the display according to your printer. For an Epson printer, you arrive at the Main tab in the Printer Properties where the current ink levels are shown, and you see a menu where you can make a choice for the paper you use, as shown in Figure 2-4.

The real power in your printer driver is in the Advanced settings. Depending on your printer, you may arrive at advanced settings when you first open the printer driver. However, in our example, Advanced settings are available when you click the Advanced tab. In the Advanced settings, you find color profile handling, as we explain later in the section "Printing with Color Profiles."

Using More Options

Click the More Options button in the Print/ Prints dialog box. The More Options dialog box opens, as shown in Figure 2-5.

When you want to manage color in Elements, as we explain later in the section "Printing with Color Profiles," you need to print from the Photo Editor. Printing from the Organizer doesn't provide you with custom profile management.

The default selection in this dialog box is Printing Choices. The choices available for printing your photos include

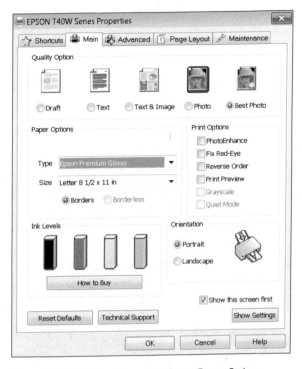

Figure 2-4: The Printer Properties for an Epson Stylus T40W printer.

✔ **Photo Details:** Select the check boxes for the detail items you want to have printed in your output below the image.

✔ **Border:** If you select the Thickness check box, you can specify the size of the border in the text box and choose a unit of measure in the

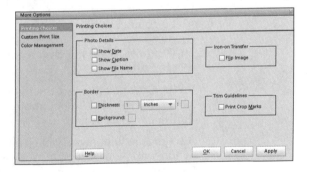

Figure 2-5: The More Options dialog box.

drop-down list. Click the color swatch to choose a color for the border.

✔ **Iron-On Transfer:** This option is used for heat transfer material: Mylar, Lexjet, and other substrates that require *e-down* printing — *emulsion-down* printing — where the negative and the image are flipped.

✔ **Trim Guidelines:** Select the Print Crop Marks check box to add marks to the print to show where the paper needs to be trimmed.

The other two items in the More Options dialog box are Custom Print Size and Color Management. Click Custom Print Size, and you can define the width and height for custom papers.

Color Management is something we cover in detail later in this chapter in the section "Printing with Color Profiles."

Printing Multiple Images

You have choices in the Organizer or the Photo Editor for choosing a command for printing multiple images as either a contact sheet or picture package. When you choose to print a contact sheet or picture package from within the Photo Editor, Elements switches you to the Organizer view. You continue the action from the Organizer and leave the Photo Editor.

Printing contact sheets

In traditional photography, people used contact sheets to view thumbnail images to decide what photos to print. Rather than viewing negatives, a photographer could see a thumbnail print of each frame on a roll in a few contact sheets. These contact sheets revealed how the frames would appear when printed.

You can get the same results in Elements by printing contact sheets from a collection of photos. By looking over the thumbnails and choosing which photos to print at larger sizes, you save money on your printer consumables.

To print a contact sheet, do the following:

1. **In Windows, open the Organizer. On the Mac, you need to open the Photo Editor.**

2. **In the Organizer, select the photos you want to print on a contact sheet. On the Mac, select photos in the Organizer and open the photos in the Photo Editor.**

   Ctrl-click in Windows (⌘-click on the Mac) to choose multiple photos in a noncontiguous selection. You can also sort photos by keyword tags, albums, dates, and so on. You then select all the sorted photos by pressing Ctrl/⌘+A. For more information on sorting files, see Book II, Chapter 2.

3. **Choose File➪Print or press Ctrl+P (⌘+P) and select a printer.**

   The Prints dialog box opens in Windows. On the Mac, choose File➪ Contact Sheet II. In the Prints/Print dialog box on Windows, select the printer you want to use for your output from the Select Printer drop-down menu. On the Mac, click OK in the Contacts Sheet II dialog box, and the photos are plotted in a new document.

4. **Select Contact Sheet on Windows from the Select Type of Print drop-down menu.**

   The Prints/Print dialog box refreshes to show your contact sheet options, as shown in Figure 2-6.

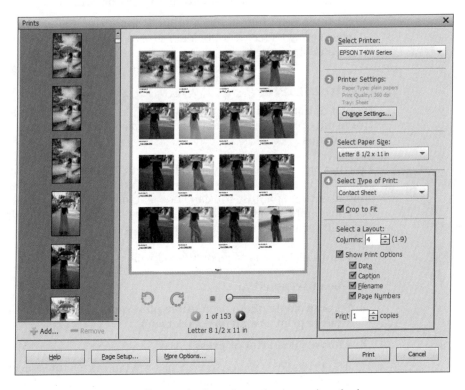

Figure 2-6: Choose Contact Sheet and select a layout for the number of columns.

5. **In the Select a Layout area on Windows, choose the number of columns you want for the contact sheet. On the Mac, these choices are made in the Contact Sheet II dialog box.**

   If you specify fewer columns, the images appear larger; as more columns are selected, the images appear smaller. Choose a size according to the number of columns that you want to print.

6. **(Optional) Select the check boxes for the items you want to be included in the captions.**

   If you want print options to be shown on your prints, select the Show Print Options check box, and the list of options is displayed below the check box. Caption items can include the date, a text line for the caption, filename, and page numbers.

7. **Click More Options on Windows in the bottom of the dialog box and select a color profile from the Print Space drop-down menu.**

   For more on printing with color profiles, see the section "Printing with Color Profiles," later in this chapter.

8. **Click OK in the More Options dialog box on Windows.**

9. **Click the Print button (back in the Prints/Print dialog box) to print your contact sheet. On the Mac, choose File⇨ Print to print the newly created document.**

Printing picture packages

Another option you have for printing multiple photos is picture packages. This feature prints multiple copies of the same photo or multiple copies of many photos.

A picture package is typically a single sheet of paper with the same photo printed at different sizes — something like your class pictures, graduation photos, or prom photos. You can choose to print a single picture package from one photo selected in the Organizer, or you can select multiple photos and print them all as multiple picture packages.

To create a picture package, do the following:

1. **Open the Organizer.**

2. **Select a single photo or multiple photos in the Organizer that you want to print as a picture package(s).**

3. **Choose File⇨Print or press Ctrl+P.**

   The Prints/Print dialog box opens on Windows. On the Mac, you are switched to the Photo Editor. Cancel out of the Print dialog box and choose File⇨Picture Package.

4. **From the Select Printer drop-down menu, select the printer that you want to use for your output.**

5. **Select Picture Package from the Select Type of Print drop-down menu on Windows.**

   The Prints/Print dialog box refreshes to show your picture package options. On the Mac, the Picture Package dialog box offers the same options.

6. **Select a layout from the Select a Layout drop-down menu.**

   As you make layout selections, you see a dynamic preview of the picture package, as shown in Figure 2-7. Select different layouts to examine the results and choose the layout you want for your picture package.

Figure 2-7: Choose Picture Package and select a layout for the package.

7. **Select a frame (optional).**

   The photos can be printed with a frame. Select an option from the Select a Frame drop-down menu or leave the default None selected to print no frame on the photos.

8. **Click the More Options button and choose a color profile from the same dialog box that appears when you print a contact sheet.**

9. **Click OK.**

10. **Back in the Prints/Print dialog box, click the Print button.**

Printing with Color Profiles

All the options we've talked about so far in this chapter give you a picture on paper, but even if you follow all the steps up to this point to a *T*, you may still not get the color right. To print the most accurate color you can on your printer, use printer profiles that are created for every printer, paper, and ink set you use.

Printer developers create printer profiles for use with the developers' inks and papers. If you decide to modify your printer and use large ink bottles or use lower-cost inks from third-party suppliers, the profiles from your printer developer aren't optimized for the change in ink pigments. Likewise, third-party papers aren't optimized for the printer profiles shipped by your printer developer.

To get accurate color when you use inks and papers different from those recommended by your printer developer, you may need to develop custom profiles for each ink set and each paper. You can search the Internet to find several sources of services that create custom profiles for you.

Working with color printer profiles

The final step in a color-managed workflow is to convert color from the profile of your color workspace to the color profile of your printer. Basically, this conversion means that the colors you see on your monitor in your current workspace are accurately converted to the color that your printer can reproduce.

Understanding how Elements uses color profiles

When using the Print dialog box (or the More Options section of the Print dialog box), you can manage color in Photoshop Elements in one of three ways when it comes time to print your files:

- **Printer Manages Colors:** This method permits your printer to decide which profile is used when your photo is printed to your desktop color printer. Your printer makes this decision according to the paper you select as the source paper used to print your photos. If you choose Epson Premium Glossy Photo Paper, for example, your printer chooses the profile that goes along with that particular paper. If you choose another paper, your printer chooses a different color profile. This method is automatic, and color profile selection is made when you print your file.

- **Photoshop Elements Manages Color:** When you make this choice, color management is taken away from your printer and is controlled by Elements. You must choose a color profile after making this choice in the Print dialog box. Desktop printers that fall in the medium to more expensive range often have many color profiles that they can install.

- **No Color Management:** You use this choice if you have a color profile embedded in one of your pictures. You'll probably rarely use this option. Unless you know how to embed profiles or receive files with embedded profiles from other users, don't make this choice in the Print dialog box.

Each of these options requires you to make a choice about how color is managed. You make choices (as we discuss later in this chapter, when we walk you through the steps for printing) about whether to color-manage your output. These selections are all unique to the Print dialog box for your individual printer.

Understanding your printer's profiles

A few years ago, we recommended using Epson printers for users who wanted to achieve the best color output from desktop printers. The reason was that Epson took the lead in color profile development and offered the best profiles one could find for these printers.

However, in recent years, we find that color profile support for the best printer developers is equally supported. You find excellent results using HP, Canon, and Epson printers. These three developers have created support and help information as well as good color profiles to support their devices.

You can find a wealth of information on the Internet for using color profiles with printers from each of these manufacturers. For starters, take a look at the following URLs for more information about printing using color profiles.

- **Epson printers:** www.redrivercatalog.com/profiles/lightroom/how-to-use-icc-color-printer-profiles-lightroom-epson-desktop-windows.html

- **HP printers (Windows):** http://h10025.www1.hp.com/ewfrf/wc/document?cc=us&lc=en&dlc=en&docname=c00286904

- **Canon printers:** www.redrivercatalog.com/profiles/lightroom/how-to-use-icc-color-printer-profiles-lightroom-canon-desktop-windows.html

Printing to Inkjet Printers

Printers are installed on your computer with printer drivers that are designed to offer you settings and controls for options that are unique to your printer. We can't hope to cover all printers and the variations you find with each device.

What we can do is give you a general idea of the printing process by showing how it's done with Epson printers — one of the more popular desktop printer manufacturers on the market. This overview gives you a basis for understanding the settings you need to adjust when printing color to desktop printers and submitting photos to service providers.

If you own a different brand of printer or use a service that uses other printers, what's important to remember in reviewing this section is the process involved in printing your files. Regardless of what type of printer you own, be aware of when a color profile is used and how color is either managed or not managed. You may have different check box selections and menu commands, but the process is the same for any printer printing your photos.

Over the past few years, at least half of the many service-provider troubleshooting tech calls coming from clients involved problems with accurate color output from Epson and some other inkjet printers. We're not talking about subtle changes between monitor and printer, but huge, monstrous color changes on output prints. As it turns out, almost all the strange output results originated from just one minor error that occurred when the file was set up to print — it involved when and how to manage color in the Print dialog box.

Color profiles also depend upon the ink being used and the paper stock you use. Refilling cartridges with generic ink can (in some cases) result in color shifts. Similarly, if the nozzles aren't clean and delivering ink consistently, your results may look very strange.

We've come up with settings that enable you to get accurate results without stress or frustration. Just remember to use the settings exactly as described, and you can achieve superior results with either desktop or professional printers.

When you install your printer driver, the installation utility also installs a number of color profiles. You can choose the profiles in the Photoshop Elements Print dialog box and control all the printing by using the profile provided by your printer manufacturer.

You can also print from the Organizer (Windows) by selecting one or more image thumbnails in the Organizer window and then choosing File➪Print. However, printing from the Organizer won't give you optimum support when using color profiles. As a matter of practice, never print from the Organizer's workspace for anything other than contact sheets. You have more control using the Photo Editor and more choices for color profile management.

You have two choices for how color profiles are used. You can

- **Choose to let your printer manage color:** The profiling selection is automatic, and you don't have to worry about making other choices in the Print dialog boxes.

- **Choose to let Photoshop Elements manage color:** In this case, you need to choose which color profile and color-management process to use.

We're talking about two very different issues here. One issue is *color management,* which ultimately comes down to whether Elements manages your color, your printer manages color, or you use no color management at all. The other issue is choosing a color profile. Therefore, you have a series of combined options to choose from. You can choose a profile and turn color management either on or off. Or you can elect not to make a profile choice and decide whether color management is on or off. The choices you make are critical to getting color right on your output.

All the methods are described in the following sections.

When printing with color management and using color profiles, print from the Photo Editor only. The Organizer Prints Color Management has fewer options than the Photo Editor Print dialog box.

Automatic profile selection for Epson printers

The automatic profile selection method exists, and depending on what model of printer you have, you may be required to make this choice.

Your options all depend on whether the printer you buy installs color profiles on your computer. If you buy some low-end color printers that cost less than $100, the installer software typically doesn't install color profiles. When no profiles are installed, the printer manages the color through built-in profiles contained in the printer's memory.

High-end models (above the $100 price range) often install individual color profiles. You might see the profiles for various papers on the Printer Profile pop-up menu in the Elements More Options dialog box. If you have one of these high-end printers, you might want to choose the profile that matches the paper you're using and let Elements manage the color.

You have two choices for your color workspace. Those choices are sRGB or Adobe RGB (1998). The workspace is used to see color on your monitor. You also need to calibrate your monitor so that the colors you see appear as close to real-world color as you can get.

When you print a picture, the color from your monitor workspace (either sRGB or Adobe RGB [1998]) is converted to your printer color. So, you want to fit all the color you see in an sRGB workspace, for example, into the printer's profile so that the print looks as close as possible to what you see on your monitor. Elements takes care of this color conversion. The only thing you need to worry about is making the right choice for how that conversion takes place.

Follow these steps (in the Photo Editor only) to print from the native color space:

1. **Open a file in the Photo Editor and choose File⇨Print.**

   The Print dialog box that opens contains all the settings you need to print a file.

   When you want to manage color, print from the Photo Editor and not the Organizer.

2. **Select the orientation of your print.**

   You can choose either Portrait or Landscape. Select the proper orientation in the Page Setup in the Prints dialog box.

3. **Select your printer from the Select Printer drop-down menu.**

4. **Set the print attributes.**

   Select the number of copies, position, scaling, and output items you want.

5. **Click the More Options button, and in the More Options dialog box, choose Color Management on the left.**

   In the Color Management area of the More Options dialog box, shown in Figure 2-8, you choose how to manage color when you print files.

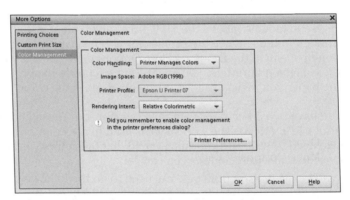

Figure 2-8: Look over the Color Management area in the More Options dialog box for options on how to manage color.

6. **From the Color Handling drop-down menu, select Printer Manages Colors; click OK in the More Options dialog box.**

   This choice uses your current workspace color and later converts the color from your workspace to the printer output file when you open the printer driver dialog box.

7. **Click the Change Settings button in the Prints dialog box (Windows).**

   The Change Settings dialog box opens.

8. **(Windows only) Click the Advanced Settings button, and the Printing Properties dialog box opens, as shown in Figure 2-9; skip to Step 10.**

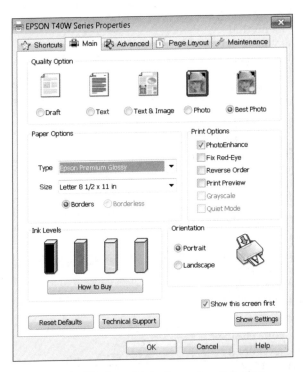

Figure 2-9: The Windows Printer Properties dialog box.

9. **On the Mac, click the Print button after you make your choices in the More Options dialog box.**

   The file doesn't print yet. You need to do the following:

   a. *Open the pop-up menu below the Paper Size item and choose Print Settings, as shown in Figure 2-10.* From the Media Type pop-up menu, choose the paper for your output.

   b. *Open the Print Settings pop-up menu and choose Color Management, as shown in Figure 2-11.* Leave the default setting at Color Controls. (This setting is used when the printer manages color.)

   On the Macintosh, click the Print button, and the file prints.

10. **Set print attributes (Windows).**

In our Epson example, select Epson Premium Glossy (or another paper from the Type drop-down menu that you may be using) and then click the Best Photo radio button. (Refer to Figure 2-9.)

Now, it's time to color-manage your file. This step is critical in your print-production workflow.

11. **Click the Advanced tab.**

The advanced settings in the Printing Properties dialog box open, as shown in Figure 2-12.

12. **Make your choices in the advanced settings of the Printing Properties dialog box.**

Here are the most important choices:

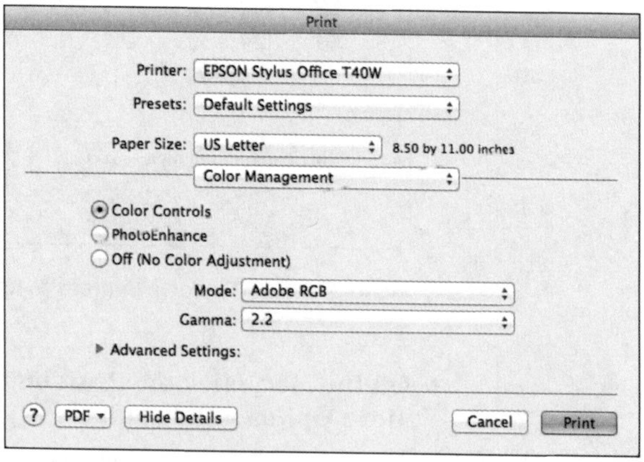

- *Select a paper type.* You selected paper already? The drop-down menu in the Paper & Quality Options section of the dialog box determines the application of inks. Select the same paper here as you did in Step 10.

- *Turn on color management.* Because you're letting the printer driver determine the color, you need to be certain that the Color Controls radio button is selected. This setting tells the printer driver to automatically select a printer profile for the paper type you selected.

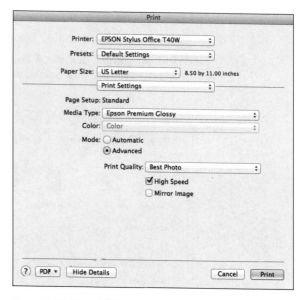

Figure 2-10: Choose Print Settings on the Macintosh and make a choice for the paper you use for the output.

Figure 2-11: Choose Color Management and make sure that Color Controls is selected.

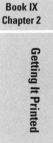

Figure 2-12: Click the Advanced tab to open advanced settings.

- *Set the color mode.* Don't use Epson Vivid. This choice produces inferior results on photos. Choose Best Photo, the Epson Standard, or Adobe RGB, depending on your printer. You need to make several test prints to find the best option for your paper and printer.

If you frequently print files using the same settings, you can save your settings by clicking the Save Settings button.

13. **To print the photo, click OK and then click OK again in the Prints dialog box.**

Your file is sent to your printer. The color is converted automatically from your source workspace of sRGB or Adobe RGB (1998) to the profile the printer driver automatically selects for you.

Selecting a printer profile

Another method for managing color when you're printing files is to select a printer profile from the available list of color profiles installed with your printer. Whereas in the preceding section, you used your printer to manage color, this time, you let Photoshop Elements manage the color.

The steps in this section are the same as the ones described in the preceding section for printing files for automatic profile selection when you're setting up the page and selecting a printer. When you choose File⇨Print in the Photo Editor, you open the Elements Print dialog box. To let Elements handle the color conversion, follow these steps in the Print dialog box:

1. **Open a photo in the Photo Editor, choose File⇨Print, and then click Color Management in the Print dialog box.**

2. **From the Printer Profile drop-down menu in the Color Management section of the Print dialog box, select the color profile designed for use with the paper you've chosen.**

3. **Click Printer Preferences in the More Options dialog box.**

   The printer's Properties dialog box opens (refer to Figure 2-9).

4. **In Windows, select the Best Photo radio button, and from the Type drop-down menu, select the recommended paper choice. On the Macintosh, make your paper choice, as shown in Figure 2-10.**

   Custom color profiles are also shipped with guidelines for selecting proper paper.

5. **In Windows, click the Advanced button to arrive at the dialog box shown in Figure 2-12. On the Macintosh, choose Color Management from the pop-up menu to arrive at the same dialog box shown earlier in Figure 2-11.**

   The paper choice selection is automatically carried over from the previous Properties dialog box. The one setting you change is in the Color Management section.

6. **In Windows, select the ICM (Image Color Management) radio button and select the Off (No Color Adjustment) check box, as shown in Figure 2-13. On the Macintosh, select the Off (No Color Adjustment) radio button.**

   Because you selected the color profile in Step 2 and you're letting Elements manage the color, be sure that the Color Management feature is turned off. If you don't turn off Color Management, you end up double-profiling your print.

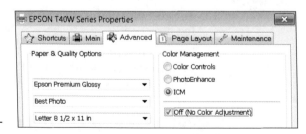

Figure 2-13: Select the ICM option and select the Off (No Color Adjustment) check box.

The choice to manage color or not to manage it is simplified in Photoshop Elements. In the Color Management area of the dialog box, a message is reported each time you make a selection from the Color Handling drop-down menu. Right below Source Space, you see a message asking whether you remembered to turn Color Management on or off. Each time you make a selection for the Color Handling, pause a moment and read the message. This is your reminder that you need to follow the recommendation to properly handle color.

Using Online Printing Services

Since Photoshop Elements 11, Adobe has partnered with a single service provider for ordering prints online. Choose the photos you want to send to the Shutterfly service in the Organizer and choose File⇨Order Prints⇨Order Shutterfly Prints. On the Macintosh, choose Adobe Elements 13 Organizer⇨ Order Prints⇨Order Shutterfly Prints.

The Shutterfly order screen opens. Follow the onscreen instructions for creating an account and placing an order.

Chapter 3: Sharing Projects with Others

In This Chapter

- ✓ **Understanding sharing options**
- ✓ **Using the Share panel**
- ✓ **Working with Adobe Revel**
- ✓ **Attaching files to email**
- ✓ **Using Photo Mail**
- ✓ **Using online sharing services**
- ✓ **Sharing creations**

You shoot photos primarily for two reasons (if you're not selling them for income): to gain personal satisfaction and revel in your own work or to share your creations with others.

Perhaps the most enjoyable aspect of photography is experiencing the appreciation of family and friends who laugh, cry, ooh, and aah when looking at your images.

Photoshop Elements provides you with a number of sharing options to get those laughs, cries, oohs, and aahs from others. When it comes down to it, the sharing of photos just might be one of the best reasons you have for using Photoshop Elements.

In this chapter, we look at the many opportunities that Elements provides for sharing photos in your living room or across the world.

Getting Familiar with the Elements Sharing Options

Before you delve into making creations for screen viewing, we want to familiarize you with the available options for not only screen images but also sharing — particularly online sharing services. You also need to know the acceptable standards for online hosts, where you eventually send your creations, and for the devices people are likely to use to view your creations.

Before you choose a sharing activity and ultimately begin work on a creation, answer these questions we explore in the following sections.

What device (s) are going to display my creations?

For viewing photos and movies, the device options include computers (including desktops, notebooks, and netbooks), handheld devices such as mobile phones, tablets such as the Apple iPad and Samsung Galaxy Tab, and TVs. If you want to make your creations accessible on all devices, the tools that you use within Elements and the file format in which you save a creation are different from the tools used and file formats you might use for showing creations on a TV or on a computer exclusively.

Issues that you need to understand regarding devices and viewing your creations include the following:

- **Adobe Flash:** Some hosts convert your video uploads to Adobe Flash. If you want to share photos with iPhone/iPod/iPad users (more than one billion and counting), you need to stay away from any host that supports Flash-only conversions. However, you should check sites regularly. Many sites are transcoding video so that people can view content on the widest range of devices that include iPad and iOS, as well as Android systems.

- **Storage space:** Hosts vary greatly in terms of the amount of space allocated for storing content. If you want to share large video files, you need to be certain that the storage host you choose allocates enough storage space to permit you to upload your files.

What storage hosts are the most popular?

From within Photoshop Elements, you can export directly to YouTube and Vimeo video sharing for computers, iOS, and Android devices; Adobe Revel; Facebook; Flickr; and Twitter. Some of these providers may be new to you. Just be aware that they all perform a similar kind of service: Each enables you to upload photos and invite people to see your creations. The online sharing services that are supported directly in Elements include the following:

- **Facebook:** Facebook (www.facebook.com) is an online service that's clearly among the most popular worldwide for sharing photos. If Facebook were a country and its users were all citizens, it would be the third largest country in the world behind China and India. Facebook offers you up to 200 photos maximum per album, up to 1024MB for each video, and unlimited space for total albums and videos.

TIP

When you submit videos to Facebook, the videos are transcoded to Adobe Flash for viewing on computers but also contain coding for viewing on an iPhone/iPod/iPad (see Figure 3-1). The process is transparent to the user. You just upload a video in any one of more than a dozen different formats, and anyone with any device can view the video. Facebook is clearly the leader for hosting all your creations.

Figure 3-1: Video on Facebook shown on an Apple iPad.

✔ **Flickr:** Whereas Facebook provides you with nearly limitless opportunity, Flickr (at `www.flickr.com` and operated by Yahoo!) is much more restrictive. Flickr assesses maximum storage per user according to bandwidth. You can upload only so many times, and then you have to wait until the next month to upload additional photos. It's much more limiting than other services, and video files are restricted to small file sizes. You can upgrade to a premium account for a fee, but why bother when you can get it all free with a much better user interface on Facebook?

✔ **Adobe Revel:** Adobe Revel (`www.adoberevel.com`) is one of the easiest methods for sharing your photos and videos. You can use the free online service to back up, view, and share up to 50 uploads per month. You can acquire additional space for a membership fee. As this book goes to press, iPhone, iPad, and Mac users can download the Revel app from the App Store to edit and access images across these devices, too, and Adobe expects to release similar support for Windows and Android devices in the near future. See the upcoming section "Working with Adobe Revel" for more details. (*Note:* Adobe Revel photo syncing is called Private Web Album in the Share Panel.)

✔ **Vimeo:** The name comes from video by replacing a *d* with an *m*. Vimeo (`https://vimeo.com`) currently has over 65 million unique users per month and is rapidly becoming a social media site for video that is supported on computers, Apple iOS, and Android devices. Vimeo offers free video uploads of up to 500MB per week.

✔ **YouTube:** YouTube (`www.youtube.com`) offers free unlimited videos up to 10 minutes in length and not exceeding 100MB.

✔ **Twitter:** Support for uploading files directly from the Organizer to Twitter (`https://twitter.com`).

You can tap into other sources that aren't direct links from within Photoshop Elements. Some of the more popular ones are shown in Table 3-1.

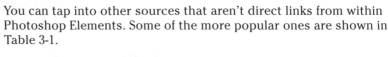

Table 3-1		Social Media Sharing Providers
Source	*URL*	*Details*
dotPhoto	`www.dotphoto.com`	Free unlimited photo uploads for one year. After one year, a paid subscription is required.
Google+	`https://plus.google.com`	Free unlimited photo and video uploads.
Myspace	`www.myspace.com`	Free unlimited photo and video uploads.
Photobucket	`http://s903.photobucket.com`	Up to 2GB photo and video uploads per month.
SlickPic	`www.slickpic.com`	Unlimited storage of up to 1600 x 1200px images and a maximum of 10MB per image.

What types of creations can I share?

Obviously, you can upload individual photos to any one of the online services. In the Elements Organizer, you can open the Share panel drop-down menu and choose from one of the listed services. If you want to share with services not directly linked to Elements in the Share panel, save your edited photos to a folder on your hard drive, open the service's URL in your web browser, and follow the guidelines for the service to upload photos and videos. In addition to uploading single photos to a service, some of the creations you might want to share include the following:

✔ **Slide shows:** In Windows, you can create a slide show and choose to export the slide show as a movie file (`.wmv`) or a PDF. On the Macintosh, you're limited to PDF only.

If you work in Windows, export to .wmv and upload your file to an online host.

If you use Facebook, users of all devices can see your creations on any device. If you add audio to a slide show, the audio plays on all devices when uploaded to Facebook. If you try to upload the same file to Flickr, more often than not, the file size will be too large to host.

TIP

On iPhones or iPads, you can view PDFs natively when the files are added to your iBooks library. However, GoodReader by Good-iWare LTD (http://goodreader.net) is, in our opinion as of this writing, one of the best PDF viewers and provides you with many options for viewing your Elements creations. GoodReader is available for both iPhone and iPad and costs $4.99 — much less than some other PDF viewers you can find in the Apple App Store.

✔ **Web hosting:** If you want to host videos on your own website and make the videos accessible to iPhone/iPod/iPad users as well as computer users, you need a little help from Adobe Premiere Elements. In Premiere Elements, you can export video for Mobile Devices, and the resultant file can be viewed on an iPhone/iPod/iPad as well as computers.

Working with Adobe Revel

Adobe Revel is a web hosting service for storing your photos in the cloud, where you can view and share your photos on all your devices, such as computers, smartphones, tablets, notebooks, and so on. When you edit a photo in Elements or via the tools in the Adobe Revel app, the photo is automatically updated on all devices.

In Elements, you can access Adobe Revel from the Import panel on the left side of the Organizer or via the Private Web Album option in the Share panel, as follows:

✔ In the Import panel, you have the Mobile Albums item appearing below the Albums button. You use the Mobile Albums link to sync photos on Adobe Revel and your computer. You can download your entire Revel library using this link, and the photos appear in the Organizer Media Browser. When you edit a photo in Elements or via the Adobe Revel app, the edited version is immediately updated in your Revel library.

✔ The Adobe Revel button in the Share panel is used to upload photos to your Revel account and share your photos with family and friends.

REMEMBER

It's important to remember that Mobile Albums is used to download and sync photos while the Adobe Revel button in the Share panel is used for uploading and sharing photos.

When you visit the Adobe Revel website at www.adoberevel.com and log in with your Adobe ID and password, you arrive at your Carousel, which displays all your photo uploads. The Adobe Revel website is limited to viewing photos and sharing your photos. As of this writing, there are no provisions on the website to edit your photos from within your web browser. On a computer, you must edit photos in Photoshop Elements. You can edit photos in Elements or use the Adobe Revel mobile application to edit photos on mobile devices.

Knowing what Adobe Revel offers you

Adobe Revel is more than just a hosting service. You can perform many tasks with Adobe Revel, such as the following:

- **Store photos and sync in the cloud:** Your photos are safely stored on the Adobe Revel website, and you can sync the photos to all your devices, such as computer, tablet, and phone.

- **Privacy:** As a default, all your photos are uploaded to your private account. Only you can see the photos you upload. When you want to share the photos, you can share them to the public or to selected users.

- **Photo albums:** You can add photos to albums and view the photos within a given album in a slide show view.

- **Edit photos:** Adobe Revel is the only photo-sharing service that offers you Adobe Lightroom performance for editing photos. As of this writing, you can edit photos with the Adobe Revel application, which is available for mobile devices using iOS and for Macs.

Downloading the Adobe Revel applications

In Photoshop Elements, you can upload and download photos through the link to Adobe Revel.

The Adobe Revel applications — which you can download for free — enable you to edit photos. When you save the edited photos, you can view the new edits on all your devices. Here's where you can find them:

- **For Macs:** You can download the application directly from the Apple App Store or through iTunes. On Windows, follow the onscreen help when you log on to Adobe Revel with your Adobe ID. Adobe will send you an email to help you with the download.

- **For iOS devices:** Adobe Revel can be downloaded to iOS devices for use on your iPhone, iPod touch, or iPad. These versions provide you with sharing and editing features. Your device needs to have iOS version 6 or greater.

- **For Android devices:** You can download Adobe Revel for Android devices; the new updated version offers you the same editing features once available to Mac users only. You can download Adobe Revel for Android from the Android Market Place, and the app requires Android version 2.2.

Understanding the Adobe Revel interface

Whether you work on a desktop or a mobile device, the Revel applications provide you with similar features, although you find some slight differences in the interfaces. Figure 3-2 shows the Revel interface on an iOS device.

Some of the main features include: Exiting the editing interface (top left), Comparing before after edits, accepting the edits (check mark), various editing options on the bottom, and cropping the photo (as shown in Figure 3-2).

The real power in Adobe Revel is editing photos, which we talk about in the next section.

Editing a photo with Revel

To edit a photo using Adobe Revel on a Mac or iOS device, do the following:

Figure 3-2: Adobe Revel application as shown on an iPad.

1. **Log in to your Adobe Revel account.**

    Launch the application on your Mac or iOS device. Sign in using your email address and password. If you haven't created an Adobe ID, you can choose the option to create a new account. After you log in, you see the photos you have in your Carousel (library) or photos you imported from a Photoshop.com library.

2. **Tap a photo in iOS or click a photo on the desktop app.**

    The view changes to an editing view, where the editing tools are available, as shown in Figure 3-3.

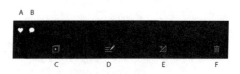

Figure 3-3: The Adobe Revel editing tools.

3. Make photo edits.

The tools available include the following:

A. *Favorites:* On iOS devices, the favorites icon is represented with a heart. On desktops, the favorites icon is a star. Tap or click the icon, and the photo you're viewing is added to your favorites.

B. *Comment:* Tap the Comment icon, and a comments panel opens so that you can type a comment.

C. *Slide Show view:* The first icon at the lower left of the window is used to run a slide show. This icon works if you tap an album. If you have a single photo selected, tapping this icon prevents you from swiping to change photos. To exit the slide show view, tap anywhere outside a photo or press the Esc key on your desktop computer.

D. *Keyboard:* Tap this icon, and the keyboard pops up on iOS devices. You can type a caption that's added at the bottom of the photo. In the desktop version, a panel opens that provides a number of different sharing options.

E. *Edit:* Tap this icon to enter editing mode. You have choices for making an auto-fix, changing white balance, adjusting exposure and contrast, making red-eye corrections, and cropping and rotating a photo. The best way to familiarize yourself with the editing tools is to play with them and make changes for auto-correction, exposure, contrast, cropping, and rotation, if needed. In Figure 3-4, you see a photo targeted for cropping.

F. *Delete:* Click the Trash icon to delete a photo.

Figure 3-4: Cropping a picture in Adobe Revel on an iPad.

4. Compare your edits with the original photo.

To make a comparison between your edits and the original photo, keep your finger pressed on the Compare icon at the top of the window. While your finger is pressed on the icon, you see the original photo before any edits. When you release your finger from the icon, you see the photo as you have edited it.

5. **Save your edits.**

   Tap the check mark at the upper-right corner of the window to save your edits and update the file. When updated, the new edited file appears the same on all your devices.

6. **Dismiss the editing mode.**

   Tap the X icon at the upper-left corner and you return to your library view. (Refer to Figure 3-2.)

Sharing photos with Adobe Revel

After you make some edits on photos and update them, you can see the new edited photos on all your devices as long as they're connected to the cloud. However, the photos are secure, and only you can view them unless you decide to share them.

Share your photos with the following steps:

1. **Select a photo in your library.**

2. **Open the Actions drop-down menu (on the Mac) or tap the Action icon on an iOS device.**

   The menu you see is different, depending on what system you use.

3. **Choose a sharing option, as shown in Figure 3-5 for Revel on the Mac, or tap Share or Share to Facebook on an iOS device, as shown in Figure 3-6.**

   If you want to share your photo via Facebook, Twitter, or Flickr, tap the corresponding option. Or tap Share to open a pop-up menu, as shown in Figure 3-6. The rest of these steps use Facebook as an example. You can find details about choosing an action from the Mac options at the end of this section.

4. **Tap an option for where you want to send the file.**

   You can email the photo to someone or send it to a sharing service. In our example, we share to Facebook.

   In the window that opens, you can type a title for your photo and identify a location, as shown in Figure 3-7.

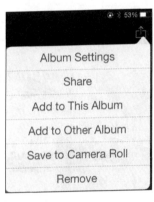

Figure 3-5: The action menu on a Mac.

Figure 3-6: The pop-up menu as shown on an iOS device.

5. **Add a title and location.**

6. **Tap the Post button to upload the photo to your Facebook Timeline.**

To share a photo from your desktop Mac, click the Action icon to choose a share option. However, the choices available to you are very different (as of this writing) than those available in iOS (refer to Figure 3-5).

Figure 3-7: When you're uploading a photo or album to Facebook, a pop-up menu opens.

You have options to share the selected album or photo to Facebook, Twitter, Flickr, Email the photo, Message (SMS), or AirDrop (a local Wi-Fi ad hoc Apple service for sharing across all Apple devices).

Choose the sharing option you want and follow the instructions provided in menus to post your photo.

Downloading images from your Revel Carousel

Your Revel Carousel contains photos you've uploaded to your Revel account. If you ever lose your photos on your hard drive or just need to access your images while you're away from your computer, you can download all the images in your Carousel or just selected photos. In this section, we focus on how to download images from Revel into the Elements Organizer.

If you want to upload images from Elements to your Revel Carousel, you can do that in the Elements Organizer, too, and we walk you through that process in the section "Getting a Grip on the Share Panel."

If you used Photoshop.com in an earlier version of Elements, a Photoshop.com library is added to your Revel account when you first log in from the Organizer. This library will exist separately from your Carousel, but you can still download all the images it contains. Note, however, that Photoshop.com is being discontinued by Adobe Systems. If you don't switch to Revel in time, you may not be able to import photos from Photoshop.com when you first create an Adobe Revel account.

Assuming you have photos uploaded to your Adobe Revel account, the photos exist online. You need to download a photo in order to edit it in the Photo Editor.

To download photos from your Revel account to your computer, do the following:

1. **Click a library in the Mobile Albums area in the Import panel.**

   The Import panel shown in Figure 3-8 displays our Photoshop.com library (we converted our Photoshop.com library to Adobe Revel) and our Adobe Revel Carousel.

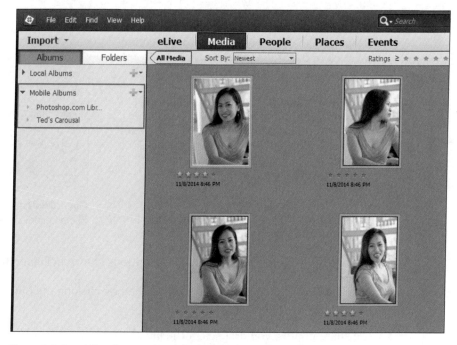

Figure 3-8: Revel libraries are shown in the Import panel.

2. **Select a photo in the Media Browser and choose Edit⇨Edit with Photoshop Elements Editor.**

   The photo opens in the Photo Editor.

   The Media Browser displays thumbnail images of the photos in your Revel libraries, but the photos are hosted online. You need to download the photo in order to edit it. As soon as you choose the menu option to edit the photo, the photo is downloaded from your Revel account to your computer.

You can choose how to sync your media in Photoshop Elements Preferences. In the Organizer, press Ctrl+K (Windows) or ⌘+K (Mac) and click Adobe Revel. You can turn the automatic sync on and off in this preference setting.

When the Revel Agent is on, new and edited photos automatically appear in the Media Browser and on all your devices running the Adobe Revel app.

Getting a Grip on the Share Panel

The Create and Share panels are available in both the Organizer and the Photo Editor and are used to make choices for assembling creations and sharing creations. For this section, we stick to the Share panel; in Chapter 1 of this minibook, we cover using the Create panel.

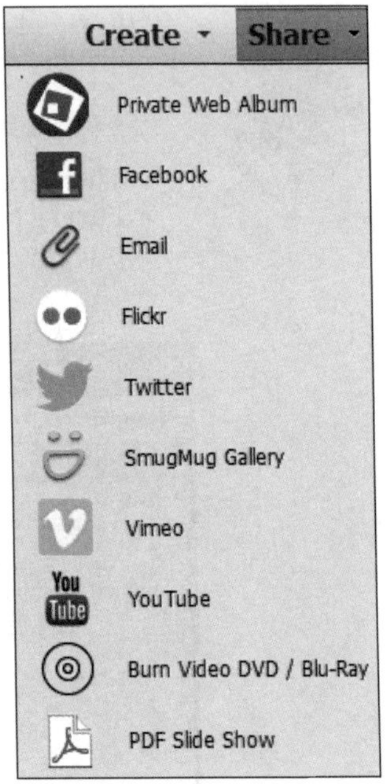

The Share panel as it appears in Windows is shown in Figure 3-9 in Windows. As of this writing Adobe has not yet finalized the user interface. By the time you read this book, Adobe may have added all the options that appear on Windows.

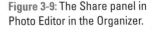

If you open the Share panel in the Photo Editor, the options are fewer and you won't find Email Attachments, Vimeo, YouTube, Burn Video to DVD Blu-Ray, or PDF Slide Show. Only the Organizer displays the complete Share options shown in Figure 3-9.

Figure 3-9: The Share panel in Photo Editor in the Organizer.

Sharing photos with Adobe Revel is handled by clicking the button labeled Private Web Album.

To share photos, you first select the images you want to share in the Organizer. Then click a button in the Share panel.

Sharing Photos on Adobe Revel

To share photos on Adobe Revel, you do the following:

1. **Click the image thumbnails in the Media Browser that you want to upload to your Revel account.**

2. **Click Share to open the Share panel and click Private Web Album.**

    The Private Web Album window opens, as shown in Figure 3-10.

3. **Choose a Library and Album or create a new album.**

    From the Library drop-down menu, choose the library to which you want to share. You can choose between your Photoshop.com library or your Revel Carousel.

If you want to share photos to an existing album, open the Album drop-down menu and select the album you want to use. If you want to create a new album, click the Plus button and you are prompted to provide a name for the new album.

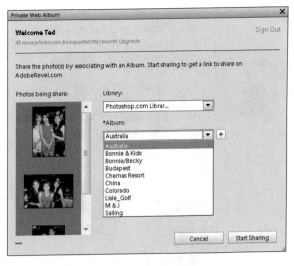

4. **Click Start Sharing to upload the photo to your Adobe Revel account.**

Figure 3-10: The Private Web Album window.

Uploading files to social media websites

When uploading files to social media websites from Photoshop Elements, you are prompted in a dialog box to authorize your account. In the Share panel, you then click the button for the social media site where you want to post your file. For example, if you select Twitter, the Twitter permission dialog box opens, as shown in Figure 3-11.

Click the Authorize button and your default web browser opens, where you type your username and password. After completing this step, return to the Organizer and click the Authorize button.

Follow the onscreen instructions to upload a photo to your Twitter account.

Figure 3-11: Permission dialog box for Twitter.

All the social media web sharing follows the same procedure, where you first authenticate an account and then proceed to upload photos.

Creating an email attachment

Elements makes it easy for you to attach photos to a new email message. You can stay in the Organizer, select photos you want to send, and email them to friends and family. You don't have to open your email client and search your hard drive to locate the photos you want to attach to an email message.

To email photos, select a photo or several photos in the Organizer and click Email in the Share panel. Adjust the size of the images (see Figure 3-12) in the Share panel and proceed through the steps in the panel to attach the files to a new email message.

Keep your file sizes small if you intend to send then to phone and tablet users.

Emailing photos is straightforward, and you should intuitively discover how easy it is to email photos.

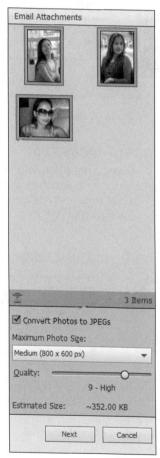

Figure 3-12: Adjust size and resolution in the Email Attachments panel.

Index

About the Authors

Barbara Obermeier is the principal of Obermeier Design, a graphic design studio in Ventura, California. She is the author of *Photoshop CS6 All-in-One For Dummies* and has contributed as author or coauthor to more than two dozen books on Adobe Photoshop, Adobe Photoshop Elements, Adobe Illustrator, Microsoft PowerPoint, and Digital Photography. She is the Interim Program Director in the Graphic Design department of the School of Film and Communication at Brooks Institute and has also taught at California Lutheran University; University of California, Santa Barbara; and Ventura College.

Ted Padova is the former chief executive officer and managing partner of The Image Source Digital Imaging and Photo Finishing Centers of Ventura and Thousand Oaks, California. He has been involved in digital imaging since founding a service bureau in 1990. He retired from his company in 2005 and now spends his time writing and speaking about digital imaging, Acrobat, PDF forms, and LiveCycle Designer forms.

For more than 17 years, Ted taught university and higher education classes in graphic design applications and digital prepress at the University of California, Santa Barbara, and at the University of California at Los Angeles. He has been, and continues to be, a conference speaker nationally and internationally at PDF conferences.

Ted has written more than 60 computer books and is the world's leading author on Adobe Acrobat. He has written books on Adobe Acrobat, Adobe Illustrator, Adobe Photoshop, Adobe Photoshop Elements, Adobe Reader, and Microsoft PowerPoint.

Dedication

It was with great sadness that we saw the passing of our long-time friend and technical editor Dennis Cohen, who worked on 15 of our previous books. Dennis was a superb editor and diligently attended to the duties of assuring our content was technically accurate. We miss Dennis and his wonderful contributions.

Barbara Obermeier: For Gary, Kylie, and Iggy, who constantly remind me of what's really important in life.

Ted Padova: For Arnie.

Authors' Acknowledgments

The authors would like to thank Steve Hayes, our acquisitions editor; Andy Cummings, Dummies Royalty; and Richard Wentk, a superb technical editor who helped us make this book much better. A huge thank-you to our project editor, Elizabeth Kuball.

Barbara Obermeier: A special thanks to Ted Padova, my coauthor and friend, who both celebrates and commiserates with me on the ups and downs of being an author.

Ted Padova: Many thanks to my dear friend and colleague, Barbara Obermeier, for asking me to join her on this project — and for a little handholding along the way, to help me get through it. Also, a special thanks to Arnie Padova, Dr. Olive De Castro, Malou and Regis Pelletier, Grace and Curtis Cooper, Irene and Bob Windley, Stefan Bergfors, George DeBoulay, Richard Leikin, and Michael Bindi for all their special modeling assistance.

Publisher's Acknowledgments

Acquisitions Editors: Aaron Black and Steve Hayes

Project Editor: Elizabeth Kuball

Copy Editor: Elizabeth Kuball

Technical Editor: Richard Wentk

Editorial Assistant: Claire Johnson

Sr. Editorial Assistant: Cherie Case

Project Coordinator: Lauren Buroker

Cover Image: © iStock.com/RooMtheAgency